*Philosophy of Criminal Law*

# Philosophy of Criminal Law

**Douglas N. Husak**

*RUTGERS UNIVERSITY*

Rowman & Littlefield
PUBLISHERS

ROWMAN & LITTLEFIELD

Published in the United States of America in 1987
by Rowman & Littlefield, Publishers
(a division of Littlefield, Adams & Company)
81 Adams Drive, Totowa, New Jersey 07512

**Library of Congress Cataloging-in-Publication Data**

Husak, Douglas N., 1948–
  Philosophy of criminal law.

  Bibliography: p. 249
  Includes index.
  1. Criminal law—Philosophy.  I. Title.
K5018.H87    1987    345'.001    86-31562
ISBN 0-8476-7550-5    342.5001
ISBN 0-8476-7563-7 (pbk.)


90  89  88  87
7  6  5  4  3  2  1

Printed in the United States of America

*To Charles and Lillian*

# Contents

# *Acknowledgments*

Of the many persons who have assisted me, I owe a special debt to George Fletcher, Stephen Hudson, Edward Sagarin, Anthony Supino, Andrew Von Hirsch, and Michael Zimmerman. Each of them should recognize how his contribution has helped to improve this book. Rutgers University has been generous in providing me with financial support.

*Philosophy of Criminal Law*

# 1

# *Orthodox Criminal Theory*

## THE NEED FOR CRIMINAL LAW REFORM

SEVERAL KINDS OF BOOKS debunk the criminal law. The most popular are sensationalistic. These are typically written by disillusioned professionals (lawyers or judges) or laypersons (defendants or victims) who emphasize the enormous gaps between the ideals of justice taught in schools and the actual administration of criminal law. The realities of our criminal justice system fall so far short of our aspirations that the resultant charade will continue to provide the content of many a best-seller. These books usually conclude with pleas for drastic reform.

The substantive criminal law is also a frequent object of attack. Some books are nonideological. Authors compile an amusing collection of antiquated laws that remain valid but are no longer enforced. More interesting critiques, however, originate from a political perspective. Radicals argue that many of our laws serve the interests of a privileged minority. Liberals lament the erosion of our civil liberties. Conservatives insist that society has become overly permissive of immorality. Libertarians maintain that too much personal freedom is sacrificed before a government bent on increasing its power. The most familiar allegation is that the criminal justice system provides insufficient protection to law-abiding citizens. Each of these complaints is supported by an examination of recent developments in the substantive criminal law. These books also contain blueprints for improvement.

This book represents yet another attempt to expose the inadequacies of the criminal law, but the target of my criticisms is less familiar. My attack aims at what I call *orthodox criminal theory*. Since it is not common knowledge that criminal law is supported by a theory, I will first introduce its nature and function. Subsequent chapters will raise difficulties with specific parts of this theory.

If my arguments are sound, it will be clear that fundamental

1

changes in orthodox theory are needed, and I will indicate the direction that such revisions should take. Instead of advocating the wholesale abandonment of orthodox theory, I will identify and retain the core of good sense in the views I replace. I will refer to the end product of my proposals as *revised criminal theory*. Unfortunately, my alternative to orthodoxy is sketchy, programmatic, and incomplete. Future theoreticians will have to decide whether the principles I defend are superior or inferior to their orthodox counterparts. At the very least, I hope to demonstrate that major revisions in orthodox theory are desirable.

The study of criminal theory is worthwhile because of its impact upon practice, and this book explores this connection. Often we read about decisions that offend our sense of justice, and we wonder why such disappointing judgments are rendered. Are our judges incompetent? Are they duped by clever lawyers? Sometimes. More frequently, however, theoretical considerations beneath the surface are at work in shaping the substantive criminal law. Unless this underlying theory is brought to the surface, we cannot begin to appreciate why the law is as it is. Much of the content of the criminal law will remain mysterious and inexplicable without an understanding of its supporting theory.

Nevertheless, the study of criminal theory does not provide a comprehensive understanding of the criminal law. Only a few of the controversies that attract media attention are substantive. The study of criminal *procedure* has become almost an obsession in contemporary America. Procedural technicalities and loopholes baffling to laypersons often contribute to decisions perceived as unjust. Our society continues to debate the rationale and limitations of, for example, Miranda warnings and exclusionary rules. Why this preoccupation with procedure to the neglect of substance? One part of the answer is that the judiciary (and Supreme Court in particular) is constrained to interpret a Constitution that has been interpreted largely (though not exclusively) as a procedural document.[1] Even so, I focus here upon the theoretical deficiencies that have a pernicious influence upon the substantive criminal law.

Substantive criminal theory is critiqued infrequently, and not only because it is less well understood. When knowledgeable authorities are asked what in our criminal justice system is most worth preserving, they are likely to respond by identifying a number of the *fundamental principles of liability* that constitute orthodox theory. Anglo-American criminal theory differs in important respects from European and Eastern traditions, and there is a strong consensus in this country about the superiority of our theory over its counterparts. Although there is wide agreement that our substantive law is in need of reform, the theoretical constraints in which improvement should take place are thought to be relatively secure. It is a testimony to the strength and influence of orthodox theory that movements to reform the criminal law almost never disregard these fundamental principles, but strain to show how the proposed changes are compatible with them. Disrespect or outright rejection of the fundamental principles of liability is almost never urged. But orthodox criminal theory, I will argue, is somewhat less worthy of preservation than is generally supposed. If the changes I recommend constitute improvements, this aspect of our criminal justice system will become even more deserving of our respect. Revised criminal theory should have a salutory impact upon the substantive criminal law.

It is timely that criminal theory should attract general attention. Although the past few decades have witnessed unprecedented change in state and federal criminal law and procedure, there is good reason to believe that these reforms signal the beginning rather than the end of a welcome trend. Despite these reforms, widespread public dissatisfaction with our system of criminal justice persists. Pressures to increase the efficiency of law enforcement exert a powerful force to compromise the content of the fundamental principles of criminal liability. We must understand when these compromises are defensible, and when they should be resisted. For example, is it really important that we continue to observe the requirement that persons be punished only for offenses that include a mens rea, if greater social protection could be achieved by dispensing with this principle? Familiarity with criminal theory is essential if this kind of question is to be answered.

Moreover, it seems apparent that our system of criminal justice is strained beyond its capacities, and may soon be on the brink of collapse. One of our most significant social and political failures has been our inability or unwillingness to develop effective noncriminal solutions to contemporary problems. Alcohol and drug abuse, for example, have ususally been addressed within our criminal justice system, largely because there has been nowhere else to turn. Had such alternatives been available, it is unlikely that the criminal sanction would be used so widely. Much behavior that constitutes a legitimate object of social concern does not fit the paradigm of blameworthy, reprehensible conduct, and seems ill suited for disposition within our criminal courts. What is urgently required is a rethinking of the kinds of conduct for which criminal penalties are appropriately imposed.[2] As we will see, this issue is absolutely central to revised (though less to orthodox) theory.

Most works by criminal theorists are exceedingly cautious and uncritical of the fundamental principles they apply. Almost all recognize flaws, but none is as sweeping in its objections as this book. The closest recent work is George Fletcher's *Rethinking Criminal Law*,[3] the most important criticism of criminal theory in several decades. It has been hailed as having exposed "the poverty of American criminal jurisprudence."[4] Fletcher's book is perhaps the first to observe that several of "the artificial words of the law" in which the fundamental principles of liability are expressed are "ambiguous beyond repair," and that criminal theory "can do quite well without them."[5] Previous theorists commonly proposed to overcome ambiguity by submitting their own technical (and equally mysterious) definitions. Fletcher, to his credit, substitutes "terms in the way they are ordinarily understood by lay speakers."[6] If his insights are heeded, future authors of criminal law textbooks need not caution readers that "there is remarkably little correlation between the common usage or dictionary meanings of words and their legal usage."[7] Thus I am overwhelmingly sympathetic to the spirit of Fletcher's remarks, although the details of our reservations about orthodox criminal theory differ substantially.

If the deficiencies in orthodox criminal theory are as glaring as I will suggest, it is important to speculate about why the great criminal theorists of this century have failed to correct them. The suggestion that orthodox theory is radically defective is likely to be dismissed unless there is good reason to believe that these defects would have escaped the notice of previous theorists. There is perhaps no single satisfactory explanation for this oversight, but the following factors are especially significant.

First, it is important to appreciate that criminal theory, like the actual practice of law, is a discipline with an internal bias toward conservatism. The legal authority may be unique in that he distinguishes himself by demonstrating that his scholarship is unoriginal. Outstanding legal research invariably builds upon the work of established experts. It is exceedingly difficult to dislodge principles that are firmly in place and upheld by the great weight of authority. Such entrenchment and widespread support are frequently cited as conclusive evidence that the principles *must* be correct. Some theorists apparently believe that legal principles should be preserved simply because they represent the accumulated wisdom of ages. Anyone who hopes to be taken seriously by legal professionals who share this methodological orientation cannot reject too much conventional wisdom all at once.

But whatever might be said about this rationale in general, it has little application to the *philosophy* of criminal law. A willingness to reconsider large parts of established theory is distinctive of the philosophy of criminal law. It is true that tens of thousands of creative and talented minds have devoted millions of hours of careful thought to the development of the criminal law, but almost all their attention has been focused in the context of specific cases. A criminal lawyer researches and reflects upon particular issues that arise in a real incident involving a person whom he prosecutes or defends. If the lawyer has sufficient experience, he may be able to relate his insights about the specific case to others that share relevant similarities. Yet he is unlikely to have an occasion to integrate his thought into a systematic theory. Thus even those most familiar with the practice of law may be remarkably unsophisticated as theoreticians. Criminal theory examines relations between issues that almost always are studied in isolation.

A discussion of how this conservative bias might be resisted suggests a second explanation for the paucity of attacks upon orthodox criminal theory. What external standards are available for testing the adequacy of the fundamental principles of liability? The answer provided here draws heavily from contemporary work in moral and political philosophy. Criminal theorists finally have begun to rediscover the intimate connections between their discipline and normative ethics. The opening sentence in Fletcher's book admits that "criminal law is a species of political and moral philosophy."[8] Hyman Gross notes that "if criminal justice is to be accepted as the rational and morally enlightened response to crime that it is said to be . . . an account is required which satisfies the demands of common sense and of morality."[9]

These remarks appear extraordinary only in the context of the almost complete absence of similar observations by criminal theorists of preceding eras. The leading authorities of the first half of this century did not acknowledge the connections between criminal theory and moral and political philosophy. Two factors conspired to prevent an earlier fusion between these disciplines. First, moral and political philosophers were preoccupied with metaethical issues and were unconcerned about substantive questions at the time these criminal theorists were educated. By contrast, philosophy journals today are filled with spirited discussions of contemporary normative controversies. Almost no respectable philosopher wrote about such topics prior to 1970. The dominant ethical theory of the earlier era, if any, was utilitarianism, and its influence on criminal law had been operative for more than a hundred years. Utilitarians who attempted to apply those principles that best promote the general interest were unable to respond to the accusation that their recommendations might violate rights and promote injustice. But the adequacy of criminal theory must ultimately be measured by reference to justice, not utility. The recent development of nonutilitarian accounts of justice, as well as a surge of interest in rights, dramatically increases the potential use of moral and political philosophy to criminal theory.

Moreover, the most influential legal philosophers on both sides of the Atlantic had officially banished ethical inquiry from criminal theory. These authorities were prepared to go to extraordinary lengths to construe their discipline as methodologically distinct from (and superior to) that of moral and political philosophy. These theorists explored differences, rather than similarities, between their principles and those of moral and political philosophy. Jurisprudence was to be scientific, objective, factual, and certain. Moral and political philosophy, by contrast, possessed none of these *desiderata.* In retrospect, it appears that these theorists suffered from what might be called "moral arguophobia," that is, a fear that their discipline might require the production and evaluation of moral and political arguments. Orthodox criminal theory is almost unintelligible unless this fear is understood, for it explains the importance attached by these authorities to a number of concepts and principles. The content of the fundamental principles of liability reflects the fantasy that criminal theory embodies no moral or political presuppositions. The pretense that the issues of concern to criminal theorists are somehow unlike those investigated by moral and political philosophers has severely stunted the development of criminal theory. As a result, criminal theory has stagnated and lost its association with moral and political philosophy. Shortcomings in orthodox theory become apparent when these connections are reestablished.

An additional reason helps explain why orthodox criminal theory has persisted so long in its present form despite its inadequacies. Consider the dominant form of contemporary legal education. Almost all law students are fed a diet of cases; it is not uncommon for a student to complete his entire legal education without having consulted (let alone read in its entirety) a single treatise. Law professors may even actively discourage the reading of textbooks. Thus the largest potential market for scholarly works in any discipline—students who hope to gain a competence in that field—is unavailable. It is not surprising that the supply is responsive to the demand, and that few critical works on criminal theory are written.

Finally, criminal lawyers and judges have a prejudice against theory that is shared by practitioners of most other professions. Theories are typically denounced as abstract, remote, and impractical. Undoubtedly the familiar phrase "that may be fine in theory, but it doesn't work in practice" was coined by a practitioner who hoped to excuse his ignorance of theory. In fact, nothing is as useful to sound practice as a good theory. I hope to show that the poverty of Anglo-

American criminal theory is among the most significant contributors to substantive injustice. Perhaps the most important thesis of this book is that attention to theory can shed light on recurrent substantive problems and thus help stimulate principled criminal law reform.

## THE FUNDAMENTAL PRINCIPLES OF CRIMINAL LIABILITY

THE RECEIVED VIEWS in orthodox theory, to be described in this section, are expressed by a number of generalizations I call the *fundamental principles of criminal liability.* Most authorities subscribe to these principles, at least in rough outline, although probably no single theorist adheres to everything I will claim on behalf of orthodoxy. Although most of the views described here have been contested,[10] each continues to represent the majority position. This summary does not elaborate orthodox criminal theory in great detail.[11] My point is to introduce a theory vulnerable to attack, and subsequent criticisms are sensible only in the context of what they reject.

One final comment about methodology should be mentioned before introducing the fundamental principles of criminal liability. The key to an understanding of any principle is to determine what would count as a violation of it. These fundamental principles are not to be interpreted as vacuous tautologies. They are alleged to express requirements to which particular offenses may or may not conform. Thus it must be possible to imagine substantive criminal laws that transgress them. My elucidation of these principles will focus on controversial areas in which it is unclear how, or whether, they apply. Uncertainty about what would amount to a violation indicates a lack of clarity about the requirements themselves. Possible violations are noted to help understand the principles.

Jerome Hall contends that "seven principles . . . underlie and permeate [criminal law]: legality, mens rea, act, the concurrence or fusion of mens rea and act, harm, causation, and punishment."[12] This list provides a sensible introduction to orthodox criminal theory. But nearly every authority, not excepting Hall, includes chapters on burdens of proof and defenses to liability. With these latter topics added to the above list, Hall has provided an accurate enumeration of the fundamental principles of liability that constitute orthodox criminal theory. In this section I briefly discuss each of these eight principles, with special focus on what they are thought to preclude.[13]

### 1. Legality
Most authorities begin their texts with the principle of legality, expressed by the maxim *nulla poena sine lege* (no punishment without

law). Impositions of liability must always be justified by reference to some criminal law that has been violated. Adoption of the principle of legality is perhaps the crucial step in the transition from the rule of men to the rule of law.

The most flagrant disregard of the principle of legality would consist in the punishment of a person known not to have committed a criminal offense. Not all punishment pursuant to law, however, would satisfy the demands of the principle of legality as it is explicated by contemporary criminal theorists. The principle is said to have four distinct but related corrolaries.

A. The first prohibits *vagueness*. The principle of legality cannot be circumvented by enacting legislation so unclear and open-ended that it could be invoked to punish anyone whose conduct is deemed objectionable. A criminal statute is defective on this ground if persons "of common intelligence must necessarily guess at its meaning and differ as to its application."[14] The vagueness rationale has been used to strike statutes that proscribe "vagrancy,"[15] or prohibit assemblies of persons who "conduct themselves in a manner annoying to persons passing by."[16] But no better example of vagueness could be produced than the infamous "doctrine of analogy" popularized under Stalin and Hitler. A (repealed) provision of the Soviet Criminal Code stated: "If any socially dangerous act is not directly provided for by the present Code, the basis and limits of responsibility for it shall be determined by application of those articles of the Code which provide for crimes most similar to it in nature."[17] In other words, any "socially dangerous act" became an offense.

B. The second corrolary prohibits the enactment of *ex post facto* criminal law. Early in the eighteenth century the Court formulated the conditions under which a criminal statute is retroactive and thus in violation of the principle of legality:

> 1st. Every law that makes an action done before the passing of the law, and which was innocent when done, criminal; and punishes such action. 2d. Every law that aggravates a crime, or makes it greater than it was, when committed. 3d. Every law that changes the punishment, and inflicts a greater punishment, than the law annexed to the crime, when committed. 4th. Every law that alters the legal rules of evidence, and receives less, or different testimony, than the law required at the time of the commission of the offense, in order to convict the offender.[18]

C. A somewhat more controversial corrolary of the principle of legality requires "strict construction" of criminal laws. Ambiguity and uncertainty in the application of criminal laws must be resolved in favor of the accused. For example, a judge refused to construe a viable fetus as a "human being" in order to find a defendant guilty of murder.[19] When reasonable persons might differ about the meaning, scope, or application of a criminal statute, that interpretation most favorable to the defendant will be adopted.

D. Finally, the principle of legality has been cited to discourage the judiciary from creating offenses not enacted by the legislature. At one time, state courts were openly permitted to punish new and ingenious forms of antisocial conduct not expressly prohibited by existing statutes. Contemporary state courts rarely fill "gaps" in the law by creating new offenses. In 1955 a defendant was convicted of making obscene telephone calls even though such conduct was not explicitly proscribed by statute or precedent.[20] The principle of legality opposes such enlargements of the common law of crimes.

Fair notice is the most frequently cited rationale for the principle of legality and its several corrolaries. Justice requires that persons have a reasonable opportunity to avoid criminal penalties by choosing to conform their conduct to law. Moreover, the principle limits the discretion of legal officials at virtually every level. Historically, unfettered discretion has been one of the most pervasive characteristics of a repressive political regime.

### 2. Actus Reus

Criminal liability requires that the conduct of the defendant includes an *actus reus*. Each offense must contain some physical, outward, external, behavioral component or manifestation in order to satisfy this fundamental principle. Controversial applications of the actus reus principle are as follows:

A. Authorities disagree about whether criminal liability was ever imposed for such offenses as "compassing or imagining the king's death." Such a statute, if interpreted to dispense with overt behavior, unquestionably would infringe the actus reus requirement. No crime can be committed simply by one's thoughts or mental states.

B. This principle has been used to prohibit *status* offenses, that is, criminal laws that impose liability for what a person *is* rather than for what he *does*. A personal condition or character trait is not a physical act, and cannot be made an offense. For example, a state cannot punish a person for being "addicted to the use of narcotics,"[21] because "criminal penalties may be inflicted only if an accused has committed some act."[22] Many authorities relate their reservations about status offenses to the proper function of the criminal justice system, which is designed to punish dangerous *behavior* rather than to apprehend and detain dangerous *persons*. Other kinds of coercive state intervention (e.g., quarantine, civil commitment) differ in this respect.

C. This principle has also been invoked to explain the disparity between acts and *omissions*. Our criminal justice system (as well as most other coercive systems) punishes positive actions far more frequently than omissions, or failures to act. When a statute (e.g., homicide) specifies some result (e.g., death) that must occur in order to give rise to liability, it is crucial to decide whether the defendant's conduct is a positive action or an omission. Persons owe duties to all others not to kill them by positive action, but a person can commit homicide by omission in only a few carefully defined circumstances.

D. It is doubtful that *possession* constitutes an act in the ordinary sense of the term. Nor does it constitute an act in the technical legal sense, if "act" is defined as bodily movement. Most American authorities, however, have managed to reconcile possessory offenses with the actus reus requirement. English courts have been less confident about this reconciliation. For example, an indictment charging possession of obscene material was held not to constitute a criminal offense, since no act was alleged.[23]

E. Many authorities have invoked the actus reus principle to disallow liability for *involuntary* conduct. According to Gross, "an involuntary act is simply not an act, just as a movie set is not a village, or an art forgery an old master."[24] The Model Penal Code, however, allows that conduct may qualify as action even though involuntary; voluntariness is included as a requirement in addition to the actus reus principle.[25]

F. Actus reus creates difficulties in imposing liability for *attempted* crimes. It is extremely difficult to determine when the defendant has made sufficient progress toward his criminal objective that he may be said to have committed an attempt. Insufficient progress that does not constitute an attempt is generally described as "mere preparation." A person has not committed an attempt unless his conduct manifests an actus reus.[26]

The requirement of an actus reus is taken for granted more frequently than it is expressly defended. Reference is sometimes made to the commitment of the criminal justice system to a conception of persons as autonomous beings possessed of free will. Philosophers and social scientists have cast serious doubts upon this understanding of personhood. But even if this conception were ultimately discredited, some criminal theorists insist that the actus reus requirement should retain its significance. Herbert Packer writes: "Very simply, the law treats man's conduct as autonomous and willed, not because it is, but because it is desirable to proceed as if it were."[27] The criminal law expresses this commitment by punishing persons only for what they do, and not for what happens to them, or for what they think, or for what they are.

### 3. Mens Rea

Perhaps the most important and perplexing principle of criminal liability is the requirement of mens rea or guilty mind, expressed by the ancient maxim *actus non facit reum, nisi mens rea sit* (an act is not guilty without a guilty mind). The meaning and application of this principle has been the subject of so much controversy that it is almost impossible to state a majority position on the matter. The closest English synonyms to mens rea are "fault" or "criminal intent." A safe generalization is that mens rea is "whatever mental element is necessary to convict for any particular crime."[28] *Any* offense, if construed to dispense with a mental element, would constitute an exception to this requirement.[29] This principle has been cited in opposition to the following kinds of criminal practices.

A. The principle of mens rea, unlike that of actus reus, is widely acknowledged to have exceptions. Offenses are said to impose *strict liability* "where no mens rea is required."[30] Such statutes have become an increasingly established part of Anglo-American criminal practice. The controversy surrounding strict liability, however, shows no signs of abating. Offenses imposing strict liability are in such disfavor that courts frequently add a mens rea requirement to a statute even in the absence of express legislative authorization.[31] Moreover, the harshness of imposing punishment without mens rea has led many authorities to conclude that strict liability should be reserved for public-welfare offenses, for which the punishment is not severe.

B. A few authorities oppose criminal *negligence* on the ground that it violates the mens rea requirement. A defendant may create a harm through inadvertence or lack of due care while his mind is a "blank." Nonetheless, most criminal theorists are satisfied that criminal liability for negligent conduct is compatible with the mens rea principle. Their ambivalence about criminal negligence is reflected in two ways. First, punishments for criminal negligence generally are much less severe than for intentional wrongdoing. Second, statutory definitions typically require that deviations from standards of due care must be "gross" or "extreme" to constitute criminal negligence.

C. The issue of mens rea is raised in the context of whether criminal liability should be based upon an "objective" or "subjective" standard. This dispute often surfaces in determinations of whether a defendant intended to bring about a given result. According to "objectivists," a person intends the natural and probable consequences of his acts, and his intention for purposes of imposing criminal liability is established by reference to the "reasonable person." If the reasonable person would have foreseen that a given consequence would follow from his conduct, then the defendant is held to have intended that result. "Subjectivists" contend that what a defendant intends depends only on what he in fact foresees. This debate is crucial in cases in which a reasonable person would have foreseen a given consequence, though the particular defendant did not.[32] Some authorities insist that the requirement that defendants conform to an "objective" standard violates the principle that criminal liability must include a mens rea.

D. Most *defenses* from criminal liability can be construed as the absence of mens rea. Thus if a defendant acts under duress or in self-defense, he may be said to have acted without mens rea. As a result, virtually any attempt to narrow or restrict the availability of a given defense is regarded by some authorities as an erosion of the significance of mens rea. For example, consider the circumstances under which mistake constitutes a defense from criminal liability. Suppose a person accused of theft convinces the jury that he mistakenly believed the stolen item belonged to him. A requirement that his mistake constitutes a valid defense only if it were *reasonable* would be resisted by many authorities as an unacceptable compromise of the mens rea requirement. Similarly, the principle that ignorance of the law is not an excuse is criticized as incompatible with the mens rea requirement. Contemporary pleas to eliminate or narrow the insanity defense also meet with this response.

E. Mens rea is said to be absent in any of the circumstances in which the conduct of the defendant is less than fully *voluntary*. For example, a person who commits what would otherwise be a criminal offense while sleepwalking lacks mens rea. Although most authorities agree that involuntariness precludes mens rea, considerable dispute concerns when conduct is truly involuntary. Few criminal theorists have been willing to extend this rationale to include conduct performed under the influence of alcohol or illegal drugs.

Even a cursory examination of mens rea is incomplete without discussion of the elusive distinction between *specific* (or special) and *general* intent. The meaning of the former is relatively unproblematic. A number of statutes expressly provide that liability requires that the defendant act with a specified mental state. For example, the offense of "assault with intent to rape" has not been committed unless the defendant acts with the specified intent. The meaning of general intent, however, is far less clear. One authority "explains" the contrast as follows: "In confusing circularity, a 'general-intent' offense can be said to be any crime that requires mens rea and that has no special or 'specific-intent' requirement."[33] Perhaps the best definition of general mens rea is "intention or recklessness with respect to all those circumstances and consequences of the accused's act (or the state of affairs) which constitute the actus reus of the crime in question."[34]

The single most impressive achievement of the Model Penal Code is its elimination of all but four of the baffling array of "mentalistic" concepts employed throughout the common law. The Code does not use such antiquated and mysterious terms as "with a depraved heart," "wantonly," or "with scienter." They are replaced by four "kinds of culpability," viz. (in descending order) "purposely," "knowingly," "recklessly," and "negligently," and each is precisely defined by the Code. The mens rea of any offense created by the Code can be specified by using one or more of these four terms.

The principle of mens rea is generally supported as a requirement of fairness to particular defendants. For the most part, our system of criminal justice exists to discourage the performance of harmful conduct. But the pursuit of this objective is qualified in a number of respects. According to one authority, "it used to be common, and it still is occasionally, to express all these qualifications to liability in terms of the requirement of mens rea."[35] Attacks on the significance of mens rea typically originate from authorities anxious to increase the efficiency of the justice system and to decrease the incidence of criminal behavior.[36] Those who emphasize fairness to defendants generally resist compromises in applications of the mens rea principle. If liability could be imposed despite the absence of criminal intent, persons would be less able to choose to follow a course of conduct that did not result in punishment.

### 4. Concurrence

Criminal liability requires that the actus reus and mens rea of a single offense *concur,* or take place simultaneously. More precisely, the defendant's mental state must "actuate" his physical conduct to give rise to a given offense. Mental states are not interchangeable between crimes. If a defendant has the mens rea of offense A and inadvertently commits the actus reus of offense B, he may be liable for neither A nor B, since the actus reus of a given offense was not "brought about" by his mens rea.

Textbooks generally use examples to illustrate the significance of concurrence. Suppose Smith resolves to kill White but performs no actus reus toward achieving his objective. Later he accidentally runs over White with an automobile. Here actus reus and mens rea do not coincide in time, and liability is precluded by the absence of concurrence. Sometimes the principle of concurrence is not satisfied even though the actus reus and mens rea are cotemporaneous. Suppose Smith resolves to kill Jones and engages in target practice while lying in wait for his victim. If his practice bullet somehow hits Jones, who happens to appear on the scene, Smith's conduct has not conformed to the principle of concurrence and he is not guilty of murder. He possessed the mens rea while performing the actus reus of murder, but since the former did not "actuate" the latter, his conduct does not satisfy the requirement of concurrence.

Real cases illustrating this principle are stranger than fiction. In one bizarre scenario, a defendant poisoned his victim with intent to kill.[37] Believing her to be dead, he transported the body to another state, where he attempted to conceal her identity by decapitation. An autopsy revealed the decapitation rather than the poison to be the cause of death. At the time the defendant possessed the mens rea to kill, he did not perform the actus reus. At the time he committed the actus reus of homicide, he lacked the mens rea. Hall describes the finding of liability for murder in this case as a "departure from the principle of concurrence."[38]

### 5. Harm

Although every criminal theorist who purports to be comprehensive examines the four principles above, discussions of harm are less frequent.[39] The major difficulty is to analyze the concept of harm so that given kinds of conduct can be shown to be harmless. Jeremy Bentham may have been the last criminal theorist to provide such an analysis,[40] and few authorities who do not follow him include a requirement of harm among their fundamental principles of liability. It is understandable that courts are reluctant to second-guess a legislative determination that conduct merits criminal penalties,[41] so judicial criteria to distinguish harmful from harmless conduct have not been developed.

In the absence of an analysis of harm, theorists are able to invoke this principle on an ad hoc basis to criticize most any law of which they disapprove (on the ground that it proscribes harmless conduct) or to support any law they favor (on the ground that the conduct it proscribes is indeed harmful). Yet it is possible to discern three controversial kinds of criminal liability against which this principle is most frequently employed.

A. It is raised in opposition to so-called "morals legislation" restricting the sexual freedom of consenting adults, especially when their conduct occurs in the privacy of their homes. These laws are frequently said to create "victimless crimes."

B. It is used to limit state power to create "inchoate" or "anticipatory" offenses. Some theorists maintain that conduct constitutes mere "preparation," and is not a criminal attempt, unless it is harmful. These theorists are apprehensive that "the law of attempts is designed to catch dangerous persons before they do harm."[42] Those who employ a harm principle generally regard it as a requirement that (as with the other fundamental principles) must be satisfied by conduct rather than by persons.

C. This principle has been used to oppose criminal *paternalism,* that is, laws that punish persons for voluntarily engaging in conduct that harms themselves. For example, statutes requiring the use of a motorcycle helmet, or proscribing the use of marijuana, are often attacked as inconsistent with the harm requirement. Here the principle that criminal liability presupposes harm is reinterpreted to require harm *to others.*

### 6. Causation

Most crimes do not require that the conduct of the defendant bring about an occurrence or specified result. These offenses are complete when the conduct is performed; there is no need to await its consequences to determine what crime, if any, has been committed. However, many crimes (most notably homicide) include some effect (such as death) that must occur before liability attaches. To have committed such offenses, the conduct of the defendant must *cause* this specified result.

Difficulties in applying this principle arise from uncertainties about whether conduct causes a given event. Textbooks and bar examinations typically include mind-boggling scenarios in which several persons independently contribute in some way to a specified result. The student is challenged to identify the defendant whose conduct caused that result. Unless the examples include collaboration, the assumption is that a unique causal agent can be chosen from among the several contributors.

Legal authorities are nearly unanimous in agreeing that conduct cannot cause an event unless that event would not have occurred "but for" the conduct. This condition usually is described as "cause in fact," and is widely regarded as unproblematic. Theorists are not especially concerned about cases of so-called "overdetermination," in which conduct is said to have caused an event even though that event would have happened whether or not the conduct had taken place.

Greater controversy arises in determining what conditions must be added to "cause in fact" to complete the analysis of causation. Clearly the "but for" condition alone is an insufficient test of causation. It is not helpful to regard the fact that the grandparents of a defendant conceived a child as the cause of any subsequent crime their grandchild performed. The missing additional condition generally is called "legal" or "proximate cause." It functions to identify an agent who causes an event from among all those whose conduct satisfies the "but for" condition. There is a lively debate among criminal theorists about the extent to which this further condition is inherent in the meaning of causation itself, or merely reflects pragmatic or policy considerations.[43]

A. The most flagrant violation of the causal principle would involve punishment of a person for a result to which he did not contribute in any way. Short of such a monstrosity, difficult problems of causation arise when the effects of conduct differ from those intended. The most important of these differences involve the persons affected, or the manner in which they are affected. When the defendant intends to harm one person but succeeds in harming another, liability has been imposed by the fiction of "transferred intent." It is well settled that "criminal homicide, battery, arson and malicious mischief do not require that the defendant cause harm to the intended victim; an unintended victim will do just as well."[44] Additional problems arise when the type of harm that befalls the victim is unlike that contemplated by the defendant. Liability is imposed when the discrepancy between intended and actual harm is minor. For example, the causal requirement is satisfied if a defendant is held liable for throwing his victim overboard with the intention of drowning him, although he is in fact eaten by sharks. But the causation requirement precludes liability when the disparity between intended and actual harm is more substantial. If a defendant shoots at a victim with intent to kill, misses him completely, but causes him to change direction, as a result of which he is struck by lightning, most authorities would resist liability for murder as a violation of the causal requirement.[45] The Model Penal Code does not resolve such questions by a precise rule, but requires the jury to determine whether the actual result is "too remote or accidental in its occurrence to have a [just] bearing on the actor's liability or on the gravity of his offense."[46]

B. Problems of causation also arise in cases of omissions. Causal difficulties are frequently raised against "good samaritan" legislation that requires persons to assist others in distress. Some theorists believe that impositions of liability for omissions require a different analysis of causation than is needed for positive actions. Hall maintains that the fact that "some goals may be attained by forbearance" demonstrates that "physical causation alone does not determine liability," and that "'legal causation' has a teleological significance that distinguishes it from mechanical causation."[47]

C. The causal requirement is difficult to reconcile with those instances in which liability is imposed on one person for the conduct of another. Especially problematic is the practice of holding defendants liable for the criminal results of their accomplices. Moreover, sometimes the law imposes "vicarious liability" upon an employer for the criminal acts of his employees.

### 7. Defenses

The first six principles discussed above include conditions that must be satisfied by offenses before criminal liability may attach. Commission of an offense, however, is not sufficient to give rise to liability. Criminal liability also requires that the defendant lacks a valid defense. Defenses to criminal liability are "extrinsic to the definitions of specific crimes but . . . further elaborate the conditions of criminal liability."[48] The two central kinds of defenses are *justifications* and *excuses.* Justifications "state exceptions to the prohibitions laid down by specific offenses"; they implicitly "qualify, supplement, and refine the proscriptions of the penal law."[49] A defendant who has a justification for committing what would otherwise be an offense commits no crime at all. A killing in self-defense, for example, is not a homicide.

Excuses, on the other hand, are not exceptions or qualifications to offenses. They do not undermine the conclusion that a crime has been committed. Instead, they function to show that a defendant should not be held criminally liable for what is admittedly an offense. Most, if not all excuses (for instance, infancy and insanity) involve some sort of personal disability. Infants and the insane can commit crimes, but should not be punished for so doing. The distinction, in other words, depends upon whether the defense shows the *behavior* not to have been criminal, or the *defendant* not to be subject to punishment *for* his behavior.[50]

An examination of the scope and limits of the several defenses to criminal liability is a massive undertaking. The most important defenses are listed by Paul Robinson:

> Alcoholism, alibi, amnesia, authority to maintain order and safety, brainwashing, chromosomal abnormality, consent, convulsion, custodial authority, defense of habitation, defense of others, defense of property, de minimis infraction, diplomatic immunity, domestic (or special) responsibility, double jeopardy, duress, entrapment, executive immunity, extreme emotional disturbance, hypnotism, immaturity, impaired consciousness, impossibility, incompetency, insanity, intoxication (voluntary and involuntary), involuntary act defenses, judicial authority, judicial immunity, justification, law enforcement authority, legislative immunity, lesser evils, medical authority, mental illness (apart from insanity), military orders (lawful and unlawful), mistake (of law and fact), necessity, official misstatement of law, parental authority, plea bargained immunity, provocation, public duty or authority, reflex action, renunciation, self-defense, somnambulism, the spousal defense to sexual assaults and theft, statute of limitations, subnormality, testimonial immunity, the unavailable law defense, unconsciousness, and withdrawal.[51]

It is dangerous and misleading to hazard a generalization about the conditions under which these defenses apply. It is said that they defeat criminal liability when they negate a general or special mens rea required for conviction. If so, it would appear that strict liability offenses, which are said to include no mens rea, admit of no defenses whatever. Many (but not all) of these defenses are examined in more detail in subsequent chapters.

### 8. Proof

Criminal liability requires that the defendant is proved guilty beyond a reasonable doubt. This final principle is unlike any of the other seven in that it pertains to how a defendant must be *shown* to have committed a criminal offense. While some authorities address this issue in discussions of criminal procedure or evidence, most textbooks in criminal law include an examination of burdens and standards of proof. This issue indicates the artificiality of too-rigid a distinction between substance and procedure.

Given the widespread public sentiment that we are losing the war against crime, it is surprising that the requirement that the prosecution prove guilt beyond a reasonable doubt has not been the subject of a general attack. It is unlikely that any other principle of criminal justice results in the acquittal of so many persons who in fact have committed offenses. Perhaps more attention should be paid to the question of what precise degree of risk of punishment of the innocent is tolerable to achieve an adequate rate of conviction of the guilty.

Compromises of this principle have been subtle rather than direct. Authorities have not been too demanding in questioning how the standard of "guilt beyond a reasonable doubt" could be made more exact. Instead, controversy surrounds what "guilt" encompasses in this formula. The Supreme Court has ruled that "guilt" includes "every fact necessary to constitute the crime."[52] This answer invites the further question: What facts *are* necessary to "constitute" given offenses? Debate centers around two issues. First, to what extent is a *defense* to criminality a fact necessary to constitute a crime? The Supreme Court has not resolved this issue by its recent holding that a state need not "prove beyond a reasonable doubt every fact, the existence or non-existence of which it is willing to recognize as an exculpatory or mitigating circumstance affecting the degree of culpability or the severity of the punishment."[53] There is a lingering suspicion that the absence of at least some defenses bears on guilt and constitutes a crime to the same extent as elements of offenses.

This first question gives rise to a second. To what extent should the distinction between the "elements" of crime (which the prosecution must prove) and "exculpatory or mitigating circumstances" (which the defendant may be required to prove) be drawn by reference to the literal wording of statutes? Does an issue become a defense as opposed to the absence of an element of an offense simply because the legislature designates it as such? Some authorites are apprehensive that attaching much significance to the fortuities of legislative draftsmanship is excessively and indefensibly "formalistic."[54] Controversy about burdens of proof will persist as long as it remains unclear what facts are necessary to constitute a crime.

This concludes the preliminary discussion of the fundamental principles of criminal liability. There is nothing magical about the number of principles I have selected; other theoreticians would add to it or subtract from it. Many of the more controversial applications of these principles will be reexamined in greater detail in subsequent chapters. This introduction should be helpful in understanding these discussions, and thus lays the foundation for the revisions in criminal theory proposed throughout this book.

## CRIMINAL THEORY AS DESCRIPTIVE

THE FOLLOWING BRIEF (and somewhat idealized) account of the origins of criminal theory will help to explain its nature and function.

The criminal law of primitive societies probably consisted of a number of taboos. As long as relatively few prohibitions existed, there was no pressing need for generalization. A set of rules as simple as the Ten Commandments, for example, needs no special organization, but the desirability of systematization became apparent when the number of offenses multiplied. Sets of offenses were collected in criminal codes, and these codes required an internal structure as they grew in complexity.

Progress toward generalization was first achieved by grouping offenses with a similar subject matter under a common heading. Perhaps the birth of criminal theory should be traced to those authorities who devised names for these common headings.[55] A miscellany of offenses, from the coloring of coins to the violation of the king's eldest unmarried daughter, became known as treason. There is no necessity that one classificatory scheme rather than another should be adopted. Whether there is a sufficient similarity between two distinct offenses to warrant their inclusion under a common heading depends upon the purpose(s) the classification is designed to serve. One system of classification can be assessed as superior or inferior to its competitors only by determining whether it serves these objectives better or worse. Implicit behind even the most rudimentary generalizations, then, is a set of purposes. These purposes provide the context against which the generalizations of theoreticians should be understood and evaluated.

Generalization did not stop at this level. Offenses with quite distinct subject matters were systematized under broader headings. The earliest works of criminal theorists organized offenses in very different ways. Some of the organizing principles once almost universally adopted are now archaic. For instance, no modern criminal theorist would continue to subdivide offenses into those against god and those against man. But a residue of this distinction—the difference between criminal and civil law—remains basic. Other distinctions of medieval origin have retained their importance. The difference between felonies and misdemeanors, for example, remains generally useful, though its significance has changed throughout legal history. Still other distinctions, such as that between offenses *malum in se* and *malum prohibitum*, have more complicated histories. This contrast once was fashionable, fell into disrepute, and is resurrected periodically. Once again, the viability of each of these broader distinctions must be assessed against a background of purposes.[56]

Generalization reached its culmination when theorists attempted to identify and analyze the conditions that are satisfied by each and every offense. The ultimate aspiration was to exhibit the components common to all offenses, the necessary conditions of criminality per se. These alleged necessary conditions were expressed in a number of fundamental principles of liability, and the content of criminal theory became a study in the meaning and application of these generalizations. At this juncture, criminal theory attained its distinctly modern form.

Yet the noble aspiration described above was doomed from its inception. The range and diversity of criminal offenses proved resistant to the formation of grand generalizations of substance. The few principles that indeed pertain without exception to all offenses have the appearance of platitudes. It is true, but hardly informative, to be assured that "the hallmark of criminality is that it is a breach of the criminal law."[57] In short, criminal theorists were able to articulate few if any significant generalizations that apply without exception to the whole of the substantive criminal law.

Virtually all criminal theorists were aware of this obstacle to the formation of universal and exceptionless principles of liability. Statements in the introductory chapters of their textbooks reflect this realization. Notice the triple disclaimer in James Stephen's influential account of "the general doctrines pervading the whole subject." He proceeds to identify a number of "positive" and "negative" conditions, "*some* of which enter *more* or *less* into the definition of *nearly* all offenses."[58] Despite such excessive caution, it is important that criminal theory be understood according to this admittedly unattainable aspiration. For much of the form and content of modern criminal theory can be conceptualized as a strategy for dealing with the fact that this obstacle to the formation of unqualified generalizations cannot be overcome. Each theorist must develop an account of why there are exceptions, whether and to what extent they are important, and how the fundamental principles of liability can be valuable if they are not universal. The writings of those criminal theorists who simply note such exceptions, without commenting upon their significance, are destined to collect dust on the shelves of law libraries.

Several strategies are available to a theorist confronted with an apparent counterexample to his requirements, and the history of criminal theory is a study in each such response. One familiar strategy is to stretch the meanings of the concepts in the generalization so that the alleged counterexample no longer constitutes a genuine exception. The prestigious Model Penal Code, for example, stipulates that "a person is not guilty of an offense unless his liability is based upon conduct which includes a voluntary act or the omission to perform an act."[59] This actus reus requirement seemingly pertains to each criminal offense. But complications arise immediately. The draftsmen were aware, of course, that all state criminal codes (as well as the Model Penal Code itself) contain a number of *possessory* offenses, for example, possession of narcotics or burglar tools. Is possession either an act or omission? Most authorities concede that "possession is not, strictly speaking, an act or omission to act."[60] Is it therefore false (or at least subject to qualification) that all criminal offenses require an act or omission? The draftsmen were unwilling to accept this result. With little or no support from standard usage, they simply assert that "possession is an act within the meaning of this section."[61] The concept of an act, then, becomes a technical term of legal art, not to be confused with its use in ordinary English. But technical terms cannot be understood unless they are expressly defined; *ex hypothesi*, we cannot rely upon standard usage to interpret them.

The draftsmen, unfortunately, do not offer a satisfactory definition. An "act" is said to consist of "a bodily movement."[62] This definition is unhelpful in this context, since it seems clear that one can possess something without having moved his body at all. As a result of this failure of definition, the generalization that all criminal liability requires an act or omission is preserved, but at a substantial price. We no longer have a precise understanding of what this generalization means; its concepts have been distorted. One of the recurrent themes of this book is that a number of criminal theorists have presided over the impoverishment of their discipline in this way. They have retained the fundamental principles of orthodox criminal theory, but no longer understand them.

This mystification of legal concepts has profound effects. The successive generations of law students who are condemned by smug professors to analyze the central terms of criminal theory cannot comply when these concepts are distorted in the above way. The Model Penal Code frequently "defines" terms by providing examples of when they do or do not apply. The draftsmen are too shrewd to offer formal definitions. But if the acknowledged experts do not understand the meanings of the central technical concepts of orthodox criminal theory, who does? Small wonder that Fletcher opts to abandon them.

It is more candid to concede that the grand generalizations of orthodox criminal theory are riddled with exceptions. Criminal theorists, of course, usually are quick to admit as much. We all understand what it means to say that a condition is necessary for criminal liability: unless that condition is satisfied, criminal liability cannot obtain. But what is the status of these principles once it is conceded that they do not represent necessary conditions of criminal liability? I will describe answers to this question as the search for a *status* for the fundamental principles of criminal liability.

No authority has adequately specified the status of the fundamental principles of liability, and few authorities even *attempt* to address this problem. Solutions must be inferred from their strategies for dealing with the exceptions to these requirements. Few works in criminal theory include an explanation of what the author hopes to accomplish. Without a statement of objectives, the reader cannot determine whether the theorist has succeeded or failed. The author simply formulates a theory, and the function of that theory is left to the imagination of the reader.

The overwhelming tendency of even the best criminal theorists is to rely on vague or metaphorical language in coming to terms with this difficulty. Once the search for a set of necessary conditions is abandoned, the precise status of the fundamental principles of liability is frequently "explained" as "giving an account of" or "identifying the salient features of" criminal offenses. What do these claims mean? Fletcher maintains that "the general part" of criminal law "has as its object the study of issues that cut across all offenses and merit analysis in isolation from their specific applications."[63] What does he mean by the suggestion that issues "cut across" all offenses? It is disquieting when legal authorities, accustomed to precision and rigor, rely so heavily on metaphor.

### CRIMINAL THEORY AS PRESCRIPTIVE

How is criminal theory important in guiding substantive law reform? Recall my earlier observation that theory construction invariably proceeds against a background of purposes or objectives. Thus far I have indicated that systematization is primarily of pedagogical use; generalizations facilitate the learning and teaching of criminal law. But soon they come to adopt an altogether different significance: they became useful as *critical* tools, as powerful instruments of legal reform. The study of how generalizations initially formulated as descriptions came to be employed as prescriptions is complex, and perhaps no criminal theorist understands this transition fully. Often it takes place without explicit comment. Some commentators expressly indicate that their project is simply to describe the majority views on substantive questions in criminal law. Yet time and time again judges cite the conclusions expressed in those treatises as *reasons* for reaching one result rather than another. Is this practice a simple conflation of what *is* with *what ought to be?* If not, why not? The tension and interplay between descriptive and prescriptive functions is perhaps the most fascinating and important aspect of criminal theory.

How and why did this transition from description to prescription occur? Earlier I indicated that a theorist may pursue several different responses when confronted with an apparent counterexample to his generalizations. One response, discussed above, is to stretch the meanings of the concepts contained in his principles to accommodate the exceptions. The resultant principles may thus become unintelligible. A second response is to preserve the original meaning of the concepts, and label the exceptions as "deviant," "aberrational," or otherwise suspect. After all, it can hardly be mere coincidence that most criminal laws share several features. It is tempting to suppose that there must be something untoward about the minority of offenses that lack these common characteristics. Criminal theorists who adopt this approach might reason as follows: if criminal liability requires an actus reus, and actus reus does not include possession, then there *should be* no possessory offenses. The existence of such statutes is proclaimed an injustice, and the criminal theorist demands their repeal. This strategy, then, merges description and prescription in a single theory. It appears to solve the prior problem of specifying the status of the fundamental principles of liability—they are said to express requirements of justice—but in turn leaves further, equally difficult questions unanswered.

Description and prescription blend uneasily in a single theory, although virtually all modern criminal theorists who comment upon the matter acknowledge that their principles serve this dual purpose. No coherent theory of Anglo-American criminal law can be purely *de*scriptive for the simple reason that the set of data (the substantive criminal law) it purports to describe is replete with contradictions. General principles cited with approval in one jurisdiction are repudiated in another, or are accepted and rejected in the same jurisdiction with no awareness of inconsistency. No theorist can deny that some legal precedents are incompatible with others. On the other hand, while it is possible to formulate a coherent theory that is wholly *pre*scriptive, no criminal theorist would be eager to do so. Since the subject matter of the theory is *our* (Anglo-American) criminal law, not some ideal system of criminal justice, no theorist would wish to disassociate himself entirely from the existing substantive criminal law. Thus it is almost inevitable that authorities would combine description and prescription in a single theory.

The major task confronting criminal theorists is to formulate principles that are plausible candidates for requirements of justice, without sacrificing their accuracy as descriptions of existing substantive law. This task is not easily accomplished. Those generalizations that best describe may not have great prescriptive appeal, while compelling prescriptive principles may lack descriptive accuracy.

When two distinct objectives are served simultaneously, there is a need to establish a priority in cases of conflict. Criminal theorists disagree about whether the descriptive function should be subordinated to the prescriptive, or vice versa. Hall expresses a preference for description:

> A theory of penal law (briefly, penal theory or criminal theory) should be tested by the significance of its explanation of existing penal law, and the scholar's primary vocation is to increase that knowledge . . . The only sound procedure is to cleave persistently to the single-minded goal of elucidating the existing penal law, asking only—which theory will maximize our understanding of that law? It also happens . . . that a rigorous adherence to theoretical inquiry inevitably uncovers areas where reforms are needed. When these discoveries are thus made, as by-products of research, the proposed reforms are apt to be defensible.[64]

Other authorities would be unhappy to describe reform as a mere "by-product" of criminal theory. In contrast, Gross seems to favor prescription:

> I do not invent a conception of criminal justice but discover it . . . Official deviations from these principles are abundant everywhere, but this need not embarrass the theorist so long as he remembers that he is not required to give an account of practices just as they are . . . The theorist's job, I think, is to make clear the ideals that generally do guide practice and that makes possible the very awareness of deviation. His job is also to show why those ideals are worthy of our acceptance, when indeed they are. The theorist thus provides the practitioner with guidance for sound practice.[65]

Regardless of whether the theorist emphasizes description or prescription,[66] he must employ some criterion for deciding when a recalcitrant part of the substantive criminal law should be accommodated by a change in general principle, or when it should be condemned as unjust. In short, he needs to know when it is appropriate to describe and when to prescribe. Any strategy that deals with counterexamples to generalizations by labeling them as injustices ripe for repeal is sound only if the fundamental principles of criminal liability can be shown to express requirements of justice. What is the warrant for believing that these fundamental principles of orthodox criminal theory have prescriptive content? Surely their status as principles of justice cannot be established by demonstrating that they accurately describe the vast majority of existing criminal offenses; the maximally descriptive set of generalizations embodied in the substantive criminal law might have little or nothing to do with justice. It would be surprising if the set of generalizations that best describe any and all criminal justice systems have prescriptive content.[67] Why assume that generalizations have a prescriptive status simply because they are inferred from Anglo-American criminal law? How is this chasm between "is" and "ought" to be bridged? It is disappointing that these crucial questions seldom are addressed, let alone resolved, by orthodox theorists. They simply assume that the fundamental principles of criminal liability share a prescriptive status, and use them accordingly.

It should be clear that only careful moral and political argument can demonstrate that the fundamental principles of criminal liability share a prescriptive status. No mechanical alternative to moral and political argument is capable of identifying injustice in the criminal law. Ultimately, the successful merger of description and prescription stands in need of a moral and political theory.[68] Throughout this book I will provide many moral and political arguments, and the reader must be prepared to become engaged in them. In sum, these philosophical arguments will show the need for revisions in the content of some of the fundamental principles of orthodox theory. The improvements I propose will help demystify the criminal law. Revised theory will become a more useful tool for critiquing the substantive criminal law, without loss of descriptive accuracy.

### NOTES

1. For one such influential treatment, see John Ely, *Democracy and Distrust*. It is noteworthy that in Great Britain (due perhaps to the absence of a written constitution) discussions of the criminal law are less dominated by procedure. I will draw freely from both British and American authorities.

2. The word "conduct" is used throughout this book to refer to *whatever* criminal liability might be based upon. Presumably criminal liability must be *for* something, and that amorphous "something" I call conduct. "Conduct" thus includes anything to which criminal liability might conceivably attach, such as action, omission, state of mind, character, status, etc. Admittedly, such a broad understanding of conduct "stretches" the ordinary usage of the word. It is far broader than the Model Penal Code's definition of

"action or omission and its accompanying state of mind." (§1.13(5)) But here the concept is expressly defined, and the word seems more elegant than the arguably more suitable "thing" or "object of criminal liability." See the usage in Glanville Williams, *Textbook of Criminal Law*, p. 153.

    3. George Fletcher, *Rethinking Criminal Law*.

    4. Thomas Morawetz, "Book Review," *Georgia Law Review* 13 (1979): 1558.

    5. Fletcher, *Rethinking*, p. 401.

    6. Ibid., p. 401. At p. 405, Fletcher writes: "In order to build a theory of criminal law, we should use concepts that we understand."

    7. Peter Low, John Jeffries, and Richard Bonnie, *Criminal Law*, pp. 204–5. For a defense of the claim that legal concepts are not technical, see Alan White, *Grounds of Liability*.

    8. Fletcher, *Rethinking*, p. xix.

    9. Hyman Gross, *A Theory of Criminal Justice*, p. 7.

    10. Glanville Williams makes the somewhat exaggerated observation that "there is no unanimity about anything in criminal law: scarcely a single important principle but has been denied by some judicial decision or by some legislature." *Criminal Law: The General Part*, p. 575.

    11. The most popular standard hornbook in America is Wayne Lafave and Austin Scott, *Criminal Law*. More recently, see their *Substantive Criminal Law*. In England, the best treatments are J. C. Smith and Brian Hogan, *Criminal Law;* and Williams, *Textbook*.

    12. Jerome Hall, *Foundations of Jurisprudence*, pp. 86–87.

    13. I have little to say about Hall's principle of punishment, since it differs in being a *consequence* rather than a *precondition* of criminal liability. Legal philosophers have been obsessed with punishment to the neglect of the other principles Hall examines.

    14. *Connally v. General Construction Co.*, 269 U.S. 385, 391 (1926).

    15. *Papachristou v. City of Jacksonville*, 405 U.S. 156 (1972).

    16. *Coates v. City of Cincinnati*, 402 U.S. 611 (1971).

    17. 1926 *RSFSR Criminal Code*, Article 16.

    18. *Calder v. Bull*, 3 U.S. 386, 390 (1798).

    19. *Keeler v. Superior Ct.*, 470 P.2d 617 (1970). But see *M.P.C.* §1.02(3).

    20. *Commonwealth v. Mochan*, 110 A.2d 788 (1955).

    21. *Robinson v. California*, 370 U.S. 660 (1962).

    22. *Powell v. Texas*, 392 U.S. 514, 533 (1968).

    23. *Dugdale v. Regina*, 118 Eng. Rep. 499 (1853).

    24. Gross, *Theory*, p. 68.

    25. *M.P.C.* §1.13(2) and §2.01(1).

    26. *Martin v. State*, 17 So.2d 427 (1944).

    27. Herbert Packer, *The Limits of the Criminal Sanction*, pp. 74–75.

    28. Francis Sayre, "Mens Rea," *Harvard Law Review* 45 (1932): 974, 1026.

    29. Some offenses, such as attempts, cannot be defined intelligibly without reference to some mental elements. This will be discussed in chapter 4.

    30. Low, Jeffries, and Bonnie, *Criminal Law*, p. 233.

    31. *Morissette v. U.S.*, 342 U.S. 246 (1952).

    32. See *D.P.P. v. Smith*, 3 All.E.R. 161 (1961).

    33. Low, Jeffries, and Bonnie, *Criminal Law*, p. 231.

    34. Smith and Hogan, *Criminal*, p. 59. See also Williams, *Criminal Law*, p. 31.

35. Sanford Kadish, "The Decline of Innocence," *Cambridge Law Journal* 26 (1968): 273, 274.

36. See Barbara Wootton, *Crime and the Criminal Law.*

37. *Jackson v. Commonwealth*, 38 S.W. 422 (1896).

38. Jerome Hall, *General Principles of Criminal Law*, p. 189.

39. According to one commentator, "with the exception of Jerome Hall, Gerhard O. Mueller and Orvil C. Snyder, there are few legal theorists who really present a clear and comprehensive view of the meaning of 'harm.' " Albin Eser, "The Principle of 'Harm' in the Concept of Crime," *Duquesne University Law Review* 4 (1966): 345.

40. *An Introduction to the Principles of Morals and Legislation.* But see Joel Feinberg, *Harm to Others.*

41. Federal courts are much more reluctant than state courts. See LaFave and Scott, *Criminal Law*, pp. 138–44.

42. Gross, *Theory*, p. 132.

43. See H.L.A. Hart and A.M. Honore, *Causation in the Law.*

44. LaFave and Scott, *Criminal Law*, p. 253.

45. See Hart and Honore, *Causation*, p. 354.

46. *M.P.C.* §2.03(2)(b).

47. Hall, *General Principles*, p. 196.

48. Low, Jeffries, and Bonnie, *Criminal Law*, p. 523.

49. Ibid., p. 523.

50. I discuss some of the important uses to which the distinction between justification and excuse has been put in chapter 7.

51. Paul Robinson, *Criminal Law Defenses*, p. 70, note 1.

52. *In Re Winship*, 397 U.S. 358, 364 (1970).

53. *Patterson v. New York*, 432 U.S. 197, 207 (1977).

54. See Barbara Underwood, "The Thumb on the Scales of Justice: Burdens of Persuasion in Criminal Cases," *Yale Law Journal* 86 (1977): 1299.

55. The authorities most frequently cited are Henry Bracton, whose *De Legisbus et Consuetudinibus Angliae* was first published in 1268, and Matthew Hale, whose *Pleas of the Crown* was first published in 1678.

56. In case there is doubt, consider Article 46 of the 1926 RSFSR Criminal Code: "The crimes dealt with in this code are classified as follows: a. Those directed against the foundations of the Soviet system established in the USSR by the power of the workers and peasants, and therefore considered to be the most dangerous; b. All other crimes."

57. P. J. Fitzgerald, *Criminal Law and Punishment*, p. 7.

58. James Stephen, *A History of the Criminal Law of England*, p. 3 (emphasis added).

59. §2.01(1).

60. LaFave and Scott, *Criminal Law*, p. 182. At common law, possession was not an act. See Williams, *Textbook*, p. 153.

61. M.P.C. §2.01(4).

62. Ibid., §1.13(2).

63. Fletcher, *Rethinking*, p. 393.

64. Hall, *General Principles*, p. 2. See also the basis for rejecting "evaluative jurisprudence" in White, *Liability*, p. 6.

65. Gross, *Theory*, p. xv. Robinson claims that "the purpose of" his treatise is "to stimulate reform." *Defenses*, p. viii.

66. "[J]urisprudence is not confined to the more commentorial interpretation of what the legislature has produced but involves also the task of providing new devices and propositions for the advancement of law and

justice . . . It is . . . a permanent obligation of criminal jurisprudence to redefine the principles of criminal liability, which, in turn, the legislators may then use to orient themselves when defining new crimes." Eser, "Harm," p. 365.

67. Some legal theorists refuse to countenance as *legal* those systems of rules that do not satisfy given normative standards. See Lon Fuller, *The Morality of Law.*

68. Unfortunately, I do not have a comprehensive moral or political theory. I hope it is clear that progress in these issues is possible in the absence of a complete theory. For expression of a similar sentiment, see Fletcher, *Rethinking*, p. 395, note 2; and Feinberg, *Harm*, p. 18.

# 2

# *Some Observations About Orthodox Criminal Theory*

## JUSTICE AND RIGHTS

In CHAPTER 1 I proposed that the fundamental principles of criminal liability have the status of requirements of justice. This book critically examines these principles as so construed. The first two sections of this chapter will discuss what it means to understand these principles as requirements of justice; the final two sections will offer some further observations about the sense in which the fundamental principles combine to form a *theory*. Most of this chapter is general and abstract. The claims made here have concrete and specific implications for the content of criminal law, but these connections will not be developed until subsequent chapters. The reader with a low tolerance for philosophical abstractions is advised to skip directly to chapter 3.

Throughout this chapter I accept the content of orthodox criminal theory as given. I do not yet propose revisions in any of the fundamental principles of liability introduced in chapter 1. Later chapters will propose changes in the *formulation*, but not in the *status* of some of these principles. If the fundamental requirements of orthodox theory are shown to be inferior to their competitors, it must be on the ground that alternative principles are superior as requirements of justice. But before such an assessment can be made, the status of these fundamental principles must be further clarified. It is impossible to identify the weaknesses of orthodox theory without first understanding how its principles are designed to function.

I construe the fundamental principles of criminal liability as requirements of justice for three reasons. First, this hypothesis explains the primary use to which these principles have been put by both theoreticians and practitioners (judges and lawyers) who shape the substantive criminal law. These principles are invoked as a basis for criticizing real or hypothetical laws that deviate from them. Second, this interpretation renders criminal theory interesting and important to the philosopher. Serious movements to reform the criminal law cannot afford to ignore criminal theory if the end product is to remain a system of criminal "justice." Finally, no other alternative is remotely appealing. This interpretation is consistent with suggestions that these principles express complex "descriptive-normative" hybrids.[1] The *normative* components of these principles, at least, should be construed as requirements of justice.

Nonetheless, my interpretation might distort what orthodox theorists may have intended. If my hypothesis does not correspond to their understanding, I apologize by protesting that they should have made their own interpretation more clear. As a last resort, my project can be defended as an investigation of some of the specific implications of orthodox criminal theory *if* its fundamental principles of liability are construed as requirements of justice. If the consequences I examine in later chapters are unpalatable to orthodox theorists, there will be an urgent need to redefine the role and status of their fundamental principles.

What does it mean to interpret a principle as a requirement of justice? I admit that I have no comprehensive theory of justice, nor am I entirely clear about all the conditions that must be satisfied before a principle qualifies as a requirement of justice.[2] Yet some progress in this direction can be made by positing a connection between justice and rights. I assume that if justice requires that something be done for someone, then he has a *right* that that something be done.[3] This assumption is crucial to understanding what it means to interpret the fundamental principles of criminal liability as requirements of justice, inasmuch as it construes transgressions of these principles as infringements of individual rights. In other words, the statement that a person is treated unjustly if he is held criminally liable for conduct that does not include a mens rea entails that he has a right not to be held criminally liable for conduct that does not include a mens rea. The statement that a person is treated unjustly if he is held criminally liable for an event he does not cause entails that he has a *right* not to be held criminally liable for an event he does not cause. And so on for each of the remaining principles.

The individual rights respected by the fundamental principles of liability should not be understood merely as *legal* rights. They may not be withdrawn at the convenience of legislators or judges (or even by constitutional amendment), as the legal system may withdraw the right of eighteen-year-olds to drink alcohol. It must be remembered that these principles function as *critical* tools; something allegedly is *objectionable* about deviations from them. I will suppose that what is objectionable about such deviations is aptly expressed by the claim that persons have a pre-existing *moral* right to be treated in accordance with these principles. Criminal theory, then, embodies a view about the moral rights citizens enjoy against state authority.

I make no systematic effort to ground the several moral rights I examine in some more basic principle or theory. Perhaps the view I defend embodies what might be described as a "respect for persons" ethic.[4] Or it might be derived from a contractarian framework.[5] Or it might be based upon a conception of equality.[6] However, I am not persuaded that a single principle can serve as the ultimate foundation for all the prescriptive claims one wants to make about the substantive criminal law.[7] While the philosophical importance of these larger projects cannot be denied, I hope it is clear that progress can be made on penultimate issues even though deeper problems remain unsolved.[8]

The supposition that persons have moral rights that the state must observe in creating law is hardly novel or unfamiliar. This supposition provides the basis for what may be the leading theory of the nature and function of the Bill of Rights. According to Ronald Dworkin, the moral rights protected legally by the Bill of Rights are independent of the existence of a legal system.[9] Unfortunately, some laws are enacted that violate these moral rights, but such laws do not generate moral duties of compliance. Persons can have no moral duty to obey a law abridging, for example, the right of free speech, because the state lacks the authority to create such a law in the first place. Such a law is inconsistent with the moral theory afforded legal protection by the Bill of Rights.

According to the interpretation advanced here, the several fundamental principles limit the authority of the state to impose criminal liability in much the same way as the rights contained in the Bill of Rights limit the authority of the state to create law generally. And for the same reason. A state that exceeds these limitations treats its citizens unjustly by violating their moral rights. Thus persons can have no moral duty to obey a law abridging, for example, the right not to be held criminally liable for conduct that does not include a mens rea.

This interpretation suggests an intimate connection between criminal theory and constitutional law. There is good reason to believe that the Constitution may be interpreted to extend legal protection to the moral rights respected by the fundamental principles of criminal liability, insofar as the Bill of Rights functions to afford legal significance to preexisting moral rights. One might assume that this suggestion could be tested by examining whether and to what extent the Supreme Court has elevated to constitutional significance the moral rights allegedly respected by the fundamental principles of criminal liability. For example, has the Supreme Court accepted or rejected the view that a person has a legal right not to be held criminally liable for an event he does not cause? Texts on constitutional law discuss these questions; they are too complicated to explore in detail here. In short, some of the moral rights respected by these principles have been "found" in the Constitution; others have not. The Supreme Court has held, for instance, that criminal sanctions for conduct that does not include an actus reus constitutes cruel and unusual punishment and thus is prohibited by the Eighth Amendment.[10] The constitutional significance of mens rea is much more complex. Herbert Packer has concluded that "to paraphrase [Supreme Court holdings]: Mens rea is an important requirement but it is not a constitutional requirement, except sometimes."[11] It is tempting to believe that those Supreme Court decisions that denied constitutional significance to the mens rea requirement create difficulties for the hypothesis that this principle respects moral rights.

Nonetheless, it is potentially misleading to attach much weight to such a constitutional inquiry. The decisions of the Supreme Court that "found" an actus reus requirement in the Bill of Rights cannot be taken as reliable authority for the constitutional significance of *everything* that principle has been construed to mean by criminal theorists. Until the meanings and implications of the central terms employed in these fundamental principles have been clarified, it cannot be determined to what extent they have been given or denied constitutional significance. Thus it would be rash to conclude that the Supreme Court has definitively decided to reject "finding" a requirement of mens rea in the Constitution. It is understandable that the Supreme Court would be reluctant to afford constitutional protection to a principle it did not fully understand and the implications of which are open to serious dispute. One commentator has argued that "one of the major impediments to converting the common law notion of mens rea into a viable constitutional standard has been the imprecision which characterized the use of the term at common law."[12] This authority predicts that the clarity achieved by the Model Penal Code definitions of mens rea removes this difficulty, and that soon the Court may be prepared to elevate this requirement to constitutional stature.

In the final analysis, the supposition that the fundamental principles respect moral rights that constrain the authority of the state to impose criminal liability does not depend upon whether or not such rights have constitutional significance. Perhaps not all moral limitations on the authority of the state to create law can be "found" in the Constitution. This issue cannot be resolved without a theory of constitutional interpretation.[13] Yet it is evident that the moral rights respected by the fundamental principles of criminal liability are novel and unfamiliar compared to those championed within the civil libertarian tradition. They are seldom included in manifestos on human rights. Persons have died on behalf of the right of free speech, for example, but no significant political movement explicitly defends the right not to be held criminally liable for conduct that does not include an actus reus. Yet the moral rights respected by the fundamental principles of criminal liability are as precious and valuable as many more familiar rights. A repressive state can do (and has done) as much damage to the freedom and well-being of its citizens by violating these novel rights as by violating those rights cherished by civil libertarians.

These moral rights are unfamiliar for a number of reasons. First and foremost, they are too abstract to be recognizable to the average citizen in the form in which they are expressed here. He would find it somewhat easier to appreciate the importance of these abstract rights if they were applied to concrete circumstances. Citizens would be outraged if they could be punished for mere religious beliefs; such liability is precluded (inter alia) by the actus reus requirement. Second, the public has little sympathy for what are perceived to be the "rights of criminals." Unfortunately, polls indicate that citizens would welcome rather than oppose many features of a more repressive state. Instead of appreciating these rights, citizens raise a public outcry at their application to defenses such as insanity. Few persons empathize with potential defendants and understand that these rights protect the general public, and are not devices contrived by clever lawyers to enable the guilty to escape their just deserts. Finally, these rights have not come under wholesale popular attack. Rights are most easily appreciated when they are violated. For the most part, courts have been vigilant in protecting these rights from occasional legislative excesses. In general, the judiciary has shown a healthy regard for the fundamental principles of orthodox criminal theory. Were it to do otherwise, it is likely that more support for the rights respected by these fundamental principles would be forthcoming. In a few areas, however, where respect for these principles has been withheld, or extended with serious qualifications, the deficiencies of orthodox criminal theory have become evident. A discussion of some of the tensions that arise within orthodox criminal theory begins in chapter 3.

### RIGHTS AND CRIMINAL THEORY

THE ASSUMPTION that the fundamental principles of criminal liability respect moral rights does not resolve all questions about how they should be interpreted. Indeed, it represents only a small beginning. It does, however, suggest the direction in which further guidance might be sought. Much of the philosophical literature about the nature and function of moral rights becomes relevant to an understanding of the fundamental principles of liability. Criminal theorists are likely to misconstrue and incorrectly apply their own principles unless they are willing to draw from the work of moral and political philosophers.

What might moral and political philosophers teach criminal theorists about the nature of the rights respected by their fundamental principles? At least three interpretations of the claim "A has a moral right to x" are available, and it makes a great deal of difference to criminal theory which interpretation is adopted. These three interpretations are most easily contrasted by the strategies they use to accommodate apparent *exceptions* to the claim that a person has a moral right to something. None of these three alternatives is a totally implausible construction of what criminal theorists might intend, nor are they examined here merely to exhaust the logical possibilities.

First, one might hold that a principle accurately expresses a requirement of justice and respects a moral right only if violations or exceptions to it are categorically condemned. According to this alternative, the statement "A has a moral right to x" is true only if all infringements of A's right are unjustifiable. It is incoherent that infringements of the principle or the right respected by it are justified. If deviations are acceptable, it follows that the statement of the principle or formulation of the right is inaccurate. All apparent exceptions are accommodated by redescribing the statement of the principle or the formulation of the right.

This first interpretation construes the fundamental principles of criminal liability as absolute, inviolable requirements of justice, admitting of no exceptions whatever. Any instance of criminal liability that dispensed with an actus reus, for example, would be unacceptable in a system of criminal justice that took seriously the moral rights of its citizens. A system would approximate perfection to the extent that it identified and repealed each law that compromised these principles.

This first interpretation probably coincides most closely with what laypersons mean by the assertion that they have a right to something as a matter of justice. A person untrained in the subtleties of legal or moral discourse would feel betrayed to learn that he has a moral right to something, even though it is permissible to deprive him of it. He *means* by this assertion that all such deprivations are wrongful. Moreover, a number of criminal theorists seem to understand the status of their fundamental principles in this way. Frequently it is suggested that any question about the justifiability of a real or hypothetical instance of penal liability can be decisively resolved by demonstrating its incompatibility with a fundamental principle. This strategy is sound only if the fundamental principles express inviolable requirements of justice.

This first interpretation, however, has attracted little sympathy among moral and political philosophers.[14] Their central criticism is that few if any accurate statements of principles of justice or formulations of rights have been provided.[15] Little ingenuity is required to devise circumstances in which infringements of a right or violations of a principle would be acceptable. Certainly the most familiar examples of principles of justice or statements of rights are not thought to be absolute or exceptionless. Consider property rights, for example. Everyone admits that in many circumstances a person's property rights may be justifiably infringed.[16] The law of eminent domain involves a justifiable infringement of property rights. Yet it hardly follows that there *are* no property rights. Nor does it follow that accurate statements of property rights include large numbers of qualifications and exceptive clauses. What probably *does* follow is that this first interpretation of what it *means* to have a property right should be rejected.

Thus it seems unlikely that the incompatibility of a real or hypothetical instance of penal liability with a fundamental principle is conclusive support for its unjustifiability. Recall that many criminal theorists do not regard possession as an actus reus.[17] This discrepancy between the actus reus requirement and possessory offenses does not entail that the latter instances of liability violate the moral rights of citizens. If such laws *do* violate rights, no one has noticed; there has been no significant movement to repeal possessory offenses.[18] Nor has this discrepancy led criminal theorists to conclude that the actus reus requirement is inaccurate or in need of qualification. What *may* follow from this incompatibility is that the actus reus requirement (as well as other fundamental principles) does not express an *inviolable* requirement of justice that respects absolute moral rights. Weaker interpretations of the status of the fundamental principles must be sought.

The alternative is to construe principles of justice or statements of rights as *prima facie* requirements. This suggestion, however, is ambiguous between the second and third interpretations of what it means to understand a principle as a requirement of justice. According to both these interpretations, a prima facie requirement is subject to exceptions. Unlike the interpretation discussed above, the admission that some instances of penal liability are justifiable notwithstanding their incompatibility with a fundamental principle does not entail that that principle is inaccurate or in need of qualification. At this point, however, the second and third interpretations diverge from their predecessor. According to the second, the principles are construed as "rules of thumb." They are analogous to rules such as "Quit when you're ahead" or "Carry an umbrella when it looks like rain." They are useful because they are true in most instances. Exceptions or violations of such rules, unless they become too frequent, are not thought to necessitate qualifications of the principles themselves. After all, these principles are not designed to be applicable in each and every situation; to suppose otherwise is to misunderstand the role and function of rules of thumb.

There is *some* indication that criminal theorists understand the fundamental principles of criminal liability to express prima facie requirements of justice according to this second interpretation. Recall Hyman Gross's observation that "official deviations from these principles are abundant everywhere, but this need not embarrass the theorist."[19] It is unclear whether Gross believes that there is something morally suspect about each and every law that violates the several principles he discusses. If not, he appears to favor this second interpretation of the status of the fundamental principles.

Yet this second interpretation does not seem wholly satisfactory. It has the merit of explaining how infringements of the fundamental principles could be justifiable, yet does not comport with the use to which many theorists seem to put these requirements. According to this interpretation, there is nothing morally suspect about each and every violation of these principles; there is no necessity that a special justification for such departures be provided. Exceptions can be ignored unless they become too frequent.

Few (if any) *moral* principles seem to have this status. On any reasonable construction, the moral principles in favor of promise-keeping or truth-telling, for example, admit of exceptions. But they are not analogous to rules of thumb that owe their usefulness to the mere fact that they are true in most instances. Departures from these principles, even when justifiable, are reasons for apology and regret. In such circumstances something of importance has been sacrificed. A special justification is required to outweigh these principles, and they continue to survive and have significance even on occasions in which they are outweighed.[20]

Thus a third interpretation of the status of the moral rights respected by the fundamental principles of criminal liability should be sought. According to this interpretation, as with its predecessor, these prima facie rights may be outweighed by more stringent moral considerations. Yet even in such circumstances the outweighed principle continues to exert some force. In this respect the third interpretation diverges from the second. A principle is not deprived of *all* weight simply because it is *out*weighed. In *each* case there is a reason (though not a *conclusive* reason) not to infringe these rights; they are not merely applicable "sometimes." These prima facie rights continue to exist in all circumstances in which they apply, even though they sometimes give way to competing moral considerations. On such occasions, an important value has been sacrificed. Thus departures from these principles are unacceptable in the absence of a special justification. I believe this third alternative is the most defensible proposal for understanding the sense in which the fundamental principles of criminal liability respect moral rights.

Nothing is mysterious or problematic about the proposal to treat the fundamental principles of criminal liability as respecting prima facie moral rights in this third sense.[21] This interpretation brings the status of the fundamental principles into conformity with more familiar moral rights protected by the Constitution. Apart from a handful of "absolutists," most authorities recognize that even the most precious constitutional rights are subject to being overridden. In such circumstances, however, the outweighed right is set aside with a deep feeling of loss and regret, and its presence continues to be felt.[22] Special justificatory considerations are required to override fundamental constitutional rights, as proposals to outweigh them require a compelling state interest, or are subject to strict scrutiny. According to the interpretation tentatively favored here, the moral rights respected by the fundamental principles of criminal liability should be treated analogously. For example, special justificatory considerations are required to hold a person criminally liable for an event he does not cause.

For the most part, criminal theorists seem to apply the fundamental principles of liability as though this third interpretation were correct. Though possessory offenses (arguably incompatible with actus reus) have not been condemned categorically, they have aroused suspicion among a few theorists.[23] Vicarious liability (probably incompatible with the causal requirement) is reluctantly accepted.[24] The use of presumptions in criminal trials (perhaps incompatible with the requirement of proof beyond a reasonable doubt) is carefully scrutinized.[25] Strict liability (almost certainly incompatible with mens rea) provides the best example. Criminal theorists have learned to live with such offenses, but few are willing to allow serious crimes to be interpreted as instances of strict liability.[26] Most theorists appreciate that these kinds of liability are suspect and require special justifications. Of course, it is quite another matter whether the special justifications they offer can withstand critical evaluation.

Although this last interpretation appears to be the most plausible of the three, one should have little confidence that it correctly captures what criminal theorists have supposed the status of their fundamental principles to be. Again, the fault lies primarily with the lack of attention and care criminal theorists have shown in addressing these issues. It is unfortunate that so much guesswork is involved in clarifying the status of these fundamental principles. But it is impossible to evaluate them unless their role and function are made more precise.

The approach defended here makes the simplifying assumption that each of the several orthodox principles shares an equivalent status. This assumption may turn out to be an *over*simplification. Perhaps some principles are absolute, others are mere rules of thumb, and still others may be overridden by more stringent considerations. But theorists have not indicated that these principles differ in their status. Since they do not conflict with one another, there is no need to order them lexically. Again, this matter deserves more careful attention than it has received from criminal theorists.

According to the interpretation tentatively favored here, the fact that a real or hypothetical law conflicts with a fundamental principle does not definitively resolve all questions about its justifiability. Such a disparity is grounds for suspicion, however. On each such occasion, it is appropriate to demand that special circumstances justify the departure. If this interpretation of the status of the fundamental principles is sound, much of the focus of criminal theory shifts to a new issue. Theorists must now address the large question of what moral considerations are sufficiently stringent to justify overriding the prima facie moral rights respected by the fundamental principles of criminal liability. A complete answer to this question requires that criminal theory be located within a broader moral and political theory. What circumstances warrant infringements of individual moral rights? Much of chapter 3 will take a very small step toward answering this question by identifying a number of considerations that are *in*sufficient to justify compromises of the fundamental principles.

First, a few additional observations about orthodox criminal theory are in order. These (somewhat vague and abstract) remarks are, I hope, interesting and important in their own right, but also contribute to a deeper understanding of the sense in which the fundamental principles comprise a *theory*. These observations should be kept in mind by anyone who seriously proposes to revise and improve upon orthodoxy.

### REDUNDANCIES AND INTERRELATIONS

EVEN THE OVERSIMPLIFIED DISCUSSION of orthodox criminal theory sketched in chapter 1 illustrates the difficulty of delineating the scope and application of the fundamental principles of liability. It is not entirely clear, for example, whether or under what circumstances mens rea is absent. These uncertainties should not be attributed merely to intellectual shortcomings on the part of theoreticians. It should be noticed that often a single injustice can be condemned as a violation of more than one principle. Frequently a judge may be convinced that criminal liability is unjust in a particular case, although he is less confident about what principle(s) is infringed. One rationale may seem as persuasive as another. Many judicial opinions include a multiplicity of rationales in support of a decision, even though theoretical clarity might have been gained by greater selectivity. As long as the result is just, there is little practical urgency that the transgressed principle(s) be precisely identified. Thus the substantive criminal law that provides the data for theory construction has not always been forced to decide *which* principles are at stake in particular disputes.

Consider an example of this phenomenon. Suppose a defendant is charged with criminal battery for injuring a person while suffering an unanticipated epileptic seizure. All would agree that criminal liability would be unjust, while disagreeing about how this result should be reached. Plausible arguments can be made from a number of different perspectives. Perhaps the most obvious injustice is the lack of mens rea, but a strong case can be made for the absence of actus reus as well. When conduct is involuntary, "we are tempted to say that even the action itself was not performed."[27] This view attaches significance to the fact that one *undergoes* or *experiences* a seizure; they happen *to* persons, and thus are not actions *of* persons. If it is impossible to act while undergoing a seizure, and battery is an action, it follows that a battery has not been committed. If this argument is sound, liability would also violate the principle of legality. The offense proscribes an actual battery, not conduct that superficially resembles a battery. A prudent lawyer would make each of these arguments in defense of his client, and a comprehensive judicial opinion might include them all.

Thus the fundamental principles of criminal liability are somewhat *redundant*. One and the same injustice may violate several principles at once. Examples of redundancy could be multiplied indefinitely. No doubt it is possible to imagine monstrous injustices that violate *each* of the above principles. Perhaps the most fascinating aspect of the controversy about whether and under what circumstances persons should be liable for their failures to act is that a number of principles conspire to render omissions problematical. This redundancy helps to explain why the scope and application of each principle have not been delineated with the precision ordinarily expected from criminal theorists. Controversy is likely to persist as long as nothing of practical significance depends upon which of several principles is selected to describe the injustice.

Redundancy impedes theoretical elegance; how might it be overcome? More precision might be achieved in a legal system that retained some of the fundamental principles of liability while rejecting others. For example, if a legal system dispensed with the mens rea requirement, judges would be squarely confronted with the issue of whether involuntariness does or does not preclude an actus reus. Liability, not mere theoretical clarity, would depend upon the outcome.[28] Implementation of this suggestion, however, would involve a related difficulty. It is seldom noticed how closely the fundamental principles of criminal theory are interrelated. The meaning of any one principle may depend upon the scope and application of another. It is doubtless an exaggeration to claim that orthodox theory stands or falls in its entirety. But the principles are not entirely independent of one another; they combine to form a *theory*. Modifications in one principle may have ramifications that echo throughout the whole of criminal theory.

Consider, for example, how different conceptions of actus reus bear upon the causal requirement. Suppose Smith, Jones, Black, and White shoot at their respective victims with the intent to kill. Smith misses his victim altogether, Jones's dies instantly, Black's is killed in self-defense, and White's survives. Which of these defendants, if any, has performed the *same* actus reus? Different responses have been provided by criminal theorists. John Salmond defined acts to include accompanying circumstances and consequences;[29] most others excluded these components.[30] It is apparent that the significance of the causal requirement depends upon how this dispute is resolved. If acts are defined to include their effects, so that two instances of conduct with different consequences necessarily involve a different actus reus, there probably is no need to retain an independent causal requirement in criminal theory.[31] A causal requirement is indispensable, however, if acts are defined to exclude their effects.

Moreover, one principle may be attractive largely because of its relation to others. The actus reus and mens rea principles combine to form an appealing model of the criminal offense as comprised of an outer, physical component, and an inner, mental ingredient. The importance to orthodox theory of this dualistic model of the criminal offense can scarcely be exaggerated. Since I will refer to this dualism

often, it will prove convenient to give it a name. Henceforth I will
refer to it as the *orthodox model of the criminal offense*. Criminal theorists
have painted many seductive pictures of this model. One of a large
number of such examples is:

> Every crime necessarily requires two elements or component parts,
> one being physical and the other mental. The physical element is the
> prohibited thing left undone, or what is called "the act." The mental
> element is the state or condition of the doer's mind which accompa-
> nies the act, the human will, otherwise known as "the intent."[32]

In colorful language, Rollin Perkins refers to the orthodox model of
the criminal offense as "the great secret of criminal guilt."[33]

If the reality of an inner dimension is challenged, the significance of retaining an outer dimension will change. The meaning of
the mental is specified in part by its contrast with the physical. As
Gross indicates, theorists strive to understand "what an act is" in order
"to make clearer the complimentary mental part of conduct . . . By
subtracting the overt elements . . . we become clearer about the
hidden inner elements."[34] If the boundaries of these dimensions are
blurred, the importance of retaining distinct principles becomes open
to doubt.

Glanville Williams, for example, defines actus reus as "the
whole definition of the crime with the exception of the mental
element—and it even includes a mental element in so far as that is
contained in the definition of an act."[35] A "mental element" *is* "contained in the definition of an act," according to Williams, largely
because he holds that involuntary conduct is not genuine action, and
that the voluntary can be distinguished from the involuntary only by
reference to the mental.[36] Thus the distinction between the physical
and the mental is deliberately blurred. The resultant model of the
criminal offense, while perhaps coherent, is considerably less attractive. What is the motivation for retaining a separate mental, nonphysi-
cal component of liability if some mental elements are assigned to the
realm of the physical? One might as well hold that two instances of
conduct caused by different mental states necessarily involve a different actus reus.[37] According to such a view, an unintentional killing
would comprise a different actus reus than an intentional killing. This
broad conception of action would threaten to swallow the significance
of the mens rea requirement altogether. The continued viability of
the orthodox model of the criminal offense depends upon the ability
to draw a relatively sharp contrast between the physical and mental
components of crime.

Thus an authority who modifies a part of criminal theory is
well advised to be sensitive to the implications upon principles not

directly considered. Moreover, he should remain attentive to whether, on balance, the revision makes the resultant theory more or less attractive.

## BLACK, WHITE, AND SHADES OF GRAY

ONE OF THE MOST STRIKING FEATURES of criminal liability is its binary or "all-or-nothing" character. Defendants are either guilty or innocent. No sense can be made within our criminal justice system of a finding of "partial" liability. Any sentiment that one defendant is *more* or *less* liable than another who has committed the same offense can be expressed only in sentencing procedures that allow for the aggravation or mitigation of punishment. Criminal justice is dispensed in two distinct stages: a defendant must be found liable (a black or white determination) before he is eligible for punishment (colored in shades of gray). Nothing is analogous in criminal law to the dissatisfaction that has led to the implementation of "comparative negligence" in tort.[38] Orthodox criminal theory itself makes no provision for degrees of liability.

The only analogue to "partial" liability admitted within orthodox criminal theory is the practice by which a jury can convict a defendant of a "lesser included offense" than the crime charged.[39] Suppose that a defendant is prosecuted for murder. If a jury believes it would be unjust either to convict or to acquit him of this offense, it may "compromise" by finding him guilty of manslaughter, since this latter, "lesser" offense is "included" within the former. By exercising this option, a jury can steer an intermediate course between what might be perceived as two unacceptable extremes: acquittal and release, or conviction for an offense with a too-severe punishment.

This procedure, however, has a very limited application.[40] First, it is viewed with suspicion in many jurisdictions, where it is construed as a device to usurp the proper function of the judiciary. Moreover, the defendant may oppose its use, for if he can force the jury to choose either of the two extremes, he will have a chance of acquittal.[41] Most important, this procedure is available only in that limited class of crimes (most notably homicide) in which lesser included offenses exist. Even in this class of crimes, this procedure cannot be used if the lesser offense is charged at the outset. Thus it does not constitute a significant exception to the rule that criminal liability has an "all-or-nothing" character. Nonetheless, the existence of this procedure is ample testimony to the strain placed upon the administration of criminal justice by the fact that liability cannot be colored in shades of gray.[42]

There is abundant evidence of this strain. Authorities have noted that a major difficulty in applying the insanity defense is that "the imposition of criminal liability must be predicated upon a categorical determination of blameworthiness, [even though] modern psychiatry conceives of most mental disorders as falling along a spectrum of degree."[43] Some commentators who take this difficulty seriously have called for "an alternative to the absolutist notion that the defendant is either completely responsible or completely irresponsible for his unlawful act."[44] For the most part, there has been no movement to implement these proposals. Once Pandora's Box is opened, the doctrine of partial responsibility could spread beyond the insanity defense. The fact that persons seldom are either "completely responsible or irresponsible" creates difficulties for the entire structure of criminal liability. Orthodox theory has not come to terms with the obvious fact that conformity to law is much more difficult for some than for others.[45]

This binary all-or-nothing feature of criminal liability is taken for granted by authorities, and is almost never the subject of explicit comment or defense. Yet it would surely surprise us were we not so accustomed to it. It is remarkable when considered in the context of other formal and informal structures in which judgments are made and sanctions imposed. Workplaces, families, and other institutions seem quite different in this respect—unless and until they begin to model themselves after legal systems. Anyone with experience in enforcing rules in such institutions quickly comes to appreciate the artificiality of supposing, in each instance, that a violation *has* or *has not* occurred, or that the accused *possesses* or *lacks* a defense. Moral theorists clearly recognize that excuses may operate to various extents. John Austin notes: "it always has to be remembered that few excuses get us out of it completely."[46] Why has this truism been overlooked by our criminal law?

To begin to answer this difficult question, consider the wide range of factors relevant in assessing the blameworthiness of conduct. Criminal justice is administered in two stages—liability and punishment—and it makes a great deal of difference at *which* stage a given factor is held to be relevant. Some factors (such as intent) typically bear on the first stage of criminal justice. They are material to *which* crime is committed, and are used to *grade* offenses. Other factors (such as motive) typically bear on the second stage of criminal justice. They are material to the *punishment* for a given crime, and operate either to mitigate or to aggravate its severity. How is it decided at which stage a given factor is relevant? Why are issues such as whether the defendant succeeded in killing his victim, as opposed to failing in his attempt, material to his liability and not to his punishment? Why are variables such as the stress of the defendant, his economic deprivation, his inherited character, his educational background, the amount of temptation, the degree of provocation, his degree of complicity in the offense, or his prior criminal record material to his punishment and not to his liability?[47] The writings of orthodox criminal theorists provide no principled answer to these vexing questions. According to one authority, "the basis for . . . assuming a clear distinction between excusing conditions, which operate to relieve a criminal defendant from liability entirely, and mitigating excuses, which are taken into account by way of sentencing discretion . . . is rarely articulated, and when it is, it seems unconvincing."[48] Yet the decision to assign a relevant factor to one stage rather than the other is crucial. It must be remembered that the fundamental principles of criminal theory pertain only to *liability*. As I have argued, these principles respect *rights*. If a relevant factor is held to bear only on the severity of punishment, *after* a finding of liability, it may fall outside the scope of the defendant's rights. If this relevant factor is ignored in discretionary sentencing, the defendant may not succeed in establishing a violation of his rights.[49]

An example helps to illustrate the importance of this distinction. Suppose that two defendants commit murder. Smith kills his victim painlessly; Jones resorts to brutal torture. Surely this difference is relevant to their culpability. A criminal justice system that ignored this important difference between Smith and Jones would violate the most basic requirement of formal justice by treating unequals equally. But at which stage of the criminal justice system should this difference be incorporated? Only two possibilities are available within orthodox criminal theory. Torture-murder (called, perhaps, one kind of "capital-murder") might be a *different* and more serious offense than "normal" murder. If so, Smith has a right not to be convicted of this more serious offense; he has not committed its actus reus. Alternatively, Jones might be thought deserving of a more severe punishment than Smith *for having committed the same offense*. If so, however, no fundamental principle of criminal liability confers Smith with a *right* to be treated more leniently than Jones. If their punishments were equally severe, Smith could not point to a fundamental principle of criminal liability that has been violated. Orthodox criminal theory must choose between these two options; rarely is there a middle ground. It is incoherent to suppose that two defendants might be liable to different extents for having committed the same offense, for liability does not admit of degrees.

Recent reforms in sentencing procedures create additional difficulties. Legislators have begun to attach "determinate" sentences to offenses that allow judges less latitude to tailor punishments to particular defendants. Thus it is imperative that offenses should incorporate whatever distinctions influence culpability. New sentencing statutes afford judges less discretion to differentiate between the punishments deserved by Smith and Jones. No longer can legislatures neglect distinctions between the culpability of defendants, expecting these oversights to be corrected by judicial discretion in sentencing.[50]

It is worthwhile to speculate whether there is something in the *nature* of criminal liability that precludes the possibility that it might be quantified. To what extent is the black-or-white character of liability an inevitable consequence of regulating conduct by reference to pre-established rules, rather than by applications of "common sense" or discretion? It is at least arguable that the application of rules is one thing, and the practice of applying them in an all-or-nothing fashion is quite another.[51]

I do not pretend to have a complete answer to these interesting (but seldom raised) questions. Nor am I entirely clear about how one might implement changes in the structure of criminal theory to allow for degrees of liability. Here I am discussing only the relationship between this "all-or-nothing" character of criminal liability and the content of its fundamental principles. It is noteworthy that satisfaction of most (if not all) of these principles does not admit of degrees. A defendant either acts or he does not; either he possesses or lacks mens rea; either his conduct causes an event or it does not. It is nonsense to contend that one action is more or less of an action than another, or that one intent is more or less of an intent than another. The harm requirement, to be sure, may be satisfied to varying extents, but authorities have been ambivalent about its place in criminal theory.[52] For the most part, the content of the fundamental principles of orthodox theory shares this binary character with judgments of liability.

It is unlikely that these phenomena are merely coincidental. If the fundamental principles could be satisfied in shades of gray, it is unlikely that judgments of liability would be colored in black or white. It is unclear, however, which of these phenomena precedes and explains the other. Perhaps the first to evolve was the sentiment that judgments of liability should not admit of degrees, and principles became fundamental to criminal theory that embodied this preference. Or perhaps principles became fundamental to criminal theory that made it incoherent to quantify liability. In any event, these phenomena are mutually reinforcing. The fact that they are closely related, if true, has important consequences for proposals to revise criminal theory. If it is believed that liability might be represented in shades of gray, there is reason to prefer fundamental principles that can be satisfied to various degrees. These (admittedly speculative) observations should be kept in mind when the process of revising criminal theory is finally begun. Before undertaking so ambitious a project, however, it is worthwhile to note some tensions that arise within orthodox criminal theory itself. Some of these difficulties substantiate the need for revisions in the content of the fundamental principles of liability.

## NOTES

1. Jerome Hall, *General Principles of Criminal Law*, p. 23.
2. The classic source is John Rawls, *A Theory of Justice*.
3. This controversial assumption depends upon deep views about the function of rights and scope of justice. Some of these issues are explored in the several essays by Joel Feinberg, *Doing and Deserving;* and Michael Zimmerman, *An Essay on Moral Responsibility* (forthcoming).
4. See John Hodson, *The Ethics of Legal Coercion*.
5. See David Richards, *The Moral Criticism of Law*, and *Sex, Drugs, Death, and the Law*.
6. See Ronald Dworkin, *Taking Rights Seriously*.
7. I am hopeful that *some* coherent rationale can be provided. For an expression of skepticism, see Mark Kelman, "Interpretive Construction in the Substantive Criminal Law," *Stanford Law Review* 33 (1981): 591.
8. See Chapter 1, note 68.
9. Dworkin, *Seriously*, p. 184.
10. See *Robinson v. California*, 370 U.S. 680 (1962), especially as interpreted in light of *Powell v. Texas*, 392 U.S. 514 (1968).
11. Herbert Packer, "Mens Rea and the Supreme Court," *Supreme Court Review* (1962): 107.
12. C. Peter Erlinder, "Mens Rea, Due Process, and the Supreme Court: Toward a Constitutional Doctrine of Substantive Criminal Law," *American Journal of Criminal Law* 9 (1981): 163, 175.
13. For one such theory, see John Ely, *Democracy and Distrust*.
14. An apparent exception is Alan Gewirth, "Are There Any Absolute Rights?" *Philosophical Quarterly* 31 (1981): 1.
15. Joseph Raz makes this criticism of Dworkin's views in his "Legal Principles and the Limits of Law," *Yale Law Journal* 81 (1972): 823.
16. See Judith Thomson, "Some Ruminations on Rights," *Arizona Law Review* 19 (1978): 45.
17. See chapter 1.
18. But see note 23.
19. Hyman Gross, *A Theory of Criminal Justice*, p. xv.
20. Herbert Morris apparently believes it is preferable to describe such rights as "absolute." See his "Persons and Punishment," *Monist* 52 (1968): 475, 498.
21. Some philosophers have concluded that the notion of prima facie rights is unsalvageable and should be abandoned. See John Searle, "Prima Facie Obligations" in Joseph Raz, ed., *Practical Reasoning*, p. 81.
22. It might be argued, for example, that less vagueness should be tolerated with legislation that jeopardizes fundamental rights. See *N.A.A.C.P. v. Button*, 371 U.S. 415 (1963). In addition, liability may be less "strict" if it has

a "chilling effect" on fundamental rights. See *Smith v. California,* 361 U.S. 147 (1959).

23. See the discussion in George Fletcher, *Rethinking Criminal Law,* pp. 197–205. Fletcher is particularly sensitive to how possessory offenses may be used to circumvent the fundamental requirement of proof beyond a reasonable doubt.

24. The classic source is Francis Sayre, "Criminal Responsibility for the Acts of Another," *Harvard Law Review* 43 (1930): 689.

25. See Harold Ashford and D. Michael Risinger, "Presumptions, Assumptions, and Due Process in Criminal Cases: A Theoretical Overview," *Yale Law Journal* 79 (1969): 165.

26. See Rollin Perkins, "Criminal Liability Without Fault: A Disquieting Trend," *Iowa Law Review* 68 (1983): 1067.

27. Jeffrie Murphy, "Involuntary Acts and Criminal Liability" in his *Retribution, Justice, and Therapy,* p. 116. See also Gross, *Theory,* p. 68.

28. See the comment about how theoretical clarity in the criminal law has been retarded by the jury's use of general rather than special verdicts. Kent Greenawalt, "The Perplexing Borders of Justification and Excuse," *Columbia Law Review* 84 (1984): 1897, 1900–1.

29. John Salmond, *Jurisprudence,* p. 401.

30. See John Austin, *Lectures on Jurisprudence,* pp. 427–28. See also *M.P.C.* §2.03.

31. "[T]o give the word 'act' such significance that the death of the victim, in a homicide case, would be a part of the act rather than a result of the act, would unduly complicate discussions in the field of causation." Rollin Perkins and Ronald Boyce, *Criminal Law,* p. 607.

32. William Burdick, *The Law of Crime,* p. 596. See also Perkins and Boyce, ibid., p. 831.

33. Perkins and Boyce, *Criminal Law,* p. 831.

34. Gross, *Theory,* pp. 49–50.

35. Glanville Williams, *Criminal Law: The General Part,* p. 18.

36. Ibid., p. 12.

37. See Donald Davidson, "Actions, Reasons, and Causes," *Journal of Philosophy* 60 (1963): 685.

38. See William Prosser, *Torts,* pp. 433–39.

39. See the experiment in *People v. Wolff,* 394 P.2d 959 (1964), subsequently "overruled" by the California legislature. English law is more congenial to "partial" defenses. See notes 44 and 46.

40. For a general discussion of some difficulties surrounding "lesser included offenses", see Christen Blair, "Constitutional Limitations on the Lesser Included Offense Doctrine," *American Criminal Law Review* 21 (1984): 445.

41. "[S]trangely, the roles of the prosecution and defence may be reversed" in trials involving the defense of diminished capacity. J. C. Smith and Brian Hogan, *Criminal Law,* p. 183.

42. Fletcher points out that such a practice "disabuses us of the view that voluntariness and freedom of the will are black-and-white issues." *Rethinking,* p. 353.

43. Peter Low, John Jeffries, and Richard Bonnie, *Criminal Law,* p. 652.

44. Note: "Graduated Responsibility as an Alternative to Current Tests of Determining Criminal Capacity," *Maine Law Review* 25 (1973): p. 343, 344.

See also the thoughtful observations in Herbert Fingarette and Ann Hasse, *Mental Disabilities and Criminal Responsibility.*

45. Arguably the difficulty of performing an action reduces the culpability of not performing it. See Andrew von Hirsch, *Past or Future Crimes,* p. 72. These issues have not been sufficiently explored. See also Jeffrie Murphy, "Marxism and Retribution," *Philosophy and Public Affairs* 2 (1973): 217.

46. John Austin, "A Plea for Excuses," in his *Philosophical Papers,* p. 123, 125.

47. Some of these examples are highly contentious. Provocation may seem to represent a counterexample. According to Williams, "murder is an exception" to the general rule that "provocation is a matter of mitigation." *Textbook of Criminal Law,* p. 524.

48. These issues have been explored most carefully in two articles by Martin Wasik, "Partial Excuses," *Modern Law Review* 45 (1982): 516, and "Excuses at the Sentencing Stage," *Criminal Law Review* (1983): 450.

49. I do not mean to imply that issues pertaining to sentencing do not raise any questions about rights. For a general discussion of rights in sentencing, see Andrew von Hirsch, *Doing Justice.* In the context of capital punishment, the presence or absence of mitigating circumstances *must* be considered by the sentencing authority. See *Lockett v. Ohio,* 438 U.S. 586 (1978) and *Bell v. Ohio,* 438 U.S. 637 (1978). But courts remain uninclined to second-guess legislative penal policy. See *Rummel v. Estelle,* 445 U.S. 263 (1980). One might well question the fixation of criminal theorists upon liability to the exclusion of an interest in sentencing.

50. See Michael Tonry, "Criminal Law: The Missing Element in Sentencing Reform," *Vanderbilt Law Review* 35 (1982): 607.

51. For distinctions between standards (viz., rules) that function in an all-or-nothing fashion and those (viz., principles) that admit of degrees, see Dworkin, *Seriously,* pp. 24–25.

52. See chapter 8.

# 3

# *Justice and Criminal Theory*

## UTILITY AND CRIMINAL THEORY

THE PROPOSAL IN CHAPTER 2 to interpret criminal theory as comprised of requirements of justice that respect prima facie moral rights has a number of extremely important consequences. Although these fundamental principles and the moral rights they respect are prima facie and therefore overrideable, the *kinds* of moral considerations that may outweigh them are significantly limited. If a person has a *right* to be treated in a given way, he *deserves* to be so treated, and many familiar reasons for withholding his deserved treatment are unpersuasive.

It is important to appreciate, however, that a number of powerful forces militate against treating defendants in accordance with their rights, that is, pursuant to their deserts. The collision of these forces with considerations of justice gives rise to tensions within orthodox criminal theory to be explored in this chapter. Here I examine problems that orthodox criminal theorists have not succeeded in resolving satisfactorily. Some of these problems indicate the desirability of changes in the content of the fundamental principles of liability, but I do not introduce these revisions until chapter 4.

The most significant implication of the proposal to construe the fundamental principles of liability as requirements of justice is that considerations of utility should not be used to restrict their scope and application. Here I presuppose without argument that principles of justice and the rights they respect may not be overridden in the pursuit of social gain. Individual desert is not a function of utilitarian calculations, and should not be sacrificed for social benefit. This conclusion about the relationship of justice and rights to utility has been endorsed by most influential contemporary philosophers. Despite profound differences in their moral and political theories, John Rawls,[1] Robert Nozick,[2] Ronald Dworkin[3] and Alan Gewirth[4] each insist upon the priority of justice and rights to utility.[5] These philoso-

50

phers present ample reason to believe that utilitarianism provides insufficent protection for moral rights. If their views are correct, and the fundamental principles are construed as requirements of justice, much of what criminal theorists have said about the scope and application of these principles must be re-examined.

Utilitarianism has exerted a profound influence upon the criminal law. Unquestionably it has been *too* influential.[6] Yet the proposal to construe criminal theory as embodying principles of justice need not purge utilitarian thinking from the law altogether. Many moral and political philosophers have noted that this presupposition about the priority of rights and justice to utility is compatible with the admission that the legislative decision to criminalize conduct may be influenced by considerations of utility.[7] It may be argued, for example, that theft should not be punished unless more utility than disutility would be promoted. Thus gains in utility might provide a necessary condition for criminalization. But this concession to utilitarianism has no straightforward implications for how the fundamental principles of liability should be understood; their scope and application should not be governed by considerations of utility. Although it is unquestioned that penal sanctions for acts of theft may be imposed, conviction for theft should not be construed, for example, to dispense with an actus reus or mens rea. To punish persons who lack mens rea for theft is to fail to treat them in accordance with their deserts; it is to do them a prima facie injustice that requires a special defense. Thus legislators and judges should resist the following line of argument: "Since punishment of theft is justifiable only if it increases utility, so punishment of thieves who lack mens rea must also be justifiable if it increases utility still more." To be persuaded by this sort of argument is to misunderstand the implications of interpreting the fundamental principles as requirements of justice that respect individual moral rights. Utilitarian reasoning cannot provide the special defense necessary to override or qualify these fundamental principles. Society has no warrant to treat persons unjustly in its pursuit of utilitarian gains.

Oliver Wendell Holmes apparently believed otherwise. He acknowledged that individual justice was at stake in applications of these principles, but maintained that it must give way to social utility. Holmes held it to be proper that "public policy sacrifices the individual to the common good."[8] Detailed critiques have been written in the century since he wrote.[9] In short, Holmes's premise that the only legitimate reason "the law-maker makes certain conduct criminal [is the] wish and purpose to prevent that conduct" simply does not entail that "prevention [is] the chief and only universal purpose of punishment."[10] Considerations of justice should constrain impositions of liability, *even if* the objectives of the legislature are largely utilitarian.

It will not do to acquiesce smugly in the injustice of compromises of the fundamental principles of criminal liability for utilitarian advantages. We should not be persuaded that rights and justice should be compromised for utilitarian benefits unless we are given a more compelling argument for this priority than Holmes offers.

Perhaps because of Holmes's enormous influence, it is, unfortunately, all too common for a judge or orthodox theorist to decide to restrict the scope of a fundamental principle for anticipated utilitarian gains. Typically this gain is the protection of society from dangerous persons. At some time or another, each of the fundamental principles has been qualified or violated in the name of social protection. Many theorists see these compromises as desirable given the perceived failures of our criminal justice system to win the "war against crime." They visualize the ideal criminal justice system as maintaining a delicate balance between fairness to defendants and protection of society.[11] Many people believe this balance has been tipped in favor of the "rights of criminals." Legal theorists are accused of disregarding the rights of society and its innocent victims.

Surely this accusation merits a careful reply. But when addressed to the criminal theorist, it threatens to conflate the function of having a system of criminal justice (which arguably is defensible along utilitarian lines) with the legitimacy of imposing liability on particular persons (which must be constrained by justice, desert, and rights). This conflation can be illustrated by an example given by George Fletcher. While the primary function of an income tax is to raise revenue, it does not follow that each decision to allow or disallow a given deduction should be resolved by reference to this overriding goal. The same is true of criminal law. It may be true that the criminal justice system *should* be more concerned with crime control and social protection, but these utilitarian benefits should *not* be purchased by violations of the fundamental principles of criminal liability or the moral rights they respect. It should now be more clear how these requirements of justice establish the constraints in which needed reform must take place.

The requirement of mens rea is the favorite target of those reformers who would compromise or qualify the fundamental principles of criminal liability in the pursuit of utilitarian gains. Total abolition of the principle of mens rea as a precondition of criminal liability has been advocated in the name of social protection. Barbara Wootton writes:

> If the law says that certain things are not to be done, it is illogical to confine this prohibition to occasions in which they are done from malice aforethought; for at least the material consequences of an action, and the reasons for prohibiting it, are the same whether it is

the result of sinister malicious plotting, of negligence or of sheer accident.[12]

This radical proposal has been discredited to the satisfaction of most legal philosophers.[13] More subtle attempts to erode the significance of mens rea are proposed routinely, and enjoy widespread support among orthodox theorists. Two examples will show how considerations of utility have been used to narrow the scope and application of a fundamental principle of liability. These examples are not isolated; they are chosen from a large number of possible illustrations of the (unfortunate) fact that justice and utility compete in interpretations and applications of the requirement of mens rea. If the philosophy of criminal law is important, it is because of the perspective it offers about issues such as these.

### Voluntary Intoxication

Consider the problem posed by a defendant who commits an offense while voluntarily intoxicated, and defends on the ground that his conduct lacks general mens rea.[14] He sheepishly protests that his judgment was impaired and his inhibitions were lowered, and he would not have committed the criminal act if sober. Suppose these claims are true. Does the defendant have a valid defense, or does his conduct contain mens rea?

Courts have been almost unanimous in finding his defense invalid.[15] Yet it is unclear how (or whether) this result can be reconciled with the mens rea requirement of orthodox criminal theory.[16] Rollin Perkins admits that "he who, while unduly excited by liquor, has committed a prohibited deed he would never have thought of doing while sober, is not in the same scale of moral culpability even if the intoxication was voluntary, as another who has done the same thing without such excitement."[17] The question is whether this disparity in moral culpability indicates a difference in mens rea, and thus to criminal liability. Perkins is ambivalent about allowing voluntary intoxication as a defense to criminality involving general mens rea, but concludes that "the matter is entitled to very thoughtful study."[18]

One authority who goes further is Glanville Williams. He queries, "if a man is punished for doing something when drunk that he would not have done when sober, is he not in plain truth punished for getting drunk?"[19] If the answer is affirmative, yet acquittal is undesirable, a possible solution is to create a new crime of "dangerous intoxication," which consists in becoming intoxicated and committing a criminal offense.[20] This proposal has attracted little sympathy from legislators, jurists, or criminal theorists.[21] What is crucial for present purposes is to understand *why* it has been rejected. This proposal should not be dismissed on the simple ground that present policy better protects society from dangerous persons. Yet the suggestion that voluntary intoxication precludes general mens rea is typically resisted for this very reason.[22] Here we find a curious willingness to allow utility to override justice.

The case of *D.P.P. v. Majewski* illustrates this reasoning.[23] In a unanimous opinion, no judge was willing to alter the established rule that voluntary intoxication does not preclude general mens rea. Lord Simon contended:

> One of the prime purposes of the criminal law, with its penal sanctions, is the protection from certain proscribed conduct of persons who are pursuing their lawful lives . . . To accede to the argument on behalf of the appellant would leave the citizen legally unprotected from unprovoked violence, where such violence was the consequence of drink or drugs having obliterated the capacity of the perpetrator to know what he was doing or what were its consequences.[24]

Lord Salmon admitted that this position could not be defended as a matter of "strict logic," but concluded that "this illogicality is, however, acceptable."[25] If a contrary position were taken, "the social consequences could be appalling."[26]

Again, it *may* be correct that mens rea is present in cases of criminality due to voluntary intoxication, but the reasoning of Lords Simon and Salmon is insufficient to support this conclusion. In fact, their opinions ignore rather than address the issue. Their arguments against acquittal could be employed with equal force against any defense, such as reasonable mistake of fact, that alleges the absence of mens rea. Perhaps more social harm is caused by persons who are intoxicated than by persons who are mistaken, but the *amount* of social harm or disutility is hardly a principled basis for "finding" mens rea in the former case but not in the latter.

Lord Edmund-Davies, to his credit, was unwilling to compromise the requirement of mens rea to protect society. Instead, he insisted that liability is just because "drunkenness is not incompatible with mens rea."[27] This conclusion was reached on the ground that "mere recklessness is sufficient to satisfy the definition of mens rea, and drunkenness is itself an act of recklessness."[28] If sound, this argument constitutes a persuasive basis for convicting intoxicated defendants without violating the fundamental principles of criminal liability. Unfortunately, the argument is unsound. The false premise identifies drunkenness as an act of recklessness. Ordinarily, recklessness is construed to require a *conscious* disregard of a substantial and unjustifiable risk.[29] Under most occasions in which defendants become intoxicated, they do not consciously disregard the risk that their condition will lead to criminal conduct. Certainly the facts of *Majewski* provide no evidence of such a conscious disregard. Lord Edmund-Davies's argument might support a conviction in the relatively rare case in which a defendant had reason to believe from prior experience that criminality would ensue,[30] or, still worse, became intoxicated in order to muster the courage to commit a crime already conceived.[31] But his reasoning leaves unresolved the general question of whether voluntary intoxication is compatible with mens rea.

Perhaps the dictates of "strict logic" do not overly concern jurists, who must regard themselves as pragmatists. But incoherence must not be tolerated by the philosopher of criminal law.[32] Here is an excellent example of the sort of question the theorist must never evade: should a distinction (in culpability) make a difference (in liability)? Undoubtedly Perkins is correct that there is a genuine distinction between the desert of the "common criminal" whose mens rea is not in dispute and the intoxicated offender who would not have committed his criminal act when sober. Should this distinction in desert give rise to a difference in criminal liability? It is noteworthy that drunkenness is frequently regarded as a ground for mitigation of punishment.[33] Moreover, a number of self-induced incapacities (other than intoxication) that lead to criminal behavior are recognized as defenses.[34] The nature of the relationship between mens rea and voluntary intoxication must be squarely addressed by theorists, who should not allow their answers to be influenced by considerations of social utility.

A number of theorists, understandably reluctant to embrace utilitarianism, argue that the invalidity of voluntary intoxication as a defense to crimes involving general mens rea can be supported on grounds of justice and desert. After all, a defendant who commits an offense after voluntarily becoming intoxicated is not *blameless*. His blame, of course, originates in his act of voluntarily becoming intoxicated. Paul Robinson states (but does not endorse) this sentiment succinctly: "the actor who is responsible for causing his own excusing condition, should not benefit from it."[35] It seems clear that this rationale has had a profound influence on the law, for it explains the disparity between voluntary and involuntary intoxication.[36] No one would hold a defendant criminally liable when his intoxication is *in*voluntary (as when he unexpectedly overreacts to prescribed medication) and he would not have committed his offense but for his intoxication.[37] Why should the law be otherwise when his intoxication is *voluntary*? In either case, the effect of intoxication upon general mens rea at the moment the offense is committed is indistinguishable. The only possible answer is that the voluntariness of the intoxication creates a mens rea that otherwise is absent.

While this rationale is appealing (and I will return to it later), it is not without serious difficulty. As Jerome Hall aptly observes: "there is a great difference between asserting that a person must voluntarily commit a certain harm to be sufficiently culpable to merit penal sanctions and asserting that he is thus culpable if he could have prevented himself from involuntarily causing an unforeseen harm."[38]

What has gone wrong? Why has the problem of the voluntarily intoxicated offender been so intractable for orthodox criminal theorists? Some authorities have noted that the inability or unwillingness to conceptualize liability in shades of gray has contributed to difficulties here.[39] A more important factor, however, is that the blameworthiness of the voluntarily intoxicated offender is expressed by a finding of *criminal* liability. Almost certainly an enlightened system of criminal justice should respond differently to "common criminals" and to voluntarily intoxicated offenders. Williams agrees that "if a man commits serious mischief when in drink, society must take steps against him."[40] On his view, the crucial issue is whether such steps should be taken within the framework of the criminal justice system. Here, as elsewhere, progress may have been retarded by the absence of effective alternative institutions of social control.[41] Judicial insistence upon mens rea might have the virtue of removing the problem of the antisocial drunk from the criminal courts, where it does not seem to belong. Such alternatives will not be developed if criminal courts remain willing to allow all problems of antisocial behavior to be thrust upon them. As long as criminal sanctions continue to be imposed upon the voluntarily intoxicated offender,[42] the difficulties raised here must be addressed, and orthodox theorists have found no satisfactory solution.

### Ignorance of Law

Under what conditions, if any, should ignorance of law be a valid defense to criminal liability? This question provides a second example of how liability might be affected by interpreting the principle of mens rea as a requirement of justice not overrideable by utilitarian considerations. The familiar rule is *ignorantia juris non excusat* for criminal offenses involving general mens rea.[43]

Does a criminal defendant who is ignorant of the law nonetheless possess mens rea in violating it? Williams's query about intoxication may be adapted in this context. If a man is punished for doing something while ignorant of law that he would not have done had he known the law, is he not in plain truth punished for being ignorant? How does ignorance of law affect just deserts?

The beginning of wisdom in answering these questions is to realize that not all cases of ignorance of law are equivalent. Sympathies for defendants are high in such cases as *State v. Striggles*.[44] Here the defendant was convicted for installing an illegal gambling device in his restaurant, after he had relied on a decision of a lower court that the machine was *not* a gambling device within the meaning of the statute. The State Supreme Court reversed the lower court decision, and Striggles was held liable. Needless to say, sympathies for defendants are lower when their ignorance of law is more unreasonable.

A number of commentators have criticized the rule of *ignorantia juris* on the ground that impositions of liability under such circumstances can have no deterrent effect. No person can be deterred by the threat of punishment for violating a law not known to exist. The assumption required to complete this argument is that liability is unjust unless it could have deterred. Jeremy Bentham employed such reasoning as the basis for all criminal law defenses.[45] *Ignorantia juris* is one of several doctrines questioned by Bentham on the ground that it inefficaciously punishes "nondeterrables."

The standard response to such reasoning, poignantly expressed by H. L. A. Hart, is that criminality is deterred by not allowing *ignorantia juris* as a defense. Hart labels Bentham's argument a "spectacular *non sequitur*": "Plainly it is possible that though (as Bentham says) the *threat* of punishment could not have operated on [nondeterrables], the actual *infliction* of punishment on those persons, may secure a higher measure of conformity to law on the part of normal persons than is secured by the admission of excusing conditions."[46] In other words, even if the defendant *himself* could not have been deterred, his punishment may serve as an example to *others*. Most courts that have commented upon the matter seem to agree with Hart.[47] Others have been unimpressed by this response. The supposition that punishment of persons ignorant of law will lead others to become informed of their legal duties has little empirical support.[48] Skeptics point out that, whatever its general force, this rationale is of limited application. Punishment of persons ignorant of law could hardly be expected to induce defendants to make more conscientious efforts to ascertain their legal duties than did Striggles.[49]

Thus the debate continues. But whatever its correct resolution, it is quite beside the point from the perspective taken here. If the principle of mens rea is construed as a requirement of justice, the relevant issue is whether and under what circumstances persons ignorant of law *deserve* criminal liability. No light is shed on this controversy by conjectures about general deterrence. Mens rea should not be deemed present because liability reduces criminality, nor should it be deemed absent if the contrary were true. It is difficult to fathom how the issue of what justice requires for a particular defendant could depend upon the impact of punishing others. Such factors have no bearing on individual desert.

Once again, there is no alternative here than to decide whether a distinction in desert should make a difference in liability. Offenders who violate laws of which they are unaware, and who would not have done what they did but for their ignorance, are unlike those who know they are acting criminally. But should this distinction in desert be reflected in liability? It is no surprise that pardons sometimes are recommended for persons who act in ignorance of law,[50] and punishment, when imposed, is frequently mitigated.[51] No principle explains why ignorance of law may influence the severity of punishment, but not liability itself. Moreover, mentally abnormal offenders are typically excused when ignorant of the wrongfulness of their conduct. Why should ignorance be irrelevant when the defendant is sane?[52] Finally, defendants are excused when their ignorance is due to the vagueness of the law.[53] Why should the result be different when their ignorance has some other cause? There *may* be good answers to these difficult questions, but the quest of utilitarian gains is not among them.

Again, there is a strong temptation to seek a compromise position. *Striggles* is unjust because the defendant *could* not have known his conduct to be illegal. In other cases, however, the failure of the defendant to ascertain his legal obligations may not be blameless. Perhaps ignorance of the law should constitute a defense when it is reasonable or without fault.[54] Surely this view represents an improvement over the harsh doctrine of *ignorantia juris*. As in the case of voluntary intoxication, however, this moderate position proves difficult to reconcile with the fundamental principles of orthodox criminal theory. To paraphrase Hall, there is a great difference between asserting that a person must knowingly violate a law to be sufficiently culpable to merit punishment, and asserting that he is thus culpable if he could reasonably have prevented himself from not knowing his conduct was illegal.[55]

## EVIDENCE AND CRIMINAL THEORY

THE ABOVE EXAMPLES indicate that utilitarian reasoning has led orthodox theorists to favor narrow and restrictive interpretations of the fundamental principles of criminal liability. The concern for social protection has a number of distinct but related manifestations. Several theorists resist applications of fundamental principles that would render liability difficult to *prove*. If liability is not easily substantiated, many guilty defendants will escape conviction by creating a reasonable doubt that some necessary condition of liability is satisfied. Punishment will become a less effective deterrent, and the welfare of society will be jeopardized. As a result, conclusions about what justice demands in a particular case are often infected with practical problems of obtaining reliable evidence. Some of the applications of these fundamental principles are virtually incomprehensible unless they are understood to represent compromises between worries about evidence and demands about what justice requires.

Anyone who has taught a course introducing criminal law appreciates how easily students conflate questions about the proper scope and application of the fundamental principles of liability with practical problems of proof. If it is proposed that defense x should be recognized, the skeptical student will ask: "How could defense x be disproved? Won't *everyone* allege x in attempts to escape conviction? Won't the guilty evade punishment?"

These questions anticipate the reactions of a great many orthodox theorists. Any proposal to recognize a defense invariably is met with apprehension about how it might be disproved. Such expressions of skepticism are typically followed by dire predictions about the social consequences of such a defense upon the welfare of law-abiding citizens. John Austin criticized the proposal that ignorance of law be recognized as a defense on the following grounds:

> If ignorance of law were admitted as a ground of exemption, the Courts would be involved in questions which it were scarcely possible to solve, and which would render the administration of justice next to impracticable. If ignorance of law were admitted as a ground of exemption, ignorance of law would always be alleged by the party, and the Court, in every case, would be bound to decide the point.[56]

Similar observations could be multiplied indefinitely, and frequently have been made as a reason to disallow voluntary intoxication as a defense to criminal liability. One judge cautioned: "All that the crafty criminal would require for a well-planned murder . . . would be a revolver in one hand to commit the deed, and a quart of intoxicating liquor in the other with which to build his excusable defense."[57]

Some familiar answers to the skeptic cannot be expected to persuade him. He is certain to be reminded that the evidence required to disprove defense x is no more difficult to assess than that involved in any number of determinations criminal courts have made for centuries.[58] But this reply is curious. The fact that criminal practice already requires juries to answer a number of exceedingly difficult questions is not a good reason to add to the list.

A better reply is available. The skeptic should be reminded that the fundamental principles of criminal liability have the status of requirements of justice. What does the defendant deserve who is *not* faking intoxication or ignorance of law? Should justice to him be sacrificed so that others do not get away with their deception? Our criminal justice system is generally unwilling to tolerate punishment of the guilty to compensate for conviction of the innocent. This "presumption of innocence" is forgotten whenever one allows his worries about evidence to infect his interpretation of a fundamental principle.

If theorists are to be taken seriously in construing these principles as requirements of justice, it is crucial that questions about evidence be placed to one side, at least temporarily. For this purpose, it is useful to assume that all the relevant facts are known when wrestling with the scope and application of these principles. Many students find this supposition fanciful and impractical. But it is not unrealistic in the context in which legal precedents actually develop. Appellate decisions are the primary source from which the content of the fundamental principles of criminal liability has been drawn. The material facts have been established at the trial level, and generally are not subject to review. Thus appellate courts *are* able to confront the issue of the just response of the criminal law *given* these facts. Theorists who specify the scope and application of the fundamental principles of criminal liability should pose the same issue, and resist the tendency to compromise their answers by practical difficulties of obtaining reliable evidence.

The scope and application of the fundamental principles of liability will differ if criminal theory is not infected by evidentiary questions. It is hardly surprising that the just outcome of a case may conflict with what is most efficient or practical. It is one thing to defend a principle as fair, and quite another to support it as the closest approximation to fairness that is possible in the real world. For example, if ignorance of law is an invalid defense, it should be because it is fair to require defendants to be aware of the law that governs their conduct, and not because too many offenders might escape their just deserts if this defense were recognized. Intellectual clarity is best served by divorcing questions of justice and evidence altogether. After these investigations are pursued independently, there *may* come a time when it is appropriate to allow the results of the latter inquiry to influence implementations of the former. It cannot be said that questions about how an issue might be proved should have no bearing whatever on the criminal law. But that result should be recognized for what it is—an unfortunate and regrettable *retreat* from what criminal theory demands as a matter of justice. Worries about evidence should not be reflected in the content of the fundamental principles of criminal liability, as long as they are to be construed as requirements of justice.

Once again, mens rea is the fundamental principle most fre-

quently compromised by practical worries about evidence. Undoubtedly this focus upon mens rea is due to the difficulty of proving what
was in the mind of the defendant at the moment of his criminal act.
Throughout legal history this problem has been exaggerated. William
Blackstone insisted that "no temporal tribunal can search the heart or
fathom the intentions of the mind, otherwise than as they are demonstrated by outward actions."[59] Some courts have indicated that there is
no fact of the matter about what a person intends. One judge wrote:
"The concept of mens rea involves what is ultimately the fiction of
determining the actual thoughts or mental processes of the accused."[60] Only occasionally are equally strong claims made in favor of
the contrary point of view. Another judge remarked that mental
states are "as much a fact as the state of a man's digestion."[61]

The formidable difficulties in proving mens rea should not
blind us to the fact that the fundamental principle indirectly jeopardized by worries about evidence is that requiring the prosecution to
establish guilt beyond a reasonable doubt. This hallowed principle has
been preserved largely because of the reluctance to allow defenses
that would almost necessarily compromise it. If criminal liability could
be established by something less than proof beyond a reasonable
doubt, legislatures and courts might be more charitable in recognizing defenses they presently are unwilling to admit.[62] Here is an
example of how conformity with a fundamental principle of liability,
superficially to the advantage of defendants, may operate indirectly to
their detriment.

In the remainder of this section I will discuss one of many
examples in which concerns about evidence have been used to narrow
the scope and application of mens rea. The conclusion of the argument may be correct on grounds other than those examined here. But
its premises are inconsistent with the interpretation of the fundamental principles of criminal liability as requirements of justice that
respect prima facie moral rights.

### Unreasonable Mistakes of Fact

Worries about evidence have been pervasive in debates about
recognizing unreasonable mistake of fact as a defense to crimes
requiring general mens rea. It is important, first, to distinguish this
controversy from closely related issues with which it might be confused.

First, this question involves the validity of the defense of
mistake of *fact,* rather than of *law.* In most instances this distinction is
easily drawn, although the difficulty of categorizing each and every
mistake as one or the other has led some authorities to repudiate the
usefulness of this distinction altogether.[63] In any event, the settled law

is more sympathetic to defendants who succeed in categorizing their mistake as one of fact rather than of law. Second, this issue arises with respect to offenses involving *general* rather than *special* mens rea. If the offense requires a special mens rea, there is little question that mistake of fact, however unreasonable, constitutes a valid defense. For example, the offense of perjury is not committed if the person under oath expresses a false statement he sincerely believes to be true, regardless of the carelessness that induced his belief.[64] Perjury requires a lie, and one does not lie unless he believes, however unreasonably, that he is not speaking the truth. Third, this topic involves *unreasonable* mistakes. Typically the defense is valid if the mistake is reasonable.[65] Finally, this controversy requires that the conduct of the defendant be noncriminal if the facts were as he mistakenly believed them to be.[66] A defendant who shoots and kills victim A, mistakenly believing him to be B, lacks a defense if he had no more right to kill B than A.[67]

Should an unreasonable mistake of fact negate general mens rea and constitute a defense to criminal liability? Many orthodox theorists believe it should not. Perkins writes: "If the offense charged requires no special mental element, but only the general mens rea, this element can be negated by a mistake that is reasonable but not by one that is unreasonable."[68] In this context, defendants are judged according to an "objective" standard: what is decisive is what they *should* have believed, rather than what they *in fact* believed.

Consider the case of *Gillum v. State*.[69] Here the defendant was convicted of bigamy despite her sincere but erroneous belief that her spouse had obtained a valid divorce. Had her belief been reasonable, there should be little doubt about the validity of her defense.[70] But her belief was based upon an unsubstantiated rumor; thus the court held it to be unreasonable and upheld her conviction.

What is the just outcome of such a case? Why should the fact that a mistaken belief is unreasonable create a mens rea that would be absent were the belief reasonable? It is doubtful that a persuasive answer to this question can be provided. Simply put, defendants who make unreasonable mistakes of fact lack mens rea for precisely the same reason as defendants whose mistakes are reasonable.[71] Of course, the former defendants may be at fault for having made the mistake, but that is quite another matter. In the first place, the prior act of making this mistake is not itself an offense. In the second place, it is mysterious how any mens rea for that prior act might "transfer" to the subsequent offense and substitute for its mens rea. The rule that mistakes of fact must be reasonable to constitute a valid defense is an unacceptable compromise of the principles of justice that constitute orthodox criminal theory. If persons have a right not to be held criminally liable for conduct that does not include a mens rea, a special justification is needed to convict those whose mistakes are unreasonable.

Why do many commentators and courts insist that mistakes of fact must be reasonable before they exculpate? One authority speculates that "some jurisdictions simply do not understand the implications" of the requirement of reasonableness.[72] According to Williams, the consequences of the view that defendants lack a defense when their mistake is unreasonable "are enough to demonstrate its untenability."[73]

Surely the appeal of this doctrine can be explained, if not justified. By far the most commonly expressed (though not the only) reason in favor of holding defendants to an "objective" standard involves the difficulty of obtaining reliable evidence. It would not be easy to prove that a defendant was aware of the truth if unreasonable ignorance of fact were available as a defense. Williams remarks: "To characterise the defendant's alleged mistake as unreasonable is often a polite way of saying 'I do not believe him.' "[74] Smith and Hogan agree that "lack of faith in the jury to detect the 'bogus defence' probably lies at the root of the objective requirements." But they immediately counter: "If the jury has the virtues which are alleged to justify its existence, it should be required to decide what [the defendant's] actual belief was."[75]

According to this analysis, the requirement of reasonableness functions (in the context of mistakes) as evidence that the defendant is sincere in alleging ignorance. It may seem that there should be no objection to using the requirement of reasonableness in this way. As a practical matter, juries can be expected to be much more suspicious that a defendant is lying when his alleged mistake is unreasonable. But on closer examination, this result is dissatisfying. The fact that unreasonableness frequently provides evidence of insincerity is no reason to disallow the defense in cases in which the defendant *is* sincere. Many unreasonable beliefs are no less sincere than those that are reasonable, and it seems that justice favors acquittal if a defendant somehow succeeds in convincing the jury that his unreasonable mistake is bona fide and not merely fabricated. Of course, many a sincere defendant who alleges unreasonable ignorance will be convicted, because the jury will not believe him to have been mistaken. Such miscarriages of justice are probably unavoidable.

As long as the principle of mens rea is construed as a requirement of justice, worries about evidence should not be allowed to restrict its application. If unreasonable mistake of fact should not be recognized as a defense, better reasons than the difficulty of distinguishing sincerity from insincerity must be provided.

### DISCRETION AND CRIMINAL THEORY

I HAVE FOCUSED on the implications of understanding the fundamental principles of criminal liability as requirements of *justice*. Here I examine the consequences of treating these principles as (prima facie) *requirements*.

Why requirements? Assuming that the fundamental principles share a prescriptive status, why not construe them as *ideals* toward which the criminal law should aspire? This alternative cannot be dismissed out of hand. Again, however, it is at odds with the primary use to which these principles have been put. Frequently they are invoked as a reason to oppose real or hypothetical instances of penal liability that violate them. These principles could not function in this way unless they had the status of requirements. The fact that a law falls short of the high standards expressed by an ideal is not a reason to demand its repeal, or to ask for the special justification that supports it. Thus I will suppose that these principles are best understood as having the status of (prima facie) *requirements* of justice.

The most important consequence of treating a principle as a requirement is that legal officials must not be given the discretion to disregard it. If an official needed no justification to infringe a principle, it would not impose a demand upon him. Exercises of discretion that benefit defendants are akin to acts of grace, which no one would regard as an effective safeguard for the protection of rights. Thus any existing discretion to disregard the implications of these principles should be removed.

Only recently have theorists begun to pay attention to the proper place of discretion in Anglo-American legal systems.[76] The less desirable aspects of discretion were frequently overlooked in efforts to emphasize its unquestioned advantages. But the focus on exercises of discretion that operate to the benefit of criminal defendants and to the overall justice of the legal system should not blind us to the *lack* of exercises of discretion that have the opposite effects. Constitutional scholars have become especially sensitive to this fact in the context of capital punishment.[77]

The crusade against entrusting rights of criminal defendants to exercises of legal discretion has been led by George Fletcher. An important theme of his *Rethinking Criminal Law* is his "unwillingness to retreat to discretion as a surrogate for the principled solution of human conflict."[78] In any number of situations it is extremely difficult to determine how the application of one or more fundamental principles should affect liability. In many of these situations there is a tendency to rely upon the good sense of legal officials. According to Fletcher, this unfortunate tendency has been a substantial "factor inhibiting [the] study of the theoretical foundations of criminal liability."[79] Robinson echoes this sentiment, contending that "the criminal law theorist suffers a moral defect when he unnecessarily defers to administrative or judicial discretion to make the criminal law just."[80]

I will identify two (of many) areas in which applications of the fundamental principles of criminal liability, interpreted as requirements of justice, undermine the proposal to entrust their implementation to exercises of legal discretion. The first example involves *judicial* discretion; the second involves *prosecutorial* discretion. Excessive reliance upon either kind of legal discretion is at odds with the aspiration to administer a government of laws and not of men.

### The "Subjectification" of Criminal Negligence

Discretion is often employed in determinations of whether a criminal defendant is negligent or reckless. Theorists have long debated whether and to what extent definitions of negligence and recklessness should take into account the peculiar disabilities or limitations of particular defendants. Invariably these definitions resort to the "objective" standard of the "reasonable person." Yet unqualified applications of this standard may result in injustice, for not everyone conforms to this ideal. For example, conduct that is deemed negligent or reckless in a blind person may be substantially different than in a sighted individual.

Legislators have relied upon discretion to prevent the injustice that would result were a single standard of liability applied to all criminal defendants. The approach of the Model Penal Code is noteworthy. Both negligence and recklessness are defined, in part, as a "gross deviation from the standard" of what the "law-abiding" or "reasonable person . . . would observe in the actor's situation."[81] What is the effect of the final clause "in the actor's situation"? The draftsmen included this phrase to allow courts to "subjectify" the otherwise "objective" standard of liability, but provided no guidance as to when this would be appropriate.

Hopefully all courts would apply different standards of liability in determinations of whether blind or sighted persons are negligent or reckless. Blindness frequently functions as a circumstance to be included "in the actor's situation." The draftsmen describe as "morally obtuse" the failure to consider such a factor.[82] But if this result is morally just, one wonders why it is not explicitly required by the Code; why is the failure to consider such a factor not also *legally* obtuse? No misapplication of *law* would be involved if a misguided judge or juror refused to allow the fact that a defendant was blind to bear on his liability. Is not the mere possibility of such an injustice sufficient reason to improve upon these standards?

The familiar answer to this question is that trust *must* be placed in the good sense of legal officials. The entire criminal justice system would collapse unless trust were warranted. But why rely on good sense when there is a better alternative? The typical response is that no better alternative exists, for it is impossible to specify in advance all the peculiarities of defendants that might bear on their liability for negligence or recklessness. It is understandable that the draftsmen were reluctant to compile a list to distinguish relevant from irrelevant characteristics. This answer seems to have satisfied most criminal theorists, though suspicion about the justifiability of criminal negligence and recklessness persists.

As a result, the relevance of a given characteristic of a defendant to liability for negligence or recklessness is unresolved by law, and is entrusted to the good sense of judges and juries. Assuming that mens rea is present in unquestioned cases of criminal negligence or recklessness, there is no guidance about what disabilities or limitations of particular defendants preclude mens rea. Is it ever relevant to "the actor's situation" that he is uneducated? Poor? Intoxicated? Easily provoked? Greedy? Apathetic? Careless? Insane? Addicted to junk food? Indeed, the list *is* endless.

Nonetheless, there is a better alternative than reliance upon judicial discretion. It is not unrealistic to hope for a *criterion* to distinguish relevant from irrelevant characteristics. Legislatures would not have to enumerate specific characteristics of defendants relevant to liability for negligence or recklessness. Instead, they could adopt a position about what *makes* a specific characteristic material.[83] If blindness is sometimes relevant and carelessness is not, blindness must possess some property (or properties) lacked by carelessness in virtue of which they have different legal significance.[84]

The supposition that mens rea functions as a requirement of justice necessitates that the property (or properties) that distinguishes relevant from irrelevant characteristics be identified and incorporated into applicable statutes. Otherwise, there is a risk that a defendant might be held liable for criminal negligence or recklessness despite having a characteristic that precludes his mens rea. Such a result would violate rights, although the fundamental principles of liability are designed to protect them.

### Choice of Lesser Evils

Some authorities confidently assert a common law defense of "choice of lesser evils" (frequently but misleadingly called "necessity"), according to which a defendant may violate a penal law if "the harm or evil sought to be avoided by such conduct is greater than that sought to be prevented by the law."[85] In fact, however, the common law is quite ambivalent about this defense, particularly in England.[86] Some jurisdictions have explicitly provided for this defense, while others have resisted.

Uncertainty about the proper rationale of this defense has contributed to misgivings about its validity. It is not surprising that many authorities support it on the ground that defendants who choose the lesser of two evils could not have been deterred from doing otherwise. This rationale may seem compelling in many cases. In the frequently cited case of *U.S. v. Kirby,* a defendant was not found liable for the offense of prison-escape when he fled from a fire he did not cause. The court solemnly pronounced: "He is not to be hanged because he would not stay to be burnt."[87] Again, however, claims about deterrence are quite beside the point. This rationale invites rejoinders of the sort made by James Stephen: it is at the "moment of temptation" that "the law should speak most clearly and emphatically to the contrary."[88] In any number of circumstances, a heroic (or foolish) person might be guided by his sense of legal duty, rather than violate the literal language of a criminal statute. A person who burns property to prevent the spread of a fire should not be guilty of arson. Yet someone might make this inferior choice if the defense of necessity were not available.[89]

Thus a better rationale must be provided. As usual, Fletcher is closer to the mark in writing that an adequate defense of choice of lesser evils requires reference to "general principles about the sort of conduct that is right and proper and therefore justifiably exempt from criminal liability."[90] The criminal law should recognize the defense of choice of lesser evils because a person who so chooses does not deserve penal liability.

Obviously, those jurisdictions that have been slow to recognize a defense of choice of lesser evils have not been content, for example, to "hang those who would not stay to be burnt." They have maintained a tolerable level of justice by relying upon prosecutorial discretion not to charge those persons who might otherwise be convicted in the absence of the defense. The English Law Commission has explicitly endorsed this approach: "We are of the view that the proper exercise of discretion in instituting proceedings . . . would render such a general defence unnecessary."[91] Lord Denning has expressed a similar view. He accepted the conclusion that the driver of a fire engine commits the offense of running a traffic light in response to an emergency, but added: "Nevertheless such a man should not be prosecuted. He should be congratulated."[92] Many theorists find this approach ludicrous. Smith and Hogan respond: "It is odd to see the Master of the Rolls finding a breach of the criminal law to be a case for congratulation. A better answer might be to make an exception."[93]

Reservations about this defense arise from examples in which it might lead to unacceptable results. The English Law Commission continues:

> 'An immediate blood transfusion must be made in order to save an injured person: the only one who has the same blood type as the injured [person] refuses to give blood. Can he be overpowered, and the blood taken from him?' The necessity defence . . . would by its terms almost certainly answer this in the affirmative. But one of those commenting . . . expressed doubts as to whether this would be regarded as a generally acceptable solution. We share these doubts. It is however, almost, if not entirely, impossible to devise any generalised exception which would exclude the availability of a general defence in this situation.[94]

More bluntly, Lord Edmund Davies has called the defense of necessity an invitation to anarchy.[95]

These difficulties are not trivial. But the other side of the coin is that *not* validating the defense might lead to injustice as well. Is it proper to risk the undeserved punishment of some, so that others are not permitted to raise a defense without merit? Our sense of justice is reluctant to allow conviction of the guilty to compensate for conviction of the innocent. Is there an alternative that minimizes the likelihood that rights will be violated?

Once again, if mens rea is absent in cases such as *Kirby,* but present in the hypothetical described by the English Law Commission, some property (or properties) must account for the disparity. After all, prosecutors are entrusted to sort cases correctly.[96] If it is too much to ask for a list of relevant and irrelevant characteristics, it is not too much to demand a *criterion* of how such a distinction might be drawn. If persons have a prima facie moral right not to be held criminally liable for conduct that does not involve mens rea, and the fundamental principle of liability that respects this right is construed as a *requirement* of justice, it is necessary that this right be protected by law. Trust in prosecutorial discretion fails to achieve this result. Should we be happy with a rule that recognizes no *legal* error by the conviction of Kirby? Here, as elsewhere, reliance upon discretion substitutes for principled argument.

Admittedly, the task of formulating rules to resolve human conflict is among the most arduous undertaken by mankind. In those instances in which plausible arguments pull in opposite directions, there is an overwhelming tendency to resort to the so-called "common sense" of legal officials. Perhaps no system of justice should strive to eliminate discretion altogether. But entrusting the rights respected by the fundamental principles of liability to the grace of officials should be a last resort. Discretion should not be hailed as a solution, but embraced only as a poor substitute for the absence of a solution.

### TAINT

SOME OF THE PROBLEMS raised in this chapter provide a clue to a "special justification" apparently regarded by many authorities as sufficient to override the prima facie right not to be held criminally liable for conduct that does not include a mens rea. I will refer to this consideration as "taint."[97] In the examples that follow, the judgment that the defendant engaged in some morally objectionable activity prior to his related criminal act is held to be a sufficient reason to "taint" him and to relax the normal requirement of mens rea. As Williams observes: "The desire of the judges to punish scoundrels who do not fall fairly within the net of the criminal law has always been a source of trouble in after years, and not least in relation to *mens rea*."[98] This section will illustrate a major theme of this book—that orthodox criminal theorists have misunderstood the proper relationship between law and morality by distorting the nature and content of morality—by examining how unsupported (and unsupportable) moral judgments influence findings of criminal liability, and result in probable violations of rights.

Perhaps the most common application of the doctrine of taint is exemplified by the problem of the relationship between voluntary intoxication and mens rea. Considerations of social utility could not account for the unwillingness of courts to recognize voluntary intoxication as a defense. As indicated above, social utility could be invoked with equal plausibility against validating *any* defense. Why single out voluntary intoxication? One answer is that the act of becoming intoxicated is regarded as morally wrongful, or at least less than morally exemplary. Thus this act "taints" the defendant with respect to subsequent criminal acts performed while intoxicated, and weakens ordinary reservations about imposing liability in the absence of mens rea.[99] Fletcher has expressed this point succinctly: "The wrongful act of becoming intoxicated in a situation where one might commit a crime is regarded as a plausible ground for not considering the impact of intoxication on the actor's culpability at the time of the act."[100] He is uncharacteristically uncritical, however, of this alleged "plausible ground" for compromising the mens rea requirement.[101] In fact, little can be said in its favor.

The central claim to be evaluated is whether the judgment that the defendant (previously) engaged in morally suspect behavior should be sufficient to "taint" him and thus override his prima facie right not to be held criminally liable for an (ensuing related) offense that does not seem to involve mens rea. It is important to distinguish this claim from a related application of the doctrine of taint that has evoked a great deal of criticism from criminal theorists, but should be less controversial.[102] This application involves the misdemeanor-manslaughter and felony-murder rules. In their least qualified formulations, these rules stipulate that anyone "who, in the commission or attempted commission of a felony [misdemeanor], caused another's death, was guilty of murder [manslaughter], without regard to the dangerous nature of the felony [misdemeanor] involved or to the likelihood that death might result from the defendant's manner of committing or attempting the felony [misdemeanor]."[103] While courts have adopted various strategies for limiting the harshness of these broad rules,[104] what is of interest is the general idea, preserved in contemporary formulations of the misdeameanor-manslaughter and felony-murder rules, that the wrongfulness of prior conduct may "taint" the defendant and thus increase his culpability for a related subsequent criminal act. It is doubtful that these rules will continue to survive the mounting criticism against them.[105] But at least they have the virtue of requiring that the prior wrongful act of the defendant sufficient to "taint" him must be *criminal*. The claim examined here does not retain this requirement. The prior act of becoming voluntarily intoxicated is lawful;[106] nonetheless, it is held sufficient to "taint" the defendant with respect to subsequent related criminal conduct. Thus this central claim should be more controversial than the felony-murder or misdemeanor-manslaughter doctrines.

It is noteworthy that the judicial attitude toward voluntary intoxication is not the only instance in which courts allow their moral judgments about the defendant's prior conduct to "taint" him and thus influence their subsequent "finding" of mens rea.[107] Earlier it was stated that reasonable mistake of fact generally constitutes a defense to criminal liability. Nonetheless, there is considerable authority for the proposition that "*some* varieties of ignorance or mistake should not be a defense, namely those which indicate that the defendant still intended to do what constitutes a . . . moral wrong."[108] The case-law involving statutory rape llustrates this proposition. Evidence that the defendant had taken precautions to learn the age of his "victim" was excluded in *Manning v. State;*[109] presumably his mistaken belief that she was not underage was reasonable. Nonetheless, the court imposed criminal liability.

Some commentators have invoked the doctrine of taint to justify the otherwise anomalous reluctance of courts to allow reasonable mistake of fact as a defense for statutory rape. Perkins is among the most emphatic. He describes recent decisions in California and Alaska that oppose the result in *Manning* as "astounding."[110] He explains: "One intending to have illicit sexual intercourse has mens rea because he is purposely engaging in a wrongful act."[111] Obviously "wrongful" in this formula means "immoral" rather than "illegal." In case there is any doubt, Perkins continues: "Conduct may be sufficiently wrongful to supply the general mens rea even if no punishment has been provided therefor, and a mistake which would merely leave the supposed deed in such a category is not exculpatory."[112] Another commentator has concluded from such observations that the defense of reasonable mistake of fact "rests ultimately on the defendant's being able to say that he has observed the community ethic."[113]

The doctrine of taint is highly problematic in *each* of its several applications. It is difficult to reconcile with the fundamental principle of concurrence, which requires that the mens rea of a single offense must "actuate" its actus reus.[114] It is hard to understand how the alleged wrongfulness of a prior act can "transfer" to the subsequent offense and substitute for its mens rea. For this reason (and others), many authorities denounce the doctrine of taint as having "no place in a rational system of substantive criminal law."[115] Much of its popularity may be due to the unavailability of alternative responses to persons who bring about their own excusing conditions.[116] Perhaps this complex and difficult problem, like many others I discuss, is better addressed outside the framework of the criminal law.

Whatever might be said about the doctrine of taint in those cases in which the prior conduct of the defendant is *criminal*, it is even less plausible when that prior conduct is lawful (or would be lawful if the facts were as the defendant believed them to be). The objection most frequently cited against this doctrine is that "moral duties should not be identified with criminal duties."[117] But skepticism about the moral judgments of those criminal theorists who defend the doctrine of taint gives rise to an equally serious difficulty. It is a continuous source of disappointment that even astute commentators, who exhibit a healthy sense of uncertainty about their ability to produce defensible principles of *law*, reveal no ambivalence whatever about the accuracy of their *moral* beliefs. Nothing less than violation of a clear and uncontroversial moral duty could conceivably "taint" a defendant with respect to subsequent criminal conduct. In the absence of an argument that defendants have moral duties to abstain from intoxication and fornication, there is no good reason to suppose that such activities are capable of tainting them. Why rely uncritically on the alleged "community morality," which in fact is deeply divided about such matters as the morality of intoxication and fornication? Surely the prima facie right of persons not to be held criminally liable for conduct that does not include a mens rea should not be overridden by prejudice masquerading as moral insight. If the fundamental principles of liability are to be interpreted as respecting prima facie moral rights, they are worthy of more protection by our criminal justice system than is afforded by these highly questionable applications of the doctrine of taint.

*    *    *

The difficulties discussed in this chapter involve unresolved tensions within orthodox criminal theory. These problems are testimony to the pervasive uncertainty among theorists about the meanings and implications of the fundamental principles of liability. A number of existing doctrines are indefensible if these principles are construed as requirements of justice that respect prima facie moral rights. As I have indicated, more sweeping reforms in the criminal law are mandated by changes in the content of these several principles. I now begin the difficult and controversial process of formulating a revised criminal theory. There is no better place to begin than with the actus reus requirement, which occupies a privileged position at the very heart of orthodox criminal theory.

## NOTES

1. John Rawls, *A Theory of Justice.*
2. Robert Nozick, *Anarchy, State, and Utopia.*
3. Ronald Dworkin, *Taking Rights Seriously.*
4. Alan Gewirth, *Reason and Morality.*
5. The view that rights and justice override utility can be challenged, though I do not do so here. Most moral and political philosophers acknowledge a "catastrophe exception" according to which considerations of rights and justice may be outweighed if the disutility is sufficiently extreme. See my "Ronald Dworkin and the Right to Liberty," *Ethics* 90 (1979): 121. See also the essays in R. G. Frey, ed., *Utility and Rights.*
6. One philosopher has described debates among criminal theorists as "largely an in-house quarrel among utilitarians." See Noel Reynolds, "The Enforcement of Morals and the Rule of Law," *Georgia Law Review* 11 (1977): 1325. The influence of deontological or rights-based theories is long overdue.
7. The view that different justifications are appropriate for the legislative and judicial functions is defended by H. L. A. Hart, "Prolegomenon to the Principles of Punishment" in his *Punishment and Responsibility,* p. 1; and John Rawls, "Two Concepts of Rules," *Philosophical Review* 64 (1955): 3.
8. Oliver Wendell Holmes, *The Common Law,* p. 41.
9. See H. L. Pohlman, *Justice Oliver Wendell Holmes and Utilitarian Jurisprudence.*
10. Holmes, *Common,* p. 40.
11. See the classic description of these conflicting models in Herbert Packer, *The Limits of the Criminal Sanction.*

12. Barbara Wootton, *Crime and the Criminal Law*, p. 51.

13. See the essays in Hart, *Punishment*.

14. The fact that most jurisdictions and authorities have been willing to allow voluntary intoxication as a valid defense to offenses involving *special* mens rea has created headaches for theoreticians. The following expression of despair is typical: "But what is a 'specific intent'? On what principle is this element distinguished from all other elements of *mens rea*? What is there about specific intent that renders it subject to negation by intoxication, whereas other kinds of *mens rea* elements are legally invulnerable to the effects of alcohol?" Herbert Fingarette and Ann Hasse, *Mental Disabilities and Criminal Responsibility*, p. 91. See also Wayne LaFave and Austin Scott, *Substantive Criminal Law*, p. 554: "It is better . . . to stay away from those misleading concepts of general intent and specific intent." ·

15. Some commentators allege a "remarkable consensus" about this point. See Peter Low, John Jeffries, and Richard Bonnie, *Criminal Law*, p. 305. It is claimed that "the modern maxim that 'voluntary intoxication is no defense' is so universally accepted as not to require the citation of cases." Fingarette and Hasse, *Disabilities*, p. 77. Yet other authorities maintain that "[i]n some jurisdictions the law on a general intoxication defense is unclear." Paul Robinson, *Criminal Law Defenses*, Vol. 2, p. 337, note 1. Robinson also claims that "there is some ambiguity about this result . . . in the Model Penal Code" (p. 248, note 8).

16. Robinson writes: "Intoxication is special among . . . defenses, however, because it is an instance in which a required offense element may be absent, yet conviction may nonetheless be permitted." *Defenses*, p. 75. Another theorist describes the law in this context as a "sad departure from principle in the name of expediency." Matthew Goode, "Some Thoughts on the Present State of the 'Defence' of Intoxication," *Criminal Law Journal* (1984): 104, 120, note 59. See also note 32.

17. Rollin Perkins and Ronald Boyce, *Criminal Law*, p. 1013. See also Jerome Hall, *General Principles of Criminal Law*, p. 544: "The solid unavoidable fact was that an injury committed under gross intoxication ought to be clearly distinguished from a like harm by a sober person."

18. Perkins and Boyce, *Criminal*, p. 1014.

19. Glanville Williams, *Criminal Law: The General Part*, p. 564.

20. This solution has been proposed in Britain by the Butler Commission on Mentally Abnormal Offenders, and discussed (as one possible alternative) by the Law Reform Commission of Canada. A number of jurisdictions have special statutes (for example, drunk driving) governing harms caused while intoxicated. See Paul Robinson, "Causing the Conditions of One's Own Defense: A Study of the Limits of Theory in Criminal Law Doctrine," *Virginia Law Review* 71 (1985): 1, 30, note 112.

21. See the objections to this alternative described in Low, Jeffries, and Bonnie, *Criminal*, pp. 311–12. See also the discussion in Eric Colvin, "Codification and Reform of the Intoxication Defense," *Criminal Law Review* 26 (1983): 43.

22. See also note 57.

23. 2 All E.R. 142 (1976). For further judicial developments in England, see *D.P.P. v. Caldwell*, 1 All E.R. 961 (1981).

24. Ibid., p. 152

25. Ibid., p. 157. See also *Regina v. Howell*, 2 All E.R. 807 (1974).

26. Ibid., p. 158. See also the exaggerated concerns of the Criminal

Law Comrs., quoted in Williams, *Criminal*, p. 565: "Were such a plea admitted, 'the pretence would be constantly resorted to as a cloak for committing the most horrible outrages with impunity; what is worse, the reality would be incurred not only to ensure safety to the most notorious offenders, but for the enabling them to inflict atrocious injuries with the greater confidence; and the very excessive brutality of an outrage would afford such evidence of the total absence of reason and humane feeling as would tend to the acquittal of the most heinous criminals.'"

27. Ibid., p. 169.

28. Ibid. See also *People v. Walker,* 396 N.Y.S.2d 121 (1977).

29. See *M.P.C.* §2.02(2)(c). But see §2.08(2): "When recklessness establishes an element of the offense, if the actor, due to self-induced intoxication, is unaware of a risk of which he would have been aware had he been sober, such unawareness is immaterial." Unfortunately, this creation of an "irrebutable presumption" of recklessness is simply ad hoc.

30. "[P]ersons who commit [serious injuries] while grossly intoxicated should not be punished unless, at the time of sobriety and the voluntary drinking, they had such prior experience as to anticipate their intoxication and that they would become dangerous in that condition." Hall, *General Principles*, p. 556. See also *Roberts v. People,* 19 Mich. 401, 422 (1870).

31. See J. C. Smith and Brian Hogan, *Criminal Law,* pp. 197–99.

32. In commenting upon this "illogicality," Williams writes that "[t]he decision in *Majewski* is a classical illustration of the truth that no authority can compel judges to arrive at a decision to which they are strongly adverse." *Textbook of Criminal Law,* p. 473. Also: "It may be said that in crimes of basic intent *Majewski* rides rough-shod over all doctrines of *mens rea* and *actus reus.*" Ibid., p. 680. See also note 16.

33. Williams, *Criminal*, p. 565. See also his remarks in *Textbook*, p. 465.

34. For a case involving criminal conduct by a diabetic who "failed to take sufficient food, following his last dose of insulin," see Smith and Hogan, *Criminal*, p. 201. They conclude that "in the case of alcohol or drugs, there is, in effect, a conclusive presumption of 'recklessness.'"

35. Robinson, *Defenses,* Vol. 2, p. 340.

36. Most authorities allow *in*voluntary intoxication as a valid defense. See *M.P.C.* §2.08(4).

37. But see Hall, *General Principles,* p. 539.

38. Ibid., p. 371.

39. See chapter 2. The remarks of Fingarette and Hasse in the context of drug and alcohol addiction are apposite here: "Undoubtedly there are those who regard possible legal approaches in polar terms: either we inflict harsh, punitive, and degrading measures on the addict, or we declare the person sick and therefore not responsible for his conduct. What is needed here is the abandonment of such extreme and fixed positions." *Disabilities*, p. 192. See also pp. 200–201, note 1.

40. Williams, *Criminal*, p. 567.

41. "The convoluted interstices of criminal law theory is no place to attempt to resolve the social problem of the effects of gross over-consumption of alcohol upon individual behavior." Goode, "Some Thoughts," p. 120. See also LaFave and Scott, *Substantive*, p. 29: "The continued existence of public drunkenness as a crime . . . can best be explained as an instance in which conduct is declared criminal so that the criminal justice process may perform social services not otherwise available."

42. "The movement to decriminalize has stalled." Note, "Alcohol Abuse and the Law," *Harvard Law Review* 94 (1981): 1660, 1665.

43. Some exceptions are discussed in Rollin Perkins, "Ignorance or Mistake of Law Revisited," *Utah Law Review* 3 (1980): 473. One class of exceptions, the scope of which is open to serious dispute, is represented by *Lambert v. California*, 355 U.S. 225 (1957).

44. 210 N.W. 137 (1926).

45. Jeremy Bentham, *An Introduction to the Principles of Morals and Legislation*, p. 161.

46. Hart, *Punishment*, p. 19.

47. See *People v. O'Brian*, 176 P. 45, 47 (1892).

48. Empirical evidence here need not be speculative, but can be drawn from the experience of other legal systems, which typically go much further than Anglo-American law in recognizing a defense of mistake of law. See George Fletcher, *Rethinking Criminal Law*, p. 747.

49. The result in Striggles is altered by *M.P.C.* §2.04(3)(b)(ii).

50. See Smith and Hogan, *Criminal*, p. 68, note 11.

51. See Williams, *Criminal*, pp. 290–91.

52. See Robinson, *Defenses*, Vol. 2, p. 374.

53. See Ronald Cass, "Ignorance of the Law: A Maxim Reexamined," *William and Mary Law Review* 17 (1976), p. 671, 688–89.

54. But see Robinson, *Defenses*, p. 13: "The 'at fault' provisions, even at best, are defective because they are oversimplified."

55. See note 38.

56. John Austin, *Lectures on Jurisprudence*, p. 498. LaFave and Scott find this explanation "somewhat more satisfying" than others. *Substantive*, p. 586.

57. *State v. Arsenault*, 124 A.2d 741, 746 (1956). See also Hall, *General Principles*, p. 530.

58. See Hall, ibid, p. 531. But see Robinson, *Defenses*, p. 376.

59. Blackstone, *Commentaries*, *21. Here Blackstone was following C. J. Bryan, frequently quoted as having said: "The intention of a man cannot be tried. The devil himself knows not the intention of a man."

60. *Bethea v. U.S.*, 365 A.2d 64, 87 (1976). Some of the reasons for believing mental events to be fictitious are discussed in Michael Moore, "The Moral and Metaphysical Sources of the Criminal Law," in J. Roland Pennock and John Chapman, eds., *Nomos XXVII: Criminal Justice*, p. 11.

61. *Edginton v. Fitzmaurice*, 29 Ch.Div. 459, 483 (1885).

62. See John Jeffries and Paul Stephan, "Defenses, Presumptions, and Burdens of Proof in the Criminal Law," *Yale Law Journal* 88 (1979): 1325.

63. Fletcher, *Rethinking*, p. 684.

64. *Commonwealth v. Brady*, 71 Mass. 78 (1855). But see Robinson, *Defenses*, pp. 250–51, note 18.

65. *State v. McDonald*, 7 Mo.App. 510 (1879).

66. *State v. Griego*, 294 P.2d 282 (1956).

67. *Jackson v. State*, 26 S.E.2d 485 (1943).

68. Perkins and Boyce, *Criminal*, p. 1036.

69. 147 S.W.2d 778 (1941).

70. *State v. Audette*, 70 A. 833 (1908). But see *Burnely v. State*, 29 So.2d 94 (1947).

71. See *M.P.C.* §2.04(1).

72. Robinson, "Causing," p. 253.

73. Williams, *Criminal*, p. 201.

74. Ibid., p. 202.

75. Smith and Hogan, *Criminal*, p. 215.

76. Concern about discretion was promoted primarily by Dworkin, *Seriously*. The most comprehensive study is Rosemary Pattenden, *The Judge, Discretion, and the Criminal Trial*.

77. See Charles Black, *Capital Punishment*.

78. *Rethinking*, p. 769. See also George Fletcher, "Some Unwise Reflections on Discretion," *Law and Contemporary Problems* 47 (1984): 269.

79. *Rethinking*, p. xx.

80. Robinson, *Defenses*, p. ix.

81. *M.P.C.* §2.02(2)(c) and (d).

82. Ibid., Comment 62.

83. Williams suggests that only *physical* handicaps are relevant, but provides no principled reason for excluding "mental" deficiencies. *Textbook*, p. 94.

84. See chapter 4, where I discuss the likelihood that the distinction between states of affairs over which persons have or lack *control* is central to revised criminal theory. This distinction has an obvious application to the present problem.

85. See *M.P.C.* §3.02(1)(a).

86. See P. Glazebrook, "The Necessity Plea: English Criminal Law," *Cambridge Law Journal* 30 (1972): 87.

87. 74 U.S. 482, 487 (1868).

88. James Stephen, *History of the Criminal Law of England*, pp. 107–8.

89. See the "danger of overdeterrence" mentioned in Meir Dan-Cohen, "Decision Rules and Conduct Rules: On Acoustic Separation in the Criminal Law," *Harvard Law Review* 97 (1984): p. 625, 638, note 29.

90. Fletcher, *Rethinking*, p. 792.

91. The English Law Commission, No. 83, *Criminal Law, Report on Defenses of General Application* (1977), pp. 19–32.

92. *Buckoke v. Greater London Council*, 2 All E.R. 254, 258 (1971).

93. Smith and Hogan, *Criminal*, p. 204. See Packer, *Limits*, p. 114. See also the comments of Lord Morris in *D.P.P. for N.Ireland v. Lynch*, AC 653, 672E (1975).

94. See note 91.

95. *Southwark London Borough v. Williams*, 2 All E.R. 175, 181 (1971).

96. See the discussion in Robinson, *Defenses*, Vol. 2, pp. 45–88. The case described by note 94 involves a physical assault upon an innocent person. The contours of the defense of necessity might well preclude (or restrict) its application to such cases.

97. I borrow the word "taint" from Fletcher, although he assigns a different meaning to it.

98. Williams, *Criminal*, p. 185.

99. The doctrine of taint probably explains (but does not justify) why criminal conduct stemming from other self-induced incapacities are treated differently from voluntary intoxication, and are held incompatible with mens rea. See note 34.

100. Fletcher, *Rethinking*, p. 277. See also Robinson, *Defenses*, Vol. 2, p. 340.

101. Elsewhere Fletcher is highly critical of the principle that "wrongdoers take the risk of their conduct turning out worse than they expected."

*Rethinking,* p. 723. Some applications of this principle, he insists, "mock the classical principles of just punishment" and involve a "truncated and distorted theory of moral retribution" (p. 730). Williams also remarks that this doctrine has "an air of practicality," although he ultimately admits that "the difficulties it presents seem to be insuperable." *Criminal,* p. 189.

102. Affinities between the law surrounding voluntary intoxication and the felony-murder and misdemeanor-manslaughter rules are noted by Hall, *General Principles,* p. 547.

103. Wayne LaFave and Austin Scott, *Criminal Law,* p. 545.

104. Fletcher notes that the harshness of this rule has been mitigated by exercises of prosecutorial discretion. See *Rethinking,* p. 320.

105. Fletcher complains that these rules "erode the link between culpability and liability." Ibid., p. 303. A similar observation could be made about each application of the doctrine of taint.

106. Sometimes public intoxication is an offense. See Robinson, "Causing," p. 29–30, note 111.

107. Some features of the defense of duress seem to involve another application of the doctrine of taint. See Robinson, *Defenses,* p. 251.

108. LaFave and Scott, *Criminal,* p. 361.

109. 65 S.W. 920 (1901).

110. *People v. Hernandez,* 393 P.2d 673 (1964), and *State v. Guest,* 583 P.2d 836 (1978).

111. Perkins and Boyce, *Criminal,* p. 917.

112. Ibid., p. 917.

113. Peter Brett, *An Inquiry Into Criminal Guilt,* p. 149.

114. See LaFave and Scott, *Substantive,* p. 582.

115. LaFave and Scott, ibid., p. 582. But see their qualification on p. 583.

116. For an interesting approach to deal with the problem of "culpability of causing" *within* the structure of the criminal law, see Robinson, "Causing." He proposes that the defendant's culpability for the ensuing offense be determined by reference to his culpability *at the time he causes the conditions of his defense.* An implication of this proposal is as follows: "Where an actor brings about the conditions of his defense but at the time has no culpability, not even negligence, as to causing or risking the commission of the subsequent offense, it is appropriate to limit his liability to that imposed by existing statutes . . . If his conduct does not constitute an offense, he faces no liability." Thus (subject to the exceptions described in notes 20 and 106) the voluntarily intoxicated offender typically will escape liability altogether. This outcome is at least questionable.

117. Graham Hughes, "Criminal Responsibility," *Stanford Law Review* 16 (1964): 470, 481.

# 4

# *The Physical Component of Crime*

## THE IMPEDIMENTS TO ASSESSMENT

No fundamental requirement of orthodox criminal theory is as deeply entrenched as the actus reus requirement, expressed by the principle that liability may not be imposed in the absence of a criminal act. Although the terms "actus reus" seem to be of relatively recent origin,[1] the requirement itself is older than any significant treatise in criminal theory.[2] It is doubtful that there ever was a time in the history of the common law when criminal liability could be imposed without an actus reus.[3] Yet despite its position at the very heart of orthodox criminal theory, it remains true that "the thorough-going analysis of the actus reus necessary for criminal liability has yet to arrive."[4]

The actus reus requirement stands alone as the single fundamental principle of criminal liability that has not been seriously challenged. Other fundamental principles of orthodox theory that once enjoyed comparable assent have been attacked in scholarly literature and compromised in criminal practice. The other half of the orthodox model of the criminal offense—the requirement of mens rea—has been subject to much more frequent criticism. To be sure, criminal theorists have long recognized that a number of controversial kinds of liability, such as conspiracy, attempt, and possession, are difficult to reconcile with this unyielding requirement. Yet the tone of their remarks is significant. Without important exception, they have not maintained that such kinds of liability represent genuine counterexamples to this requirement. Instead, they have struggled to show how, appearances notwithstanding, the actus reus requirement is preserved by these kinds of liability.

The actus reus requirement is so firmly established in orthodox theory that it may prove impossible to dislodge. An unbiased assessment of this principle poses acute difficulties, for orthodox theorists show an extraordinary deference toward it. Three distinct indications demonstrate this veneration. Consider first the nature of their attempts to analyze the concept of an act. What *is* an actus reus? Is it true, as a matter of fact, that all criminal liability involves an actus reus? One might reasonably expect that some theorists would answer these questions by formulating an independent conception of an act, and then employing it to test the hypothesis that all criminal liability requires such an act. Invariably, however, the approach proceeds in the opposite direction. The actus reus requirement is unquestioned, and those criminal theorists who have sought to explicate the concept of an act have formulated analyses designed to assure the inviolability of that requirement. John Austin and John Salmond, for example, disagree radically in their analyses of an act. According to Austin, all acts are intentional.[5] Thus it seems to follow that liability for negligence is suspect, since negligent "acts" can be performed unintentionally. Whatever one believes about the soundness of this argument, it is clear that its validity presupposes the actus reus requirement as a suppressed premise. Unless all criminal offenses require an act, the alleged fact that acts are intentional could not be used to oppose liability for negligence.

Without debating the actus reus requirement itself, Salmond turns Austin's logic on its head. Austin's analysis of an act must be too narrow, he insists, because "intention is not a necessary condition of legal liability, and therefore cannot be an essential element in those acts which produce such liability."[6] Since criminal liability may attach to unintentional conduct, it must be incorrect to suppose that an act is necessarily intentional. The disagreement between these theorists is important and profound. But it is noteworthy that neither questions the actus reus requirement itself. Both assume that *however* the concept of an act is explicated, the analysis must preserve the truth of the actus reus requirement. Neither theorist entertains the possibility that the best analysis of the concept of an act might render the actus reus requirement false or subject to qualification. Small wonder that no challenge to that principle has emerged from the work of those few orthodox criminal theorists who were sufficiently ambitious to undertake an analysis of the concept of an act. Existing analyses effectively immunize the requirement from criticism.

Further evidence of the deference of orthodox criminal theorists toward the actus reus requirement is provided by their curious willingness to accept that principle while confessing to uncertainty about what it is they have accepted. After presenting criticisms of traditional analyses of the concept of an act, Hyman Gross admits that "the act itself, or rather the very idea of an act, still remains veiled in mystery."[7] Against this confusion, he asks the sensible question of "why we want to understand the concept of an act?"[8] His answer, in part, is that "it is only acts that we regard as a proper basis for criminal liability."[9] Surely this approach must be interpreted as an expression of faith, for it puts the cart before the horse. How can such confidence in the actus reus requirement be warranted in the absence of a tolerably clear understanding of actus reus?

Finally, orthodox criminal theorists share a nearly universal tendency to attach almost *any* meaning to the concept of actus reus—regardless of how peculiar—in order to ensure the truth of the requirement. A consequence of this tendency is that the principle comes to adopt the guise of a tautology or conceptual truth. At some time or another, it is likely that *each* of the several fundamental principles of criminal liability has been "defended" by being converted into a tautology. Since more scholarly debate has surrounded the meaning of mens rea, it is instructive to borrow from the history of that controversy to illustrate this point. Many "defenses" of the mens rea requirement proceed little further than to stipulate that mens rea is a technical term of legal art with no precise translation in ordinary language. The definition of mens rea most indicative of this strategy is "whatever mental element is necessary to convict for any particular crime."[10] Even theorists who propose such definitions admit that they "say very little about any mens rea."[11] They have the "virtue" of salvaging mens rea as a precondition of criminal liability, but do so in a most uninformative way. The principle that criminal liability requires a mens rea becomes tautologous: as so defined, no conceivable instance of criminal liability could dispense with mens rea. The parallel strategy (now beginning to appear in treatises) to preserve the truth of the actus reus requirement is to define actus reus as any "events or states of affairs for which a person might be responsible."[12] It is not clear how this requirement, as so elaborated, might be challenged. The truth of the requirement is purchased at the price of its triviality. It no longer has any potential to illuminate or to contribute to our understanding of the substantive criminal law.

It is doubtful that the fundamental principles of orthodox criminal theory can be of much value if they are interpreted as tautologies. Surely nothing in the *concept* of criminal liability necessitates the occurrence of an actus reus; the requirement is substantive rather than conceptual.[13] Nor is the concept of an actus reus infinitely elastic; orthodox criminal theory loses significance if theorists preserve this requirement by enlarging the scope of actus reus whenever novel kinds of liability are invented. Of course, it must not be assumed that the concept of an act contained in the analysis of the actus reus requirement must be identical to the best philosophical account of action, or to the sense of action expressed in ordinary language.[14] Yet it is surely a *desideratum* that the concepts contained in the fundamental principles of liability are reasonably close in meaning to their nonlegal analogues. The potential to mislead laypersons and legal theorists alike is reduced to the extent that concepts with both legal and nonlegal uses share related meanings.

The philosopher of criminal law who hopes to *assess* the actus reus requirement should resist the extraordinary deference shown by orthodox theorists toward the principle. From a critical perspective, those analyses of the concept of an act that are designed to preserve the inviolability of the requirement are question-begging. Nor should we accept the requirement without at least a rough understanding of what we have accepted. Finally, we must not succumb to the temptation to construe the principle as a tautology.

It would be incredible to suppose that a principle that has gone virtually unchallenged throughout the long history of criminal theory did not express a substantial and important insight. I will attempt to identify, elaborate, and preserve this insight. To this limited extent, I defend the actus reus requirement. But my overall strategy is a good deal more critical than defensive. Having identified what is correct about this principle, I will argue that that insight is misleadingly expressed by the claim that criminal liability presupposes an act. I will argue (with a few reservations) that an alternative, competitive principle—*the control principle*—expresses more perspicuously the good sense embodied in the actus reus requirement. I will contend, in other words, that the principle I propose to substitute for the actus reus requirement at the heart of revised criminal theory is a more illuminating principle than that which it replaces. To this extent, I attack the actus reus requirement. My conclusion is that orthodox criminal theorists have vastly overrated the significance of the distinction between action and whatever is contrasted with it.

This strategy is viable only if it is relatively clear what is meant by the claim that a given principle "illuminates" criminal law better than its competitors. The criteria of adequacy according to which the fundamental principles of criminal liability should be assessed have been sketched in chapters 1 and 2. I assume that, like the other fundamental principles of criminal liability, the actus reus requirement has a dual role and function. Initially, it is formulated as an inductive generalization to describe accurately the existing substantive criminal law. Its more interesting and important use, however, is to express a requirement of justice. In other words, orthodox criminal theory maintains that persons have a prima facie right not to be held liable for conduct that does not include an actus reus. If this supposition about the status of this requirement is correct, there

should be something suspicious about those real or imaginary instances of penal liability that violate it, and impose criminal liability
despite the absence of an actus reus. Theorists should be unwilling to
allow such laws to become part of our criminal practice unless a
special justification is offered in their favor. If there is nothing
objectionable about such laws, the actus reus principle does not
express a requirement of justice. If the principle does *not* express a
requirement of justice, it does not belong at the heart of criminal
theory, and orthodox theory is ripe for revision.

It is safe to anticipate that criminal liability *will* be objectionable
in the vast majority of cases in which it is imposed in violation of the
actus reus requirement. Accordingly, the relevant inquiry shifts to
two sets of questions. First, is what is objectionable about liability in
the majority of cases in which an actus reus is absent best expressed by
the claim that an act has not occurred? Or does some other feature
better explain what is objectionable about such liability? Second, what
should be said about the small minority of cases in which liability
seems *un*objectionable despite the absence of an actus reus? Does the
"other feature" mentioned above provide a better explanation of why
such cases are acceptable within our criminal practice? Answers to
these questions are significant in laying the groundwork for a principle designed to replace the actus reus requirement at the heart of
criminal theory.

A criminal theorist cannot assess the actus reus requirement
unless he is confident about his ability to identify real or hypothetical
instances of criminal liability that violate it. Again, the key to understanding a principle is to appreciate what would count as an infringement of it. As George Fletcher indicates, "to clarify the proposition
that criminal liability presupposes a human act, we need to consider
. . . contrasting situations in which 'an act' is arguably absent."[15] There
is, however, considerable dispute among theorists about what these
situations might be. Recurrent patterns can be discerned in the way
that orthodox theorists have treated those real or hypothetical instances of liability that appear to violate this principle. With respect to
each kind of liability, some theorists (a) hold it to be inconsistent with
the actus reus requirement, and thus suspect, while others (b) believe
it to be reconcilable after lengthy (and sometimes tortured) analysis,
and still others (c) deny the existence of a problem to be resolved.
Such widespread disagreement indicates the confusion about the
meaning of the actus reus requirement itself. Again, assessment of
this principle is tenuous in view of such uncertainty about its meaning. With much apprehension, I turn to a critical discussion of those
instances of criminal liability that seemingly violate this fundamental
principle.

## CRIMINAL LIABILITY WITHOUT ACTION

IN THIS SECTION I identify four distinct areas in which it is arguable that the actus reus requirement is violated. A few other instances of criminal liability may be equally difficult to reconcile with this requirement,[16] though the following discussion should provide a sufficient basis to assess the principle. I will conclude that the actus reus requirement is problematic both as a descriptive generalization about existing criminal practice and as a prescriptive precondition to just punishment. The presence or absence of action turns out to have little to do with the distinction between unobjectionable and objectionable instances of criminal liability. In the subsequent section I return to these four areas of liability in the hope of demonstrating that the competitive "control principle" provides a better solution to the difficulties left unresolved by the actus reus requirement.

### Omissions

Omissions, or failures to act, constitute one of the most puzzling tests of the actus reus requirement in both its descriptive and prescriptive formulations. First, it is surprisingly difficult to identify those instances in which the criminal law imposes liability for omissions. Is a doctor's refusal to utilize extraordinary life-support systems for a terminally ill patient an instance of positive action or omission? What if the required "therapy" is as routine as a blood transfusion or intravenous feeding? Or if the patient is not terminally ill? It would be a mistake to suppose that difficulties of categorization result from a few stubborn, borderline cases. To a great extent, this uncertainty results from the lack of adequate analyses of the concepts of action, omission, and the distinction between them.[17] Few theorists have questioned whether such a distinction can be drawn, although its significance has been challenged.[18]

Anglo-American criminal law seemingly imposes liability for omissions in three different kinds of circumstances. First, a number of statutes expressly proscribe failures to act, for example, the failure to file a tax return or to register for the Selective Service. Second, criminal negligence or recklessness may be committed by failing to act in conformity with a standard of care. Finally, some offenses typically committed by action, such as homicide, may be committed by omission as well. While each of these three circumstances may generate unique problems and require independent solutions, the differences between them are perhaps less important than their similarities.[19] Is there a generic problem of criminal omissions that is common to all three categories? How is criminal liability for *any* omission reconciled with the requirement of an actus reus?

Criminal theorists have suggested three very different answers to this question. First, one might simply contend that punishment for omissions constitutes an extension of criminal liability beyond its legitimate theoretical boundaries. This alternative is implicit in those theorists who combine the actus reus principle as a requirement of justice with an analysis of acts as bodily movements.[20] The total implausibility of this view is betrayed by the fact that almost no theorist explicitly embraces it. For example, no theoretical considerations are sufficiently compelling to place beyond criminal sanctions the failure of a wealthy parent to feed his seriously malnourished infant. If the actus reus requirement had such counterintuitive implications, it would not deserve to be taken seriously as a requirement of justice. Indeed, more criminal theorists favor enlarging than narrowing the scope of duties to prevent harm.[21]

Nonetheless, many theorists express skepticism about whether a person should *ever* be punished for a failure to act. Some authorities admit "grave doubts on the appropriateness of holding someone responsible for the harm he omits to prevent."[22] Fletcher suggests that there "might be good reasons for legislatures to tread carefully in enacting statutory duties to act and for courts to apply special criteria for assessing the culpability of breaching a statutory duty to act."[23] These reservations are what one would expect if liability for omissions were incompatible with a fundamental principle of criminal liability that respects prima facie rights.[24] A special justification would be required before criminal liability could be imposed for an omission.

A second alternative is to demonstrate how, appearances notwithstanding, action *is* present in cases in which persons are held criminally liable for failures to act. Some theorists allege that, on close inspection, punishment in these cases is for action rather than inaction. Omissions, according to Gross, "always prescribe what must be done *when something else is done or takes place*."[25] He continues:

> Criminal omissions occur when there is a failure to do something specified by the law. It is this specification of what must be done that creates the illusion that liability for an omission . . . is simply liability for failing to do what is required. In fact, however, liability for criminal omissions is complex, and can be understood only when the act required is seen in relation to the legitimate (though problematic) activity that prompted what the law requires. *That* legitimate activity is the conduct necessary for liability, and so in laws creating criminal omissions there is conduct required for liability, though liability is not for that conduct alone.[26]

Fletcher adopts a similar strategy in his treatment of negligent omissions. He cites a number of examples of negligence that might be subject to punishment, such as a driver who fails to turn on his lights, a railroad switchman who omits to keep a lookout, and a surgeon who neglects to remove a sponge from a patient after an operation—and seeks to explain how liability in such cases attaches to *action* after all. He contends that

> these negligent failures are embedded in larger activities. In these particular cases, the negligent breach of duty converts the driving, the railroad crossing, and the medical operation into unexpected hazards. The negligently managed activity creates a substantial and unjustified risk of harm. If the harm materializes, the cause appears to be the negligent activity as a whole rather than the isolated failure to exercise due care.[27]

Before critically examining these proposals, it is important to become clear about the theoretical motivation for conceptualizing omissions as disguised actions "embedded in larger activities." Whenever appearances are said to be deceptive or illusory, it is safe to assume that a theory looms beneath the surface. The conceptualization pursued by Gross and Fletcher would have little appeal were it not for an actus reus requirement that is difficult to reconcile with cases of criminal omissions. Replacement of the actus reus requirement with a competitive principle might undermine the motivation for providing such a peculiar account of omissions.

In any case, the above proposals are riddled with difficulties. Most any conduct, act or omission, can be regarded as "embedded in larger activities." On what independent basis is it decided whether to treat conduct as so embedded? Most important, it is doubtful that this analysis addresses the difficulty it presumably is designed to resolve. The inescapable fact is that what renders the "activity as a whole" *criminal* in each of the above cases is the *failure* to act; the activity as a whole would be perfectly legal but for the given omission. Hence it seems disingenuous to conclude that criminal liability is not really *for* the omission, but rather for the "complex action" in which the omission is "embedded."[28]

The third and final strategy for treating criminal omissions is simply to redefine the actus reus requirement itself so that the problem dissolves. Actus reus, on this account, includes either action or omission, the latter sometimes described as "negative action."[29] Subtle variations on this strategy claim either that no meaningful distinction between acts and omissions can be drawn,[30] or that actus reus encompasses the admittedly distinct categories of acts and omissions.[31] Criminal theorists unsympathetic to a critical assessment of the actus reus requirement are unlikely to regard this strategy as ad hoc or suspicious. Actus reus, after all, is a technical term of legal art, so there is little basis for objecting to any definition of those terms a theorist may stipulate.

On the other hand, there is something dissatisfying about this alternative. *Any* proposed kind of liability could be reconciled with *any* fundamental principle as long as the theorist were permitted to characterize that principle as he saw fit. If ordinary language, philosophical analyses, and legal precedents distinguish acts from omissions,[32] there is some oddity about a usage that subsumes both under a generic concept of a criminal act. Moreover, there *is* one problem with criminal omissions that this facile solution seems incapable of addressing: our criminal justice system (and perhaps every such system) proscribes actions far more frequently than omissions. Statutes typically are worded "do not" rather than "do." It would be unfortunate to exclude the possibility that an explanation of this disparity could be found in whatever considerations seemingly support actus reus as a precondition of criminal liability. The pervasive belief that the punishment of omissions gives rise to special justificatory difficulties cannot be explained by this third strategy for reconciling existing criminal practice with the actus reus requirement.

It seems fair to conclude that each of the above three strategies for dealing with omissions within orthodox criminal theory is somewhat problematic. It would be preferable to avoid the difficulties that arise from the inclusion of an actus reus requirement within criminal theory by replacing this principle with an alternative requirement.

### Status Offenses

A second challenge to the actus reus requirement in both its descriptive and normative formulations is posed by *status* criminality. Authorities disagree sharply about the acceptability of finding persons liable for their status. Some commentators indicate that the mere fact that the state endeavors to punish a status rather than an act creates, at the very least, a strong presumption of unconstitutionality.[33] In his discussion of drug addiction, Gross writes, "the reason that being an addict cannot be a crime is that it is not an act, which means in part that nothing amenable to a judgment of responsibility has occurred."[34] Others suggest that a constitutional defect does not automatically attach to each and every status offense.[35] Rollin Perkins insists that "there is no legal objection to the punishment of one who has a socially objectionable status."[36] This disagreement is due largely to confusion about whether and to what extent the criminalization of status is incompatible with the actus reus requirement.

What *are* status offenses? Insofar as definitions are proposed,[37] the most familiar is that status crimes "are defined in terms of *being* rather than in terms of *acting*."[38] If this definition is acceptable, it is doubtful that all such offenses are objectionable. They "have a long history in the common law and in statutory law; they have not been fundamentally challenged by the Court."[39] Such offenses are seldom found defective *qua* status crimes, that is, on the ground that they violate the actus reus requirement. A more typical basis of unconstitutionality is vagueness.[40] Still other authorities seem to understand status offenses quite differently. One commentator writes: "In the case of a status crime, i.e., the possession of an involuntary condition or illness . . ."[41] It is apparent that this commentator equates a status with an *involuntary* condition. If this latter criterion is acceptable, it would be obvious that all status offenses are objectionable, since the state can no more punish an involuntary condition than an involuntary act.[42] In the following discussion, it will be assumed that the former criterion is preferable, since the latter fails to identify textbook examples of paradigm illustrations of status crimes.[43] Hence a status crime will be understood as any offense defined in terms of *being* rather than *acting*. As so defined, one searches the works of criminal theorists in vain for a persuasive argument against status criminality *per se*.

But first it may be important to note the connection between the absence of an actus reus and the particular defects found in several status offenses that have been declared unconstitutional. Consider why it is so difficult to remove the vagueness from a statute that attaches liability to a status. One explanation of this difficulty is that it is often unclear *how* one acquires a given status. For example, does a person become a homosexual (or bisexual) by having a single sexual experience with a partner of the same sex? Is it possible to be a homosexual prior to having any such experience? How does one lose this status once it is acquired?[44] No doubt these (and other related) difficulties have led many authorities to denounce status crimes categorically. But though it does seem plausible to hold that many of the defects commonly associated with status criminality could be removed by rewriting statutes to proscribe a specific actus reus, it is doubtful that status offenses are objectionable simply *because* they are not acts. Consider the status crime of being an alien crewman who willfully remains in the United States in excess of the number of days allowed in any conditional permit.[45] As this example indicates, not every status crime need be vague.

An adequate understanding of the law with respect to status crimes necessitates the extremely difficult task of interpreting *Robinson v. California*[46] in the light of *Powell v. Texas*.[47] In *Robinson*, the Court held that a statute making it illegal to be "addicted to the use of narcotics" constitutes "cruel and unusual punishment."[48] In *Powell*, however, no constitutional defect was found in a statute proscribing "being found in a state of intoxication."[49] The process of reconciling *Powell* with *Robinson*, and determining to what extent the Court retreated from its earlier position, has stimulated an extraordinary amount of critical discussion. The most familiar strategy to render these decisions consistent is to claim that the statute in *Powell,* unlike that in *Robinson,* was construed to require an actus reus. Justice Marshall writes in *Powell:*

> On its face, the present case does not fall within [*Robinson*], since appellant was convicted, not for being a chronic alcoholic, but for being in public while drunk on a particular occasion. The State of Texas thus has not sought to punish a mere status, as California did in *Robinson* . . . Rather, it has imposed upon appellant a criminal sanction for public behavior . . . The entire thrust of Robinson's interpretation of the Cruel and Unusual Punishment clause is that criminal penalties may be inflicted only if the accused has committed some act, has engaged in some behavior, which society has an interest in preventing, or perhaps in historical common law terms, has committed an *actus reus.*[50]

Many commentators, attracted to this facile basis for reconciling *Powell* with *Robinson,* claimed considerable explanatory power on behalf of the distinction between status and action.[51] These decisions were cited in virtually every treatise in criminal law for the principle that the actus reus requirement precludes the punishment of status. But this interpretation, though superficially appealing and reinforced by the Court's own language, is problematic for at least four reasons.

First, it should be noted that the *Powell* Court interprets the actus reus of the Texas statute as "being in public while drunk." Note that this statute, like that in *Robinson,* is defined in terms of *being* rather than *acting.* Thus it is apparent that a status offense (as here understood) *can* constitute a legitimate exercise of state authority. *Both* the California and Texas statutes proscribe a status.

Second, given a principle of statutory construction in favor of constitutionality,[52] one must wonder why the *Robinson* Court failed to construe the statute as involving an actus reus. Subsequent decisions easily avoided the force of *Robinson* by interpreting statutes proscribing "being or becoming" a drug addict to require one or more acts of drug use.[53] In fact, most statuses entail one or more acts;[54] sometimes the distinction between status and non-status offenses appears merely verbal. Hence the suggestion that *Robinson* should be interpreted to bar punishment for only those status offenses that exclude acts indeed "restricts that decision to factual situations which will only infrequently, if ever, arise."[55] For not even *Robinson* falls under such a narrow rule; the status of being addicted to narcotics, like most other statuses, typically requires an actus reus.

A third difficulty with this interpretation derives from the already noted tendency to redefine the scope of actus reus to encompass any kind of criminal liability the theorist wishes to include. It may be strained to analyze statuses in terms of acts, but theorists have not balked at the difficulties of analyzing *omissions* in terms of acts. No one who favors liability under the facts of *Robinson* need be deterred by the apparent absence of an actus reus; he simply would redefine that requirement in such a way that an actus reus could be said to be present in status offenses. One can safely predict that theorists unsympathetic to the result in *Robinson* will resort to this device in future treatises: status will become another variety of actus reus.[56] Theorists who approve of the result in *Robinson* will continue to employ a more traditional interpretation of the actus reus requirement as the basis for an objection to status criminality.

Finally, the explanation that emphasizes the dichotomy between status and actus reus fails to account for the willingness of courts to uphold other status offenses that, like *Robinson*, do not explicitly require an actus reus. The sweeping predictions in the wake of *Robinson* and *Powell* that each and every status offense will be found unconstitutional simply have not come true.[57]

A more promising basis for distinguishing these cases must focus on other characteristics of the conduct the state sought to make criminal, regardless of whether that conduct is categorized as a status or an act. The key to reconciling these decisions is to examine the important differences between the respective statuses involved. Hence one should be suspicious of the conclusion that *Robinson*, unlike *Powell*, was constitutionally defective simply because it failed to predicate liability on an actus reus.

Confidence in the claim that the *Robinson* and *Powell* courts attached dispositive significance to the presence or absence of an actus reus is eroded further by examining the prescriptive application of the actus reus requirement to preclude status criminality. What is it about status per se that allegedly renders it an inappropriate subject of penal legislation? Frequently it is stipulated that judgments about persons, as opposed to acts, fall outside the criminal law.[58] Those authorities who endeavor to support this conclusion produce objections long on rhetoric and short on argument. Status offenses have been denounced as "a cruel anachronism in our free society."[59] They have been said to be incompatible with "notions of a decent, fair, and just administration of criminal justice."[60] Surely it is not unreasonable to hope for more detailed criticisms. Although such offenses are perhaps particularly susceptible to abuses such as discriminatory enforcement, it is not clear that all offenses defined in terms of being rather than acting need give rise to such difficulties. In some occasions the punishment of a status rather than an act may be the more appropriate means to secure an unquestionably legitimate legislative end.[61] No argument to be found in the writings of criminal theorists supports a blanket rejection of all status offenses; one needs to know precisely *which* status is proscribed before a statute can be evaluated. The subsequent process of distinguishing between acceptable and unacceptable status offenses will divert attention from the presence or absence of an actus reus, and will focus instead upon a deeper, more significant principle that underlies our prescriptive judgments about status criminality. Perhaps this deeper principle will also shed light on the task of reconciling *Robinson* and *Powell.*

### Involuntary Conduct

All criminal theorists agree that involuntary conduct should not (except perhaps under extraordinary circumstances) give rise to liability.[62] The controverted substantive issues are two. First, what conduct should be deemed involuntary?[63] Second, on what theoretical basis should liability be opposed?[64] Many theorists invoke the actus reus requirement as the central premise in attempts to resolve both issues. According to this account, the actus reus principle functions descriptively in proposing that conduct otherwise criminal is involuntary when it expresses no actus reus. In addition, it functions prescriptively to oppose liability *because* of the alleged absence of an actus reus. Are these two claims illuminating? Does involuntary conduct contain no actus reus? Is the alleged absence of an actus reus a good reason to oppose liability for involuntary conduct? These are the issues the philosopher of criminal law should address.

On what ground(s) can it be maintained that those whose conduct is involuntary commit no actus reus in performing what otherwise would be a criminal offense? Presumably all theorists oppose liability when, for example, a driver becomes unconscious without prior warning and is charged with violating a statute proscribing dangerous or reckless driving.[65] But it is quite debatable whether this conclusion should be reached by supposing that in such circumstances "the accused could not really be said to be driving at all."[66] A more obvious defense is the absence of mens rea, and the onus is on those who claim that involuntariness precludes an actus reus to show why their reasoning should be preferred.[67] This onus is not satisfied by the simple assertion that when conduct is involuntary "we are tempted . . . to say that no true human action has been performed at all."[68] One might wonder whether such alleged temptations should be dispositive of controversies in criminal theory. More to the point, it is dubious whether this assertion accurately reports ordinary linguistic usage, according to which the notion of an involuntary act seems coherent.[69] Such usage recognizes that action may be either voluntary or involuntary.[70] Many criminal theorists (with close parallels to their treatment of omissions) resort to definitional *fiat* to ensure the result that actus reus precludes involuntariness. But definitional stipulations are a poor substitute for substantive argument. What can be said in favor of the view that involuntary conduct can express no actus reus?

This view draws support from two sources, the first theoretical and the second substantive. The theoretical basis, called the "orthodox" analysis,[71] understands acts as external manifestations of internal volitions.[72] If the "will" is inoperative, no act can occur. The thesis that acts are bodily movements caused by internal volitions has been widely discredited,[73] and these criticisms need not be repeated here.

Perhaps more compelling is the substantive basis for excluding involuntary conduct from the scope of actus reus. It is widely asserted that "the attraction of stating the defence of involuntariness in terms of there being no act on the part of the accused is that this will be a defence even in cases of strict liability."[74] The reasoning here is roughly as follows: a defense should *always* be available to those whose allegedly criminal conduct is involuntary. All (substantive) defenses can be categorized as the absence of either actus reus or mens rea. Defendants can commit a strict liability offense even though they lack mens rea. Thus, if defendants whose conduct is involuntary are to escape liability for apparent violations of any given offense, including those of strict liability, the only available defense is the absence of actus reus. This reasoning is seductive, although it can be attacked on a number of distinct grounds.[75]

There is one powerful objection against the view that involuntariness precludes actus reus. As indicated in chapter 2, much of the appeal of the orthodox model of the criminal offense as divisible into actus reus and mens rea derives from the belief that outward physical conduct, when accompanied by the appropriate mental state, may give rise to criminal liability. This (admittedly attractive) model is undermined by including voluntariness within the scope of actus reus. If all acts are voluntary, proof of actus reus would require evidence of the inner, mental state (the "will") of the defendant;[76] no longer would the scope of actus reus be confined to the external and physical. Hence definitions of actus reus that include voluntariness become confusing at best and useless at worst. Glanville Williams, it should be recalled, defines actus reus as "the whole definition of the crime with the exception of the mental element—and it even includes a mental element insofar as that is contained in the definition of an act."[77] A "mental element [is] contained in the definition of an act," according to Williams, largely because he holds that involuntary conduct cannot be genuine *action*.[78] Thus the distinction between actus reus and mens rea, initially tolerably clear,[79] is deliberately blurred.[80] Unless the dichotomy between the physical and the mental can be preserved, the orthodox model of the criminal offense has little to recommend it.

Thus it seems preferable to side with those theorists who maintain that "in cases in which a man is able to show that his conduct . . . was involuntary, he must not be held liable for any harmful results produced by it: what has been done is an actus reus, but his defence is that he is *not legally responsible* for this actus reus."[81] This treatment preserves the distinction between actus reus and mens rea. But the cost of this preservation is noteworthy: the actus reus requirement no longer functions as a descriptive generalization to preclude criminal liability for involuntary conduct.

Nonetheless, in a significant class of cases the issue of whether persons *should* be held liable for their involuntary conduct is open to serious dispute. In these cases, the plausibility of the actus reus requirement as a prescriptive basis for objecting to liability for involuntary conduct is called into question. Such controversial cases involve what might be called *self-induced incapacitation* in which a defendant foresaw, but failed to take reasonable steps to prevent, harm caused by his involuntary conduct. Sometimes persons behave involuntarily because of their prior voluntary act or omission, and it is foreseeable that criminal conduct might ensue at the moment they incapacitate themselves. There is room for disagreement when, for example, a driver who is aware of his susceptibility to epilepsy fails to take his medication, experiences a seizure, runs over a number of pedestrians, and is charged with violation of a statute proscribing "criminal negligence in the operation of a vehicle resulting in death."[82] Case law is sparse here, and it is difficult to hazard generalizations with any degree of confidence.[83] Apparently most courts impose liability under such circumstances,[84] although a few theorists remain skeptical.[85]

It is less important to resolve this controversy here than to note the problems inherent in attempts to resolve it by reference to the actus reus requirement. A theorist who holds that involuntariness precludes an actus reus must strain to reach liability in these cases,[86] since this view entails that "we cannot while unconscious 'operate' a car in a culpably negligent manner or in any other 'manner.' "[87] It is ad hoc to impose liability on the ground that the foresight of the likelihood of oncoming involuntariness somehow restores an actus reus that generally is precluded from involuntariness by definition. It is obvious that the distinction between these cases in which liability arguably is appropriate, and more typical cases of involuntariness in which liability clearly is inappropriate, has nothing to do with the presence of action in the former but not in the latter cases: *action* is simply not the relevant variable here. The foresight of harm *might,* however, restore a mens rea that ordinarily is precluded when involuntariness cannot be anticipated. Hence theorists sympathetic to (or undecided about) liability in cases of self-induced incapacitation with foreseeable harm are advised to resist the view that involuntariness is incompatible with actus reus. It remains to be seen whether an alternative principle proposed to replace the actus reus requirement at the heart of criminal theory can provide a preferable perspective from which to assess this very difficult class of cases.

### Thoughts

No application of the actus reus principle is believed to be less problematic than its use to preclude liability for thoughts. Some criminal theorists apparently regard the proscription of punishment for thoughts as *the* meaning of the actus reus requirement.[88] It might seem that this requirement is unassailable here, both descriptively and prescriptively. Perhaps no Anglo-American jurisdiction has even sought to punish persons for thoughts not manifested in action. This apparently unblemished record might be explained by pondering why a secular state would *want* to punish mere thoughts. Among the diverse range of mental phenomena categorizable as thoughts, *intentions* represent the only plausible candidates for liability. Thus it seems fair to restrict the broad discussion of punishment for thoughts to the more narrow area of punishment for intentions. Perhaps the temptation to impose liability for intentions is greatest in the law of *attempts,* and it is here that the maxim *cogitationis poenam nemo patitur* has its most significant application.

Before examining the relationship between the actus reus requirement and criminal liability for attempts, it is worthwhile to digress and mention some unexplained perplexities in the supposition that punishment for intentions is precluded by the alleged absence of an actus reus. Why is it assumed that intentions cannot constitute an actus reus? This question could be answered easily if theorists were entitled to rely on an analysis of acts as involving bodily movements. Such an analysis, however, is incompatible with the (almost) indisputable fact that some omissions give rise (and ought to give rise) to criminal liability. Apart from reliance on such a widely discredited analysis, it is not obvious why at least *some* thoughts may not constitute "mental acts." A number of philosophers[89] and legal theorists[90] have been willing to countenance mental acts. A broader definition of actus reus as a "state of affairs"[91] is not helpful, since an intention *can* be a state of affairs. If an independent analysis of the concept of action cannot demonstrate why the notion of a mental act is incoherent, it is hardly surprising that the application of the actus reus requirement to the more controversial cases of omissions, status, and involuntariness is so problematic. A definitive demonstration of the incompatibility of the actus reus requirement with liability for thoughts awaits a more satisfactory analysis of actus reus than has yet been provided by orthodox theorists.

What of criminal liability for attempts? Orthodoxy holds that liability for attempts attaches when conduct passes beyond the stage of what is called "mere preparation." The actus reus requirement is invoked to describe this elusive boundary. Preparation ceases and attempt begins when the defendant commits an actus reus. One authority writes: "It is a legal commonplace that attempting to do an act and preparing to do it need differ in no way other than that identified by an actus reus test for attempt."[92] The task of the philosopher of criminal law is to assess whether this application of the actus reus requirement to the law of attempts is descriptively and prescriptively illuminating.

What *is* the actus reus of attempt that is lacked by preparation? This question has proved extremely difficult to answer. One authority aptly notes that "the law as to the actus reus for attempts is in an uncertain and underdeveloped state and many of the decisions are arbitrary and contradictory."[93] Despite various nuances,[94] it is crucial to appreciate that only two basic kinds of criteria are available for drawing the distinction between preparation and attempt. Liability may attach when the conduct of the defendant either *does* or *does not* "show criminal intent on the face of it."[95]

The first alternative seems unnecessarily restrictive. Why is conduct disqualified as a criminal attempt unless it manifests mens rea "on its face"? As Williams observes, a man approaching a haystack with a match may intend either to light his pipe or to set a fire.[96] If it were known that his intent is criminal, why should liability not be imposed?[97] There is an overwhelming tendency to answer this question by raising worries about evidence, as though the formidable problem of proving intent disposes of the question of whether there are principled objections to the punishment of intentions that *are* proved. As I have indicated, difficulties in obtaining reliable evidence should not infect the content of the fundamental principles of criminal liability. To show the irrelevance of questions about evidence to the present problem, suppose that the defendant confesses to his state of mind. As Williams remarks: "If the accused confesses it does not matter, so far as proof of *mens rea* is concerned, that his acts are ambiguous, being consonant equally with an innocent and a guilty mind."[98] His external conduct might remain equivocal, that is, would not become reus, until it had passed beyond the stage of attempt and become a choate offense. Small wonder that only a handful of orthodox criminal theorists oppose criminal liability until the conduct of the defendant unequivocally exhibits criminal intent. Such a test "would acquit many undoubted criminals."[99]

The second alternative has more to recommend it. Criminal liability for an attempt may attach before the conduct of the defendant exhibits criminal intent "on its face." But if liability may arise though the actus is equivocal, it is difficult to resist the implication that punishment is *for* the intention rather than for the action.[100] Criminal liability cannot plausibly be construed as *for* the act, since the act itself is innocuous (or at least equivocal). In short, the actus in these cases simply is not reus, yet liability is imposed. This is especially evident when liability is imposed for notorious "impossible attempts," that is, attempts that could not possibly succeed in resulting in a choate offense.[101] A number of theorists have appreciated these difficulties. Williams, following Austin, contends that "in attempt the party is really punished for his intention, the act being required as evidence of a *firm* intention. There is much to be said for this."[102] This position, of course, threatens to make hash of the use of actus reus to distinguish between preparation and attempt. If attempts are not reus, no longer can liability for preparations be resisted on the ground that they are not reus.[103] These implications prove devastating to orthodox criminal theory. The conclusion that criminal liability may be imposed for intentions is so unpalatable that many authorities have mustered extraordinary ingenuity to resist it. Others, upon appreciating these (and other) problems, have called for the abolition of liability for some—or even all—attempts.[104] Rejection of the actus reus requirement at the heart of criminal theory may have the merit of removing the chief obstacle to candor in admitting that liability for attempts sometimes, quite properly, punishes persons for their intentions.

One unsatisfactory device to avoid this conclusion is noteworthy. The Model Penal Code defines an attempt as "an act or omission constituting a substantial step in the course of conduct planned to culminate in [a] crime."[105] The actus reus requirement seemingly is preserved here. But the draftsmen fail to offer a principled account of when a "step" toward attainment of a criminal objective can be identified as "substantial." The only guide is that a step is *not* substantial unless it is "strongly corroborative of the actor's criminal purpose."[106] Actus reus is important here only insofar as it provides *evidence* of criminal intent; the requirement has no *independent* significance.[107] Hence it appears inescapable that liability is really *for* such an intent. The failure to assign a non-evidentiary significance to actus reus becomes important when one asks why liability should be precluded in those cases in which evidence of intent somehow is gained despite the absence of an actus reus. Orthodox criminal theory provides no convincing answer to this question.

If the law of attempts imposes liability for intentions, why do orthodox criminal theorists confidently maintain that the actus reus requirement precludes punishment for thoughts? What general arguments are offered against liability for intentions? It is noteworthy that the writings of orthodox criminal theorists provide no entirely convincing reason why punishment for thoughts is so widely regarded as outrageous. A number of purported explanations are little more than unsubstantiated rhetoric. The alleged unwillingness of our criminal justice system to punish intentions has been hailed as a "contemporary scientific insight" as well as a "political expectation of democracy."[108] Unfortunately, the precise connection between the actus reus requirement and either science or democracy is left to the imagination of the reader. Herbert Morris has argued, somewhat convincingly, that a system that punished persons solely for intentions, and never for actions, would deviate in a number of important specified respects from standard and familiar examples of legal systems.[109] But such a conclusion fails on its own terms to explain what is objectionable about each and every statute that punishes persons for intentions.

It has been alleged that criminal liability for intentions represents "a radical change from conduct-regarding princples of liability to person-regarding principles."[110] This allegation is difficult to assess, since (as I will indicate later) the connection between "person-regarding" (agent morality) and "conduct-regarding" (act morality) principles is extremely complex and controversial. Insofar as there is a "radical departure," it is not clear that it is indefensible. In chapter 2 I cautioned against conflating the purpose of implementing a system of criminal justice (which may be influenced by utilitarian considerations) with the legitimacy of imposing liability on particular persons (which must be constrained by justice and rights). Some criminal theorists charge that the use of our criminal justice system to punish intentions betrays this very conflation,[111] and involves an objectionable confusion of "administrative and legal processes."[112]

*Why* is it thought that the criminal justice system should not be used to identify and restrain dangerous persons? Three distinct answers are provided, and they indicate that there are important limitations on the extent to which the criminal justice system may be used for this purpose. First, persons cannot be said to be dangerous unless they have dispositions to engage in dangerous conduct in the future. Unfortunately, our social science has not progressed to the point where it can accurately predict whether persons will perform dangerous acts. Hence we could not identify and restrain dangerous persons effectively, even if the criminal justice system were construed to have this function.[113] Second, if the evaluation of persons were the business of the criminal law, there would be no point to restricting evidence at criminal trials to the alleged criminal conduct of the accused. Has the defendant performed valuable community service? Has he been a good citizen? If "whole persons" were assessed, such questions would be material, and criminal trials would become a fiasco.[114] Finally, evidence about the dangerousness of persons probably could not be gathered without objectionable infringements of individual rights, especially rights to privacy.[115] Thus it is concluded that the criminal justice system should not adopt this function.

But such objections, though forceful in other contexts, are of limited relevance to the present proposal. The proposal to punish persons for firm intentions to commit crimes *need* not require dubious predictions of dangerousness, trial fiascos in which "whole persons" are judged, or unwarranted intrusions into privacy.[116] Admittedly, use of the criminal justice system for this purpose *would* be objectionable if it violated rights. But what injustice is committed by punishing a person who firmly intends to commit a crime though his overt conduct does not yet manifest criminal intent? The facile response that such punishment would violate the right of persons not to be held liable for conduct that does not include an actus reus is question-begging, for I am challenging here whether such a right exists. And I caution that it may be unwise to adopt too narrow a view of *the* proper function of the criminal justice system (as though there were only one).

None of the foregoing is designed to remove all doubts about the propriety of punishing persons for their intentions. My more modest conclusion is that what allegedly renders liability for intentions objectionable is quite mysterious, and is not perspicuously expressed by the claim that intentions are not an actus reus.

Unless the actus reus requirement is an unilluminating tautology, it must be possible to identify real or hypothetical instances of criminal liability that violate it. This task has proved more difficult than might have been anticipated. Moreover, it is not clear that the presence or absence of an actus reus is a crucial variable in drawing the distinction between just and unjust instances of penal liability. Against this uncertainty, the stage is set to introduce a competitive principle that better illuminates criminal law.

## CONTROL

FORMULATING A PRINCIPLE designed to replace the actus reus requirement at the heart of criminal theory is a daunting task. It may be unrealistic to suppose that a single principle can account for what is suspect about liability for omissions, status, involuntary conduct, and intentions. Still, as H. L. A. Hart has observed, "the itch for uniformity in jurisprudence is strong."[117] A single principle seems to explain much of our reasoning about these different areas of liability after all. Thus I turn attention to the *control* principle which, despite difficulties of its own, represents an improvement over actus reus as a fundamental requirement of criminal liability.

Simply expressed, the control principle states that criminal liability is unjust if imposed for a state of affairs over which a person lacks control. We have a prima facie moral right not to be held criminally liable in violation of this requirement. The phrase "state of affairs" should present no difficulties in understanding and applying this principle. Liability is always *for* something, and this amorphous "something" may be called a state of affairs.[118]

The term "control" raises far greater difficulties. The core idea is that a person lacks control over a state of affairs if he is unable to prevent it from taking place. If the state of affairs is an action, he must have been capable of not performing that action; if it is a consequence, he must have been able to prevent that consequence; if it is an intention, he must have been capable of not having that intention; and so on. The philosophical literature that discusses whether and under what conditions a person could have done otherwise than he did, and the relationship between this debate and questions of culpability, is both voluminous and tortuous.[119] Though I do not dispute the relevance of these issues to criminal theory revised to include the control principle, a critical examination here would take us too far afield. Though perhaps disappointingly little is said here, I hope that the notion of control is able to withstand the great intuitive weight I place upon it.

Yet one matter deserves explicit comment. Control, unlike actus reus or mens rea, admits of degrees. It is difficult to anticipate the profound ramifications of including a principle within criminal theory that may be satisfied to various extents.[120] Any attempt to apply this requirement must confront the issue of what degree of loss of control is sufficient to preclude liability. The answer to this (already difficult) question is (further) complicated by the fact that control may vary from person to person. Orthodox criminal theory has not fully come to terms with the indisputable fact that the capacity to conform conduct to law is not equally distributed throughout the whole population. Arguably, the difficulty of performing an action reduces the culpability of not performing it.[121] It may be true that all but the seriously disabled possess *some* degree of control over their criminal tendencies, but it is doubtful that loss of control need be total to preclude liability. The test to be applied is a normative standard of what is reasonable to expect from a defendant in his particular circumstances. In any number of occasions it is unreasonable to demand that persons should successfully control their conduct and avoid violations of the criminal law. An examination of case law involving such defenses as diminished capacity and duress may help to locate this elusive boundary.[122] But many unanswered questions remain. Under what conditions, if any, does economic deprivation or an inadequate education impair control? Perhaps the greatest merit of revised criminal theory is that it raises questions neglected by its orthodox counterpart,[123] questions that are among the most vexing issues raised by applications of revised criminal theory.[124] My modest contribution here is not to answer these questions, but to provide a theoretical framework in which they can assume their proper significance.

The initial disappointment resulting from my failure to propose a more thorough analysis of the concept of control is mollified by the following three considerations, each of which involves a comparison with the actus reus requirement. First, orthodox criminal theorists have produced nothing even remotely resembling an adequate analysis of the concept of a criminal act, despite having had several centuries in which to do so. If no satisfactory account of actus reus exists, the corresponding failure to produce a precise analysis of control does not render the control principle inferior to its competitor. Second, the term "control," unlike "actus reus," has a familiar, nonlegal usage. Hence an analysis of that term is not needed as urgently as if it functioned as a technical term of legal art. Laypersons and legal theorists alike can be expected to be better at deciding whether a state of affairs is under personal control than at determining whether an actus reus has occurred. Finally, like the actus reus requirement, the control principle is best understood by examining its implications upon the substantive criminal law. If these implications can be drawn with tolerable accuracy, the absence of a thorough philosophical analysis of the concept of control will not be crucial. I am painfully aware, however, that more must be said about the concept of control than I am able to deliver here.

When is a person unable to prevent the occurrence of a state of affairs, and thus ineligible for liability under the control principle? This question is best addressed by examining the implications of the control requirement upon the four areas of liability identified as problematic by the actus reus principle.

### Omissions

The implications of the control principle upon the area of omissions are radical. It seems clear that in *many* cases (though not the majority) persons have as much control over consequences that result from their omissions as from their positive actions. When such control exists, revised criminal theory provides no basis for supposing that, *ceteris paribus,* liability for a failure to prevent harm requires greater justification *qua* omission than does liability for actively harming.[125] Once control rather than actus reus is identified as the relevant variable, the distinction between action and omission per se loses any significance it might have been thought to possess.

It is important to appreciate how this approach to the problem of omissions improves upon the more familiar strategy of subsuming them under the scope of actus reus. This latter strategy fails to explain why omissions are proscribed much less frequently than positive actions. The control principle seems capable of providing such an explanation. One can account for this asymmetry by noting that, as a matter of fact, persons generally exercise far less control over what happens as a result of their omissions than as a result of their positive actions. Control over a consequence is typically exercised by positive action. Ordinarily, one is better able, for instance, to bring about a death by positive action than by omission. But the multitude of cases that represent counterexamples to this generalization pose no problem for revised criminal theory. If one happens to be in a position to bring about a death by omission, the fact that his conduct does not involve a positive action is irrelevant to revised criminal theory.[126] Thus this approach offers an explanation—which the simple categorization of omissions as actus reus does not—of why our criminal justice system (and perhaps each such system) proscribes positive actions more frequently than omissions. The prohibition of positive actions is usually the more effective means to ensure that certain undesired consequences will not take place.

### Status Offenses

Application of the actus reus requirement to status criminality led to both descriptive and prescriptive difficulties. The initially promising distinction between status and action ultimately fails to reconcile *Robinson* with *Powell.* Moreover, the reason a number of status crimes seem unjust has little connection to the alleged absence of an actus reus.

The control principle seems capable of providing an improved account on both these scores. As a descriptive generalization, the control principle requires that persons not be punished for conduct over which they lack control, regardless of whether that conduct is characterized as status or action. It seems impossible to reconcile *Robinson* with *Powell* without focusing on particular features of the conduct the state sought to proscribe. The *Robinson* opinion attaches great significance to the affinities between narcotics addiction and disease.[127] These references cannot be explained by the supposition that *Powell* did not follow *Robinson* simply because Texas, unlike California, sought to punish an actus reus rather than a status. Presumably the point of the comparison is that punishment for narcotics addiction is objectionable for the same reason as is punishment for disease—both impose sanctions for conduct over which persons lack control. Surely the different outcome in *Powell* is partially due to the reluctance of the Court to believe that alcoholism inhibits control to the same extent as does narcotics addiction.[128] The subsequent unwillingness of the Court to extend the scope of *Robinson* to conduct allegedly "occasioned by a compulsion symptomatic of the disease" may reflect skepticism that such conduct (such as stealing to acquire narcotics) is compelled.[129] Even the issue of whether the narcotics addict lacks control over his condition, so confidently embraced in *Robinson,* has been challenged.[130] Surely it is improvident for the Court to lay down fixed constitutional rules in the face of medical uncertainty about the extent to which chronic users of narcotics and alcohol exercise control over their conditions. But in cases in which there is no doubt that control is absent—illustrated by many cases of somatic disease—it seems safe to read *Robinson* as authority for the proposition that criminal liability is unconstitutional.[131]

Whether or not this interpretation is helpful in distinguishing *Robinson* from *Powell,* it rests upon a more secure prescriptive foundation than the distinction between status and actus reus. Many statuses that result from the possession of character traits are quite properly regarded as the objects of moral evaluation, either praise or condemnation. It is appropriate to admire those who are courageous, generous, or benevolent, and to criticize those who are cowardly, selfish, or wicked. Yet other statuses, such as lack of intelligence, are not suitable candidates for moral evaluation. The distinction between statuses that are and are not regarded as proper objects of evaluation coincides closely with the distinction between statuses that are and are not under personal control.[132]

One might, of course, regard the above as a reasonably accurate account of certain features of moral evaluation while resisting its application to the sort of evaluations involved in the criminal law.[133] Though arguments are produced infrequently, the criminalization of status is held by many authorities to be beyond the scope of legitimate state authority. But there are occasions in which criminal offenses might better be expressed in terms of *being* rather than *doing.* Suppose that a fatal communicable disease could be contracted only by bacteria that live in facial hair, and the state passed a statute that punished persons for having beards. It may be controversial whether conviction under such a statute would require an actus reus. But it is crucial to appreciate that such a controversy has little or no relevance to the issue of whether this statute would be a legitimate exercise of state authority. There is no good reason to suppose that this statute should violate a fundamental principle of criminal liability, despite its likely exclusion of an actus reus. One would hardly feel confident about citing *Robinson* as authority that this statute would be unconstitutional. Since the status of being bearded is (typically) under personal control, the presence or absence of an actus reus seems quite unimportant to the issue of its justification. Thus, both descriptively and prescriptively, the control principle seems superior to the actus reus requirement in its implications for status criminality.

### Involuntary Conduct

Both the actus reus requirement and control principle might be thought to provide equally satisfactory implications for the issue of whether criminal liability may be imposed for involuntary conduct. For the most part, persons are unable to control their involuntary conduct, and the reason for believing liability to be unjust on such occasions might be expressed by citing either the lack of control or the absence of an actus reus. Indeed, it is probable that the presence or absence of control is an essential criterion by which difficult borderline cases of conduct are categorized as voluntary or involuntary. After surveying cases in which liability was imposed despite allegations of involuntariness, one authority concludes: "What emerges from these different types of case is that the accused should have had the ability to control his movements."[134] It seems likely that the control principle underlies the tendency to use the actus reus requirement to preclude liability for involuntary conduct.

So far the implications of the two principles upon involuntariness coincide. But the probable superiority of the control principle emerges by returning to those unusual cases in which control may be present despite the fact that conduct is involuntary. If it is coherent to suppose that persons somehow were able to control an instance of their involuntary conduct, it would be difficult to construct a convincing argument against liability. The sorts of cases that seemingly combine control with involuntariness are those involving self-induced incapacitation, in which persons foresaw but failed to take reasonable steps to prevent harm brought about by their involuntary conduct. A more detailed explication of the control principle is required before its implications upon such difficult cases can be stated confidently. But it seems plausible to hold that if a person foresees impending involuntariness (such as an epileptic seizure) and fails to take sensible steps to prevent ensuing harm (that is, stops driving), he may be held liable for the simple reason that it was reasonable for him to exercise control over its occurrence.[135] Many authorities agree that the defense of lack of control "should be excluded in those cases where the accused either brought about his own lack of power or control, or foresaw that he might lack control and took no precautions."[136] Perhaps it should be reminded that the competing view, according to which involuntariness precludes an actus reus, must strain to reach liability in these cases. If, for example, a person cannot be "driving" during an epileptic seizure, he cannot be "driving recklessly" even if his seizure were foreseeable and preventable. Whether the probable implications of the control principle upon such difficult cases of "self-induced incapacitation" are preferable to those of the actus reus requirement represents yet another test of its superiority over its competitor.

### Thoughts

Unquestionably the greatest challenge to the substitution of the control principle for the actus reus requirement consists in its implications for the justifiability of holding persons liable for thoughts. To examine these implications, it is necessary to take note of what must be regarded as a psychological fact: some, but not all, of the mental processes crudely categorized as "thoughts" are under personal control. At or near one extreme on the continuum of control are the thoughts that occur in dreams. Examples of thoughts under personal control are provided by the careful and calculated intentions of the noncompulsive embezzler. I will make no effort to provide a principled account of the difficult and elusive distinction between mental processes that are and are not under personal control.[137] The important point is that such a distinction undoubtedly exists,[138] wherever it is drawn, and however stubborn cases are categorized.

Given this psychological fact, two serious problems are encountered by placing the control principle at the heart of criminal theory. The easier of these difficulties will be addressed first. Consider that class of thoughts over which persons lack control. All theorists agree that liability for any such thought would be outrageous.[139] The interesting issue is whether objections to such liability are perspicuously expressed by the control principle. There is some precedent among criminal theorists for an affirmative answer. Nearly a century ago, one authority noted that "it may perhaps be doubted whether the mental provision is sufficiently under one's control to justify legal results being based upon it."[140]

The second difficulty is far more troublesome. The control principle seems to provide *no* basis for opposing liability for thoughts that *are* under personal control. This result may seem so devastating to orthodox criminal theorists that it is likely to be regarded as a *reductio ad absurdum* of the entire project of replacing the actus reus requirement with the control principle. Surely, it will be protested, liability for *any* thought is outrageous. Moreover, this implication will be said to grossly distort existing criminal practice, which recognizes no distinction among mental states depending upon whether or not they are subject to personal control. Both descriptively and prescriptively, these implications of the control principle seem less acceptable than those of the actus reus requirement.

As I have argued, however, the dogmatic insistence that criminal liability is never imposed for intentions is falsified (or at least rendered problematic) by the law of attempts. Despite ingenious devices to salvage the principle here, an actus reus is required only to provide *evidence* of criminal intent. It is not sensible to insist that an actus reus must occur when reliable evidence of intent is gained without it. If an actus reus is required only to provide evidence of what is already known independently, the requirement becomes purposeless, and is preserved merely to maintain consistency between the law of attempts and a principle of orthodox theory that has little to recommend it. No authorities who have placed the actus reus requirement at the heart of criminal theory should be comfortable with this result.[141] But their dissatisfaction should find expression in a revision of orthodox criminal theory, not in an ill-conceived reform of the substantive law of attempts.

Does revised criminal theory enact *any* barriers to punishment for thoughts? Of course. Even those theorists inclined to agree that the law of attempts involves punishment for thoughts oppose liability until the criminal plan of the defendant passes beyond the mere daydreaming stage, over which persons have little or no control, to the point at which the intention becomes "firm." According to this account, "firm" intentions are those over which persons have control. Of course, as a practical matter of evidence, this transitory point almost always will prove impossible to locate in the absence of an actus reus.[142] But the control principle would not hold liability to be unjust in those rare cases in which evidence of a firm intention to commit a crime is gained even though no actus reus has been committed.

Admittedly, less radical strategies for dealing with these controversial implications of the control principle are available. One might insist that the replacement of the actus reus requirement by the control principle has *no* substantive implications for this area of criminal law. This result could be achieved if, in each case in which a given intention were under personal control, liability were precluded neither by the rejected actus reus requirement nor by the substituted control principle, but rather by some additional consideration. Perhaps the imposition of liability for even those intentions over which persons have control can be resisted on the ground that such a policy would make criminals of too many of us,[143] or could be enforced only by objectionable means,[144] or might be too minimal a concern to warrant the costly use of the criminal sanction.[145] My own view is that to the extent that liability for thoughts is to be condemned, it should be on the ground that (a) few thoughts are immoral, and (b) only the immoral is an appropriate subject of criminal liability. Neither of these claims, however, is congenial to orthodoxy. It is important to emphasize that the removal of the actus reus requirement from criminal theory is not the first step toward an Orwellian nightmare of thought control; several other well-established principles severely restrict the wholesale punishment of intentions. In any case, it is important to realize that these cautious strategies do not return full circle to the approach toward liability for intentions adopted within orthodox criminal theory. No fundamental principle of revised theory is preserved by assigning it an evidentiary role. Revised criminal theory does not regard control as evidence of anything further that is needed to allow liability.

*    *    *

The foregoing reexamination of omissions, status criminality, involuntary conduct, and thoughts further undermines the plausibility of the actus reus requirement in both its descriptive and prescriptive formulations. The cases in which liability does not and ought not to exist correlate more closely with the lack of control than with the absence of an actus reus. Hence both the descriptive and prescriptive implications of the control principle upon the substantive criminal law are superior to those of its competitor. But a preference for these implications does not exhaust the reasons that can be invoked in favor of the control principle. Arguments independent of these implications support the principle as well. The next section shows that considerations typically advanced by orthodox criminal theorists in support of the actus reus requirement, insofar as they are compelling, actually constitute *better* support for the control principle. Thus there is a sense in which the control principle preserves the core of good sense embodied in the actus reus requirement.

## ARGUMENTS FOR CONTROL

ONE STRATEGY TO HELP CLARIFY the meaning of the actus reus requirement is to investigate why orthodox criminal theorists have been so persuaded by it. An examination of treatises in search of rationales for this principle is disappointing, for theorists offer not one but several arguments in favor of the actus reus requirement, and none is entirely convincing.[146] But this result is unsurprising; it may be unreasonable to expect that a single rationale would support a principle with so many distinct applications. Nonetheless, it is possible to identify a few common concerns that underlie a number of the more plausible defenses of the actus reus requirement. These common concerns, however, provide even better support for the control principle.

Defenses of the actus reus requirement can be sorted profitably into two categories. The first, which should be dismissed quickly, treats the requirement as serving an important "practical" function. Usually, but not always, this function is said to be evidentiary—without an actus reus, it could not be *known* that persons had committed a particular offense. Blackstone defended this requirement by insisting that "no temporal tribunal can search the heart or fathom the intentions of the mind, otherwise than as they are demonstrated by outward actions."[147]

Worries about evidence continually reappear in defenses of the actus reus principle. But they constitute insufficient support for this requirement for at least five reasons. First, they rest on dubious premises. Sometimes the intentions of persons, although not manifested by an actus reus, *can* be ascertained with sufficient reliability, for example, by confessions.[148] Second, they are inadequate to support the principle in its full generality. The actus reus requirement has been invoked to preclude punishment not only for thoughts, but also for a host of other kinds of liability. For instance, reservations about status offenses cannot be derived from difficulties in proving intent. Third, they render the importance of actus reus parasitic upon a defense of mens rea; they confine the importance of actus reus to its tendency to provide evidence of the elusive mens rea. On the contrary, one might reasonably expect actus reus to function as an independent requirement of criminal liability,[149] especially insofar as several offenses have been construed to dispense with mens rea. Fourth, they fail to explain the significance within orthodox theory of the fundamental principle of concurrence. The insistence that liability is unjust unless an actus reus coincides with, or is actuated by, a mens rea is not sensible if an evidentiary status is assigned to the actus reus requirement. An actus reus that coincides with a mens rea is no better evidence of mens rea than an actus reus that does not. Finally, they are disingenuous. Even if means could be perfected to enable authorities to ascertain the intentions of persons who had not committed an actus reus, few defenders of the actus reus requirement would be inclined to abandon it in virtue of such developments. The reluctance to jettison a principle when its express rationale is discredited indicates that it is supported by reasons that withstand any technical improvements in the ability to gather reliable evidence.

The last of these grounds is also forceful against many other "practical" (but non-evidentiary) rationales in favor of the actus reus requirement.[150] Some criminal theorists have called attention to the difficulties of enforcing laws that do not include an actus reus. One authority contends: "Even if it were thought desirable to have such control over man's thoughts, the enforcement of such control might well be impossible."[151] Theorists who stress the difficulties of enforcement generally reveal their true sympathies when pressed to answer the hypothetical question of whether they would continue to oppose legislation that dispensed with an actus reus even if such problems could be overcome. It is fair to conclude that some deeper, "nonpractical" rationale underlies the entrenchment of the actus reus requirement within orthodox criminal theory.

These deeper rationales take seriously the proposal to treat the actus reus principle as a requirement of justice. Orthodox criminal theorists have advanced a variety of reasons purporting to show why penal legislation that dispensed with an actus reus would be unjust. The most important distinction is between consequentialist and non-consequentialist defenses of this requirement. Some authorities insist that punishment in the absence of an actus reus is objectionable because "there has been no 'social harm.'"[152]  Others concede that "although . . . intentions to commit crimes are potentially harmful,"[153] the grounds for requiring an actus reus are sufficiently compelling to override those gains in social protection that might be achieved by dispensing with it. These latter rationales seem a good deal more plausible. As the discussion of attempts indicates, society would receive better protection if liability did not presuppose an actus reus. An adequate defense of the actus reus requirement must explain why these added benefits of social protection are not worth the sacrifice of individual justice. Why is justice thought to require a criminal act?

One might reply (with some impatience) that the search for justification must terminate somewhere, as any principle invoked in support of a normative claim may itself be challenged as standing in need of justification. Thus, one might simply contend that it is axiomatic or self-evident that actus reus should be an ingredient of each criminal offense.[154] But this position is hardly plausible. The substantive law involving, for example, omissions and attempts is anything but self-evidently just. Surely deeper justificatory principles must be available.

On close examination, the most appealing rationales in behalf of the actus reus requirement actually provide better support for the control principle. Oliver Holmes writes: "The reason for requiring an act is, that an act implies a choice, and that it is felt to be impolitic and unjust to make a man answerable for harm, unless he might have chosen otherwise."[155] Though this rationale is clearly on the right track, it does not quite support the conclusion that Holmes drew. For if Holmes is correct in identifying *choice* as crucial, it should be pointed out that the objects of choice are not always acts. Persons may choose, for example, not to act, or to be of a given status, or to incapacitate themselves so their harmful conduct will be involuntary, or to have firm intentions. A similar observation can be made about the defense proposed by Williams, who argues in favor of the actus reus requirement by calling attention to the "difficulty of distinguishing between day-dreams and fixed intentions."[156] The importance of the distinction between such mental states as day-dreams and fixed intentions is based upon the control principle: one has little or no control over day-dreams, but (at least under ordinary circumstances) substantial control over intentions that can be described as "fixed."

It might be questioned whether the control principle is what orthodox criminal theorists have meant by the actus reus requirement all along. Why suppose that the control principle is better regarded as an *alternative* to the actus reus requirement than as an *interpretation* of it? After all, the control principle incorporates the core of good sense embodied in the actus reus requirement. "Actus reus" is a technical term, to be defined as the criminal theorist stipulates. Indeed, Salmond construes "acts" as "any event which is subject to the control of the human will."[157] And Gross writes, "an act consists of events or states of affairs for which a person might be held responsible . . . and so an act has taken place when such events occur or when such states of affairs exist."[158] If it is true that the class of "events or states of affairs for which a person might be held responsible" is a subset of that over which he has control, Gross's stipulation simply *redefines* actus reus as control. It is tempting to believe that the difference between these suggestions and that proposed here is solely terminological. Both analyses limit the class of states of affairs for which it is just to ascribe liability to that over which persons have control. Gross merely contends that it is advisable to accomplish this result by redefining the actus reus requirement rather than by abandoning it.

The most straightforward reason to prefer my solution to Gross's is that it is less misleading.[159] Gross's identification of actus reus with the concept of responsibility makes perfect sense of *reus*. But what happened to the *actus*? It seems wrong-headed to characterize acts as whatever has taken place when a state of affairs exists for which a person might be held responsible. It is clear, for example, that a parent is ordinarily more responsible for failing to feed his infant than for failing to feed the infant of his neighbor.[160] But is this difference perspicuously expressed by contending that the parent has *acted* in the former but not the latter case? A more plausible explanation of this difference would not focus on the concept of action, but rather on the family of concepts such as ability, opportunity, and expectation, which are closely associated with the concept of control. The foregoing discussion of omissions, status, involuntary conduct, and thoughts reveals some of the substantive differences between the control principle and the actus reus requirement as interpreted within orthodox criminal theory. What is required to resolve the state of confusion about these areas is not new stipulative definitions of old terms, but a more fundamental revision of criminal theory.[161]

One should expect little controversy about the control principle.[162] Few theorists approve of liability for a state of affairs that is beyond the control of a defendant. Yet some skepticism—especially in the context of the insanity defense—has been expressed.[163] On closer inspection, however, most hostility toward the control principle has been based upon difficulties of accurately determining when conduct is truly beyond personal control.[164] Practical experience has shown such problems to be formidable.[165] But difficulties in assessing the reliablity of evidence do not discredit the control principle itself.

Thus the control principle is accepted, for the most part, by orthodox criminal theorists. Where, then, is the novelty in revised criminal theory? My answer is that orthodox criminal theory does not award a central place to the control requirement, instead reserving that privilege to less illuminating principles such as actus reus. Control is not regarded as an organizing principle by reference to which the immense body of substantive criminal law can be understood and assessed. No leading authority includes in his treatise a separate chapter on the concept of control or its place in criminal theory, and few orthodox theorists even include an entry for control in their indexes. If the concept of control is as illuminating as I have claimed, it deserves a place at the heart of criminal theory.

Is it possible to defend a secure justificatory foundation for the control principle? Arguments in favor of the actus reus requirement were not especially persuasive, and there seemed nothing self-evident about the claim that liability without an actus reus is unjust. The principle that liability is unjust for states of affairs over which persons lack control has more intuitive support.[166] Yet even if one denies that the control principle is self-evident, a more satisfactory rationale (than that for its competitor) can be constructed. It is important to resist consequentialist reasoning in support of the control principle. Considerations about deterrence are quite beside the point. Justice simply is not a function of the effect of liability upon oneself or others.[167] Thus Gross's argument in favor of the control principle must be rejected:

> If the law is enforced only when a rule is broken by someone who is able to observe it, so that inability to observe it is a defense against enforcement, the law will not as a result be weakened in the eyes of others, nor in the future will it be less a restraint upon those who were for some reason unable to abide by the law on the present occasion. No one will be thought by others to have gotten away with a violation of the rules when he could not help violating them, and no one will be encouraged by his exemption from liability under such circumstances to engage in crime at another time.[168]

A more plausible rationale appeals to views about the source of legitimacy of the criminal law. These views, more fully elaborated elsewhere, can only be sketched here.[169] An adequate justification for a system of criminal law should speculate about what life would be like in its absence. The existence of a reasonably efficacious and just system of criminal law increases the extent to which each person is able to plan his life and destiny. The punishment of violators decreases the likelihood that individuals will be victimized and thus prevented from attaining their goals. The absence of a criminal justice system would reduce the opportunities of persons to plan their lives and destinies, consistent with the opportunities of others to do likewise.[170]

Thus the concept of control plays a key role in providing the general justifying aim for adopting an institution of criminal justice. A reasonably effective system of criminal law provides persons with greater control over their lives. Law enforcement, however, must not exceed limits, and these limits are derived from considerations of justice. The concept of control is equally important here. To be just, sanctions must not be inflicted upon persons who cannot plan to avoid them. If criminal liability could be imposed for states of affairs persons were powerless to prevent, we would lose control over our lives. Thus, liability that violates the control principle would undermine the purpose of adopting a legal system in the first place.[171] As David Richards has noted:

> The moral principle underlying actus reus as a constitutional requirement is the limitation of criminal liability coherent with the values of . . . maximum autonomy and predictability in planning one's actions and their consequences. . . . The subject of criminal liability is thus to be limited to conduct over which an agent has planful control. Accordingly, penal liability should be limited to such acts or omissions to act.[172]

Until the final "accordingly," the argument in this quotation is sound. Richards has, perhaps unwittingly, supported the control principle rather than the actus reus requirement. The inconsistency he notes need not result from punishing persons who have not acted—since the objects of control are not always acts—although the inconsistency clearly results from punishing persons for states of affairs over which they lack control. The control principle therefore rests on a more secure justificatory foundation than the actus reus requirement.

What accounts for the tendency to retain an actus reus requirement despite all that can be said against it? Perhaps much of its appeal is due to the methodological bias mentioned earlier. Action is the subject matter of behavioral psychology. A criminal theory built upon this foundation may seem to qualify as an empirical science. Here is the great myth of orthodox criminal theory. The discussion throughout this chapter illustrates how the concept of actus reus is not nearly as "objective" as many theorists pretend. Moral and political argument is required to interpret and apply this requirement. But there seems even less hope that the concept of control could be given a factual analysis; its presence or absence is not amenable to empirical verification or falsification. The issue of whether or not a person has acted may appear to be a matter of fact, but the question of whether or not a person has control over a state of affairs is more clearly evaluative. Authorities who cling to the misguided ideal of criminal theory as a science will tend to resist these proposed revisions in the content of its fundamental principles. But the inclusion of the control principle should be welcomed by those who seek to reestablish neglected connections between criminal theory and moral and political philosophy.

### NOTES

1. Professor Turner has speculated that the terms were coined by Kenny, who used them in his lectures. See Jerome Hall, *General Principles of Criminal Law*, p. 222, note 24.

2. Ibid., p. 176.

3. W. Hitchler, "The Physical Element of Crime," *Dickenson Law Review* 39 (1934): 95. One authority dismisses apparent evidence to the contrary, and concludes that "there never was a time when . . . criminal liability could be rested upon mere intent as evidenced by an overt act rather than upon the overt act itself." See Francis Sayre, "Criminal Attempts," *Harvard Law Review* 41 (1928): 821, 826.

4. D. O'Connor, "The Voluntary Act," *Medical Science Law* 15 (1975): 31.

5. "The bodily movements which immediately follow our desires of them, are the only human *acts,* strictly and properly so called. For events which are not *willed,* are not *acts.*" John Austin, *Lectures on Jurisprudence,* p. 432.

6. John Salmond, *Jurisprudence,* p. 400.

7. Hyman Gross, *A Theory of Criminal Justice,* p. 133. See also Glanville Williams, *Textbook of Criminal Law,* p. 147: "Considerable confusion reigns, both in ordinary and in legal speech, on what is meant by an act."

8. Gross, *Theory,* p. 133.

9. Ibid., p. 133.

10. Francis Sayre, "Mens Rea," *Harvard Law Review* 45 (1932): 974, 1026.

11. Hall, *General Principles,* p. 70.

12. Gross, *Theory,* p. 56.

13. But see Herbert Morris, "Punishment for Thoughts," in Robert Summers, ed., *Essays in Legal Philosophy,* p. 95. Morris construes the actus reus requirement as a conceptual truth about the nature of criminal liability. His only apparent reason for this curious interpretation is that the principle must be construed as a conceptual truth in order to be philosophically interesting.

14. "Unfortunately, theories that are correct philosophically may not always be the most useful for the analysis of problems in the criminal law. And what is most useful for criminal lawyers may unhappily entail serious philosophical fallacies." George Fletcher, *Rethinking Criminal Law,* p. 438. But see Alan White, *Grounds of Liability.*

15. Fletcher, *Rethinking,* p. 420–21.

16. See Fred Abbate, "The Conspiracy Doctrine: A Critique," *Philosophy and Public Affairs* 3 (1974): 295.

17. See, e.g., the analyses of acts and omissions offered in Eric D'Arcy, *Human Acts;* Miles Brand, "The Language of Not Doing," *American Philosophical Quarterly* 8 (1971): 49; Roderick Chisholm, *Person and Object*; and Judith Thomson, *Acts and Other Events.* But see Michael Bayles, "The distinction between omissions and commissions is frequently difficult, if not impossible, to make. . . . There is no way to completely classify all conduct as a commission or an omission." *Principles of Legislation,* p. 72.

18. See James Rachels, "Active and Passive Euthanasia," *New England Journal of Medicine* 292 (1975): 78; Micheal Tooley, "An Irrelevant Consideration: Killing Versus Letting Die," in Bonnie Steinbock, ed., *Killing and Letting Die,* p. 56. See also chapter 6.

19. Fletcher insists that the problems associated with the third kind of liability are greater than with the previous two. He puts forward the "experimental" thesis that criminal liability for such omissions is "derivative", and raises difficulties akin to those with accessorial liability. *Rethinking,* pp. 581–85.

20. Despite criticism sometimes amounting almost to ridicule, the view that acts consist of bodily movements continues to attract widespread support. See Austin, *Lectures,* p. 432; Oliver Wendell Holmes, *The Common Law,* p. 45; Walter Cook, "Act, Intention and Motive in the Criminal Law," *Yale Law Journal* 26 (1917): 645; and *M.P.C.* §1.14(2). Paul Robinson adopts this definition after noting that "[o]ne can define 'act' in many ways." *Criminal Law Defenses,* Vol. 2, p. 230. Williams writes: "The most acceptable language is to say that an act means a willed bodily movement." *Textbook,* pp. 147–48. See

also Wayne LaFave and Austin Scott, *Substantive Criminal Law,* pp. 272–73: This definition of acts "is adopted here because it is [the] most meaningful in discussing the requirement of an act."

21. See Jeremy Bentham, *An Introduction to the Principles of Morals and Legislation,* p. 293, note u. See also chapter 6.

22. Elazar Weinryb, "Omissions and Responsibility," *Philosophical Quarterly* 30 (1980): 1, 3.

23. Fletcher, *Rethinking,* p. 425.

24. Of course, the fundamental principle of criminal liability compromised here may not be the actus reus requirement. According to Fletcher, "the critical distinction between commission by act and commission by omission is not to be found in the contrast between bodily movement and standing still. The issue is imposing liability in the absence of the actor's causing the required result." Ibid., p. 423. See chapter 6.

25. Gross, *Theory,* p. 63.

26. Ibid., pp. 63–64.

27. Fletcher, *Rethinking,* pp. 586–87. See also Robinson, *Defenses,* Vol. 2, p. 229, note 19.

28. See the criticisms of Gross in J. C. Smith, "Liability for Omissions in the Criminal Law," *Journal of Legal Studies* 4 (1984): 88.

29. This usage is approved in Rollin Perkins, "Negative Acts in Criminal Law," *Iowa Law Review* 22 (1937): 659. See also Salmond, *Jurisprudence,* p. 399.

30. See note 18.

31. The Model Penal Code uses "conduct" as generic for acts and omissions. §1.13(5).

32. "[I]t would require bold judicial interpretation to read 'act' to include 'omission.' " J. C. Smith and Brian Hogan, *Criminal Law,* p. 263. Williams cites authority that "a statute forbidding the 'doing' of something did not cover an omission." *Textbook,* p. 151. At p. 150, Williams remarks that "it is stretching things" to suppose that *killing* can be performed by omission. At p. 410, he writes that "the word 'act' in a statute should not include an omission." See also note 16.

33. "Most status crimes are probably unconstitutional." Dale Broder and Robert Merson, "Robinson v. California: An Abbreviated Study," *American Criminal Law Quarterly* 3 (1965): 203, 205. "There is a growing body of authority [that crimes of personal condition] are unconstitutional." Wayne LaFave and Austin Scott, *Criminal Law,* p. 181. See also *Lanzetta v. N.J.,* 306 U.S. 451 (1939). According to Williams, some "offences of this kind strike one as being particularly tyrannical." *Textbook,* p. 157. "Potential objects of criminal law . . . are *not* . . . situations to which the law attaches sanctions purported to prevent or cure a condition qua status." Helen Silving, *Constituent Elements of Crime,* p. 4.

34. Gross, *Theory,* p. 146.

35. In the context of discussing vagrancy statutes, one authority notes that "nowhere has the claim been accepted that vagrancy is immune simply because it is a status. . . . It is implausible to read *Robinson* to announce a new constitutional doctrine declaring crimes of status generally to be outside the scope of the criminal law." Herbert Fingarette, "Addiction and Criminal Responsibility," *Yale Law Journal* 84 (1975): 413, 417–18, note 24.

36. Rollin Perkins and Ronald Boyce, *Criminal Law,* p. 497.

37. Sometimes definitions must be inferred from lists of status crimes. Perkins apparently regards possessory offenses as instances of status criminality. Ibid., p. 497.

38. Forrest Lacey, "Vagrancy and Other Crimes of Personal Condition," *Harvard Law Review* 66 (1953): 1203, 1204. Another commentator defines status as "the [legal] condition or state of being of a person." John Silber, "Being and Doing: A Study of Status Responsibility and Voluntary Responsibility," *University of Chicago Law Review* 35 (1967): 47, note 2.

39. Fingarette, "Addiction," p. 417. See also Herbert Fingarette and Ann Hasse, *Mental Disabilities and Criminal Responsibility*, p. 142. But see Robinson, *Defenses*, Vol. 2, p. 453: "Legislatures recently have taken an active role in eliminating 'status' crimes."

40. See *Wheeler v. Goodman*, 306 F.Supp. 58 (1969). The vagueness doctrine is said to be the "most obvious federal constitutional attack" on status crimes. Anthony Amsterdam, "Federal Constitutional Restrictions on the Punishment of Crimes of Status, Crimes of General Obnoxiousness, Crimes of Displeasing Police Officers, and the Like," *Criminal Law Bulletin* 3 (1967): 205, 216.

41. Anthony Cuomo, "Mens Rea and Status Criminality," *Southern California Law Review* 40 (1967): 463, 507.

42. See "Criminal Liability Without Action: Involuntary Conduct," this chapter.

43. See the examples provided in LaFave and Scott, *Criminal*, p. 166.

44. Some courts object to status criminality on the ground that a status is necessarily "chronic rather than acute," or that it "continues after it is complete, and thereby subjects the offender to arrest at any time before he reforms." *People v. Craig*, 91 P. 997, 1000 (1907). But this generalization simply is not applicable to all statuses. The status of "being younger than 21 years of age" is not "chronic," nor does one lose this status by "reforming."

45. See *U.S. v. Cores*, 356 U.S. 405 (1958).

46. 370 U.S. 660 (1962).

47. 392 U.S. 514 (1968).

48. *Robinson*, p. 660.

49. *Powell*, p. 516.

50. Ibid., pp. 532–33.

51. A typical comment describes the "narrow interpretation" of *Robinson* as one which "substantively limited the states' power to punish 'status' alone." Mike Stevenson, "Chronic Alcoholism and Criminal Responsibility," *Gonzaga Law Review* 4 (1969): 336, 338. See also Robinson, *Defenses*, Vol. 2, p. 452: "*Robinson* is now viewed as holding that liability must be based on an *act*."

52. *Nicol v. Ames*, 173 U.S. 509 (1899). Also noteworthy is the principle of statutory construction according to which a statute worded unclearly on the question of whether an actus reus is required should be construed to require an act. *Baender v. Barnett*, 255 U.S. 224 (1921).

53. *State ex.rel. Blouin v. Walker*, 154 So.2d. 368 (1963).

54. The plausible claim that most statuses entail one or more acts must be distinguished from the implausible claim that most statuses are *reducible* to one or more acts. Though most statuses contain one or more acts in their analysis, each analysis will contain one or more elements other than acts, such as dispositions or propensities to continue to perform such acts. Without these dispositions or propensities, it would seem more accurate to say that a person *had* or *was* of a given status than to say that he is of that status.

55. Robert Keller, "Constitutional Law: Cruel and Unusual Punishment," *Buffalo Law Review* 18 (1969): 337, 352.

56. Note that the definition of actus reus as "events or states of affairs for which a person might be held responsible" does not, contrary to the author's own opinion, preclude status criminality. See Gross, *Theory,* p. 56. Smith and Hogan subsume status under the ambit of actus reus. *Criminal,* p. 41.

57. "Statutes creating crimes of this sort . . . have often been upheld notwithstanding their definition . . . in terms of 'being' rather than 'acting.'" LaFave and Scott, *Substantive,* p. 279.

58. Gross, *Theory,* p. 77.

59. John Murtaugh, "Status Offenses and Due Process of Law," *Fordham Law Review* 36 (1967): 51, 58.

60. Arthur Sherry, "Vagrants, Rogues, and Vagabonds—Old Concepts in Need of Revision," *California Law Review* 48 (1960): 557, 567.

61. See "Control: Status Offenses," this chapter.

62. The necessity that conduct be voluntary is described by some authorities as the "fundamental requirement of all criminal liability." J. Edwards, "Automatism and Criminal Responsibility," *Modern Law Review* 21 (1958): 375, 379.

63. For an indication of how far some courts are willing to go in characterizing involuntariness, see *People v. Newton,* 87 Cal.Rep. 394 (1970). See the discussion in Williams, *Textbook,* pp. 665–76.

64. Oftentimes this debate is framed in terms of whether the recognition of excuses such as involuntariness can or should be justified within deterrent, or retributive theories of punishment. See H. L. A. Hart, "Legal Responsibility and Excuses," in his *Punishment and Responsibility,* p. 28.

65. See *People v. Baker,* 268 P.2d 705 (1954).

66. *Hill v. Baxter,* 1 Q.B. 277, 283 (1958).

67. Smith and Hogan remark that whether involuntariness is precluded by actus reus or mens rea "is a matter of convenience only." *Criminal,* p. 37. Williams writes that the view that involuntariness precludes actus reus involves an "unnecessary refinement" of "pure theory." Textbook, p. 663. Later (p. 677) he characterizes some applications of the doctrine that actus reus precludes involuntariness as "absurd from start to finish." See also Robinson, *Defenses,* Vol. 2, p. 264.

68. Jeffrie Murphy, "Involuntary Acts and Criminal Liability," in his *Retribution, Justice, and Therapy,* p. 116. Murphy writes: *"Involuntary* acts or omissions . . . fail to satisfy the law's minimal condition for liability—the requirement of an actus reus." See also Smith and Hogan, Criminal, p. 35–36.

69. See Hart, "Acts of Will and Responsibility," in his *Punishment,* p. 90: "The phrase 'sleep-walking' is alone sufficient to remind us that if the outward movements appear to be co-ordinated as they are in normal action, the fact that the subject is unconscious from whatever cause does not prevent us using an active verb to describe the case, though we would qualify it with the adverb 'unconsciously' or with the adverbial phrases 'in his sleep', 'in a state of automatism', etc. So in the case of 'driving' it would be natural, as a matter of English, to distinguish those cases where the movements of the body are wild or spasmodic or where the 'driver' simply slumps in his seat or collapses over the wheel, from cases where, though unconscious, he is apparently controlling the vehicle, changing gears, steering, braking, etc. In the latter case it might well be said that he drove the vehicle, changed gear,

braked, etc. 'in his sleep' or 'in a state of automatism'. Such cases can certainly occur." Further indication of the oddity of the claim that an involuntary actus reus is incoherent is provided by the fact that Murphy (who makes such a claim) later goes on to defend a criterion of when acts are involuntary. Murphy, "Involuntary." See also the ambivalence in Gross, *Criminal,* pp. 68–69.

70. See *M.P.C.* §1.14(2). See also S. Coval, J. Smith, and Peter Burns, "The Concept of Action and its Juridical Significance," *University of Toronto Law Journal* 30 (1980): 199, 207; P. Sim, "The Involuntary Actus Reus," *Modern Law Review* 25 (1962): 741, and White, *Liability,* chapter Five.

71. This adjective is used by Gross, *Theory,* p. 70. Murphy refers to this account as the "classical analysis." "Involuntary," p. 117.

72. See note 20.

73. See Hart, "Legal Responsibility"; Fletcher, *Rethinking,* p. 421; Gross, *Theory,* p. 70; Herbert Morris, "Book Review," *Stanford Law Review* 13 (1960): 185; and White, *Liability,* p. 31. See also O'Connor, "Voluntary," p. 31, who describes the orthodox Austinian model as a "grossly inaccurate analysis of the actual physiological and psychological process." But see Michael Zimmerman, *An Essay on Human Action.*

74. Patrick Fitzgerald, "Voluntary and Involuntary Acts," in Anthony Guest, ed., *Oxford Essays in Jurisprudence,* p. 1, 17. See also Hart, "Legal Responsibility," pp. 107–8; and Robinson, *Defenses,* Vol. 2, p. 265.

75. See chapter 5.

76. I assume that the distinction between voluntariness and involuntariness cannot be drawn without reference to the mental. For some *apparent* doubts, see Gross, *Theory,* p. 30.

77. Glanville Williams, *Criminal Law: The General Part,* p. 18.

78. Ibid., p. 12. But see his later qualifications in note 67.

79. But see the complications discussed in A. C. E. Lynch, "The Mental Element in the Actus Reus," *Law Quarterly Review* 98 (1982): 109.

80. Those criminal theorists anxious to maintain that "intent and act are separable concepts" recognize the "confusion" in requiring that "acts" must be "willed" or "voluntary." See Justin Miller, *Criminal Law,* p. 94. See also Francis Jacobs, *Criminal Responsibility,* p. 105. Williams himself admits that his approach "makes the legal distinction between an act and a state of mind a jagged one." *Criminal,* p. 14.

81. Courtney Kenny, *Outlines of Criminal Law,* p. 30. See also Robinson, *Defenses,* Vol. 2, p. 267.

82. *People v. Decina,* 138 N.E.2d 799, 808 (1956).

83. Williams writes: "No case before 1973 suggested that a defense of automatism is excluded because the condition was produced by the defendant's fault, other than voluntary intoxication." *Textbook,* p. 681. The forseeability of harm in these cases distinguishes them from the related problem of the voluntarily intoxicated offended discussed in chapter 3.

84. *People v. Freeman,* 142 P.2d 435 (1943); *State v. Gooze,* 81 A.2d 811 (1951); and *R.v. Quick,* QB 910 (1973). But see *Fain v. Commonwealth,* 78 Ky. 183 (1879). The Model Penal Code sidesteps this difficulty by requiring that liability be based on conduct that "includes" a voluntary act. See §2.01(1).

85. Gross, *Theory,* p. 293; Murphy, "Involuntary"; and Williams, *Textbook,* pp. 681–83. The central difficulty is how criminal liability can be reconciled with the fundamental principle of concurrence. Mens rea at one time (when involuntariness is self-induced) does not "transfer" to create mens

rea at a later time (when the criminal conduct is performed). See Paul Robinson, "Causing the Conditions of One's Own Defense: A Study of the Limits of Theory in Criminal Law Doctrine," *Virginia Law Review* 71 (1985): 1. See also chapter 3.

86. Smith and Hogan describe such cases as "one exception to the rule requiring proof that a relevant act was voluntary." *Criminal*, p. 36.

87. *People v. Decina*, p. 808 (Desmond, J., dissenting).

88. See Torcia, *Wharton's Criminal Law*, Vol. 1, p. 115.

89. See Peter Geach, *Mental Acts*.

90. "The unconcern with intention, unless and until the intention is manifested in an overt act, does not arise from any view that making up the mind is in fact no act at all; for it is an act and as much a fact as the state of a man's digestion." Orvil Snyder, *Criminal Justice*, p. 110. See also Salmond, *Jurisprudence*, p. 399; and Austin, *Lectures*, p. 376. Austin, however, subsequently revised his original views, indicating how they tended to "darken their subjects . . . it is utterly absurd to apply such terms as 'act' and 'movement' to *mental* phenomena" (p. 433).

91. Smith and Hogan, *Criminal*, p. 41.

92. Barbara Levenbook, "Prohibiting Attempts and Preparations," *University of Missouri at Kansas City Law Review* 49 (1980): 41, 50.

93. Donald Stuart, "The Actus Reus in Attempts," *Criminal Law Review* (1970): 505, 510. Smith and Hogan claim that endeavors to describe the boundary between preparation and attempt are "capricious in their operation or simply unhelpful." *Criminal*, p. 260. Williams indicates that "none of them gave much assistance, and one or two of them were positively misleading." *Textbook*, p. 411.

94. For a list of the various tests of when preparation ends and attempt begins, see LaFave and Scott, *Criminal*, pp. 432–38.

95. This criterion was devised by Salmond, *Jurisprudence*. Different versions of this criterion have been formulated. The "equivocality" test, seemingly part of English law, holds that attempt liability attaches when the conduct of the defendant "cannot reasonably be regarded as having any other purpose than the commission of the crime." Archbold, *Archbold's Criminal Pleading, Evidence and Practice*, §4104.

96. Williams, *Criminal*, p. 630.

97. "If a locksmith is found next to a bank safe with his tools of trade, it would be ludicrous to exclude a confession or other evidence that his intention had been to steal." Stuart, "Actus Reus," p. 507.
See also Williams, *Criminal*, p. 620.

98. Williams, *Criminal*, p. 620. But see his later claim: "An act does not become an attempt merely because the *mens rea* is obvious." (p. 414).

99. Ibid., p. 630.

100. "Whereas in most crimes it is the actus reus, the harmful conduct, which the law desires to prevent, while the mens rea is only the necessary condition for the infliction of punishment on the person who has produced that harmful result, in attempt the position is reversed, and it is the mens rea which the law regards as of primary importance and desires to prevent." J. Turner, "Attempts to Commit Crimes," *Cambridge Law Journal* 5 (1934): 230, 235. See also note 102.

101. The literature on impossible attempts is voluminous. See Arnold Enker, "Impossibility in Criminal Attempts—Legality and the Legal Process," *University of Minnesota Law Review* 53 (1969): 665.

102. Williams, *Textbook,* p. 631.

103. Some authorities favor criminal liability for preparations. See Levenbook, "Prohibiting."

104. For the more radical attack on attempts, see P. Glazebrook, "Should We Have a Law of Attempted Crime?" *Law Quarterly Review* 85 (1969): 28. For an attack directed largely to so-called impossible attempts, see Enker, "Impossibility."

105. *M.P.C.* §5.01(1)(c).

106. Id., §5.01(2).

107. See Fletcher, *Rethinking,* p. 168. Fletcher himself, however, does not draw the conclusion reached here. For a contrary interpretation of the import of the Model Penal Code, see Enker, "Impossibility," p. 676.

108. Helen Silving, *Criminal Justice,* Vol. 1, p. 319.

109. Morris, "Punishment."

110. Gross, *Theory,* p. 132. A similar observation is made by Fletcher, *Rethinking,* p. 172, and LaFave and Scott, *Substantive,* Vol. 2, p. 18.

111. Gross, *Theory,* p. 132.

112. Fletcher, *Rethinking,* p. 174.

113. Gross is especially sensitive to the difficulties in inferring that a single dangerous act is reliable evidence of a dangerous person. *Theory,* pp. 340 and 386. See Andrew Von Hirsch, *Doing Justice.*

114. See Andrew von Hirsch, "Desert and Previous Convictions in Sentencing," *University of Minnesota Law Review* 65 (1981): 591.

115. Some of these difficulties are discussed in Michael Bayles, "Character, Purpose, and Criminal Responsibility," *Law and Philosophy* 1 (1982): 5.

116. Williams expresses a view similar to that defended here, but adds that "this opinion is not generally held in the legal profession." *Criminal,* p. 632.

117. H. L. A. Hart, *The Concept of Law,* p. 32.

118. A fundamental insight of Fletcher's book, as I understand it, is that this amorphous "something" to which criminal liability may attach (which I call "conduct") is distinguished profitably into three "patterns." The phrase "states of affairs" is sufficiently broad to encompass each "pattern."

119. I do not examine the question of whether or in what sense criminal liability presupposes "free will." Most philosophers subscribe to what is called "the principle of alternate possibilities," according to which a person is responsible for what he does only if he could have done otherwise. This principle, which has great intuitive appeal, might best be understood by examining how it has been challenged. See Harry Frankfurt, "Alternate Possibilities and Moral Responsibility," *Journal of Philosophy* 46 (1969): 829. For useful rejoinders to Frankfurt's challenge, see Peter van Inwagen, "Ability and Responsibility," *Philosophical Review* 87 (1978): 201; and John Fischer, "Responsibility and Control," *Journal of Philosophy* 79 (1982): 24.

120. See chapter 2.

121. See Michael Zimmerman, *An Essay on Moral Responsibility* (forthcoming).

122. See Smith and Hogan, *Criminal,* pp. 186 and 209.

123. For a pessimistic outlook about why these questions are not raised, see Mark Kelman, "Interpretive Construction in the Substantive Criminal Law," *Stanford Law Review* 33 (1981): 591.

124. See E. O'Doherty, "Men, Criminals, and Responsibility," *Irish Jurist* 1 (1966): 285, 288, and Comment, "Graduated Responsibility as an Alterna-

tive to Current Tests of Determining Criminal Capacity," *Maine Law Review* 25 (1973): 343, 356.

125. See note 18 and chapter 6.

126. Perhaps there are difficulties involving legality and causation. See chapter 6.

127. *Robinson v. California,* pp. 666–67: "It is unlikely that any State at this moment in history would attempt to make it a criminal offense for a person to be mentally ill, or a leper, or to be afflicted with a venereal disease . . . In the light of contemporary human knowledge, a law which made a criminal offense of such a disease would doubtless be universally thought to be an infliction of cruel and unusual punishment . . . We cannot but consider the statute before us as of the same category." But compare *Reynolds v. McNichols,* 488 F.2d 1378 (1973).

128. *Powell v. Texas,* p. 526: "It is one thing to say that if a man is deprived of alcohol his hands will begin to shake. . . . It is quite another to say that a man has a 'compulsion' to take a drink. . . . It is simply impossible, in the present state of our knowledge, to ascribe a useful meaning to the latter statement. This definitional confusion reflects, of course, not merely the undeveloped state of the psychiatric art." The defendant's claim in *Powell* that his conduct was beyond his control was seriously undermined by his admission that he had refrained from heavy drinking on the day of trial.

129. *People v. Borrero,* 227 N.E.2d 18 (1967).

130. Fingarette, "Addiction," p. 444.

131. The major impediment with the foregoing attempt to reconcile *Powell* with *Robinson* is that it is inconsistent with some of the language of the *Powell* Court. See 392 U.S. 514, 533 (1968): "It is suggested in dissent that *Robinson* stands for the 'simple' but 'subtle' principle that 'criminal penalties may not be inflicted upon a person for being in a condition he is powerless to change'. . . Whatever may be the merits of such a doctrine of criminal responsibility, it surely cannot be said to follow from *Robinson.*"

132. See Charles Taylor, "Responsibility for Self" in Amelie Rorty, ed., *The Identities of Persons,* p. 281. See also Harry Frankfurt, "Freedom of the Will and the Concept of a Person," *Journal of Philosophy* 68 (1971): 5. But see Robert Adams, "Involuntary Sins," *Philosophical Review* 94 (1985): 3.

133. The actus reus requirement frequently has been held to differentiate moral from criminal responsibility. See chapter 5.

134. Fitzgerald, "Voluntary," p. 17. See also White, *Liability,* p. 53.

135. "That element of choice which is fundamental to criminal liability is present in these cases, for the individual has exercised his choice by allowing to supervene an incapacitating condition." A. Ashworth, "Reason, Logic, and Criminal Liability," *Law Quarterly Review* 91 (1975): 102, 124.

136. Fitzgerald, "Voluntary," pp. 20–21. But see the thoughtful proposal in Robinson, "Causing."

137. See Barnard Williams, "Deciding to Believe" in his *Problems of the Self,* p. 136. See also Michael Stocker, "Responsibility, Especially for Beliefs," *Mind* 91 (1982): 398.

138. But see a review of Morris's "Punishment," where a philosopher remarks: "As to beliefs, [Morris] does not make what seems to be the obvious point, that one cannot choose whether or not to believe something; and that it is obviously objectionable to create a criminal offense as to which people cannot choose whether or not to commit it." Warnock, G. J., "Review: *On Guilt and Innocence,*" *Nous* XIV (1980): 134–35. See also Abbate, "Conspiracy," p.

303: "if we made the mere having of certain intentions punishable, the element of individual control of one's behavior would be significantly diminished."

139. An extreme example: the emperor Dionysius is said to have executed a subject who had dreamed of killing him.

140. William Keener, *Selections on Jurisprudence,* p. 169.

141. "This requisite act should not be regarded as being merely for the purpose of evidencing the intent; it is a separate and independent part of the crime, as necessary and substantial as the intent itself." Robert Skilton, "The Requisite Act in Criminal Attempt," *University of Pittsburgh Law Review* 3 (1937): 308, note 1.

142. Williams, *Criminal,* p. 2. See also Gerald Dworkin and David Blumenfeld, "Punishment for Intentions," *Mind* 75 (1966): 396, 401: It is "a rather hazy matter to know just when a person is intending rather than wishing."

143. Perkins and Boyce, *Criminal,* p. 605. James Stephen also notes that such a doctrine would have the consequence that "all mankind would be criminals." *History of the Criminal Law of England,* p. 78.

144. Fitzgerald, "Voluntary," p. 3. See also Bayles, "Character."

145. Herbert Packer, *The Limits of the Criminal Sanction,* p. 74.

146. Even theorists unshaken in their confidence in the actus reus requirement admit that its "rationale is obscure." Snyder, *Criminal,* p. 110.

147. Blackstone: *Commentaries,* Vol. 4, *21.

148. It is noteworthy that the ascendancy of the actus reus requirement within orthodox criminal theory coincided with misgivings about the reliability of confessions. See Snyder, *Criminal,* p. 111.

149. See note 141.

150. Not all "practical" rationales in favor of the actus reus requirement will be discussed. One theorist speculates that the principle minimizes the likelihood of multiple prosecutions. See Abe Goldstein, "Conspiracy to Defraud the United States," *Yale Law Journal* 68 (1959): 405, 406.

151. Fitzgerald, "Voluntary," p. 3. See also Bayles, "Character."

152. Perkins and Boyce, *Criminal,* p. 605.

153. Fitzgerald, "Voluntary," p. 3.

154. Some philosophers characterize the unwillingness of our criminal justice system to dispense with an actus reus as a "datum" by which "to test the adequacy of a number of plausible contemporary" theories. See Dworkin and Blumenfeld, "Punishment," p. 396.

155. Holmes, *Common,* p. 54.

156. Williams, *Criminal,* p. 2.

157. Salmond, *Jurisprudence,* p. 381. See also Keener, *Selections,* p. 164.

158. Gross, *Theory,* p. 56.

159. The implications of the control principle upon omissions, status criminality, and involuntary conduct are less likely to be appreciated by redefining rather than by abandoning the actus reus requirement. Gross, it may be recalled, categorically resists status criminality on the ground that a status is not an act (p. 146). But to the extent that persons have control over some statuses, and persons may be held responsible for states of affairs over which they have control (p. 60), it is likely that Gross has failed to recognize the implications of his own position.

160. See *Jones v. U.S.,* 308 F.2d 307 (1962).

161. Most of the more sophisticated analyses of the concept of action distinguish it from control. See Coval, Smith, and Burns, "Concept," p. 211.

162. Occasionally dissent is encountered. See Robert Adams, "Involuntary Sins," *Philosophical Review* 94 (1985): 3. See also T. M. Scanlon, "Quality of Will and the Value of Choice" (unpublished).

163. "[T]he central issue in the debate about the insanity defense is whether impairment of volitional capacity should have independent exculpatory significance." Peter Low, John Jeffries, and Richard Bonnie, *Criminal Law*, p. 692.

164. "[M]ost opponents of the control [test of insanity] have concentrated their criticism on the difficulty of administering such a test in the light of present knowledge." Ibid., p. 693. See *U.S. v. Lyons*, 731 F.2d 243 (1984).

165. See *U.S. v. Moore*, 486 F.2d. 1139 (1973). See also Barbara Wootton, *Crime and the Criminal Law*.

166. "It might even be argued that it would be contradictory to say that a person was morally responsible for something over which he had no control whatever." Jacobs, *Criminal*, p. 11.

167. See chapter 3.

168. Gross, pp. 11–12.

169. Hart appeals to such a view as a justification for recognizing excuses. "Responsibility," p. 47. Lon Fuller regards some version of the control principle as a necessary condition before a system of norms can qualify as a *legal* system. See *The Morality of Law*, chapter two.

170. Surely all rational persons would consent to be governed by institutions that contribute to their autonomy, if such hypothetical agreement were thought necessary to the justification of institutions. See John Rawls, *A Theory of Justice*.

171. It must not be supposed that this inconsistency entails that there are no conceivable circumstances in which the control principle should be infringed. After all, the fundamental principles of criminal liability are only prima facie requirements.

172. David Richards, *The Moral Criticism of Law*, p. 201.

# 5

# *The Mental Component of Crime*

## THE ORTHODOX MODEL OF THE CRIMINAL OFFENSE

Oɴᴇ sʜᴏᴜʟᴅ ɴᴏᴛ ᴛᴀᴍᴘᴇʀ with a part of orthodox criminal theory without attending to the implications upon the remainder. If the concept of actus reus is abandoned, what becomes of mens rea, the other half of the orthodox model of the criminal offense? I make no pretense that my answer to this question is comprehensive; I barely scratch the surface in examining the multitude of problems surrounding the mental component of crime.

It is clear that the control principle cannot simply substitute for the actus reus requirement alongside mens rea. Mens rea is the complement of a concept that is outward, behavioristic, and physical, and the concept of control has none of these characteristics. It eludes categorization as either mental or physical. As Hyman Gross observes: "Control (and its failure or absence) is sometimes a mental matter, sometimes a physical matter, and sometimes a matter belonging to neither category."[1]

It should be obvious that whether a person has control over a state of affairs is a function of his physical capacities. What may be less clear is that information about his mental state is needed as well. Consider *ignorance of fact,* always treated within orthodox criminal theory as the absence of mens rea. Suppose a person has the means to prevent a harm, but is unaware of this fact (and could not reasonably have been expected to be aware of it). Does he have control over its occurrence? Definitive answers to such questions must await a more detailed analysis of the control principle than is provided here. But frequently the answer is negative. It seems facetious to hold, for example, that a medieval doctor had control over the death of his poisoned patient when an antidote was readily available, yet no one at that time was aware of its medicinal effects. Such examples indicate that a hybrid of revised criminal theory, which includes a control principle, and orthodox criminal theory, which includes a requirement of mens rea, is redundant. It makes little sense to retain a purely mental component to pair with what is not wholly nonmental.

The conviction among orthodox theorists that criminal offenses are divisible into distinct physical and mental components has always been contrived and artificial.[2] This "dualistic" model, long discredited philosophically, cannot survive careful scrutiny. It is quite remarkable that the orthodox model of the criminal offense has persisted, for there are any number of instances of liability that falsify it. Attempts provide the best counterexamples. It is impossible to identify the actus reus of an attempted offense as distinct from criminal intent. If a defendant shoots at his victim with intent to kill but misses, he is guilty of attempted murder, but only because of his mental state. The actus reus of the offense is not shooting and missing; shooting and missing is not attempted murder. The outward, physical component of the defendant's conduct simply does not constitute the "forbidden act" of attempted murder unless accompanied by criminal intent.[3]

Any systematic endeavor to sift the mental component from a criminal attempt in order to isolate the physical residue leads to absurd and extraordinary results. Consider the case proposed by Glanville Williams:

> Suppose that D puts an aspirin in P's tea, thinking that it is the sweetening tablet for which P has asked. This act is innocent; it harms no one; yet it is the *actus reus* of attempt to murder. For if D intended to poison P, and believed that an aspirin would kill him, his administration of it would be an attempt to murder.[4]

According to this view, each of us commits the actus reus of attempted murder thousands of times every day. Virtually *any* act becomes the actus reus of *any* attempted offense! One can only wonder how the concept of actus reus, as so understood, can be useful to criminal theory.

Many theorists allege that attempts represent a "special case," or an "anomaly" for the orthodox model of the criminal offense. In fact, however, attempts provide only the most obvious, although not the only counterexamples. A great many verbs that appear in criminal statutes imply intentionality.[5] One cannot "appropriate," "possess," "permit," "impersonate," "bribe," "marry," or "fight" (to name only a few) without the appropriate mental state. A defendant can swing his arms and land blows on another either intentionally or unintentionally, but no one would describe his conduct as "fighting" unless he intended to fight.[6] Here again, the attempt to subdivide offenses that include these verbs into distinct inner and outer components is a hopeless endeavor.

Consider the offense of perjury. This may be construed as "making a statement, whether true or not, on oath in a judicial proceeding, knowing it to be false or not believing it to be true." What would orthodox criminal theorists identify as the actus reus of this offense? When reference to the mental is deleted, the physical part of perjury can only be "making a statement under oath in a judicial proceeding." Some orthodox criminal theorists explicitly endorse this conclusion. According to their view: "When we say then that a certain event is the *actus reus* of a crime what we mean is that the event would be a crime if it were caused by a person with *mens rea*. The description of it as an *actus reus* implies no judgment whatever as to its moral or legal quality."[7] This view, however, encounters two formidable difficulties. First, it allows that an actus reus may not be "reus." Obviously, the "actus" of testifying under oath is innocuous, or even exemplary. "Actus reus" becomes a misnomer. Second, it is likely that the authors of the above quotation equivocate in their two uses of the word "event." An event "caused by a person with mens rea" is a *different* event than that *not* caused by mens rea. The event of "shooting in the direction of a victim" (without intent to kill) is almost certainly a different event from that of "attempting to kill." How can two descriptions refer to the same event if the events have different causes?[8] When mens rea is subtracted from offenses that contain verbs implying intentionality, the "event" itself may be altered as well.

The fact that the alleged actus reus is frequently changed by the addition of mens rea is particularly evident in the case of offenses that require that the defendant act with a specified purpose. Consider the offense of acting "with intent to impede [the] apprehension" of a person who "has committed an arrestable offense." When divorced from intent, the actus reus of this offense can only be action that in fact results in impeding a lawful arrest or prosecution. A pedestrian who happens to slow the pursuit of a police car unwittingly commits the actus reus of a felony. Small wonder that the application of the orthodox model to such offenses has been described as "unhelpful."[9]

A few theorists appreciate these difficulties, and have concluded that the orthodox model of the criminal offense "works well enough" only in the special case of so-called "result crimes," such as homicide.[10] Since only a minority of offenses are "result crimes," this admission all but rejects the orthodox model. Even here, however, it is unclear what the actus reus of these offenses should encompass, due to uncertainty about whether the proscribed result, for example, death, should be included. Two alternatives are available. On the first, death is *not* part of the actus reus. The actus reus of homicide *causes* death, so that death is a consequence of the proscribed act rather than a component of it. According to this view, an element of liability is part of neither the actus reus nor the mens rea. It may seem odd to suppose that one can commit the actus reus of homicide before anyone has died, but this first view entails this oddity. On the second alternative, death *is* part of the actus reus. According to this view, the actus reus of homicide includes death, so that the actus reus has not been committed unless and until the victim dies. This alternative, too, is troublesome. Since a killer may predecease his victim, a defendant may continue to be engaged in the commission of the actus reus of murder even after he has died. It is strange to think that a dead defendant may be capable of action. Neither alternative is unproblematic, and a viable theory need not be forced to choose between them.[11]

If these difficulties are not sufficient to cast serious doubts upon the cogency of the orthodox model in the special case of "result crimes," where it is alleged to "work well," evidence of further confusion can be cited. Even criminal theorists with a reputation for care and precision sometimes express "the rule, which is almost invariable, that [the defendant must] have caused the *actus reus*."[12] Is what causes an actus reus itself an act, different from the actus reus that is caused? Compare this locution with a familiar definition of actus reus as "such result of human conduct as the law seeks to prevent."[13] Does this definition imply that a dead man with a bullet in his brain *is* the actus reus of murder? I will not hazard guesses about how orthodox criminal theorists might best resolve these problems. Instead, I propose that there is something defective in the theory that gives rise to them.

I do not insist that any of these difficulties is fatal to the "great secret of criminal guilt," as Rollin Perkins describes the orthodox model of the criminal offense.[14] Orthodox theorists have expended much ingenuity in attempts to overcome them (though often they are conveniently ignored). But when a theory gives rise to oddities and strange results, it becomes appropriate to inquire whether an alternative can preserve the advantages of that theory while escaping its difficulties. What would be sacrificed if the orthodox model of the criminal offense were abandoned? What is gained by the attempt to subdivide offenses into distinct physical and mental ingredients? Why is it thought important that a mental component to crime exists that is distinguishable from external behavior? Unless the philosopher of criminal law can answer these questions, it is doubtful that the immense intellectual energy required to salvage the "great secret" of the orthodox model of the criminal offense is worth the bother.

Revised criminal theory retains the concept of an *offense,* as something distinct from the absence of various *defenses* that can be invoked to preclude liability. These offenses in turn may be subdivided into *elements*, but no significance attaches to whether these elements are categorized as physical or mental. No longer is *fault* conceptualized as an exclusive function of mental state, but as an indivisible product of both what one thinks and what one does. This view, I submit, represents common sense.[15] Consider murder. Is the fault in murder a function of what one thinks or what one does? The answer is that it is both. If fault were an exclusive function of what one *thinks*, killing would be no more culpable than intending to kill. Almost no one explicitly endorses such a result,[16] despite the fact that it is implied by views defended by a number of theorists. If fault were an exclusive function of what one *does*, intentional killing would be no more culpable than accidental killing. Again, almost no one accepts this result. The attempt to subdivide offenses into distinct physical and mental parts, and to identify one as the unique locus of fault, is hopeless. It is no small advantage of revised criminal theory that it does not embrace such absurdities.

I trust I will not be misunderstood in proposing that the orthodox model of the criminal offense should be abandoned, and the distinct mental component of crime denounced as fictitious. I am not doubting the reality of mental phenomena in denying that conduct can be divided into separate physical and mental components. Still less am I advocating that culpability is unimportant in criminal law and that all offenses should be converted into "strict liability." It would be a step backward to remove from the Model Penal Code the four "terms of culpability" that constitute (or replace) mens rea. I depart from orthodoxy only in denying that these terms are purely mental, or are the sole constituents of fault.

These so-called mental states are not the sole constituents of fault; nor do they refer to what is purely mental. Even "knowledge," thought by orthodox theorists to be a paradigm mental state, incorporates nonmental elements. A person who believes a proposition cannot be said to *know* it unless his belief is both true and justified.[17] Neither truth nor justification can plausibly be regarded as purely mental. Is knowledge therefore to be included within actus reus? Of course not; the correct inference is that the orthodox model of the criminal offense cannot be sustained. As H. L. A. Hart has prophetically remarked: "If knowledge (the constituent *par excellence* of *mens rea*) may be counted as part of the *actus reus*, it seems quite senseless to insist on any distinction at all between the *actus reus* and the *mens rea*, or to develop a doctrine of criminal responsibility in terms of this distinction."[18]

Revised criminal theory does not hold distinctions between so-called mental states to be irrelevant to criminal liability. In fact, the inclusion of the control principle in revised criminal theory *may* provide a *better* explanation than its orthodoxy of why distinctions between "mental" states should make a difference to liability. Gross inquires why the four "terms of culpability" in the Model Penal Code are scaled as they are. Why should what is done "purposely" be more culpable than what is done "knowingly," "recklessly," or "negligently"? The draftsmen of the Code offer no principled answer. Gross suggests that these terms are scaled in descending order because they involve different degrees of control:

> As the scale is ascended, conduct of each degree leaves succeedingly less room for chance to determine the occurrence of harm. Because of that the harm (whether actual or in prospect) is attributable to the actor more and more as the scale is ascended. It is then more within or under his control, and it is fair as well as reasonable to blame the actor more when the harm is more subject to his control and less as a matter of chance.[19]

In chapter 4 I argued that the control principle underlies and explains the core of good sense embodied in the actus reus requirement of orthodox criminal theory. If the above remarks by Gross are correct, the control principle may underlie and explain much of the appeal of the mens rea requirement as well. It would be fascinating to determine to what extent this is so. The absence of control constitutes the underlying rationale for a great many excuses conceptualized within orthodox theory as negating mens rea. Not all excuses, however, derive their validity from the control principle, and attempts to subsume them under this rationale are contrived and artificial.[20] It is unreasonable to expect that a single rationale can explain the great variety of excuses recognized within the criminal law. Although the concept of control may be adequate in replacing actus reus, it cannot suffice as the single pillar of revised criminal theory.

Professionals skilled in the daily practice of law are likely to regard this proposed departure from orthodoxy as trivial and insubstantial. The process of defending or prosecuting a defendant does not require the viability of a distinction between actus reus and mens rea. Practitioners can agree that "the only concept known to the law is the crime. . . . Once it is decided that an element is an ingredient of an offence, there is no legal significance in the classification of it as part of the *actus reus* or the *mens rea*."[21] Yet it would be a mistake to conclude from this observation that the orthodox model of the criminal offense is unimportant to the theory of which it is a part. In fact, the assumption that mens rea and actus reus are distinct components of liability has a number of important uses in orthodox criminal theory.

In this Chapter I will critically examine a number of the various uses to which the orthodox model of the criminal offense has been put, and conclude that the absence in revised criminal theory of a distinct mental component of crime should not be lamented. This discussion is necessarily inconclusive, as there may be important uses of this model I do not consider.[22] Much speculation is involved; the significance of this model of the criminal offense may not be fully appreciated even by orthodox theorists themselves. It remains to be shown by orthodox theorists that revised criminal theory suffers from the absence of a distinct mental component of crime.

## LEGAL AND MORAL OBLIGATION

FEW PROPOSITIONS HAVE BEEN CITED more frequently by authorities than the claim that the criminal law is unconcerned with moral obligations per se. Sometimes it is baldly asserted that "mere moral wrongs are regarded by the criminal law as none of its business."[23] This proposition is puzzling. If the word "mere" is deleted, the proposition becomes patently false; it is obvious that all sorts of moral wrongs, such as theft and murder, are quite properly the "business" of the criminal law. Inclusion of the word "mere," however, does not do much to clarify matters. If "mere" is construed to mean "insignificant" or "trivial," then the proposition correctly asserts that a given threshold of immorality must be exceeded before it becomes appropriate to invoke the criminal law. But this interpretation accepts rather than rejects a connection between law and morality. Alternatively, if "mere" is synonymous with "harmless," the proposition suggests that some conduct may be immoral though harmless—a very controversial claim about moral theory. Finally, if "mere" means "moral offenses not recognized by the criminal law," the proposition becomes tautologous. Despite these puzzles, this proposition is repeated consistently in the writings of orthodox theorists as expressing an important insight. What could it mean?

Perhaps the key to an understanding of this proposition is to attend to its use. Frequently it is expressed by judges in opinions that reach a result perceived as contrary to justice.[24] It might be thought that apology and regret should accompany such decisions. Should we *ever* be content to allow the criminal law to reach a result conceded to be morally unjust? The claim that justice in law is something different from justice in morality has been accepted altogether too uncritically. Morally unjust results *should* be a cause of alarm and deep concern. What is most disturbing about this proposition is that it is often trumpeted as a sound policy reason for reaching unjust decisions, rather than as a source of embarrassment to be justified by special considerations. In this section I will critically examine one of many possible theoretical bases for the claim that "mere moral wrongs" are not the "business" of the criminal law.[25]

Sometimes it is alleged that morality and law, or moral and legal obligation, differ in their subject matters. This claim is vague and imprecise, and I will not make a systematic effort to render it more clear. But if some version of this doctrine were true, it would not be surprising if some moral wrongs were not illegal or, conversely, if some legal wrongs were not immoral. The nature of the obligations recognized by law would be different from those countenanced by morality. There would be a principled reason why criminal justice would differ from moral justice. But is it true? In what respect(s) is the subject matter of morality unlike that of law?

The most familiar answer to this question in legal history depends heavily upon the orthodox model of the criminal offense. Mens rea, as something different from actus reus, is used to differentiate moral from legal obligation.[26] One authority contends that "in failing to punish evil intent alone criminal justice parts from the moral law."[27] Another seeks to expound upon the "truth" in the "formula" that "law is concerned with external conduct, morality with internal conduct."[28] Yet another writes: "In the field of ethics, as in the teachings of the Church, guilt depends upon the state of mind alone."[29] Perhaps the clearest example of this use of the orthodox model is as follows:

> In requiring a physical act as a condition of liability the criminal law differs from the Divine law . . . It also differs from principles of ethics or moral philosophy, by which the mental element is sufficient to constitute guilt. Morality is internal. The moral law has to be expressed in the form, "Be this," and not in the form "Do this."[30]

Obviously, this attempt to differentiate between the subject matters of moral and legal obligation presupposes the adequacy of the orthodox model of the criminal offense. If the physical and mental ingredients of offenses cannot be separated—if there is no distinct mental component of crime—this basis for contrasting the subject matters of morality and law cannot be sustained.

The above quotations embody so many confusions that one hardly knows where to begin in addressing them. Most important, they grossly distort the nature of moral theory. These remarks represent a ludicrous oversimplification in light of the enormous complexity and difference of opinion in the long history of philosophical thought. The claim that moral theory is (necessarily?) concerned solely with the "internal" is simply mistaken. Both consequentialist and deontological traditions in ethics evaluate (inter alia) action. It is difficult to understand what function moral philosophy could be thought to serve unless it is construed as action-guiding.[31] The fact that a particular moral theory is unable to guide action is generally regarded by philosophers as a fatal flaw. A morality concerned exclusively with the "internal" could not be expected to perform this vital function. The legal theorists cited above, in short, have misrepresented the nature of moral theory in order to drive a conceptual wedge between the subject matters of morality and law.

It is true that moral philosophers have been anxious to evaluate dimensions largely neglected by the criminal law. Moral philosophers, interested in the appraisal of persons as well as behavior, have formulated theories of *agent morality* in addition to theories of *action morality*. Philosophers continue to debate the similarities and differences between the principles of agent and action morality,[32] but none would hold them to be identical. The evaluation of persons is clearly distinct from, although related to, the evaluation of action. Any plausibility the several above quotations from orthodox theorists might appear to possess derives from the mistaken supposition that morality is solely concerned with the evaluation of agents. It is not surprising to discover contrasts between the principles used by moral philosophers to evaluate persons, and those used by criminal theorists to evaluate action. But when the proper comparison is made—viz., between the principles both moral philosophers and criminal theorists use to evaluate *action*—these contrasts evaporate. An adequate theory of *agent* morality would attach different evaluations to person A, who believed that he was engaged in wrongdoing but in fact was not, and person B, who knew he was engaged in wrongdoing. But it would be mistaken to use this fact as evidence of an important theoretical distinction between the subject matters of moral and legal obligation. Principles of *action* morality would afford no more basis for distinguishing between the behavior of A and B in morality than in law. If the criminal law were used to evaluate persons—as sometimes may be appropriate—it too could be expected to recognize a distinction between A and B.[33] The unwillingness of criminal theorists to hold A liable follows from a simple application of the fundamental principle of legality. Presumably an adequate theory of action morality contains an analogous principle, and would not condemn behavior that is not an instance of "objective" wrongdoing.

What seemingly underlies these errors about the alleged theoretical difference between moral and legal obligation, then, is a misapprehension about the nature of moral theory. Why would orthodox criminal theorists mistakenly suppose that moral theory is concerned exclusively with the appraisal of persons? Perhaps this view is the product of a pervasive conflation of morality and religion. In defending the actus reus requirement in the context of criminal attempts, Justice Holmes writes that "the aim of the law is not to punish sins, but to punish certain external results."[34] When an orthodox theorist hears "morality," he thinks "religion"; when he hears "immorality" he thinks "sin."[35] Perhaps so-called "divine justice," as interpreted within the Judeo-Christian tradition, makes responsibility solely a function of mental state. But moral justice does not, and it is moral justice against which the criminal law must be measured. Here again, misplaced confidence among orthodox criminal theorists in their understanding of moral philosophy has contributed to unfortunate results.[36]

One cannot but wonder why orthodox theorists have been so eager to drive a wedge between the subject matters of moral and legal obligation in the first place. Rather than attempt to understand the "truth" in the "formula" that "law is concerned with external conduct, morality with internal conduct," it is disappointing that more authorities have not been anxious to avoid injustice by repudiating this pernicious doctrine and bridging the alleged conceptual gap between moral and legal obligation.

In fact, the doctrine that morality and law have different subject matters is extremely radical, with implications that surely are unacceptable to orthodox theorists who pause to consider them. If this doctrine were true, it would be impossible for *any* legal decision to be criticized from a moral perspective; *no* legal judgment could be morally unjust. Only authoritarians anxious to immunize their judgments from criticism would welcome this result. In short, there is no need to retain the orthodox model of the criminal offense in order to contrast the subject matters of moral and legal obligation, for such a contrast should not be tolerated. At bottom, the doctrine that justice in law is different from justice in morality is only a nice way of admitting that justice in law may not be justice at all.

Substitution of the actus reus requirement by the control principle removes one source of the temptation to embrace a theoretical distinction between the subject matters of morality and law. As indicated above, much of the appeal of the concept of actus reus is its apparent potential to serve as the foundation of a scientific, empirical, or objective theory of criminal liability. The inclusion of the control principle abandons this fanciful aspiration. If criminal theory were revised to include the control principle, it would be brought into closer harmony with moral theory, which traditionally has failed to impose blame for states of affairs over which persons lack control. Moral philosophies typically include some version of the doctrine that "ought implies can,"[37] which is the analogue of the control principle in criminal theory. It is highly desirable to place analogous principles at the hearts of moral and criminal theory. Of course, there may be good reasons not to convert each moral obligation into a legal duty. But the basis for resisting such a conversion requires a special justification, and should derive no support from the fundamental principles of criminal liability.

## CRIMINAL NEGLIGENCE

CRIMINAL LIABILITY FOR NEGLIGENCE has long been a subject of heated debate among orthodox theorists. Here conjectures about deterrence abound, as is to be expected in disputes about any controversial kind of liability. Does the imposition of criminal liability for negligence ever stimulate either the offender himself or prospective offenders to become more careful? Theorists provide radically different answers. Jerome Hall alleges that "there is no evidence that . . . punishment . . . will sensitize thoughtless individuals to the rights of other persons."[38] Williams disagrees: "it is possible for punishment to bring about greater foresight, by causing the subject to stop and think."[39] This controversy, I submit, is largely irrelevant. The central issue is whether persons who act negligently *deserve* criminal liability. Do persons have a (prima facie) moral right not to be held criminally liable for harm they did not foresee? Typically this question is approached by inquiring whether negligence is a form of mens rea. If it is not a form of mens rea, it would seem to follow that negligence should not be a basis for criminal liability, whatever the truth about its effectiveness as a deterrent. (I will soon indicate, however, why framing the issue of negligence in terms of mens rea is potentially misleading.)[40]

*Should* negligence be countenanced as a form of mens rea? Some theorists think not, and conclude that negligence should not give rise to criminal liability.[41] At the risk of oversimplification, the central argument in favor of this conclusion is as follows:

(1) Criminal liability without fault (mens rea) is unjust.
(2) Criminal liability for negligence is imposed according to "objective" standards, regardless of the state of mind of the defendant.
(3) Fault is a "subjective" state of mind (mens rea) of the defendant. Therefore,
(4) Criminal liability for negligence is unjust.

Needless to say, criminal liability for negligence is an established part of our criminal practice. Unless we follow Holmes and shrug off injustice,[42] the criminal theorist who accepts the legitimacy of liability for negligence must show the above argument to be unsound. Which premise is most vulnerable? This question cannot be addressed without examining whether and under what conditions criminal defendants may be held liable according to "objective" as opposed to "subjective" standards.

Premise (1) appears to be unexceptional. It is remarkable, then, that a number of orthodox theorists reject it. Why would anyone tolerate criminal liability without fault? I will return to this question later.

Premise (2) follows from statutory definitions of negligence as conduct that fails to conform to an "objective" standard of care. And "objective" standards, by definition, do "not depend upon a finding of what passed in the defendant's mind."[43]

The controversy, then, centers around premise (3). It is clear that this premise presupposes the adequacy of the orthodox model of the criminal offense. It presupposes that offenses may be subdivided into distinct physical and mental components, and that fault is a function of the latter. If the orthodox model is abandoned—if there is no distinct mental component of crime to serve as the locus of fault—premise (3) is false, and this objection to the legitimacy of criminal negligence fails. But if the orthodox model is retained, this argument becomes powerful.

Hence consistent champions of the orthodox model are uneasy about accepting criminal negligence. The difficulty is that they are also uneasy about rejecting it. This ambivalnce manifests itself in some strange results. Consider the concluding paragraph of Perkins's treatment of negligence and recklessness:

> So far the attempt to eliminate the concept of criminal guilt based upon objective fault has been rejected. But the time may come when we shall insist that any true crime requires a mind subjectively at fault,—that criminal guilt depends upon what is actually in the mind of the actor and not upon what *should* be in his mind. If that time comes . . . criminal negligence will be recognized as a non-criminal offense. As such, it would be appropriate to deal with it by the imposition of a fine, or some other penalty such as suspension or revocation of a driver license—but *not by imprisonment.*[44]

Perkins's predicament, as I understand it, is as follows. Although he relies heavily upon the orthodox model and thus cannot enthusiastically embrace criminal negligence, he cannot quite bring himself to abandon it. Thus he "compromises" by inventing a new, intermediate category of the "noncriminal offense" (or "quasi-crime"), punishable only by fine or revocation. But punishment is still punishment whether lenient or harsh, and objections to punishment without fault should persist regardless of its severity.[45] If we are to follow Perkins and impose only light punishments for criminal negligence—as seems just—we should do so because the fault in negligence is relatively minor, and not because negligence is not a "true crime."

Other orthodox theorists come to terms with the above argument against the criminalization of negligence somewhat differently. Unable to resist either liability for negligence or the orthodox model of the criminal offense, they conclude that premise (1) must be rejected. Some theorists reason that both criminal negligence and strict liability are instances of liability without fault, so that if the former is acceptable, then the latter is too.[46] It seems fair to speculate, then, that the orthodox model of the criminal offense has indirectly contributed to perhaps the greatest monstrosity tolerated within orthodox theory—criminal liability without fault.

There is no end to the ingenuity that has been expended in attempts to preserve the premise that fault is a state of mind. Michael Zimmerman insists that a person may not be held responsible for a consequence unless he actually, consciously foresaw it.[47] One might expect that he would disapprove of criminal liability for negligence, but his purpose is to show how this requirement of conscious foresight is compatible with such liability. This result is achieved by developing an account of "inadvertence cum advertence." Although a defendant did not consciously advert to a harm at the moment he performed his negligent conduct, he must have foreseen its possibility at an earlier time. If there were no such previous time, Zimmerman concludes that criminal liability for negligence would be unjust. This extraordinary account is motivated, no doubt, by the desire to preserve the premise that fault requires that defendants possess a given state of mind, in this case, the peculiar state of mind described by the phrase "inadvertence cum advertence."

Thus the grip of the orthodox model remains tight. Again, it becomes appropriate to ask: why would anyone believe that fault is an exclusive function of mental state? I have provided a partial answer to this question in the preceding sections, although two new considerations emerge in the context of criminal negligence. One source of confusion derives from an important ambiguity in the concept of mens rea itself. Smith and Hogan explain:

> Writers differ as to whether negligence can properly be described as
> *mens rea*. If that term is used simply as a compendious expression for
> the varieties of fault which may give rise to criminal liability, then it
> does of course include negligence. If it is taken in its more literal sense
> of "guilty mind," the usage is inappropriate.[48]

In other words, mens rea in the sense of *fault,* as in premise (1), should not be confused with mens rea in the sense of *guilty state of mind,* as in premise (3). To insist that persons could not be at fault *unless* they acted with a certain state of mind simply begs the question in favor of the orthodox model that identifies states of mind (as something distinct from behavior) as the exclusive locus of fault. This ambiguity in "mens rea" has lent false support to the orthodox model.

A second source of confusion derives from the use of "objective" standards of negligence. Here, as elsewhere, the supposed dichotomy between the "objective" and the "subjective" gives rise to headaches. If fault is a function of mental state, as the orthodox model requires, then only "subjective" standards should give rise to criminal liability. After all, the application of "objective" standards may result in punishment even though, in Williams's words, the defendant "was doing his level best."[49] It seems harsh to be told that one's best is not good enough. This difficulty, however, may be overcome by the further "subjectification" of "objective" standards[50] as proposed by Hart. Before liability for criminal negligence could be imposed, Hart would require that each of two questions be answered affirmatively: "(i) Did the accused fail to take those precautions which any reasonable man with normal capacities would in the circumstances have taken? (ii) Could the accused, given his mental and physical capacities, have taken those precautions?"[51] In other words, it is important to distinguish between two reasons why a person might fail to conform to an "objective" standard of care. First, he may have lacked the capacity to do so. Second, he may have failed to exercise his capacities to do so. Hart is persuasive in arguing that only the second of these reasons should give rise to criminal liability for negligence.[52] Thus criminal liability for negligence would not be imposed in opposition to the control principle. It does not follow, however, that criminal liability is imposed only for a state of mind.[53]

Moreover, Hart's approach brings criminal liability for negligence into closer conformity with liability for recklessness, which is much less controversial. American courts have construed recklessness to involve a *conscious* disregard of a risk.[54] In this decade, however, English courts have begun to impose criminal liability for recklessness on occasions in which the defendant was not actually conscious of a risk, although he *would* have been conscious of it had he stopped to think.[55] This result has been roundly criticized by authorities,[56] who have noticed that it blurs, almost beyond recognition, the distinction between recklessness and negligence.[57] This approach, although arguably an indefensible extension of liability for recklessness, is a more appropriate standard for negligence. Although a negligent defendant does not consciously advert to a risk, it is reasonable to require that he be capable of so doing; this condition is satisfied by requiring that he would have foreseen the risk had he stopped to think.[58] This requirement would implement Hart's sensible recommendation for the "subjectification" of criminal negligence.

Though the arguments against the legitimacy of criminal liability for negligence are unpersuasive,[59] it remains to be seen what can be said in its favor. The answer is simple. As Hart has noted:

> After all, a hundred times a day persons are blamed outside the law courts for not being more careful, for being inattentive and not stopping to think; in particular cases, their history or mental or physical examination may show that they could not have done what they omitted to do; but *if* anyone is *ever* responsible for *anything*, there is no general reason why men should not be responsible for such omissions to think, or to consider the situation and its dangers before acting.[60]

Many acts of negligence, in short, are blameworthy. In the absence of a persuasive argument against punishing harmful, blameworthy conduct, the case in favor of criminal liability for some acts of negligence is compelling.[61]

My tolerance of criminal negligence may seem at odds with positions I defend elsewhere, such as my largely "subjectivist" views about voluntary intoxication, mistake of fact, and mistake of law. Are these positions consistent with my "objectivist" sentiments about negligence? I believe it is necessary to incorporate both subjectivist and objectivist perspectives into revised criminal theory.[62] Criminal liability must not be imposed in the absence of fault, but this requirement does not entail a wholesale endorsement of subjectivism. Liability may be imposed despite the absence of a subjective mental state, as long as this is allowed by whatever general rationales support subjective standards. The control principle provides one such rationale. Subjectivism is attractive largely insofar as it precludes liability in the absence of control.[63] But conformity with the control principle does not always yield results congenial to the subjectivist, as the example of negligence illustrates. Negligence is punishable as long as the defendant fails to exercise the control he possesses, despite the fact that it requires no state of mind.

## WHEN IS LIABILITY "STRICT"?

PERHAPS NO TREND[64] in the criminal law has attracted as much attention from legal philosophers as strict liability. Almost all authorities express grave reservations about the justifiability of such offenses,[65] although a handful have welcomed them as the product of an enlightened, scientific jurisprudence.[66] It is obvious that meaningful debate about the propriety of strict liability presupposes that the concept itself is clearly understood. The orthodox model of the criminal offense is widely believed to be necessary for this purpose. Strict liability offenses are generally defined as those for which "no mens rea is required . . . the 'act' *(actus reus)* alone being sufficient."[67] Needless to say, if actus reus cannot be distinguished from mens rea, such definitions are nonsensical (or at least impossible to apply).

Reliance upon the orthodox model of the criminal offense in defining strict liability is indicated by the ease with which theorists equate conviction without mens rea to conviction without fault. Many commentators characterize strict liability as "criminal liability for conduct unaccompanied by fault, that is, without a requirement that the actor have any particular mental state."[68] Most of the criticisms of strict liability are sensible only if mens rea is identified with fault. If the orthodox model is abandoned, these criticisms will have to be reformulated, for revised criminal theory cannot accept the above definition of strict liability. If it is impossible to effectively separate actus reus from mens rea, how can the concept of an offense that (allegedly) requires only proof of actus reus be understood? How can it be determined whether liability is strict without presupposing the orthodox model of the criminal offense?

Before these difficult questions can be answered, it is important to address an ambiguity in orthodox definitions of strict liability. For two distinct reasons, proof of mens rea may not be required. First, mens rea might be totally irrelevant to conviction; its presence or absence may not be material to liability in any way. I will call this the "substantive" interpretation of strict liability. Second, proof of the presence of mens rea may not be required *by the prosecution,* although proof of the absence of mens rea adduced *by the defendant* might nonetheless preclude liability. According to this second, "procedural" interpretation, an offense is an instance of strict liability if the burden of proof concerning mens rea is placed upon the accused. Such offenses involve what might be called a "presumption of mens rea" that can be rebutted by the defendant in order to escape liability.[69] This procedural device relieves prosecutors of the formidable burden of proving mens rea, though ultimately it remains material to liability. Many offenses thought to create strict liability in the former sense have been construed by courts to impose it only in the latter. Perkins claims: "In fact, it is no longer proper to say that offenses *mala prohibita* are enforced on the basis of liability without fault. They are enforced on the basis that fault is presumed unless the defendant introduces evidence to establish clearly that there was no fault."[70] The use of such presumptions raises a distinct (though related) set of issues from those with which critics of strict liability are typically concerned. Arguably, these procedural devices are unconstitutional, and compromise the fundamental principle of criminal liability that requires that defendants be proved guilty beyond a reasonable doubt.[71] But the more impressive objections against strict liability are not directed at improper allocations of the burden of proof. They are concerned with the justifiability of making mens rea totally irrelevant to criminal liability. In what follows I will focus upon the propriety of "substantive" strict liability.

It is noteworthy that the arguments about the justifiability of strict liability follow familiar patterns previously discerned in the controversy surrounding criminal negligence. There are various schools of thought about the effectiveness of strict liability in inducing persons to adopt extraordinary precautions against the occurrence of harm.[72] These exchanges avoid the central issue of desert. Some authorities allege that the absence of fault is unimportant because strict liability offenses do not constitute "true crimes," but instead are called "violations," "quasi-crimes," "civil offenses," "public welfare offenses," or "regulatory offenses."[73] This "solution" is a terminological evasion.[74] Other theorists cannot bring themselves to admit that, in the real world, conviction for strict liability offenses dispenses with actual fault. Faith is entrusted in the good sense of prosecutors to charge only those defendants who in fact acted with mens rea.[75] But this argument "amounts not to any defense of strict liability, but rests instead on the assumption that a wise administration of these statutes avoids their admitted evil."[76] Discretion is not a reliable substitute for getting the rules right in the first place.[77] A few commentators have allowed their reservations about liability without fault to be mollified by recommendations that punishments be lenient,[78] but most recognize this response as an apology, rather than as a justification, for dispensing with fault.[79] In any event, the actual practice of criminal courts undermines these flimsy rationales. Judges have imposed liability on persons whose conduct could not be construed as blameworthy by any stretch of the imagination,[80] and some judges have imposed severe punishments for strict liability offenses.[81] Finally, other theorists concede the injustice of strict liability, but retort that "the unfairness is morally tolerable" as long as it is confined to "selected areas of conduct where such a standard of liability [serves] social utility."[82] This defense fails to explain why criminal punishments are appropriate to attain these goals. In this context, Williams voices a recurrent theme of this book: "The whole problem . . . arises from using the criminal process for a purpose for which it is not suited."[83]

To return to the central question, is revised criminal theory impoverished by its rejection of the orthodox model, since it has no way to characterize the nature of strict liability? Not at all. In fact, the orthodox model is unnecessary to understand the concept of strict liability, and actually contributes to confusion about it. The best indication that the definition of strict liability within orthodox theory is unhelpful is that it has never been satisfied by any actual offense. It is unlikely that *any* instance of criminal liability has dispensed with mens rea altogether.[84] Perhaps the term *absolute* liability should be coined to describe those purely hypothetical offenses that do not require mens rea at all. The fact that strict liability falls short of absolute liability must prove embarrassing to orthodox theorists. Authorities who decry the "trend" toward strict liability would be less vehement if they were convinced that no such offenses exist according to their own definition. Revised criminal theory cannot be condemned as deficient because it fails to include an unsatisfactory definition.

How, then, *should* strict liability be understood? A clearer picture emerges from a careful examination of actual cases said by orthodox theorists to represent examples of strict liability. These cases differ from others in which liability is alleged not to be strict because a given defense is not accepted as valid.[85] Thus offenses can be said to impose strict liability when one or more defenses, usually recognized as valid, do not preclude conviction. This usage comports with what a number of criminal theorists have said about strict liability in their more reflective moments.[86] It is noteworthy that applications of this definition do not require the viability of a distinction between actus reus and mens rea, and thus do not presuppose the accuracy of the orthodox model of the criminal offense. The only distinction presupposed by this definition is that between the elements of offense and the absence of defenses. Admittedly, this distinction is problematic,[87] though less so than that between actus reus and mens rea. In any event, both orthodox and revised criminal theories require the viability of the former distinction, and it is no small advantage of revised theory that it does not also require the latter.

This improved understanding of strict liability has benefits. The orthodox definition of strict liability as requiring only actus reus and not mens rea renders incoherent the suggestion that one offense could be more or less strict than another.[88] This revised account of strict liability makes possible the development of a rich taxonomy of offenses depending upon their "degree of strictness." The theorist might grade offenses along a "continuum of strictness," depending upon whether a greater or lesser number of defenses are recognized as valid.[89] The end point of this continuum would be the mythical (and monstrous) category of "absolute" liability.

Placement of a given offense along this continuum would invite comparisons and contrasts with other offenses, and would focus attention on the central issue: Should a given defense be recognized as valid? Often this question is extremely difficult; no theoretical analysis will render it easy. But the task should not be needlessly complicated. Use of the baffling distinction between actus reus and mens rea only confounds this crucial question. This can be seen by returning to a loose thread from chapter 4. Recall that some criminal theorists favor treating involuntariness as incompatible with actus reus in order to preclude conviction for offenses of strict liability.[90] If strict liability is defined so that the absence of mens rea is irrelevant, the orthodox theorist who favors a defense of involuntariness for such offenses has no option but to regard voluntariness as entailed by actus reus. This result, however, has the considerable disadvantage of blurring the distinction between the inner (mental) and the outer (physical) components of crime. Thus it met with resistance from a number of orthodox theorists, even the best of whom doubted that involuntariness should be recognized as a valid defense for offenses of strict liability.[91] The headaches caused by this controversy can be cured by revised criminal theory. The issue of whether involuntariness should be recognized as a valid defense to a given offense should be addressed squarely on its own merits. No progress toward resolution of this (not so difficult) issue is achieved by the tortured analysis pursued above.

Moreover, the use of such a continuum would facilitate the drawing of connections between issues that seldom are seen to be related. For example, the reluctance of orthodox theorists to recognize ignorance of law as a valid defense can be seen to make liability more strict.[92] For the most part, orthodox theorists have not conceptualized the invalidity of the defense of ignorance of law as a kind of strict liability.[93] In fact, many of the general arguments about the pros and cons of strict liability are applicable to debates about the propriety of recognizing ignorance of law as a defense.

Frank recognition that strict liability admits of degrees should help to end the fruitless debates about whether or not strict liability per se is justifiable. This question is not especially meaningful in the general way it is typically raised. The issue cannot be addressed profitably unless it is specified *which* offenses and *which* defenses are involved. A given defense may be valid for one offense but not for another; these fine distinctions are unlikely to be drawn as long as the legitimacy of strict liability per se is thought to be a sensible inquiry.

How *should* it be decided whether or not to recognize a defense as valid for a given offense? It is impossible to answer this question in its full generality, but one factor—control—stands out as especially significant. Consider the issue faced in the leading case of *U.S. v. Park:*[94] Should unawareness of wrongdoing constitute a defense to the charge of selling adulterated food as brought against a corporate officer? The Court held that it should not. Crucial to its decision was the fact that the defendant had the power "to prevent . . . the violation."[95] It is not surprising that the dissent stressed the alleged injustice of imposing liability in the absence of mens rea, and thus of fault. But if it is reasonable to blame those who fail to exercise control over a harmful state of affairs, there is no obvious reason why liability should be precluded by the alleged absence of mens rea. In other words, the defendant *is* at fault if he failed to exercise the control he possessed that is fair to demand of him; his absence of mens rea as conceptualized within orthodox theory is not a good reason for acquittal. A finding that defendants lacked the requisite degree of control probably provides the rationale in the majority of cases in which convictions for violations of strict liability offenses have been overturned.[96] The opinion in *Park* explicitly allowed the accused to defend on the ground that he was "'powerless' to prevent or commit the violation."[97] Liability without control is both pointless and unjust.[98] Again, judgments about the propriety of punishment even for so-called strict liability offenses coincide more closely with the presence of control than with the existence of either actus reus or mens rea.

### BIFURCATED TRIALS AND THE INSANITY DEFENSE

THE INADEQUACIES OF THE ORTHODOX MODEL of the criminal offense have become painfully evident to most well-intentioned theorists who have attempted to simplify and improve upon the cumbersome procedures for adjudicating the insanity defense. One of many concerns is to limit the role and influence of psychiatric testimony. To minimize jury confusion brought about by a bewildering conflict of expert opinion, a number of theorists have argued that the insanity defense should be bifurcated into two distinct stages, with psychiatric testimony admissible only in the second.[99] A number of jurisdictions have implemented various forms of this basic scheme.

Have these efforts proved successful? Reviews are mixed. The primary difficulty is to decide precisely *which* issues are to be litigated in each stage. Two alternatives are available, and neither is unproblematic. The California bifurcation experience, pioneered in 1927, illustrates the first option. In *People v. Wells,*[100] the California Supreme Court held that the first stage of the bifurcated trial is designed to establish guilt or innocence, the second to determine the psychological state of the defendant at the time of the offense. This interpretation, unfortunately, undermined much of the simplicity the proposal had sought to achieve. Guilt, the court noted, includes mens rea. Thus evidence of the presence or absence of mens rea is material at the first stage of the trial. Psychiatric testimony may be relevant to the question of whether the defendant lacked mens rea. Thus the bifurcated procedure is redundant; frequently mens rea is litigated twice. A system designed to streamline adjudication achieves exactly the opposite effect. One commentator observes:

> The separate trial procedure, as it stands today, results in duplication. The proof admissible to show defendant's mental state at the time of the crime is substantially the same as that admissible to show insanity. No workable rule has been formulated, and probably none can be fomulated, that would effectively differentiate between the two types of evidence.[101]

This unfortunate result has not persuaded all authorities to abandon hopes that litigation of the insanity defense should be bifurcated. It is widely held that the California experience failed because of a misunderstanding about the issues that should be litigated at each stage. As long as the first stage determined guilt or innocence, it is difficult or impossible to bar psychiatric testimony. Alternatively, it was proposed that the first stage should assess whether the actus reus of the offense had been committed, with psychiatric input and the determination of mens rea postponed to the later inquiry.[102] It seems likely that this division corresponds to the original intent of the California legislature. Some authorities confidently predicted that this approach would finally improve upon the litigation of criminal insanity.

It is obvious that the viability of this proposal depends upon the ability to effectively distinguish actus reus from mens rea. If the orthodox model of the criminal offense is deficient, confusion in implementing this strategy for bifurcating the insanity defense is inevitable. Not surprisingly, problems were encountered almost immediately.

This proposal was adopted in Wyoming. A statute provided that the first stage of the bifurcated proceedings should determine "whether the defendant in fact committed the acts charged in the alleged criminal offense," while the second should consider "the remaining elements of the alleged criminal offense and . . . the issue of the mental responsibility of the defendant."[103] The drawbacks of this plan became evident in *Sanchez v. State*,[104] as the court struggled to identify the actus reus of rape and attempted rape. The trial court had concluded in the first stage of the bifurcated proceedings that the defendant had "unlawfully touched" the victim "in an attempt to have sexual intercourse with her." Psychiatric testimony was held inadmissible at this stage because it was not material to the actus reus of these offenses.

The difficulties in identifying the above as the actus reus of rape or attempted rape should be familiar. First, as I discussed earlier, physical behavior cannot be understood to constitue an *attempt* without reference to intention. If psychiatric testimony established the inability of the defendant to entertain the requisite intention, it would suffice to demonstrate that he could not have attempted to rape. Second, "touching" the victim can be deemed "unlawful" only in the absence of consent. Therefore, it was implicit in the finding of the trial court that the defendant did not believe the victim to have consented. Again, psychiatric testimony might be material to whether the defendant held such a belief. Thus the court concluded that the Wyoming bifurcation statute was unconstitutional in excluding relevant evidence at the first stage.

The above problems are not peculiar to the particular offenses involved in *Sanchez*. Difficulties in effectively distinguishing the two components of the orthodox model are apparent in those jurisdictions that construe involuntariness as negating actus reus rather than mens rea. In *People v. Grant*,[105] the defendant was convicted of aggravated battery despite evidence of epilepsy and grand mal seizures indicating that he was unaware of what he was doing at the time of the alleged offense. If this evidence is construed as undermining his actus reus, it cannot be held inadmissible at the first stage of the bifurcated proceedings, and once again the door is open to psychiatric experts.

Despite these difficulties, a number of commentators continue to hope that the advantages of bifurcated procedures to adjudicate the defense of insanity outweigh its disadvantages.[106] Regardless of whether this plan has merit, it seems clear that procedures for litigating the insanity defense are in need of improvement, and this strategy should not be dismissed in the absence of preferable alternatives. Nonetheless, the implementation of various proposals to bifurcate the insanity defense will continue to encounter serious obstacles unless the orthodox model of the criminal offense can be salvaged.

### THE IRRELEVANCE OF MOTIVE

ONE OF THE MOST IMPORTANT CONSEQUENCES of the use of the orthodox model of the criminal offense is that factors *not* subsumed under actus reus or mens rea are deemed irrelevant to liability. The orthodox model is important to criminal theory not only because of what it includes, but also because of what it excludes. A number of mental states almost certainly affect the blameworthiness of conduct but are not thought to be part of mens rea, and are held by orthodox theorists to be immaterial to criminal liability. Foremost among these is *motive*. The suggestion that motive might be relevant to culpability though it cannot be subsumed under mens rea is heresy to orthodox opinion. According to Hall, "hardly any part of penal law is more definitely settled than that motive is irrelevant."[107] Many authorities add that motives "are important for discretionary decisions about prosecution and punishment."[108] In other words, although a good motive might mitigate punishment (or encourage prosecution), and a bad motive might aggravate punishment (or discourage prosecution), it is a truism within orthodoxy that motive has no bearing on liability itself.

It is unfortunate that orthodox criminal theorists do not scrutinize this issue more critically. The exceptional significance attached by the criminal law to intention stands in stark contrast to its almost complete disregard of motive. Nothing written by moral philosophers supports the unimportance of motive. It is doubtful that this feature of criminal theory is reproduced in other institutions in which rules are enforced, judgments rendered, and sanctions imposed. Schools, places of employment, and families all regard motive as crucial. Why should the criminal law do otherwise? Here we have a moral distinction, with no corresponding difference in liability. Frequently the failure of the criminal law to attach significance to a factor relevant to the blameworthiness of conduct provokes outrage from theorists. But few tirades are expressed about the immateriality of motive. The doctrine that motive is irrelevant has contributed to a number of unjust decisions that should be denounced in the strongest possible language. Perhaps a convincing case against the significance of motive to liability could be constructed; it is disappointing that this matter is taken for granted and seldom addressed.

In fact, what little is said by orthodox theorists about the nature and irrelevance of motive is ample testimony to further confusion about the mental component of crime. The following discussion illustrates a recurrent theme of this book: criminal theorists, uncritically attempting to make sense of a principle, frequently "defend" it by construing it as true by definition. What initially is put foward as an important substantive claim is interpreted as an uninformative tautology.

It might be thought that a clear distinction between intention and motive can be drawn, given the radical difference in treatment that follows from categorizing a mental state as one or the other. In fact, however, the distinction has long bedeviled law students and criminal theorists alike. Many theorists observe that since "definitions are less than completely satisfying, it is typical to clarify the difference with an illustration."[109] One colorful example is provided by Gross: "If a rich man has an ugly daughter, he is concerned about her suitor's motives. But a poor man with a beautiful daughter is concerned about her suitor's intentions."[110]

Of course, the problem with "definition by illustration" is the inability to generalize from the example. Williams and Gross have given this issue the most extensive treatment among contemporary orthodox theorists, but their accounts differ markedly. According to Williams, motives are one species of the genus intention. He writes: "motive is ulterior intention—the intention with which an intentional act is done. Intention, when distinguished from motive, relates to the means, motive to the end."[111] This use of the means/ends distinction is problematical, for the end of one action may be the means toward another. Williams is aware of this complication: "Much of what men do involves a chain of intention (D pulls the trigger of his revolver in order to make the bullet enter P's body in order to kill P in order to get him out of the way, etc.), and each intention is a motive for that preceding it."[112] Since "each intention is a motive for that preceding it," the only intention that is *not* (also) a motive is that currently entertained by the defendant: "It is only the immediate physical act that can never be called a motive."[113] The difficulty with this account is that it relativizes the distinction between intention and motive to moments of time. An intention ceases to remain a motive as soon as it becomes immediate. When actions are examined retrospectively, as in criminal trials, there may be *no* intentions that are not also motives. It is difficult to understand how the criminal law could attach such extraordinary significance to the distinction between intention and motive as so construed.

Thus it is not surprising that other orthodox theorists endeavor to provide an account of motives that differentiates them from intentions altogether.[114] According to Gross, motive and intention are logically distinct types:

> Motives differ from intentions with respect to both duration and function. Though some motives are more ulterior than others, any motive for doing something relates to the ulterior thing to be achieved or satisfied through the act. It is thus more abiding than an intention, whose life must end with the act that fulfills it. With respect to function, motives differ from intentions in that motives are the source of *power* for the act, while intentions supply the *direction* . . . [A] motive can be distinguished from an intention by the fact that the intention but not the motive has a beginning and an end . . . [A] motive can be distinguished from an intention as an explanation of an act and not a description of it.[115]

One difficulty (among many) with this account is that it does not make sense of Gross's own example. Why does the (alleged) intention of the suitor to marry the beautiful (but poor) daughter have a "beginning and an end," while the (alleged) motive of the suitor to marry the rich (but ugly) daughter have no beginning or end? Does the intention of the former suitor *describe* his act; does the motive of the latter suitor *explain* it? Perhaps a clear account of the distinction between intention and motive can be stipulated, but it is not to be found in the writings of orthodox criminal theorists.[116]

It is unlikely, moreover, that this distinction, once drawn, would support the doctrine that theorists have prepared for it. On even the most superficial understanding of the nature of motives, the alleged truism that they are irrelevant to criminal liability, when interpreted descriptively, must be qualified for at least two reasons. First, the validity of any number of defenses to criminal liability is inexplicable unless motive is held to be material. Consider the defenses of duress or necessity. Both preclude criminal liability if the defendant acted with a specified purpose. A necessary condition of the defense of duress is that the defendant must have committed the illegal act *in order to* avoid an unlawful threat of harm from another person. A defendant may not use an unlawful threat as an opportunity to escape liability for a crime he would have committed in the absence of that threat; the defense should be available only if he acted *because* of the threat.[117] Thus *why* the defendant committed the crime is crucial. The same is true of necessity, and probably of self-defense.[118]

Second, many offenses explicitly prohibit an act only when done with a specified purpose. The most obvious example is burglary, defined at common law as "breaking and entering . . . with the intent to commit a felony therein."[119] The reason *why* the defendant breaks and enters is crucial in characterizing his conduct as a burglary. Forgery, kidnapping, criminal libel, and conspiracy provide other examples, and the list could be expanded at great length.

Of course, one might insist that motive is irrelevant to the crime of burglary by denying that the purpose to "commit a felony therein" is a motive.[120] The statute itself describes this purpose as an intention. This controversy cannot be resolved in the absence of a clear distinction between intention and motive. But it is certainly question-begging and unhelpful to designate this purpose as an intention simply *because* it is relevant to criminal liability.[121]

Thus motive may be relevant to the issues of whether the defendant has committed an offense or possesses a valid defense. Hence motive is material to criminal liability after all. When is this so? Perhaps the safest *descriptive* generalization is that motive is relevant when the law says as much, and irrelevant otherwise. According to this view, the claim that motive is immaterial is a simple corrolary of the fundamental principle of legality: no factor is relevant to criminal liability except as is provided by law. Of course, the same could be said of actus reus, mens rea, or causation. LaFave and Scott express this conclusion well:

> The notion that motives are irrelevant in the substantive law requires that the word "motive" be defined as those purposes, ends, and objectives which are deemed irrelevant, which brings one full circle. One might well take the position that it would be better to abandon the difficult task of trying to distinguish intent from motive and merely acknowledge that the substantive criminal law takes account of some desired ends but not others.[122]

Thus the claim that motive is irrelevant to criminal liability (like the claim "the best team always wins") is either false or tautologous.[123] This result cannot provide the principled defense of the irrelevance of motive that the philosopher of criminal law seeks.

Can anything be said in favor of the *prescriptive* thesis that motives *should* be largely immaterial to criminal liability? Perhaps this doctrine has been an accepted truism within orthodox theory for so long that authorities feel no pressing need to defend it.[124] It is sometimes alleged that motives are irrelevant because the criminal law judges actions rather than persons.[125] Hall writes: "when we ask questions about a person's motives, we are asking for data relevant to the evaluation of his character."[126] This argument, however, is flawed on a number of grounds. First, it fails to explain why the criminal law attaches such supreme importance to intentions. If intentions enter into the evaluation of actions (the alleged proper concern of the criminal law), there is no obvious reason why motives should not do so as well. Second, this rationale requires a sharper contrast between intentions and motives than has been drawn by orthodox theorists thus far. We cannot be confident that motives, unlike intentions, are part of the evaluation of persons without understanding this distinction with reasonable precision. Moreover, this supporting premise is in need of a defense. Why should the criminal law be totally unconcerned with the evaluation of persons?[127] Finally, if this argument were persuasive, special justificatory considerations would be required to support the several above qualifications to the rule against the relevance of motive. In fact, however, no outcry is expressed by orthodox theorists against the legitimacy of such offenses as burglary, kidnapping, etc. (which include motives in their definitions), or the validity of such defenses as duress, necessity, etc. (which also depend upon motives). The truism that motive is irrelevant to criminal liability fails to withstand critical scrutiny when interpreted either descriptively or prescriptively.

Nonetheless, this doctrine has had a pernicious impact upon the disposition of a number of cases, most notably those involving benevolent euthanasia. It is monstrous that a defendant should be convicted of the most serious offense known to the criminal law when he lovingly and regretfully complies with a request to kill his suffering and incurable spouse.[128] Only very powerful arguments could support such an injustice. Instead, however, such decisions are typically "justified" by the doctrine that motives are irrelevant to criminal liability. It is difficult to understand how a tautology could be expected to satisfy those who believe that such disappointing decisions require a special justification.

Of course, few defendants are actually convicted in the above circumstances. As Yale Kamisar writes in this context: "The Law In Action is as malleable as The Law On The Books is uncompromising."[129] Kamisar seems content to allow prosecutorial and judicial discretion to rectify injustice. I have expressed reservations about allowing the dispensation of justice to be entrusted to discretion.[130] Williams, to his credit, attempts to avoid injustice by improving the substantive law of homicide. He lists three possible "lines of argument [that] can be used to exempt [persons who commit beneficient euthanasia] from liability,"[131] but he is appropriately skeptical of each.[132] What is noteworthy is that the *need* to construct such rationales arises only from the lack of candor in admitting what is patently the case, viz., that a laudable motive should preclude liability.[133] Were this sentiment not shared, no one would strain to invent fantastic reasons to acquit persons who commit acts of benevolent euthanasia.

Perhaps it is too much to hope that some of these unfortunate results could be avoided by rethinking orthodox views about the mental component of crime. The requirement of mens rea as a fundamental principle of criminal liability, coupled with the tendency to equate it with intent, surely contributes to the unsatisfactory treatment of motive in orthodox theory. Abandonment of the orthodox model of the criminal offense might overcome a major theoretical obstacle to candor about the relevance of motive to criminal liability, and thus remove one source of injustice from the criminal law.

## NOTES

1. See Hyman Gross, *A Theory of Criminal Justice*, p. 89.
2. For a discussion of how a criminal theorist may be led to "great incoherence in the division of the ingredients of a crime between *mens rea* and

*actus reus*, see H. L. A. Hart, "Negligence, Mens Rea, and Criminal Responsibility," in his *Punishment and Responsibility*, pp. 136, 140.

3. A. C. E. Lynch, "The Mental Element in the Actus Reus," *Law Quarterly Review* 98 (1982): 109, 118. Lynch retains the concept of actus reus by including some mental elements within its scope. In my view, this device seriously undermines the viability of the distinction between actus reus and mens rea.

4. Glanville Williams, *Criminal Law: The General Part*, p. 642.

5. See the examples in Elizabeth Anscombe, *Intention*.

6. Does the verb "driving" imply intentionality? See *Hill v. Baxter*, 1 Q.B. 277 (1958).

7. J. C. Smith and Brian Hogan, *Criminal Law*, p. 30. See also Glanville Williams, *Textbook of Criminal Law*, p. 147, and *Textbook*, p. 642.

8. Difficulties in the philosophy of action are among the most vexing problems for criminal theorists. See Donald Davidson, "Actions, Reasons, and Causes," *Journal of Philosophy* 60 (1963): 685.

9. Lynch, "Mental Element," p. 127.

10. Ibid., p. 112.

11. Some of these perplexities are explored in Michael Zimmerman, *An Essay on Human Action*, pp. 108–9; and Alan White, *Grounds of Liability*, p. 35.

12. Smith and Hogan, *Criminal*, p. 41. Elsewhere (p. 40) these theorists describe a case in which a defendant is alleged to have "failed to bring about the *actus reus* of the crime."

13. Courtney Kenny, *Outlines of Criminal Law*, p. 17.

14. Rollin Perkins and Ronald Boyce, *Criminal Law*, p. 831.

15. Jerome Hall notwithstanding. See his allegations about the "plain man's morality" in *General Principles of Criminal Law*, pp. 133–34.

16. But see Stephen Schulhofer, "Harm and Punishment: A Critique of Emphasis on the Results of Conduct in the Criminal Law," 122 *University of Pennsylvania Law Review* 122 (1974): 1497.

17. See the problems discussed by Edmund Gettier, "Is Justified True Belief Knowledge?" *Analysis* 23 (1963): 121.

18. Hart, "Negligence," p. 145.

19. Gross, *Theory*, pp. 87–88.

20. See George Fletcher's reasons for not subsuming all categories of excuse under a single rationale of compulsion in "Criminal Theory as an International Discipline: Reflections on the Freiburg Workshop," *Criminal Justice Ethics* 4 (1985): 60.

21. Smith and Hogan, *Criminal*, p. 30.

22. See Lynch, "Mental Element," p. 112, for an argument that the orthodox model is necessary in order to "define when a crime has terminated."

23. This proposition is repeated too frequently to merit citation. See Gross, *Theory*, p. 16.

24. See, e.g., *People v. Beardsley*, 113 N.W. 1128 (1907). For a civil case, see *Buch v. Amory Mfg.Co.*, 44 Atl. 809 (1897).

25. Many other bases are available, and are examined in chapter 8.

26. Jerome Hall cryptically remarks that "the restriction of 'act' to overt movemement was probably first suggested by a doctrine of political ideology—that distinguished law from morals." *General*, p. 176.

27. William Clark and William Marshall, *A Treatise on the Law of Crimes*, p. 161.

28.  Herbert Morris, "Punishment for Thoughts," in Robert Summers, ed., *Essays in Legal Philosophy*, p. 96.

29.  Perkins and Boyce, *Criminal*, p. 830.

30.  W. Hitchler, "The Physical Element of Crime," *Dickenson Law Review* 39 (1934): 96.

31.  "The function of moral principles is to guide conduct. . . . And this is what makes ethics worth studying." R. M. Hare, *The Language of Morals*, p. 1.

32.  See, e.g., A. N. Prior, "The Virtue of the Act and the Virtue of the Agent," *Philosophy* 26 (1951): 121.

33.  George Fletcher observes that we do not hold persons criminally liable when they believe, incorrectly, that their conduct constitutes an offense because the criminal law judges conduct, not persons. See his *Rethinking Criminal Law*, p. 559.

34.  *Commonwealth v. Kennedy*, 48 N.E. 770, 772 (1897).

35.  This conflation pervades the work of Patrick Devlin, *The Enforcement of Morals*. See also chapter 8.

36.  "It is a mark of the unhappy separation of legal and moral theory that legal theorists accept a definition of morality that is, for a moral theorist . . . transparently inadequate." David Richards, *Sex, Drugs, Death, and the Law*, p. 85.

37.  See William Frankena, "Obligation and Ability" in Max Black, ed., *Philosophical Analysis*, p. 157.

38.  Hall, *General*, pp. 138–39. See also Gross, who suggests that the alleged advantages of negligence as a deterrent are "untrue to the facts." *Theory*, p. 351.

39.  Williams, *Criminal*, p. 123. See also Hart, who supports the "common sense belief that in some cases we may make people more careful by blaming or punishing them for carelessness." "Intention and Punishment" in Punishment, pp. 113, 133.

40.  "For the substantial issue is not whether negligence should be called *'mens rea'*; the issue is whether it is true that to admit negligence as a basis of criminal responsibility is eo ipso to eliminate from the conditions of criminal responsibility the subjective element which, according to modern conceptions of justice, the law should require." Hart, "Negligence," p. 140. See also note 48.

41.  "The thesis that inadvertent damage reflects a moral fault is difficult to accept." Hall, *General*, p. 136. See also Gross, *Theory*, p. 421: "Negligent conduct is not itself wrong." See also Norval Morris, *Madness and the Criminal Law*, p. 70: "Clearly one cannot lapse into moral fault by failure to recognize the existence of a risk of injury to another or to property; the argument in these cases is opportunistic not moral." Williams is of two minds. *Textbook*, p. 91.

42.  Oliver W. Holmes, *The Common Law*.

43.  Williams, *Textbook*, p. 88.

44.  Perkins and Boyce, *Criminal*, p. 851.

45.  See Francis Jacobs, *Criminal Responsibility*, p. 105.

46.  Hart attributes this view to Turner in "Negligence."

47.  Michael Zimmerman, "Negligence and Moral Responsibility," *Nous* (forthcoming).

48.  Smith and Hogan, *Criminal*, p. 82.

49. Williams, *Textbook*, p. 90.

50. See chapter 3.

51. Hart, "Negligence," p. 154.

52. Ibid., p. 154. Hart's views probably are subject to a qualification in cases of self-induced incapacities. See also Fletcher, *Rethinking*, p. 512: "There is nothing in the nature of law that precludes a two-tiered process of legal analysis. The question of wrongdoing is governed by 'standards of general application.' The question of attribution might properly be analyzed with a full consideration of individual differences and capacities." But see his remarks on p. 514.

53. "[T]o have a standard set by the capacities of the average man does not entail that the capacity of the individual to conform to the standard must be tested by the average man's capacities." Jacobs, *Criminal*, p. 134.

54. But see the exception in cases of voluntary intoxication discussed in chapter 3.

55. *R. v. Caldwell*, 1 All E.R. 961 (1981).

56. It is criticized by Smith and Hogan, *Criminal*, pp. 52–57; and by Williams, *Textbook,* pp. 106–9. See also John Smith, "Subjective or Objective? Ups and Downs of the Test of Criminal Liability in England," *Villanova Law Review* 27 (1981–82): 1179.

57. "The number of instances of gross negligence which do not amount to Caldwell recklessness will be very small." Smith and Hogan, *Criminal*, p. 57. See also Williams, *Textbook*, p. 108.

58. Smith, in "Subjective," writes: "The very fact that we have to assume that the defendant had thought about the matter removes any significant distinction between him and the reasonable man. Where we all sometimes differ from the reasonable man is in failing to consider whether there is a risk. Such failure may be attributed to a number of internal states, such as fatigue, excitement, anger, anxiety, or absent-mindedness. The hypothesis that the defendant had thought about it removes any distinction, unless he is an abnormal person" (p. 1201).

59. I do not pretend to have responded to all the arguments against the criminalization of negligence. Hall lists six distinct arguments in *General*, pp. 138–39. See the "deterministic" reservations expressed by Williams, *Criminal*, p. 122. See also the *concern* (though the authors do not construe it as an objection) that "negligence is . . . faulty . . . as a character defect." Jeffrie Murphy and Jules Coleman, *The Philosophy of Law*, p. 160, note 27.

60. Hart, "Negligence," pp. 150–51. See also note 41.

61. Some authorities, who do not take seriously the possibility that all acts of negligence are blameless, maintain that "the fighting issue" about criminal negligence is "whether the 'quantum of blame or punishment' for thoughtlessness or carelessness is sufficient to justify use of the criminal sanction." Peter Low, John Jeffries, and Richard Bonnie, *Criminal Law*, p. 224.

62. "Both objective and subjective standards may have their own respective proper roles to play in determining culpability." Celia Wells, "Swatting the Subjectivist Bug," *Criminal Law Review* (1982): 209, 211. For doubts about whether a "wholly subjectivist test for blame is practically comprehensible," see Kent Greenawalt, "The Perplexing Borders of Justification and Excuse," *Columbia Law Review* 84 (1984): 1897, 1917.

63. "The underlying rationale of subjectivism appears to be that it

allows punishment only where a person has exercised some choice and that it prevents the natural converse, the punishment of those who had no choice." Wells, "Swatting," p. 212.

64. One and the same authority is inconsistent in commenting upon whether strict liability, unknown to common law, continues to represent a growing trend. In *Criminal*, p. 906, Perkins and Boyce write: "Today the trend seems to be in the direction of requiring conviction to be supported by at least objective fault." Also, at p. 910: "The resurgence of strict liability has passed its peak." But elsewhere Perkins contends: "Recent criminal cases reveal an increasing reliance on notions of strict liability and its concomitant punishment without fault." "Criminal Liability Without Fault: A Disquieting Trend," *Iowa Law Review* 68 (1983): 1067, 1068. Some authorities contend that strict liability has reached its "nadir." Smith and Hogan, *Criminal*, p. 99.

65. "[A]cademic opinion has been almost unanimously hostile to any degree of strict liability." Jacobs, *Criminal*, p. 111.

66. See Barbara Wootton, *Crime and the Criminal Law*. See also Richard Wasserstrom, "Strict Liability in the Criminal Law," *Stanford Law Review* 12 (1960): 731.

67. Perkins and Boyce, *Criminal*, p. 901. See also *In Re Marley*, 175 P.2d 832, 835 (1946): "The doing of the act constitutes [the] crime." See also Williams, *Textbook*, p. 142: "Here it is sufficient for the prosecution to prove the doing of the prohibited act."

68. Wayne LaFave and Austin Scott, *Criminal Law*, p. 218. See also Williams, *Textbook*, p. 74: "Offences not involving legal fault are those of strict liability." Francis Sayre writes that these offenses involve "no moral delinquincy" and proceed "without proof of any individual blameworthiness." See "Public Welfare Offenses," *Columbia Law Review* 37 (1933): 55, 70. See also Herbert Packer, *The Limits of the Criminal Sanction*, p. 13. See also Murphy and Coleman, *Philosophy*, p. 132.

69. English courts refer to a "presumption of mens rea" much more frequently than their American counterparts. See *Sherras v. De Rutzen*, 1 Q.B. 918, 921 (1895). But see *Sheppard*, 3 All E.R. 899 (1980).

70. Perkins, "Disquieting," p. 1079. See also Smith and Hogan, p. 105. Some authorities construe what I call "procedural strict liability" as "a method which falls midway" between "substantive strict liability" and "ordinary" liability. LaFave and Scott, *Criminal*, p. 221. See also the insightful discussion in Fletcher, *Rethinking*, pp. 717–19.

71. See *In Re Winship*, 397 U.S. 358 (1970), and *Mullany v. Wilbur*, 421 U.S. 197 (1977).

72. See the discussion and references in Hall, *General*, pp. 345–48. See also Williams, *Criminal*, p. 931.

73. See Perkins and Boyce, *Criminal*, p. 887; and *M.P.C.* §1.04(5).

74. "The difficulty with trying to establish a category of this kind is to say exactly what it means." Williams, *Textbook*, p. 936. See also Packer, *Limits*, p. 131.

75. Williams, *Textbook*, p. 928. He does not, however, endorse this rationale in favor of strict liability. His true sympathies are revealed in *Criminal*, p. 256: "The effect of the law is that the police or other enforcement authorities hold what amounts to an informal trial of what they conceive to be the accused's culpability." See also Low, Jeffries, and Bonnie, *Criminal*, p. 371, note c: "It appears that a judgment as to fault is highly relevant to the likelihood of prosecution."

76. Hall, *General*, p. 343.

77. See chapter 2.

78. "[T]he penalty in such cases is so slight that the courts can afford to disregard the individual in protecting the social interests." Sayre, "Public," p. 60.

79. Hall, *General*, p. 342. See also Williams, *Criminal*, p. 255: "It is not easy to see why the slightness of the penalty should justify an abandonment of the requirement of culpability."

80. The most celebrated case is *Larsonneur*, 24 Cr.App. Rep. 74 (1933), called by Hall "the acme of strict injustice" in *General*, p. 329. See also *Parker v. Alder*, 1 Q.B. 20 (1899), and the discussion in Williams, *Textbook*, p. 931.

81. "Certainly, the courts do not seem to have been deterred in recent years from imposing strict liability in the case of offences carrying heavy maximum sentences." Smith and Hogan, *Criminal*, p. 98. See *U.S. v. H.Wool & Sons, Inc.*, 215 F.2d 95 (1954).

82. Murphy and Coleman, *Philosophy*, p. 135. The authors contend (at p. 136) that this "complex" and "sophisticated" defense defeats the "knee-jerk liberal grumbling about the 'unfairness of it all.' "

83. Williams, *Criminal*, p. 264.

84. See Smith and Hogan, *Criminal*, pp. 100–101. See also Hart, "Acts of Will and Responsibility," in *Punishment*, p. 90. See also Perkins and Boyce, *Criminal*. p. 898: "Let us hasten to recognize frankly that we have no offenses enforced on the basis of absolute liability. No doubt minor traffic violations would be high on the list claiming such a position, but it is submitted that if gangsters, fleeing from the scene of their robbery, should 'commandeer' a car stopped for a red light and force the driver, under threat of death at pistol-point, to proceed without waiting for the signal to change and at a speed in excess of that permitted by law, this compulsion would be recognized as an excuse." See also Packer, *Limits*, p. 126.

85. Throughout this book I use the term "valid" to refer to defenses that succeed in precluding criminal liability. See chapter 7.

86. There is much disagreement among criminal theorists about *which* defenses are valid for offenses of strict liability. Williams writes: "Strict liability is sometimes called 'absolute liability,' but this, although accepted usage, is a misnomer, because all the usual defences are available except the defences of lack of intention, recklessness or negligence." *Textbook*, p. 142. Contrast Fletcher: "We define strict liability to mean liability imposed for an act or omission in violation of the law, without considering at trial whether the defendant may exculpate himself by proving a mistake or accident bearing on the wrongfulness of his violation." *Rethinking*, p. 716. Also contrast Smith and Hogan: *Criminal*, p. 100: "When the court holds that it is an offence of strict liability . . . it decides that a reasonable mistake . . . is not a defence. It does not decide that any other defence is unavailable . . . There is no reason why all other defences should not be available as they are in the case of offences requiring full *mens rea*."

87. See chapter 7.

88. Confusing locutions such as "partial absolute liability" have appeared in the literature. See Gerhard Muller, "On Common Law Mens Rea," *Minnesota Law Review* 42 (1955): 1043, 1068. The degrees of strictness in liability are noted in Wasserstrom, "Strict," p. 12.

89. Admittedly, the model suggested here is oversimplistic for at least two reasons. First, no single continuum could determine whether offense A is

more strict than B if defense x is valid for A but not for B, and y is valid for B but not for A. Second, liability might be more strict for some elements than for others. As Williams indicates, "an offense may carry strict liability in one respect but not in all." See *Textbook*, p. 927.

90. See chapter 4.

91. See Hart, "Negligence."

92. See chapter 3.

93. A notable exception to orthodoxy is Fletcher, *Rethinking*, p. 730.

94. 421 U.S. 658 (1975).

95. Ibid., p. 674

96. See *Lim Chin Aik*, 1 All E.R. 223, 228 (1963). See also the cases discussed in Perkins, "Disquieting."

97. 421 U.S. 658, 673 (1975). See also Wayne LaFave and Austin Scott, *Substantive Criminal Law*, p. 357.

98. See Jacobs, *Criminal*, pp. 113–14.

99. Bifurcation has been proposed for many reasons other than the desirability of restricting psychiatric testimony. Wootton favors it as a step toward purging criminal justice of its unenlightened retributivist legacy. See her *Crime*.

100. 202 P.2d 53 (1949).

101. David Louisell and Geoffrey Hazard, "Insanity as a Defense in the Bifurcated Trial," *California Law Review* 49 (1961): 805, 829–30.

102. Ibid.

103. Wyo.Stat. §7-242.5(a) (1957 & 1975 Cum.Supp.)

104. 567 P.2d 270 (1977).

105. 360 N.E.2d 804 (1977).

106. See Donald Hermann, "Assault on the Insanity Defense: Limitations on the Effectiveness and Effect of the Defense of Insanity," *Rutgers Law Journal* 14 (1983): 241, 291–310.

107. Hall, *General*, p. 88. He claims that "it is doubtful whether one is responsible for his motives" (p. 90).

108. Gross, *Theory*, p. 104. "Indeed, criminal justice is seriously impoverished if motives are disregarded as mitigating and as aggravating factors."

109. LaFave and Scott, *Criminal*, p. 204.

110. Gross, *Theory*, p. 111.

111. Williams, *Criminal*, p. 48.

112. Ibid., p. 48.

113. Ibid., p. 48, note 2.

114. Hall criticizes Salmond's treatment of motive as a kind of intention as "unfortunate." See *General*, p. 85.

115. Gross, *Theory*, pp. 107–8, 111.

116. There is some indication among orthodox criminal theorists that philosophical analyses of motive are not especially helpful. See Hall, *General*, p. 85, note 67. Recall also the comment by Fletcher, *Rethinking*, p. 438.

117. Causation generally is included in descriptions of the defense of coercion. See LaFave and Scott, *Criminal*, p. 374. See also *M.P.C.* §2.09(1).

118. See Fletcher, *Rethinking*, pp. 552–69. But see Paul Robinson: "A Theory of Justification: Societal Harm as a Prerequisite for Criminal Liability," *University of Southern California Law Review* 23 (1975): 266.

119. LaFave and Scott, *Substantive*, p. 708.

120. LaFave and Scott suggest: "Intent relates to the means and motive to the ends, but . . . where the end is the means to yet another end, then the

medial end may also be considered in terms of intent." *Substantive,* p. 320. Williams maintains that "whenever an intention to commit another crime is involved in the definition of a crime, it is generally referred to as intention and not as motive [because] it would be confusing to use the same word 'motive' both for the burglar's intention to commit larceny in the house and for his intention to use the proceeds of the larceny to provide for his paralytic daughter." *Criminal,* p. 49. Gross describes this use of "motive in the definition of the offense" as "a special use of the term intent." *Theory,* p. 112.

121. Smith and Hogan are sensitive to the fact that mental states are arbitrarily classified as intentions or motives depending upon whether or not they are relevant to criminal liability. See *Criminal,* p. 67.

122. LaFave and Scott, *Criminal,* p. 206.

123. Williams is aware of this result. In *Criminal,* p. 49, he writes: "It becomes tautologous to say that motive is irrelevant to legal responsibility. For as soon as the word 'motive' is uttered, it is impliedly asserted to be irrelevant to responsibility." See also Smith and Hogan, *Criminal,* p. 67: "Motive, by definition, is irrelevant to criminal responsibility."

124. Fletcher admits that bad motives "make a voluntary, intentional act arguably more culpable in some persons than in others," but defends their irrelevance, uncritically deeming them as "foreign to our experience of crime and punishment." *Rethinking,* p. 463.

125. In his discussion of the limited relevance of motives, Gross insists that "the blameworthiness of a person falls outside the concern of the criminal law." See *Theory,* p. 77.

126. Hall, *General,* p. 93.

127. See chapter 4.

128. One of many such cases is *People v. Roberts,* 178 N.W. 690 (1920).

129. Yale Kamisar, "Some Nonreligious Views Against Proposed 'Mercy-Killing' Legislation," *Minnesota Law Review* 42 (1958): 969.

130. See chapter 3. Williams, responding to Kamisar's confidence in discretion, writes: "It is hard to understand on what moral principle this type of ethical ambivalence is to be maintained." " 'Mercy-Killing' Legislation—A Rejoinder," *Minnesota Law Review* 42 (1958): 1043.

131. Williams, *Textbook,* p. 280.

132. One of the rationales depends upon the contrast between positive acts and omissions. See chapter 6.

133. Fletcher is reluctant to allow motives to become relevant in this context because such a policy "would legitimate cases of overtly terminating the lives of persons who either desire to die or whose lives are deemed unworthy." *Rethinking,* p. 607. It is difficult to understand why he believes the criminal law would find it so hard to distinguish between good and bad motives.

# 6

# *Omissions, Causation, and Criminal Liability*

### SUBSTANTIVE INJUSTICE

No area of the substantive law can rival omissions in generating apparent injustice.[1] The most disappointing criminal decisions are exemplified by *People v. Beardsley*[2] and *Jones v. U.S.*[3] In *Beardsley,* the defendant failed to call for help after he watched a prostitute ingest several grams of morphine. The woman died after receiving no medical assistance. The Supreme Court of Michigan found the defendant innocent of manslaughter. *Jones* represents a similar but even more extreme case. Here the defendant was entrusted with the care of a neighbor's infant. The ten-month old baby died of malnutrition, having received no medical care. The Federal Court for the District of Columbia reversed a manslaughter conviction.

The criminal law does not hold a monopoly on apparent injustice in the area of omissions. *Osterlind v. Hill*[4] is one of several comparable tort cases. Here the intoxicated plaintiff overturned a canoe rented from the defendant. Although an excellent swimmer, the defendant sat passively on the dock, boat and rope at hand, smoked a cigarette, and watched the plaintiff drown. The Supreme Court of Massachusetts imposed no civil liability.

Crucial to each of these decisions was the contention that the defendant owed no legal duty to the decedent. It is, of course, impossible to violate a nonexistent duty. Thus authorities frequently begin a discussion of omissions by remarking that "the difficulty" in establishing liability "is to determine whether the criminal law imposes a duty to act."[5] This requirement of a legal duty does not identify a distinction between the preconditions of liability for omissions as opposed to positive actions. *Each* imposition of criminal liability presupposes a legal duty, regardless of whether conduct is

156

categorized as a positive action or an omission. Admittedly, the question of whether a legal duty exists does not arise in allegations of homicide by positive action. But this question is unimportant *not* because it is not a necessary condition of criminal liability for positive action, but because it *is* a necessary condition *that is always satisfied.* In other words, every person owes a legal duty to every other person not to commit homicide by a positive action. When the alleged homicide is committed by an omission, however, a legal duty exists in only a few narrowly defined circumstances.

Under what circumstances does the criminal law impose a legal duty such that homicide can be committed by omission? Although Anglo-American jurisdictions differ, *Jones* provides the following summary:

> There are at least four situations in which the failure to act may constitute breach of a legal duty. One can be held criminally liable: first, where a statute imposes a duty to care for another; second, where one stands in a certain status relationship to another; third, where one has assumed a contractual duty to care for another; and fourth, where one has voluntarily assumed the care of another and so secluded the helpless person as to prevent others from rendering aid.[6]

None of these circumstances was clearly present in *Beardsley, Jones,* or *Osterlind,* and thus the defendants were not held liable.

A number of authorities have questioned the accuracy of this summary of circumstances that give rise to liability for homicide by omission. George Fletcher argues that these conditions are redundant, and would subtract from the list.[7] Paul Robinson contends that they are incomplete, and would add to the list.[8] But the important and indisputable point is that the criminal law imposes a *universal* duty not to commit homicide by positive action, but recognizes a duty such that homicide can be committed by omission in only a few circumstances. Since the existence of a legal duty is satisfied trivially in cases of positive action, the question of whether a legal duty exists assumes significance only in cases of omission.

Why this disparity? Why does it matter to the criminal law that a harm is "brought about" by positive action rather than by omission? Legal authorities are neither incompetent nor insensitive to considerations of justice. The opinions of the judges in each of these decisions included apologies for the fact that the law departed so far from morality. Indeed, these decisions have been condemned by several authorities in the strongest possible language. William Prosser describes *Osterlind* as "shocking in the extreme" and "revolting to any moral sense."[9] Generally, the sentiment has favored enlarging rather than narrowing the scope of criminal liability for omissions.[10] Many theorists have lamented the failure of Anglo-American law to go as far as Western European systems in enacting so-called "good Samaritan" legislation.[11] In the light of such reactions, it must be asked why the criminal law continues to attach such importance to the difference between omission and positive action.

To answer this question, it is necessary to interpret some of the fundamental principles of liability that comprise orthodox criminal theory. When apparently unjust and disappointing decisions are rendered systematically, it is safe to predict that powerful theoretical considerations are at work. One cannot begin to understand the rationale for the disparity between positive actions and omissions without an appreciation of the influence exerted by orthodox criminal theory upon the substantive law.

No less than three fundamental principles of orthodox criminal theory conspire to support the disparity between omissions and positive actions. The first of these has been discussed at length in chapter 4. Some authorities interpret the actus reus requirement to preclude (or at least to render problematic) criminal liability for omissions. Complications are all but guaranteed by those theorists who analyze actus reus in terms of bodily movement, for it seems clear that the conduct of the defendants in each of the above cases involved no motion.[12] Liability for omissions has been proclaimed to be so "uncongenial" that some authorities have denied its existence.[13] In this chapter I will not return to the complications for omissions occasioned by the actus reus requirement.

Applications of the principle of legality create a second difficulty with liability for omissions. Homicide statutes typically require that the defendant "kill" a human being. Can a person "kill" by omission, or does a killing invariably require a positive action? More specifically, were the victims *killed* by the defendants in *Beardsley, Jones,* or *Osterlind?* Criminal theorists divide into two (or three) camps in answering these difficult questions. Fletcher has little doubt that "a parent might starve a child to death by refusing to feed it. A water company might poison the public by systematically omitting to purify the water. These 'motionless' activities are appropriately described by an affirmative verb of killing."[14] Glanville Williams is more ambivalent. He writes: "The parents who bring about their child's death through want of medical treatment are regarded in law as killing the child, but it is stretching things."[15] Other authorities are equally emphatic in denying that defendants can kill by omission.[16]

Why would anyone suppose that killings could *not* be committed by omission? An answer to this question gives rise to the third fundamental principle that can be invoked against criminal liability for omissions. When an offense requires the occurrence of some specified result, (that is, death), criminal liability is alleged to be unjust unless the conduct of the defendant *causes* that result. This is the causal requirement of orthodox criminal theory; it is the fundamental principle upon which most of this chapter will focus. Under what circumstances, if any, does a defendant cause a result when his conduct consists in an omission rather than a positive action? Does a negative answer to this question remove all doubts about whether such cases as *Beardsely, Jones,* and *Osterlind* were decided correctly? Or does revised criminal theory sometimes allow liability for a result a defendant did *not* cause?

Matters might be clarified if the central issue of this chapter were recast as a response to the following syllogism:

(1) Omissions, as distinguished from positive actions, cannot be causes of results;
(2) Persons have a prima facie moral right not to be held criminally liable for results they do not cause; therefore
(3) Criminal liability is unjust in cases such as *Beardsley, Jones,* or *Osterlind.*

My main concern is to critically evaluate the above argument. The next sections consider premise (1); discuss premise (2); inquire whether (3) follows from (1) and (2); examine whether sense can be made of this argument, or whether its central terms ("positive actions" and "omissions") are too vague and unclear to bear the heavy weight they are assigned within orthodox criminal theory.

Before undertaking this assessment, however, two brief caveats are necessary. First, it is helpful to place the problem of omissions in a broader perspective, for uncertainty about actus reus, legality, and causation do not provide the only reasons that such liability is widely regarded as problematic. Two familiar reservations are not considered here. First, it is frequently alleged that liability for omissions represents a greater deprivation of liberty than liability for positive actions, since a person who is *prohibited* from performing some positive action is left with a greater number of permissible options than is a person who is *required* to perform a given positive action. Since liberty is valuable, we should prefer laws that restrict it minimally.[17] Second, a number of theorists have warned against taking the first step down the "slippery slope" toward creating criminal liability for omissions. They caution that there would be no principled stopping point once a precedent in favor of criminal liability for omissions is introduced.[18] I will not address these interesting objections here.

Perhaps they constitute good reason to "tread carefully" in creating criminal liability for omissions,[19] but it is doubtful that they are sufficient to conclude that *all* such liability as unwarranted.

Finally, it should be pointed out that a few thinkers may not share my conviction that the results in such cases as *Beardsley, Jones*, or *Osterlind* seem unjust and thus in need of special theoretical justification. Here is a (surprisingly rare) instance of an irreconcilable conflict of moral intuitions beneath which it is perhaps impossible to probe. Fortunately, those who believe that persons are not morally blameworthy for their omissions, and who defend this judgment as a matter of intuition rather than by applications of theoretical considerations, are few and far between. When pressed, most persons who resist criminal liability for omissions offer principled reasons for this conclusion. Most share the opinion of the judges in these cases that a moral duty exists, but believe that there are good reasons not to incorporate such a moral duty into the criminal law.[20] The central topic of this chapter is whether such reasons can be derived from the fundamental principle of causation.

## CAN OMISSIONS BE CAUSES?

IF IT IS ASSUMED that the causal requirement in orthodox criminal theory is acceptable, the question arises: under what circumstances, if any, can omissions be causes? If omissions have causal effects in precisely the same sense as positive actions, the causal requirement will not create special difficulties in imposing liability for omissions. But do they? A plausible case can be defended for both positive and negative answers to this question.

It should come as no surprise that orthodox criminal theorists reach diametrically opposed answers to this question. At one extreme is the view of Rollin Perkins: "For the most part the problems of causation are the same whether the harm is alleged to have been caused by positive action or by negative action."[21] At the other extreme is the position that omissions cannot be causes.[22] Fletcher *sometimes* appears to endorse this position. He writes: "The critical distinction between commission by act and commission by omission is not to be found in the contrast between bodily movement and standing still. The issue is imposing liability in the absence of the actor's causing the required result."[23] At other points, Fletcher seems less certain. Although he holds that cases of "letting die" are instances of omissions, he admits that "there might be some cases of 'letting die' that could arguably be described as causing death."[24] His more considered judgment seems to be that "the failure to intervene does not cause death *in the same sense* that shooting or strangling the victim does."[25] Thus his "official" view seems to be that both positive actions and omissions *can* be causes, though in somewhat different senses. If this view is correct, orthodox criminal theorists are faced with at least two important questions: First, in what precise sense is the causal efficacy of positive actions different from omissions? Second, is this alleged difference important to criminal liability?

Answers to these difficult questions may seem to require a complete analysis of the concept of causation. If so, it is unrealistic to hope that they can be resolved, for no satisfactory theory of causation has yet been provided, despite several centuries of sustained effort by theorists from many different disciplines. Fortunately, however, an entire theory of causation may not be needed. There is sufficient agreement about a number of issues to hope for progress in answering these difficult questions. Orthodox criminal theorists are nearly unanimous in supposing that the causal requirement condemns criminal liability as unjust unless two distinct conditions are satisfied. First, the conduct of the defendant must be what is typically described as a "cause in fact" of the result. Second, the conduct of the defendant must be what is generally called the "proximate cause" of that result. My strategy in the remainder of this section is to inquire whether the application of either condition shows that omissions cannot be causes.

### Cause in Fact

Nearly every criminal theorist begins his analysis of causation by insisting that conduct cannot cause an event unless it satisfies a condition variously described as "cause in fact," "sine qua non," "cause in the scientific sense," or "but for causation."[26] According to this first condition, conduct A does not cause consequence x unless x would not have taken place "but for" A. Difficulties of so-called "causal overdetermination," in which A causes x notwithstanding the fact that some other simultaneous conduct B is sufficient to cause x, are typically dismissed as impossible[27] or "not of immediate concern."[28] This complication aside, nearly all criminal theorists agree[29] that this first condition is central to any adequate analysis of causation.

A stubborn intuition insists that omissions *cannot* be "causes in fact," at least not in the same sense as positive actions. The primary reason for believing that the conduct of the defendants in *Beardsley, Jones,* or *Osterlind* did *not* cause death is that each of the three victims would have died even if the defendants had not been present. Harvey Green expresses this position as follows: "A's refraining from preventing B's death is not a causally necessary condition for B's death since B would have died even if A had been absent or unable to prevent B's death."[30]

Does this "intuition" establish a difference between the senses in which actions and omissions are causes in fact? Again, authorities disagree.[31] Some retort that the fact that B would have died even if A had not been present does not entail that B's death would have occurred notwithstanding A's conduct. In *Beardsley, Jones,* and *Osterlind,* the defendants *were* present; they *did* omit to do something they could have done to prevent death. But for these omissions, the consequence would not have taken place. Green continues:

> It is true that had A been absent or unable to prevent B's death, B would still have died. And in that case of course A's refraining from preventing B's death is not a necessary condition for B's death, since it would not be possible for A to refrain from preventing B's death. In the case in which A is present and able to prevent B's death, however, it is possible for A to refrain from preventing B's death. [sic] and in such a case, had A not refrained from preventing B's death—that is, had A prevented B's death—B would not have died. This means that while A's refraining from preventing B's death is not a causally necessary condition for B's death where A is absent or unable to prevent B's death, where it is possible for A to prevent B's death, A's refraining from doing so is a causally necessary condition to B's death.[32]

If this observation is correct, the first condition of an adequate analaysis of causation fails to substantiate the claim that positive actions and omissions are causes in a different sense.

Robinson remains unconvinced. He admits that "one can speak of but-for relationships between omissions and results," but adds that "the meaning is dramatically different from the meaning of but-for in the commission context."[33] This alleged "dramatic difference" is expressed as follows: "The problem here, and with causation by omission generally, is that every other person in the world also satisfies the but-for cause requirement; 'but for' the omission of every one of us, the [consequence] would not have [occurred]."[34] Thus he concludes that "for omission liability, the cause-in-fact requirement is nearly useless as a test for assigning liability."[35]

Robinson's argument is suspect for two reasons. First, it is simply false that "every other person in the world satisfies the but-for cause requirement"; the conduct of many persons fails this test. The omission of a person to rescue a drowning victim is not a cause in fact of death unless he could have prevented (that is, was in a position to prevent) that death. Moreover, the fact that this condition may be easily satisfied in cases of omissions is not a good reason to conclude that its meaning has changed, for the application of this test to positive actions yields precisely the same result. The fact that the grandparents of John Wilkes Booth conceived a child was a cause in fact of the assassination of Lincoln. The fact that applications of this "cause-in-fact" condition result in too many candidates for criminal liability for a given event merely demonstrates that it is not a *sufficient* test of causation. All authorities agree that a second condition must supplement the first in an adequate analysis of causation.

I conclude that we should suspend judgment about whether an alleged difference in causal efficacy between positive actions and omissions can be located in this first condition of an adequate analysis of causation. Perhaps those theorists who insist that omissions cannot be causes can better support this claim by applications of the second condition.

### Proximate Cause

There is far less unanimity about what this second condition should be called, or how it should be formulated. "Primary cause," "efficient cause," "efficient proximate cause," "efficient adequate cause," "legal cause," "jural cause," and—the term favored here— "proximate cause"—have all been put forward as candidates.[36]

When is a cause in fact of a given event also the proximate cause of that event? For present purposes, it is less important to defend a complete answer to this question than to notice that attempts to answer it divide into two camps.

A.  Proximate Cause as Evaluative

According to the majority of orthodox criminal theorists, there is nothing in the *facts* of causation to further narrow the candidates for liability for a "result crime." There are no empirical, scientific, objective facts (beyond the first condition) that preclude describing the relationship between *any* conduct and event as one of proximate cause. This second component of causation merely reflects considerations of justice or "social policy." Robinson's remark is typical: "The determination here is not a scientific one at all."[37] Instead, following the approach of the Model Penal Code,[38] findings of proximate cause are said to be "left to the discretionary judgment of the trier of fact using intuitive notions of justice."[39]

If this majority view is correct, it is crucial to note the difficulties in opposing liability for omissions on the ground that they cannot be proximate causes of harm. Such reasoning is tantamount to contending that "intuitive notions of justice" oppose liability for omissions. The assertion "omissions cannot be proximate causes of harm" *appears* to be a nontautologous reason to conclude that criminal liability for omissions is unjust. But if determinations of proximate cause are nothing more than considerations of justice disguised in the language of causation, this assertion is cast in an entirely different light. It now becomes equivalent to the claim that "intuitive notions of justice oppose holding persons criminally liable for their omissions." This latter claim is difficult to reconcile with the widespread sentiment that considerations of justice apparently *favor* liability in such cases as *Beardsley, Jones,* and *Osterlind.* Thus some authorities conclude that the "problem of causation in omission cases . . . disappears once it is acknowledged that the question of causation is . . . a question of policy on imputing or denying liability."[40]

Moreover, if value judgments constitute the real objection to impositions of criminal liability for omissions, it would be less misleading simply to identify and assess these values without the inevitable confusion that arises from framing the issue in terms of causation. If the sense of causation in the first condition is scientific, objective, and factual, and the sense of causation in the second condition is not, it can only mislead to use the same concept. Candor is not served by couching moral arguments in the language of causation.

### B.  Proximate Cause as Descriptive

But the majority view discussed above may not be correct. Perhaps there *is* something scientific, objective, or factual (above and beyond cause in fact) in determinations of whether conduct is the proximate cause of a result. Against the majority view of orthodox criminal theorists stand H.L.A. Hart and A.M. Honore, whose seminal work *Causation and the Law* represents the most impressive and comprehensive treatment of causation yet produced in Anglo-American legal philosophy. Hart and Honore endeavor to show that most orthodox theorists are mistaken in supposing that judgments of proximate cause are simply expressions of "intuitive notions of justice." They admit that *some* determinations of whether the conduct of the defendant is the proximate cause of a harm are insoluble without recourse to moral evaluations.[41] But their research

> does not confirm the modern view that in using the language of causation [courts] have merely given effect to their conceptions of justice, expediency, or chosen policy. Over a great area of the law they have, in using causal language, sought to apply a group of causal notions embedded in common sense. . . . So on our view the modern way is too short a way with problems of proximate cause: there is more to be said about the actual practice of courts than the blend of sine qua non and policy to which such problems are now customarily reduced.[42]

In short, "ordinary language" and "common sense" lead Hart and Honore to conclude that "an act is the cause of harm if it is an intervention in the course of affairs which is sufficient to produce the harm without the co-operation of the voluntary actions of others or abnormal conjunctions of events."[43]

Do these "facts of causation" contained in Hart and Honore's analysis of proximate cause provide any reason to believe that omissions cannot be causes? Not at all. Like Perkins (who differs in regarding these questions as largely matters of policy), Hart and Honore conclude that "there is no special difficulty about omissions."[44] The authors are so uninclined to take the contrary position seriously that they do not devote a single subchapter, much less an entire chapter, to the question of whether omissions can be causes. It is clear to them that omissions, like positive actions, can represent "interventions" in the normal course of events. They write:

> In circumstances where the cause of the flowers dying is said to be the gardener's failure to water them the only alternative to citing this omission as the cause would be to cite the later physical conditions which led to their death. But to cite these would not satisfy the special interest in the particular case: it would show what *always* happens when flowers die, why *flowers* die: whereas an explanation is wanted not of that, but of the death of *these* flowers when normally *they* would have lived: what made *this* difference was the gardener's omission—an abnormal failure of a normal condition.[45]

Fletcher's remark that omissions and positive actions differ in their causal efficacy would baffle them.

Perhaps, however, Hart and Honore are mistaken in their analysis of causation. Their careful account, while universally respected, has been "rejected for the most part in the legal literature."[46] Many critics allege that their account is even less "factual" or "objective" than they suppose. In particular, it has been noted that the distinction between "normal" and "abnormal" events, on which their analysis depends, is not statistical, but incorporates value judgments.

But perhaps an improved account of the factual component in proximate causation would reveal that omissions cannot be causes. We cannot rely uncritically upon Hart and Honore for having definitively demonstrated that there is "no special difficulty about omissions." Thus I suspend judgment about whether omissions can or cannot be causes. But what are the implications of such indecision for a revised theory of criminal liability? In the following section I will attempt to show that no "fact of the matter" about causation should persuade us that persons should not be held criminally liable for (some of) their omissions.

### THE CAUSAL REQUIREMENT

EVEN IF HART AND HONORE are mistaken about whether omissions can be causes, there are two good reasons to believe that no "fact of the matter" about either cause in fact or proximate cause can be used to show the injustice of holding defendants criminally liable in such cases as *Beardsley* or *Jones*. A brief discussion of these reasons will lead to an assessment of the causal requirement itself.

First, the claim that omissions cannot be causes, when paired with the causal requirement as a necessary condition for criminal liability, has implications that are unacceptable to any reasonable person. No one doubts that liability is just in cases involving "special relationships," for instance, when a parent deliberately and maliciously starves his infant to death.[47] Those who emphasize the alleged injustice of holding persons criminally liable for their omissions are embarrassed when confronted with these obvious counterexamples. Richard Epstein's strategy for accommodating such cases is particularly disingenuous. In the course of arguing that it is unjust to hold persons liable for their omissions, he proposes to "put aside . . . all those cases in which there are special relationships between the plaintiff and the defendants: parent and child, invitor and invitee, and the like."[48] But any theory can be preserved as long as the theorist permits himself the luxury to "put aside" those cases that falsify it. Epstein must appreciate that an honest attempt to deal with such cases would force him to admit either (a) that some omissions are causes or (b) that the causal requirement must be qualified or overridden.

Moreover, even if the facts of causation somehow demonstrate that omissions cannot be causes, nothing compels us to use these facts as a reason to preclude liability in cases in which a harmful result is not caused. Hart and Honore are perfectly clear about this point: "There is nothing to compel any legal system to accept a causal connexion with harm as either necessary or sufficient for liability, and, where it seems just to do so, it may introduce special principles of 'policy' or scope rules to enlarge or cut short liability independently of causal connexion."[49] If considerations of justice support the conclusion that the defendants in *Beardsley, Jones,* or *Osterlind* should be held criminally liable, and the best analysis of causation reveals that omissions *cannot* be causes, the proper response is *not* to acquiesce in injustice, but rather to abandon or qualify the causal requirement. Criminal theory would be undeserving of our respect if its fundamental principles placed such conduct beyond the reach of punishment. Thus it is sensible to propose that the defendants in the above cases be held criminally liable even if the their omissions did not cause the deaths of their respective victims.

These latter remarks challenge the causal requirement itself. Why have orthodox criminal theorists been so attracted to it? There is no simple answer. For the most part, criminal theorists do not directly address this question. Even Hart and Honore, after remarking that nothing *compels* us to "accept a causal connexion with harm as . . . necessary . . . for liability," elect to do so.[50] They support their decision by observing that the contrary view "is not, however, the present position in Anglo-American law: causal connexion is very generally required as a ground of liability."[51] Here there is a curious willingness to accept the causal requirement without supporting argument. Is it possible to improve upon this reasoning? Why have orthodox criminal theorists been so inclined to use the concept of causation to limit the results for which persons may be held liable? In the remainder of this section I will evaluate the reasoning that may have led a number of orthodox criminal theorists to uncritically accept the causal requirement. Unfortunately, this task requires much speculation, since the causal requirement typically is taken for granted rather than explicitly defended.

The scientific connotation of the concept of causation provides one clue to its powerful appeal. We previously have encountered (and will continue to encounter) strong resistance to the suggestion that criminal theory presupposes the application of a moral and political philosophy. Most orthodox theorists like to believe that their discipline is scientific and empirical. Undoubtedly this aspiration is a major factor in the almost universal tendency to employ the concept of causation to describe the relationship that must obtain between the conduct of the defendant and the proscribed result before criminal liability may attach. Causation, after all, is a term borrowed from the natural sciences. Its use helps perpetuate the myth that the methodology of criminal theorists is scientific and empirical.

One might think that few modern theorists continue to cling to this misguided ideal, inasmuch as it is widely acknowledged that proximate cause includes "intuitive notions of justice." Nonetheless, expressions of the aspiration to rely upon empirical science rather than moral and political philosophy can be detected among even those authorities who emphasize the role of justice in determinations of proximate causation. One theorist admits that "the choice of the proper test [of causation] is . . . ultimately a matter of legal policy rather than of science or philosophy," but immediately adds:

> This does not mean, however, that scientific and philosophical tests are irrelevant in determining the choice of policy, for sound policy must be oriented to scientific data and philosophical criteria . . . When the legislator limits or extends responsibility to situations in which causation prevails, he in a sense indicates that he does not wish to be

limited to an exclusively legal criterion of responsibility but chooses to invoke the aid of disciplines other than law—philosophy and the sciences—in which the concept of causation is at present rooted.[52]

The dream to develop a "science of jurisprudence" does not die easily. It finds contemporary expression in the above claim: if science cannot determine liability, at least it can identify the outer boundaries that liability may not exceed. The concept of causation is attractive for this purpose. Again, one must not forget that the "choice to invoke the aid of disciplines other than law" must be defended as a matter of moral and political philosophy.

The scientific, factual, empirical flavor of the concept of causation lends itself to yet another favorite doctrine of orthodox criminal theorists: the alleged distinction between moral and legal obligation. Those authorities who contend that causation is and ought to be a necessary condition for criminal liability, and go on to express moral regret about legal judgments rendered accordingly, implicitly adopt a view about the differences between the preconditions of moral and legal obligation. They are committed to the claim that criminal wrongdoing, unlike moral wrongdoing, requires a causal connection between conduct and result. A number of legal philosophers explicitly embrace this thesis. Hart and Honore maintain that "in all legal systems, liability to be punished . . . depends on whether actions (or omissions) have caused harm. Moral blame is not of course confined to such cases of causing harm."[53] This view about the different preconditions of moral and legal obligation is controversial and in need of a defense. If there are good reasons why a person is not and should not be held criminally liable for a result he does not cause, why should he be held morally responsible for that result? Here again, legal authorities exhibit remarkable but totally misplaced confidence in their sophistication as moral philosophers. To turn the question around, if moral responsibility does not require causation, why should criminal liability be otherwise? In short, why should this (implausible) view about the different preconditions of moral and legal obligation be welcomed?

No sound arguments in support of this view about the different preconditions of moral and legal obligation have been (or could be) provided. Hart and Honore do not offer a general argument in favor of this thesis, but are content to substantiate it by examples. In the sentence immediately following the above quotation, they write: "We blame a man who cheats or lies or breaks promises, even if no one has suffered in the particular case."[54] These observations about moral blame are true but quite irrelevant. These examples of moral wrongdoing *sans* causation are not analogous to "result crimes" in which blame depends upon the occurrence of a proscribed consequence.

One might as well seek to refute the causal requirement of orthodox theory by citing examples of criminal liability that are not "result crimes," such as larceny. Defendants are criminally liable for this offense even if they return the stolen item before anyone has noticed its absence so that "no one has suffered in the particular case." Questions about causation simply do not arise unless criminal liability requires a *consequence* as something distinct from the conduct of the defendant.

The only kind of example that could support the claim that criminal liability, unlike moral responsibility, requires (and ought to require) causation (for "result crimes") is a case in which a person is morally blameworthy, though he is not (and should not be) liable for a consequence he did not cause. It is doubtful that such an example could be constructed. There are at least two reasons why the *Beardsley, Jones,* or *Osterlind* cases do not provide persuasive illustrations. First, it is controversial whether the conduct of the defendants in these cases was a cause of death. Second, it is question-begging to insist that criminal liability would be unjust here. Attempts to employ the concept of causation to distinguish between moral and legal obligation fare no better than those that depend upon the orthodox model of the criminal offense.

The central question of this section remains unanswered: why are orthodox criminal theorists so convinced of the causal requirement? A second possible answer is derived from a curious application of the presupposition that criminal liability for a result cannot admit of degrees,[55] and must be imposed, fully or not at all, upon a single defendant. One philosopher remarks: "Our idea of responsibility requires that it should be uniquely ascribed, [and] in many situations causation is the only means by which we can satisfy the uniqueness requirement."[56] This reasoning is especially significant in the context of omissions. In many situations in which criminal liability is urged for an omission, there are too many candidates on whom it might be imposed. Apparently, dozens of people failed to assist Kitty Genoveese; it might seem absurd to hold each of them liable.[57]

But this ground in favor of the causal requirement is almost certainly unsatisfactory as it stands. If conduct is culpable, it seems peculiar to resist liability because too many people engage in it. Such a policy would require the elimination of criminal penalties for income tax evasion, to cite just one example. This objection is usually supplemented to add to its plausibility. Another philosopher continues: "If there are a hundred independent defaulters . . . and one death, each carries a hundredth of a murderer's guilt."[58] But the suggestion that liability be diminished in proportion to the number of perpetrators is odd at best, and has no analogue elsewhere in the law. If Smith and

Jones conspire to kill, their liability would not (and should not) be lessened by the discovery of a third conspirator. The claim that the "idea of responsibility requires that it should be uniquely ascribed" cannot withstand critical scrutiny.[59]

Nonetheless, surely *some* general principle(s) should limit liability for a proscribed result. The fundamental principles of criminal theory should provide some basis for resisting liability for a result with which a defendant is not appropriately connected. The difficulty is to understand whether the concept of causation should be used to describe this "appropriate connection." It is true that one cannot fail to be impressed by the correlation between cases in which the conduct of A does not cause result x and cases in which A should not be held liable for x. Does this correlation support the causal requirement?

One useful strategy in an attempt to answer this question is to assess possible *alternatives* to causation. Perhaps some theorists are drawn to the causal requirement because they cannot envisage a competing "appropriate connection" between conduct and result before liability is not unjust. But such alternatives may be available. The correlation between the absence of *control* and the injustice of liability may be stronger than that between the absence of *causation* and the injustice of liability. Perhaps the plausibility of the causal requirement can be explained by the fact that persons have control over most of the harm they cause and lack control over most of the harm they do not cause. But liability clearly is unjust in those cases in which persons have no control over harm they cause (for example, they injure someone while acting involuntarily). Conversely, liability should *not* be precluded as unjust in those cases in which persons *have* control over harm they (arguably) do *not* cause. Perhaps *Beardsley, Jones,* and *Osterlind* provide illustrations of control sans causation. It is unquestionable that there *is* a connection between conduct and result in these cases; it may or may not be correct to describe that connection as causal. The point is that it is *this* connection, however it is best described, that should function as a necessary condition for criminal liability (for "result crimes") in revised criminal theory. *Whether or not* a causal connection exists in these cases between conduct and harm, criminal liability should not be precluded as unjust. I submit that it is because the defendants failed to exercise control over the deaths of their respective victims that their conduct is regarded as morally outrageous. Even if one became convinced of an analysis of causation that entailed that there were no causal connection between conduct and harm in these cases, our outrage would persist because of the failure of these defendants to exercise control.

I suggest that the control principle is a preferable alternative to the causal requirement of orthodox criminal theory. But this preference must remain tentative pending a more detailed explication of the concept of control, and its differences from causation.[60] Orthodox criminal theorists will demand that such an analysis be formulated before they will agree to substitute the control principle for the causal requirement. On one level, this demand is perfectly reasonable. On another level, however, this demand may appear almost perverse, since orthodox theorists have accepted the causal requirement without a clear understanding of it. The concept of control seems no less amenable to a precise analysis than that of causation, and should prove more useful to criminal theory than those it is designed to replace. Again, I hope that the concept of control can withstand the great intuitive weight I place upon it here.

## CRIMINAL OMISSIONS WITHOUT CAUSATION

WHAT LEGAL REFORMS are needed in order to impose criminal liability in cases comparable to *Beardsley, Jones,* and *Osterlind?* In the preceding sections I have supposed that the causal requirement constitutes the primary theoretical obstacle to liability. Thus I examined whether omissions can be causes, and questioned whether the causal requirement should be retained within revised criminal theory. In this section I will argue that liability can be imposed even if retain the causal requirement and we accept the conclusion that omissions cannot be causes.

There are two strategies for imposing liability on the bad Samaritan. The first is judicial. Existing homicide statutes might be construed to warrant the punishment of the defendants in the above cases. Difficulties with this approach have been noted: reasonable minds disagree about whether Beardsley "killed" his victim. Those who seek to prevent the erosion of the fundamental principle of legality are likely to oppose this judicial enlargement of crime.[61]

The second strategy is legislative. New statutes might unambiguously impose liability on the bad Samaritan regardless of whether his conduct is construed as a positive action or an omission. This strategy poses no threat to the principle of legality. It concedes that the defendants in the above cases escaped liability through an unfortunate gap in the law, and rectifies this oversight through improved legislation. Those jurisdictions most successful in proscribing bad Samaritanism, such as Vermont,[62] have opted for a legislative rather than a judicial solution.

This second strategy has an additional advantage. A lively philosophical debate concerns whether, and under what circumstances, homicide by omission is as culpable as homicide by positive action.[63] Any difference in culpability should be reflected in a just statutory scheme. The attempt to impose liability under existing homicide statutes blurs any distinction between the culpability of defendants who commit homicide by omission and those who kill by positive action.[64] I have not insisted that positive actions are as culpable as omissions, but only that their relative culpability should not be derived from the fundamental principles of liability.

It is tempting to believe that this second strategy is no more compatible with the causal requirement than the first. The basis of such skepticism is as follows: if the causal requirement constitutes the primary theoretical obstacle against liability for omissions, why suppose that the problem can be overcome by the simple expedient of drafting new statutes? No legislative act can confer causal effects upon omissions if they have none. If persons have a prima facie right not to be held criminally liable for results they do not cause, and it is at least doubtful that omissions can be causes, then a statute that imposes liability for an omission represents a prima facie injustice. This is the very sort of injustice that the fundamental principles of criminal liability are designed to prevent.

This skepticism is unwarranted, since good Samaritan legislation need not compromise the causal requirement. The key to understanding how such statutes can be construed as compatible with the causal requirement is to return to the distinction between "result" and "non-result crimes."[65] Only a handful of offenses, such as homicide and arson, require the occurrence of a specified consequence that is conceptually distinct from the defendant's conduct. Liability for such offenses cannot be imposed until that consequence, such as death, occurs. In the case of "non-result crimes," such as larceny or perjury, liability attaches at the moment the defendant acts, and does not require the occurrence of any conceptually distinct consequence.

It should be clear that not all omissions for which criminal liability is imposed are "result crimes." The criminal law proscribes, for example, the failure to file an income tax return. Liability for such an offense need not await the occurrence of some specified consequence to which the defendant's conduct is causally related. This statute is violated as the time for filing a return expires. It is important to appreciate that the difficulties with criminal omissions discussed in this chapter do not pertain to such "non-result crimes." The requirements of legality are satisfied.[66] More important, the causal requirement has no application to such offenses. Since liability need not await the occurrence of a conceptually distinct consequence to which the conduct of the defendant must be causally related, questions of causation do not arise in these cases.[67]

Good Samaritan legislation may be construed as an instance of

a "non-result crime" committed by omission. According to this interpretation, the defendant who fails to act pursuant to the statutory
requirements is not punished *for* the harm suffered by the victim;
liability is complete at the time he omits to offer assistance. Those
philosophers who have argued that the causal requirement creates
difficulties for good Samaritan legislation have implicitly assumed
that liability under such statutes must be *for* the subsequent harm.[68]
But the liability of the bad Samaritan need not be construed in this
way. Unlike "result crimes," liability may attach whether or not harm
occurs. Even if the victims in *Beardsley* or *Jones* had been saved by the
unanticipated heroism of a third party, making it impossible to
convict for bringing about a result, the defendants should be held
liable for failing to behave as good Samaritans. Legislation that does
not require a result need not run afoul of the causal requirement,
even if it is conceded that omissions cannot be causes.

## THE DISTINCTION BETWEEN ACTS AND OMISSIONS

IT IS ARGUABLE that the inquiry in the preceding sections places
the cart before the horse. One cannot decide whether the disparate
treatment of positive actions and omissions is warranted unless the
distinction itself is clearly understood.[69] When the moral relevance of
a distinction is endorsed by some and challenged by others, it is at
least possible that they draw the distinction somewhat differently.
Perhaps confusion about how the distinction should be drawn has
contributed to uncertainty about the difficult question of whether
omissions can be causes. In light of the importance of the classification, one might hope that orthodox criminal theorists have developed
reasonably precise criteria for sorting particular instances of conduct
into one category or the other. But many criminal theorists are so
anxious to support (or attack) the disparate treatment of positive
actions and omissions that they pay insufficient attention to the prior
question of how this distinction should be drawn.[70]

If we hope to decide whether it is (ceteris paribus) less culpable
to bring about a harm by omission than by positive action, we must
have an independent, value-neutral criterion to sort instances of
conduct into these two categories. Such a criterion must be independent and value-neutral in order to avoid question-begging. It is
circular to classify conduct as an omission on the ground that it is less
culpable than a positive action that produces the same harm. Any
criterion that places conduct in one of the two categories by reference
to its culpability would convert into an uninformative tautology the
claim that it is more culpable to bring about a harm by positive action

than by omission.[71] Presumably orthodox criminal theorists intend this claim to be understood as a substantive insight, rather than as a conceptual truth.

In this section I will argue that the distinction between positive actions and omissions is partly evaluative rather than purely descriptive. In other words, the tendency to categorize an instance of conduct as a positive action rather than an omission is not based upon objective, scientific, empirical fact, but is strongly influenced by judgments of its culpability.[72] Courts and theorists alike deem conduct to be a positive action when they want to impose criminal liability, and pronounce it to be an omission when they want to resist (or lessen) liability.[73] The disparity between positive actions and omissions is "justified" by incorporating (or smuggling) moral evaluations into the distinction itself.

The thesis I am defending about the distinction between positive actions and omissions is analogous to the thesis about the distinction between proximate causation and its absence, which many orthodox criminal theorists have appreciated for some time. Most authorities acknowledge that the premises "A's conduct is the proximate cause of harm x" and "B's conduct is not the proximate cause of harm x" do not constitute a (non question-begging) reason for holding A rather than B liable for x; these premises already incorporate this conclusion. A's conduct (rather than B's) would not have been identified as the proximate cause of x unless it were thought more appropriate to impose liability upon him.[74] Although it is widely acknowledged that determinations of whether conduct is or is not the proximate cause of harm embody values, there is almost no sensitivity that the determination of whether conduct is a positive action or an omission does so as well. Neither of these determinations is entirely value-neutral; both presuppose the application of a moral and political theory. If I am correct, the claim "a defendant is more culpable if his conduct brings about a harm by positive action than by omission" is as trivially true as is the claim "a defendant is more culpable if his conduct is the proximate cause of a harm than if it is not." Both claims are disguised tautologies.

### Bodily Movements

It will be instructive to apply this thesis to the most familiar criterion to distinguish positive actions from omissions, viz., bodily movements. Although Fletcher remarks that "it is hard to find anyone today who seriously argues that omissions should be defined as the 'absence of movement,' "[75] this criterion continues to attract wide support. It is simple and *seems* to satisfy the desideratum of value-neutrality. While this criterion has been vigorously attacked,[76] no satisfactory alternative has emerged to take its place. Orthodox criminal theorists are understandably reluctant to abandon an analysis of so important a distinction unless a preferable criterion can be formulated.

The following discussion is not designed merely to provide yet another refutation of the view that positive actions can be distinguished from omissions by bodily movement. The important point to notice is that this criterion, insofar as it has any prospects for plausible application, is *not* value-free. I hope to create doubt that *any* satisfactory criterion can be value-neutral.

How are values incorporated in the determination of whether bodily movement has taken place? Is it not possible to devise scientific, empirical tests to detect the presence or absence of movement? Consider the following difficulty. Notice that a person can, and usually does, perform an omission although his body is constantly in motion. The defendant in *Osterlind* smoked a cigarette while he watched the victim drown. Surely these movements would not persuade anyone that he acted rather than omitted; we remain inclined to say that he let his victim die. But why? Defenders of this criterion will respond by admitting that a defendant need not be absolutely motionless before his conduct is properly categorized as an omission. Though the defendant in *Osterlind* moved his body, he did not do so in the appropriate way, and thus he let his victim die. The difficulty, of course, is to specify which movements are "appropriate." It is tempting to respond that his movements were inappropriate because they were not designed to save the life of the victim. But the defendant in *Beardsley* advised his victim to rest in the hope that she would recover. Suppose, moreover, that he had knelt and prayed for her. These movements, although designed to save the life of the victim, presumably are "inappropriate" to falsify the judgment that he let her die, because they should not have been thought sufficient, given the exigency of the circumstances, to preserve her life. We reasonably expect that persons should summon a doctor when a victim has ingested large amounts of morphine. But surely our "reasonable expectations" about what persons should do are influenced by, if not based upon, our moral assessments of what they ought to do. The concept of reasonableness has proved stubbornly resistant to a value-neutral analysis. In introducing such concepts as reasonable expectations, we have moved far beyond the simple presence or absence of bodily movement that can be detected by factual, empirical inquiry.

Although reliance upon bodily movement in an attempt to formulate a value-neutral distinction between positive actions and omissions fails, some satisfactory criterion may eventually emerge to take its place. I am unable to *prove* that a value-free criterion will not be forthcoming. My strategy to support my thesis that the distinction between positive actions and omissions is partly evaluative, rather than wholly descriptive, is to examine two kinds of cases: (a) those involving apparent omissions, although courts and theorists have strained to categorize the conduct as a positive action in order to "find" culpability; and (b) those involving apparent positive actions, although courts and theorists have strained to categorize the conduct as an omission in order to "find" little or no culpability. Both types of cases support Williams's astute observation that frequently "the defendant's conduct can be looked upon from one point of view as a forbidden act and from another point of view as an omission."[77] I hope it will become clear that which point of view is preferred depends primarily upon whether or not liability is desired. In both sorts of cases courts have made the decision to categorize the conduct as a positive action or an omission by first determining what degree of culpability, if any, is involved. Conduct is not categorized as positive action or omission in order to determine the proper extent of culpability; instead, the process proceeds in the opposite direction. Courts and theorists have found it easy to manipulate the distinction to reach the desired degree of culpability because the distinction itself is partly evaluative rather than purely descriptive.

### Apparent Omissions Categorized as Positive Actions

Perhaps the best examples of cases in which courts have strained to construe the conduct of the defendant as a positive action in order to impose liability are those involving a sequence of events. Two such cases are as follows.[78] In R v. Miller,[79] the defendant went to sleep holding a lit cigarette. He awoke to find his mattress smoldering, but simply moved to another room and fell back asleep. He was accused of arson after the house burned. In Fagan v. Metro. Police Com.,[80] the defendant accidentally parked his car on a policeman's foot. After becoming aware of what he had done, he deliberately delayed moving, and reveled in his victim's suffering. He was accused of assaulting a police officer. Authorities have maintained that "common sense" upholds liability,[81] but these results have proved difficult to reconcile with orthodox criminal theory. At what time did Miller "burn" the building or Fagen "assault" the policeman? No one would suggest that these offenses were committed at the moment the mattress caught fire or the car came to rest. Can the subsequent failure to rectify these situations constitute arson or assault?

A third case of interest may not seem to involve a "sequence" of events comparable to that of Miller or Fagan. In R v. Speck,[82] a man stood motionless for several minutes while an eight-year-old girl rubbed and aroused him through his trousers. The defendant had done nothing to encourage her precocious behavior, but was accused of "gross indecency with a child." Did Speck have a duty to actively discourage the child's advances even though he had not actively initiated them?

First consider the two "sequence" cases, in which there are essentially two theoretical paths toward liability. First, one might hold that the defendants in these cases are properly liable for their omissions.[83] This alternative has not attracted unanimous favor from orthodox theorists.[84] Second, one might deem the conduct of the defendants to be positive action, in which case liability is not imposed for an omission. Williams writes: "An unintentional act followed by an intentional omission to rectify it can be regarded *in toto* as an intentional act."[85] This rationale finds support in tort law, where some authorities would describe the conduct of the defendants in these cases as "pseudo-misfeasance."[86]

The difficulty of categorizing the conduct in *Speck* is amenable to a similar solution. Here the court construed the sustained inactivity of the defendant as constituting "an invitation to the child to undertake the act."[87] In other words, a sequence is involved here as well, since liability would have been unjust had the defendant removed the child's hand immediately. And this sequence (of omissions?) might be deemed an "act of invitation."

A number of judges have accepted Williams's "single act" rationale for liability in *Miller* and *Fagan*,[88] but J. C. Smith has vigorously attacked it. He regards the "deeming" of the sequence as a single act to be a "fiction" with "no place in the modern criminal law": "Let us by all means have regard to reality and common sense and no more of this 'damned deeming.' "[89] If we assume that liability is just,[90] should the conduct of Speck be categorized as a positive action or an omission? Should the conduct of the defendants in *Miller* and *Fagan* be categorized as a single positive action or as a positive action followed by an omission?

Fortunately, I need not hazard an answer to this difficult question in order to support my thesis. My position is that there is no *fact of the matter* about how the conduct of these three defendants should be categorized. Clearly, the tendency to categorize the conduct of these defendants as positive action derives not from the application of a value-neutral criterion to distinguish positive actions from omissions, but rather from the judgment that their conduct is culpable and that liability should be imposed. This thesis may be supported by noting a serious difficulty with the "single act" rationale. Inasmuch as almost all conduct that culminates in liability involves a sequence of events, one must have some criterion to decide when it is appropriate or inappropriate to construe a sequence "in toto" as a "single act." Any plausible criterion to "deem" a given sequence as a "single act" must be made by reference to whether liability is regarded as just or unjust. Any criterion to decide when a sequence should be construed "in toto" must include a test of proximity to determine when events separated over long periods of time may be deemed a "single act." It is likely that an adequate test of proximity (as with proximate causation) must incorporate values.

The following example should illustrate the need for a test of proximity. Suppose the defendant manufactures cars and deliberately cuts corners by installing defective emergency brakes. A year later he notices one of his cars parked on a hill. Because the emergency brake is defective, it rolls backwards and comes to rest on a policeman's foot. The defendant fails to assist the policeman for several moments, reveling in his suffering. Here the defendant initiated a causal chain culminating in harm. Is this sequence to be "deemed" a "single act" comparable to *Fagan*? There is no fact of the matter about how this question should be answered.[91]

### Apparent Positive Actions Categorized as Omissions

If liability were regarded as unjust in the above cases, there would be no inclination whatever to "deem" conduct involving a "sequence of events" as positive action. Some resistance to conceptualizing sequential conduct as positive action is encountered in examples in which a defendant *justifiably* creates a dangerous situation and subsequently fails to rectify it. Such cases parallel *Miller* and *Fagan*, but differ in that the initial positive action of the defendant is justified.[92]

One such case is *King v. Commonwealth*.[93] Here the defendant failed to summon a doctor to assist a plaintiff he had justifiably shot and wounded while protecting his father from the plaintiff's unlawful attack. Authorities differ about whether liability should be imposed under such circumstances.[94] Those who oppose liability will tend to categorize the conduct of the defendant as an omission. Those who prefer liability will prefer to conceptualize the conduct of the defendant "in toto" as a "single act." One can only wonder why the "single act" path toward liability was not embraced in *Beardsley* and *Osterlind*.

Courts and theorists are especially inclined to construe conduct as an omission when it arises from good motives. The clearest illustration of a killing from good motives involves beneficent euthanasia. Fletcher asks: "Is the physician's discontinuing aid to a terminal patient an act or omission?"[95] Why does Fletcher raise this question? Because "if turning off the respirator is an 'act' under the law, then it is unequivocally forbidden. . . . If, on the other hand, it is classified as an 'omission,' the analysis proceeds more flexibly."[96] This "flexibility" in imposing liability for omissions allows Fletcher to conclude that, under some circumstances, doctors are not culpable for committing beneficient euthanasia.

But why is it appropriate to categorize some cases of beneficient euthanasia as an omission? Here Fletcher relies on the "linguistic sensitivity" of "native speakers of English."[97] Cases in which such speakers describe the relationship between conduct and result as "permitting" are categorized as omissions. Fletcher writes: "permitting harm to occur should be sufficent for classification as an omission."[98]

Is Fletcher's "ordinary language" criterion for distinguishing positive actions from omissions value-neutral?[99] The answer to this question depends upon *how* native speakers of English decide whether to describe the relationship between conduct and result as "permitting death" rather than as "killing." Psychological data about how speakers decide to describe events would be helpful here. It would not be surprising if a preference for one description over another were based largely upon the objectives that speakers hoped to achieve. Uncertainty about whether the conduct is culpable might be reflected in a tendency to regard *both* descriptions as apt. There is no reason why it *must* be inaccurate to describe a single instance of conduct as both positive action and omission.

Fletcher himself seems close to agreeing with my thesis, since he writes: "The logic of classification is ineluctable. Cases of permitting harm . . . cannot be classified as cases of acts: to do so would avoid excusing the harm."[100] In other words, one does not conclude that "liability should not arise because the conduct is an omission," but rather "the conduct is an omission because liability should not arise." The contrast between positive actions and omissions is not invoked to *support* the judgment that liability is unjust; it is applied *after* this judgment is reached on other unexplained grounds.[101] The disparity between positive actions and omissions cannot be assessed until these other unexplained grounds for categorizing conduct are identified. In the context of beneficient euthanasia, I believe the good motive of the physician accounts for our tendency to categorize his conduct as an omission.[102] If the physician had a bad motive, for example, "pulled the plug" in order to collect an early inheritance, no one would describe his conduct as an omission. It seems clear that if Fletcher were opposed to all such conduct, he would have no inclination to construe any instances of benevolent euthanasia as an omission.[103]

Frequently the basis for categorizing a case of beneficient euthanasia as an omission rather than as a positive action involves a comparison of examples said to be relevantly similar. Is withdrawing the tube of a drip feed that keeps a patient alive a positive action? Is the failure to replace an emptied bag an omission?[104] Smith and Hogan write: "It seems offensive if liability for homicide depends on distinctions of this kind."[105] This approach does not show that beneficient euthanasia is not culpable. The relevant similarity between such cases does not support the conclusion that both should be regarded as omissions; it is equally persuasive to support the conclusion that both should be regarded as positive actions. Instead, such examples underscore the futility of invoking the distinction between positive actions and omissions in the first place.[106] Eventually criminal theorists must begin to wonder whether the struggle to draw and apply this distinction is worth the effort. *Should* the liability of doctors who commit beneficient euthanasia depend upon whether their conduct is active or passive? If my thesis is correct, it is apparent that orthodox theory is not posing the right questions.

I would like to caution against a possible objection to my thesis. It might be responded that at most I have shown that the distinction between positive actions and omissions is value-laden and blurred at its outer boundaries. But the existence of troublesome borderline cases need not undermine the value of a distinction. Aren't there any number of clear cases? If so, the usefulness of this distinction might be salvaged.

I am not altogether certain how to respond to this objection. I confess that I have no clear intuitive sense of a distinction between positive actions and omissions that remains to be captured by a philosopher sufficiently clever to formulate the correct analysis. Thus I am unable to estimate with any confidence whether the alleged "borderline cases" are numerous or rare. It seems likely, however, that *most* cases in which liability is imposed for alleged positive action involve a "sequence of events" that, to borrow Williams' phrase, can be conceptualized from different "points of view." Suppose a driver deliberately runs over a pedestrian. I would think that this example represents something close to a "paradigm case" of a positive action. No one would be persuaded that his conduct should be conceptualized as an omission on the ground that harm resulted because he failed to apply his brakes. But why not? Our unwillingness to construe his conduct in this light may simply reflect our certainty that his culpability is high and liability is just. It is doubtful that the distinction between positive actions and omissions does any independent work even in this "paradigm" case.

I have provided reasons to believe that the decision to categorize conduct as a positive action or an omission is conclusory; it does not function as an independent reason to impose or resist liability. What then is the function of this distinction? I am skeptical that the contrast between positive actions and omissions has a proper place in revised criminal theory. The appropriate question is whether the defendant had *control* over a harmful result, for liability is unjust if he lacked the ability to prevent the result. The presence of control helps explain why liability should not be precluded in *Miller, Fagan,* or *Speck.*

Does the use of the control principle in this context require that doctors who perform beneficial euthanasia are murderers? Not at all. It is true that no fundamental principle of revised criminal theory exempts them from punishment. But the real basis for opposing liability in these cases should be openly acknowledged; we must recognize that sometimes good motives are relevant to liability. Once this sentiment is recognized, there is no longer a need to invoke the baffling distinction between positive actions and omissions in a circular attempt to demonstrate the injustice of liability.

### NOTES

1. I do not distinguish between inactions, refrainings, nondoings, failings to act, neglectings to act, and omissions. For a systematic account of how these various distinctions might be drawn, see Joel Feinberg, *Harm to Others,* p. 258. I use the terms "positive actions" to contrast with omissions. "Actions" is simpler but may be misleading, since some theorists regard omissions as a kind of action. Again, I use "conduct" as generic for all states of affairs for which persons may be held criminally liable, subsuming both positive actions and omissions.

2. 113 N.W. 1128 (1907).

3. 308 F.2d 307 (1962).

4. 160 N.E. 301 (1928).

5. J. C. Smith and Brian Hogan, *Criminal Law,* p. 43.

6. See note 3, p. 310. See also the list compiled by the English Criminal Law Revision Committee, reproduced in Helen Beynon, "Doctors as Murderers," *Criminal Law Review* (1982): 17, 23–24.

7. See the insightful discussion in George Fletcher, *Rethinking Criminal Law,* pp. 611–18.

8. Paul Robinson, *Criminal Law Defenses,* pp. 440–48. In tort, it appears that "courts have increased the number of special relationships that require one person to aid another in peril." See Ernest Weinrib, "The Case for a Duty to Rescue," *Yale Law Journal* 90 (1980): 247, 248.

9. William Prosser, *Law of Torts,* pp. 340–41.

10. For the classic defense of enlarging the scope of criminal liability for omissions, see Jeremy Bentham, *An Introduction to the Principles of Morals and Legislation,* p. 293, note u.

11. See the discussion of comparative law in Feinberg, *Harm,* p. 127.

12. But see, in this chapter, "The Distinction Between Acts and Omissions: Bodily Motions."

13. See chapter 4.

14. Fletcher, *Rethinking,* p. 601.

15. Glanville Williams, *Textbook of Criminal Law*, p. 150.

16. See Richard Epstein, *A Theory of Strict Liability*. See also Eric Mack, "Causing and Failing to Prevent," *Southwestern Journal of Philosophy* 7 (1976): 83; and Feinberg, *Harm*, p. 181: "If we say that A *killed* B this will probably be taken as passionate hyperbole, the equivalent of claiming that he is 'no better than a murderer,' which is surely true, even if he did not literally kill."

17. See the excellent discussion in John Kleinig, "Good Samaritanism," *Philosophy and Public Affairs* 5 (1976): 382. See also P. J. Fitzgerald, "Acting and Refraining," *Analysis* 37 (1967): 133; and Fletcher, *Rethinking*, pp. 602–6.

18. Weinrib describes this argument as "the most powerful objection that can be made to the judicial creation and enforcement of a duty to effect an easy rescue." "Duty to Rescue," p. 268. The classic source is Thomas Macaulay, "Notes on the Indian Penal Code," in Peter Low, John Jeffries, and Richard Bonnie, *Criminal Law*, p. 118.

19. Fletcher, *Rethinking*, p. 425.

20. Epstein's remark is typical: "It may well be that the conduct of individuals who do not aid fellow men is under some circumstances outrageous, but it does not follow that a legal system that does not enforce a duty to aid is outrageous as well." *Strict Liability*, p. 65. Elsewhere Epstein adopts a different line. He writes (at p. 64): "The common law position on the Good Samaritan problem is in the end consistent with both moral and economic principles." See also P. J. Fitzgerald, "In respect of omissions . . . law and morals part company." *Criminal Law and Punishment*, p. 95.

21. Rollin Perkins and Ronald Boyce, *Criminal Law*, p. 773. See also John Harris, "The Marxist Conception of Violence," *Philosophy and Public Affairs* 3 (1974): 192.

22. "In omission no human agent causes the patient's death, either directly or indirectly." Paul Ramsey, *The Patient as Person*, p. 151. See also Mack, "Causing"; Elazar Weinryb, "Omissions and Responsibility," *Philosophical Quarterly* 30 (1980): 1; Epstein, *Strict Liability;* and John Hodson, *The Ethics of Legal Coercion*, p. 39. Hodson adopts this interpretation "largely as a matter of convenience" to preserve the "uncontroversial character [of] the harm principle."

23. Fletcher, *Rethinking*, p. 423.

24. Ibid., p. 602. Here Fletcher is following Phillipa Foot, "Euthanasia," *Philosophy and Public Affairs* 6 (1977): 85.

25. Ibid., p. 582 (emphasis added). Also (p. 590): "Our aim is to develop a theory of causation that will give adequate expression to the difference between acts resulting in consequences such as human death and omissions that fail to prevent these consequences."

26. These words are used throughout the discussion of Wayne LaFave and Austin Scott, *Criminal Law*, pp. 249–50.

27. "[A]ny doubt about factual causation here is the result of faulty analysis." Perkins and Boyce, *Criminal*, p. 773.

28. Fletcher, *Rethinking*, p. 589, note 6. Some commentators seem to believe that problems of overdetermination can be circumvented by defining cause-in-fact in terms of a "substantial factor." See Wayne LaFave and Austin Scott, *Substantive Criminal Law*, pp. 394–95.

29. H. L. A. Hart and R. M. Honore would disagree somewhat. They allege that there are cases in which "a causally relevant factor is not a condition sine qua non." *Causation in the Law*, p. 121.

30. O. Harvey Green, "Killing and Letting Die," *American Philosophical Quarterly* 17 (1980): 195, 202. Green does not endorse the view I quote here; see note 32.

31. Even philosophers who are sympathetic to the view that omissions can be causes tend to describe the relationship between conduct and harm in cases of positive actions differently from that in cases of omissions. John Kleinig prefers describing omissions as "causal factors" rather than as "causes" of harm. "Good Samaritanism," p. 382.

32. Green, "Killing," p. 202.

33. Robinson, *Defenses*, p. 461.

34. Ibid., p. 461.

35. Ibid.

36. These terms are collected in Perkins and Boyce, *Criminal*, p. 775.

37. Robinson, *Defenses*, p. 462. See also Jerome Hall, *General Principles of Criminal Law*, p. 196; and Epstein, *Strict Liability*, p. 18.

38. *M.P.C.* §2.03(2).

39. Robinson, *Defenses*, p. 462.

40. LaFave and Scott, *Criminal*, p. 189. See the astute comment by Fletcher, *Rethinking*, p. 597: "One wonders whether this commonsense concept of causation is well suited to function as a basic building block in a theory of criminal liability."

41. Hart and Honore, *Causation*, pp. 68 and 123.

42. Ibid., p. 123.

43. Ibid., p. 5.

44. Ibid., p. 131.

45. Ibid., p. 36. See also Fletcher, *Rethinking*, p. 596.

46. Epstein, *Strict Liability*, p. 17. See also Joel Feinberg, "Causing Voluntary Actions," in his *Doing and Deserving*, p. 152.

47. See Hall, *General*, p. 195. Liability in these cases "is not even doubted."

48. Epstein, *Strict Liability*, p. 51, note 1. Fletcher also proposes that we "leave aside" such cases. *Rethinking*, p. 601.

49. Hart and Honore, *Causation*, p. 124.

50. But see ibid., p. 63.

51. Ibid., p. 125.

52. Paul Ryu, "Causation in Criminal Law," *University of Pennsylvania Law Review* 106 (1958): 773, 785.

53. Hart and Honore, p. 59. See also Fitzgerald, *Criminal*, p. 97.

54. Ibid., p. 59.

55. See chapter 2.

56. Weinryb, "Omission," p. 9. See also Fletcher, *Rethinking*, p. 369: "The inquiry into causation is categorical. A death is attributable to someone or it is not. There is no room for a compromise verdict."

57. "[W]hen many people have stood by and let someone die, either we have too many candidates for liability or we have none at all." Fletcher, *Rethinking*, p. 604. See also Joel Feinberg, "The Moral and Legal Responsibility of the Bad Samaritan," *Criminal Justice Ethics* 3 (1984): 56.

58. L. Jonathan Cohen, "Who Is Starving Whom?" *Theoria* 47 (1981): 65, 75.

59. See Michael Zimmerman, "Sharing Responsibility," *American Philosophical Quarterly* 22 (1985): 115.

60. For an expression of skepticism that control does not differ from causation, see John Harris, "Bad Samaritans Cause Harm," *Philosophical Quarterly* 32 (1982): 60.

61. "[C]ourts should not create liability for omissions without statutory authority. Verbs used in defining offences and prima facie implying active conduct should not be stretched by interpretation to include omissions." See Glanville Williams, "Letter to the Editor," *Criminal Law Review* (1982): 773.

62. *Vt. Stat. Ann.* tit. 12, §519 (1973): "(a) A person who knows that another is exposed to grave physical harm shall, to the extent that the same can be rendered without danger or peril to himself or without interference with important duties owed to others, give reasonable assistance to the exposed person unless that assistance or care is being provided by others."

63. See James Rachels, "Active and Passive Euthanasia," *New England Journal of Medicine* 292 (1975): 78; and Michael Tooley, "An Irrelevant Consideration: Killing Versus Letting Die," in Bonnie Steinbock, ed., *Killing and Letting Die,* p. 56.

64. See LaFave and Scott, *Criminal,* p. 191.

65. Although I believe the label "result crimes" was coined by Gordon, the concept receives its most detailed elaboration in Fletcher's discussion of "the pattern of harmful consequences." See *Rethinking,* pp. 388–90.

66. Thus Fletcher writes that liability for violations of such statutes is not "derivative." Ibid., pp. 585–88.

67. "With all such crimes there is no need to worry about causation." LaFave and Scott, *Substantive,* p. 390. But questions about causation may arise in *all* offenses if the connection between mens rea and actus reus is described as causal, that is, if a mens rea must "actuate" an actus reus to satisfy the fundamental requirement of concurrence within orthodox theory. If so, "result crimes" can be differentiated from "non-result crimes" in that they raise issues of causation on two distinct levels.

68. See the remark (attributed to Epstein) in Eric Mack, "Bad Samaritanism and the Causation of Harm," *Philosophy and Public Affairs* 9 (1980): 230, 231: "Bad Samaritan laws would assign liability for injuries where the crucial condition for the proper assignment of liability, namely causation of injury, was absent."

69. " 'Act' must be defined before an omission can be distinguished; and no agreed juristic concept of an act exists." Graham Hughes, "Criminal Omissions," *Yale Law Journal* 67 (1958): 590, 597.

70. "In theory the difference between the two is simple and obvious; but in practice it is not always easy to drawn the line." Prosser, *Torts,* p. 339. Prosser does not indicate, however, how this "obvious" distinction might be drawn "in theory."

71. See the remarks about the "responsibility thesis" in Mack, "Samaritanism," pp. 235–41.

72. Most orthodox criminal theorists have simply assumed without argument that the distinction between positive actions and omissions could be drawn by morally neutral criteria. For a criticism of this assumption, see Nancy Davis, "The Priority of Avoiding Harm," in Steinbock, *Killing,* p. 172.

73. I do not deny, of course, that a morally neutral distinction between positive actions and omissions can be *stipulated.* Anyone can simply announce that he understands the distinction to be such-and-such. The writings of philosophers are filled with such stipulations; for the most part, I will spare the reader the tedious exercise of examining their strengths and weaknesses.

See the various analyses discussed in Michael Gorr, "Omissions," *Tulane Studies in Philosophy* 28 (1979): 93.

74. But see note 42.

75. Fletcher, *Rethinking*, p. 591. See also the criticisms in Hyman Gross, *A Theory of Criminal Justice;* and Carolyn Morillo, "Comments on Gorr and Green," *Tulane Studies in Philosophy* 28 (1979): 125, 134: "I remain convinced that the difference between a decision to *move* my body in some way and the decision *not* to move it is in itself quite morally irrelevant."

76. See chapter 4.

77. Williams, *Textbook*, p. 152.

78. I describe these cases as involving "apparent" omissions because I am uncertain how the distinction between positive actions and omissions should be drawn.

79. 1 All ER 978 (1983). See also *Commonwealth v. Cali*, 141 N.E. 510 (1923).

80. 1 Q.B. 439 (1969).

81. See J. C. Smith, "Commentary," *Criminal Law Review* (1982): 527–28.

82. 2 All ER 859 (1977).

83. "The *reality* is that [Miller] is held liable because he omitted to put out the fire which he had started." Smith, "Commentary," p. 528.

84. See note 61.

85. Glanville Williams, "Criminal Assault—Parking on a Copper's Foot," *Cambridge Law Journal* (1969): 16, 17.

86. This expression was coined by Harold McNiece and John Thornton, "Affirmative Duties in Tort," *Yale Law Journal* 58 (1949): 1272. The authors fail, however, to provide a general account of how "misfeasance" and "pure nonfeasance" may be distinguished from "pseudo-nonfeasance."

87. *Speck*, p. 861.

88. The "single act" rationale was explicitly used to support the conviction in *Fagan*, but was rejected in *Miller* on the ground that it was too difficult "to explain to a jury." *Miller*, p. 983.

89. Smith, "Commentary," p. 528.

90. *Fagan* provoked a dissent, in which J. Bridge confessed his inability "to find any way of regarding the facts which satisfies me that they amounted to the crime of assault." He indicated, however, that he had "no sympathy at all for the appellant, who behaved disgracefully." *Fagan*, p. 440.

91. This kind of difficulty is noted by Weinrib, "Duty to Rescue," p. 256, note 34. Although he apparently does not regard it as insurmountable, he provides no indication about how it might be overcome.

92. See note 78.

93. 148 S.W.2d 1044 (1941).

94. "There is no reason why the case of any person who innocently creates a dangerous situation should be judged differently from that of the bystander who sees a person in danger of life and limb and does not assist him." Otto Kirchheimer, "Criminal Omissions," *Harvard Law Review* 58 (1942): 615, 627. The law may be changing. See Prosser, *Torts*, pp. 342–43.

95. George Fletcher, "Prolonging Life: Some Legal Considerations," *Washington Law Review* 42 (1967): 999, 1005.

96. Ibid., p. 1006.

97. Ibid., p. 1007.

98. Ibid., p. 1014.

99. See the criticisms in I. M. Kennedy, "Switching-off Life Support Machines: The Legal Implications," *Criminal Law Review* (1977): 443. For criticisms of linguistic criteria generally, see Richard Trammell, "A Criterion for Determining Negativity and Positivity of Duties," *Tulane Studies in Philosophy* 33 (1985): 75.

100. Fletcher, "Prolonging," p. 1012.

101. "There is something unquestionably bizarre about equating this medical decision with a gunman's killing in cold blood." Fletcher, *Rethinking*, p. 607.

102. See Smith and Hogan, *Criminal*, p. 277. See my discussion in chapter 5.

103. Fletcher himself opposes recognizing good motives as a defense on the ground that such a policy "would legitimate cases of overtly terminating the lives of persons who either desire to die or whose lives are deemed unworthy." *Rethinking*, p. 607. This ground involves undue pessimism about our ability to distinguish good from bad motives.

104. See Beynon, "Doctors."

105. Smith and Hogan, *Criminal*, p. 44.

106. Consider the following from Hughes, "Omissions," pp. 598–99: "The nature of certain offenses may make classification difficult. Examples may be drawn from the offenses of practicing certain callings without a license. Does the offense lie in practicing—commission—or in failing to obtain a license? The question is clearly absurd. . . . It is clearly the most tedious kind of verbal dispute to argue about the proper description of his offense in terms of action or omission."

# 7
# *Substantive Defenses*

## A TAXONOMY OF DEFENSES

L<small>EGAL PHILOSOPHERS HAVE BEEN FAMILIAR</small> with the distinction between justification and excuse since at least 1957, the date of publication of John Austin's "A Plea for Excuses."[1] Austin writes: "In the one defense, briefly, we accept responsibility but deny that it was bad: in the other, we admit that it was bad but don't accept full, or even any responsibility."[2] Austin thought that attention to this distinction would illuminate a wide range of substantive problems. But he could not have anticipated the extraordinary explanatory power some criminal theorists would claim on behalf of this distinction. A few theorists have been so adamant in supporting the utility of this distinction that it has almost become part of orthodoxy.[3] This chapter will critically discuss this distinction, with special emphasis on the various uses to which it has been put.

In this section I will present this distinction uncritically, and supplement it with another required to complete a taxonomy of substantive defenses. This taxonomy comprises the various ways a person can defend himself from an accusation that he is liable for having committed a criminal offense. A defendant who possesses a substantive defense merits no punishment (or perhaps a less severe punishment than he would otherwise deserve). A number of defenses, of course, are not substantive, and do not respect rights or reflect requirements of justice merited by defendants. Our criminal justice system recognizes a host of defenses designed to promote objectives quite apart from treating particular defendants according to their deserts. Jurisdictional and venue rules ensure that persons are judged by proper tribunals; exclusionary rules penalize illegal law enforcement; statutes of limitations guarantee that trials are timely; entrapment discourages overzealous law enforcement; proscriptions of double jeopardy protect defendants from harassment and anxiety, etc. These might be called *procedural defenses*.[4] Society pays a high price for recognizing some of these procedural defenses, and their validity continues to be a subject of heated political debate. The distinction between substance and procedure is notoriously elusive; I have no clear way to draw it.[5] I simply presuppose the rough accuracy of a distinction between defenses that reflect the merits of a case as contrasted with the proper means for ascertaining them.

In the first three sections of this Chapter I present a sketch of the logic or structure of substantive criminal law defenses. Such defenses are of three general kinds: denials, justifications, and excuses.[6] This project is termed an inquiry into the logic or structure of substantive defenses because the proposed taxonomy does not beg questions about whether a particular defense should be recognized as valid for a given offense.[7] It is conceivable (though draconian) that a given offense should admit of no justifications or excuses whatever. But it is more plausible that a specified justification or excuse, generally recognized, should not be valid for a particular offense. Perhaps, for example, duress or necessity should not constitute a defense to murder.[8] This taxonomy is not designed to resolve such controversies, although it is useful for providing the framework in which these disagreements can be expressed. Additional substantive argument is needed to determine which defenses should be recognized as valid for given offenses, just as substantive argument is required to determine which kinds of conduct should be criminalized. Moral and political arguments are needed if these difficult questions are to be resolved. But this taxonomy would not be worthy of study if there were no connections between the logic or structure of defenses and such substantive issues. Some of these connections will be explored in the final two sections of this chapter, and the topic clearly is ripe for further discussion. After long neglect, criminal theorists have finally begun to appreciate the practical applications of a proper understanding of the logic or structure of criminal law defenses.[9]

I begin with the notion of *criminal offenses* as something distinct from criminal law *defenses*.[10] Each offense has components known as *elements*.[11] Murder might be defined to require that a defendant (1) intentionally (2) kills (3) a human being. Element (2) might be further subdivided into (2a) causes and (2b) the death of. However, no important questions depend upon the *number* of elements that constitute a given offense, as long as there is agreement that each subdivision is included within an element expressly listed. But the failure to explicitly dissect offenses into their component elements may conceal important disagreements. It could be argued, for example, that one can *kill* without *causing* death.[312] Thus it is advisable to subdivide offenses into the maximum number of elements of which they are composed.

The first and simplest kind of defense to an existing criminal offense is to *deny* commission of one or more of its elements. Denials are of two types. In the first, one denies that a condition or state of affairs described by an element obtained, as when one defends against the above accusation by alleging that no one was killed, or that the victim was not a human being. These sorts of denials might be called *denials of the occurrence of the offense*. In the second type, one denies that an element was committed by the defendant, as when one claims not to have been the killer. These sorts of denials might be called *denials of agency*. The first denies that the offense was committed, while the second denies that the offense was committed by the person accused. Criminal theory provides for both types of denials by a simple application of the fundamental principle of legality. Each type of denial, if valid, establishes the innocence of the defendant.

A somewhat more complex kind of defense is a *justification*. A defendant who alleges a justification contends that his conduct was not legally wrongful in his particular circumstances, even though it may (or may not) have satisfied each of the elements of a criminal offense. For example, a defendant might contend that his intentional killing of a human being took place in circumstances that constitute self-defense, and that a killing in self-defense is not wrongful. The conduct of a defendant who acts under a justification may be exemplary and socially encouraged, but more typically is permissible and socially tolerated.[13]

The several justifications known to the criminal law are frequently conceptualized as exceptions to the offenses for which they are valid, that is, as qualifications, exceptive clauses, or implicit elements amended to the otherwise incomplete specification of offenses.[14] I will describe this understanding of justifications as the "implicit elements" approach.[15] Alternatively, one can treat persons who act under a justification as having a license, liberty, or privilege to commit a given offense.[16] I will refer to this understanding of justifications as the "license" approach. A few criminal theorists employ both characterizations.[17]

*Excuses* are the third and final kind of substantive defense. Unlike denials and justifications, excuses cannot be used to show that the conduct of the defendant was not legally wrongful. Instead, an excuse provides a reason why the accused should not be punished, at least not to the extent typically deserved,[18] even though his conduct might (or might not) satisfy each of the explicit elements of a criminal offense without justification. Most valid excuses refer to some characteristic of the defendant (sometimes called a disablity)[19] in virtue of which punishment should not be imposed, or at least decreased in severity. For example, a defendant who claims to have been insane at the time of his offense does not dispute the wrongfulness of his conduct, but rather alleges that the severity of punishment ordinarily deserved by persons who commit such offenses would be excessive and unjust if imposed upon him. Murders committed by the sane and insane are equally wrongful. There should be no temptation to assimilate excuses to the "license" approach to justifications, and construe defendants who act under an excuse as having a privilege or liberty to commit a given offense, as though the insane possess an extraordinary "license to kill."[20]

This taxonomy is reasonably familiar to orthodox criminal theorists.[21] Nonetheless, confusion about how these distinctions should be drawn has given rise to a number of problems. Awareness of these difficulties requires that the distinctions in this taxonomy be further clarified and refined.


## ADVANTAGES OF THE TAXONOMY

CARELESSNESS IN DRAWING the distinctions in the taxonomy of substantive defenses should be avoided for two reasons. First, it gives rise to puzzles that are easily avoided; second, it misleads some theorists to believe that they have solved some genuine and important problems. This taxonomy is useful in showing their solutions to be spurious; thus the problems they have claimed to solve should be reopened. In this section I will identify some of these advantages of the taxonomy.

### Two Accounts of Justifications

Two conceptions of justifications have been presented in this chapter. According to the "implicit elements" approach, justifications are construed as exceptions or qualifications to criminal offenses. According to the "license" approach, justifications are construed as liberties to commit criminal offenses. Although few theorists are sensitive to the difference, it is important to appreciate that these conceptions are incompatible.

The inconsistency between these two approaches should be evident. According to the "implicit elements" approach, a defendant who acts under a valid justification *cannot* commit the offense charged. His conduct may have satisfied each of the explicit elements of a given offense, but complete offenses are comprised of *all* their elements: unless the conduct of the defendant satisfies the implicit as well as the explicit elements, he has *not* committed the offense. This approach would add (at least) a fourth (implicit) element to the offense of murder, viz., (4) without self-defense. A defendant needs no license to commit what is not a criminal offense. On the other hand, according to the "license" approach, a defendant who acts under a justification *can* (and frequently *does*) commit the offense charged. The commission of the offense is not undermined by establishing a justification, although the presumption that the offense constitutes a legal wrong is rebutted. This approach does not amend the earlier description of first degree murder; it is complete as originally specified. In short, the "implicit elements" approach conceptualizes justifications by refining the descriptions of offenses, while the "license" approach construes justifications as properties possessed by defendants in virtue of the circumstances surrounding their conduct. Which approach is preferable?

It should be noted that the distinction between denials and justifications is threatened by the "implicit elements" approach. One might conclude that there can be *no* justification for commiting an offense by construing each alleged justificatory condition as the absence of an implied element. According to this approach, persons who act under a valid justification do not commit offenses for the same reason as persons who allege a valid denial—each element of the offense has not been satisfied. Justifications negate "implicit" elements; denials negate "explicit" elements. Thus the distinction between justifications and denials is at least eroded and at most collapsed by the "implicit elements" approach. This distinction is eroded because justifications, like denials, negate elements of offenses; this distinction is collapsed altogether if there is no important difference between implicit and explicit elements of offenses. Thus a persuasive case in favor of the "license" approach awaits a demonstration of the substantive importance of preserving the distinction between denials and justifications.[22] Nonetheless, an inconclusive and tentative defense of the "license" approach can be sketched prior to an understanding of the utility of this distinction.

First, an intuitive difference between denials and justifications defies any attempt to erode or collapse it. We are all familiar with the distinction between defenses that are preceded by "no, I didn't do it" rather than by "maybe I did do it, but." Moreover, if justifications are construed as negating implied elements of offenses, it follows that actual descriptions of most (or perhaps all) offenses are incomplete. It is doubtful that anyone has succeeded in completely describing the offense of larceny, for example, since any attempt to do so would require an exhaustive list of those circumstances in which it is not legally wrongful to satisfy its explicit elements. Persons who teach and work with the law would be dismayed to learn that their statements of offenses are only incomplete approximations. Our understanding of the fundamental principle of legality might have to be revised if criminal theory entailed that few (if any) offenses could be accurately described. One could seek to remedy this difficulty by including the word "unlawfully" or the clause "without justification" as an element of each offense, but this solution would undermine the precision achieved by dissecting offenses into elements. In light of these advantages of the "license" approach (neither of which is decisive), it becomes appropriate to explore what can be said in favor of the alternative "implicit elements" approach.

Admittedly, there is a great resistance to supposing that persons who act under a valid justification commit a criminal offense, and this resistance explains much of the appeal of the "implicit elements" approach. A defendant who killed in self-defense would be indignant to learn that he had committed a criminal offense. Moreover, the "license" approach may give rise to a confusion between justifications and excuses. It is clear that "acts are justified; agents are excused."[23] The "license" approach, however, may foster the misapprehension that justifications derive from characteristics of defendants rather than of their conduct. To be precise, justifications *are* possessd by agents, but arise because of circumstances that indicate that their *conduct* is not wrongful. Finally, the suggestion that it is not always legally wrongful to commit a criminal offense is bound to cause puzzlement. These results, however, are not theoretically devastating. According to the "license" approach, persons who act under a valid justification *can* commit an offense, though they are not *liable* for so doing. Criminal liability does not result from the simple commission of an offense, but rather from the commission of an offense *without justification or excuse.* To underscore this point, I will speak of offenses, and the absence of justifications and excuses as the *three components of criminal liability.*

I believe the advantages of the "license" approach outweigh those of the "implicit elements" approach. But the issue is not clear-cut; it is unwise to be emphatic here. It is at least arguable that different justifications are amenable to different approaches; the structure or logic of each justification need not be identical. Still, problems and confusions can be avoided by appreciating the differences, and thus the drawbacks, of each approach.

### Ignorance of Law and the Modification of Offenses

Some arguments advanced by orthodox theorists are unsound because they fail to apply the taxonomy of criminal law defenses developed above. Perhaps the best example is the reasoning of Jerome Hall that purports to show why ignorance of law should not be a defense from criminal liability. According to Hall, the consequences would be absurd if *ignorantia juris* were valid. He begins with the sensible premise that the fundamental principle of legality requires that the conduct of persons be judged according to "objective" law. He then attempts to show that this principle implies that ignorance of law should be an invalid defense. Legality could not allow the criminal law to change in conformity with whatever misapprehensions defendants might have about its content. Yet those who favor a defense of ignorance of law are said to be committed to this very absurdity. He writes:

> If that plea were valid, the consequences would be: whenever a defendant in a criminal case thought the law was thus and so, he is to be treated as though the law were thus and so, i.e., *the law actually is thus and so*. But such a doctrine would contradict the essential requisites of a legal system, the implications of the principle of legality.[24]

Thus Hall concludes that ignorance of law should not be recognized as a valid defense in any system of criminal justice that respects legality.

Unfortunately, Hall's argument for rejecting this defense has persuaded many a criminal theorist. Herbert Packer agrees that "once the conduct has been so defined [as criminal], one cannot usurp the lawmaking function by pleading that his ignorance must mean that the conduct is not criminal as to him."[25] Even Paul Robinson, who refines a taxonomy that should enable him to refute Hall's argument, concurs that the validity of the defense of *ignorantia juris* "makes it more difficult to maintain the integrity of the prohibition violated."[26]

Nonetheless, the defect in this argument should be evident to anyone who understands the taxonomy of defenses developed earlier. Not all defenses have the effect of modifying the content of offenses; some defenses can be recognized as valid without altering the description of offenses one whit. The objectivity of law, required by the fundamental principle of legality, is not undermined by each and every defense. The contrary view supposes that the validity of all defenses must be conceptualized as implicit elements of various offenses. But excuses do not negate implicit elements, and (on the preferred "license" approach) neither do justifications.[27] Of course, to the extent that ignorance of law should be a valid defense to criminal liability, there is no doubt that it should be categorized as an excuse.[28]

The refutation of Hall's argument amply illustrates the virtues of a taxonomy of substantive defenses. The case against the validity of the defense of ignorance of law, once widely regarded as decisive, is easily seen to be unpersuasive. Criminal theorists should be willing to reopen the question of under what conditions, if any, ignorance of law should be recognized as a valid defense.[29]

### The Serial View of Defenses

According to Robinson, the several different kinds of defenses may be placed along a continuum: "Each successive type of defense need be considered only if those preceding it are unavailable."[30] If a defendant denies the commission of a criminal offense, issues pertaining to other defenses cannot arise, and so on along the defense spectrum: "Justifications and excuse are serial rather than alternative determinations. One asks whether an actor should be excused only after he has determined that the act was not justified. If the act was justified, there would of course be nothing to excuse."[31] I will refer to this sequential conception as the *serial view of defenses*. Virtually all criminal theorists who present a taxonomy suppose that defenses are ordered in some sort of sequence.[32] According to this conception, a defendant who alleges a given defense should be understood to concede the unavailability of each defense prior to it along the spectrum.

Fletcher maintains that this serial view is supported by ordinary language.[33] Robinson observes that one is always justified or excused *for something*. Perhaps so; but what is supposed to follow from this observation? Although it is clear that an excuse is not required unless one is *accused* of criminal conduct, it is not as clear that one who alleges an excuse thereby *concedes* that criminal conduct has taken place.

One basis for suspicion about the serial view of defenses is that theorists who subscribe to it provide radically different sequential orderings.[34] Robinson's claim that the allegation of an excuse concedes the absence of a justification is typical, but by no means universal. A few theorists contend that at least some excuses should be placed first on the continuum of defenses.[35] If a defendant is excused for his conduct, why should it matter whether he has committed a criminal offense without justification? Still other theorists seem to believe that the use of either defense concedes the absence of the other. Austin, whose quotation introduced this chapter, writes that persons who offer a justification "accept responsibility," while those who allege an excuse "admit that it was bad." This vast difference of opinion should encourage theorists to reconsider whether defenses are serially ordered at all.

In sharp contrast with the serial view, I believe it is preferable to understand the several defenses in the taxonomy so that the use of one does not preclude the use of any other. A defendant who alleges an excuse cites some property or characteristic in virtue of which he should not be held liable *whether or not* he has committed the offense charged; he categorically concedes neither the commission of the offense nor the absence of justification. Similarly, a defendant who alleges a justification claims that his conduct was not wrongful *whether or not* he has committed the offense charged; he categorically concedes neither the commission of the offense nor the absence of excuse. I will refer to the view that the use of any given type of defense does not preclude the use of any other type of defense as the *nonserial view of defenses.*

The superiority of the nonserial view of defenses can be demonstrated by an illustration. The following example presupposes that (nonmistaken) self-defense functions as a justification, and accident and mistake as excuses.[36] Suppose that Sue is attacked without provocation in her home by a thug wielding a knife. She retreats to her bedroom with her assailant in hot pursuit. The thug provides every indication of his intent to kill her. Sue is an extreme pacifist who would rather lose her own life than kill another. Still, she hopes to scare her attacker away by brandishing a hunting rifle she reasonably believes to be unloaded. Much to her horror, the rifle is loaded; she accidentally fires it, and kills her assailant.

Several valid defenses are available to Sue in the unlikely event that she is charged with murder. She can *deny* that her killing was intentional; she can *justify* her conduct as involving self-defense; or she can *excuse* her killing as mistaken or accidental. Given her pacifist convictions and the remorse she would be expected to feel about her conduct, it would not be surprising if her inclination were to excuse her killing. Use of this defense, however, should not be taken as an admission that no denial or justification is available. But the serial view of defenses entails these very concessions. According to this view, it is incoherent for Sue to defend by alleging a denial or justification in the event that her excuse is disbelieved or for some reason not recognized as valid. This scenario, however, is preserved as coherent by the nonserial view of defenses, in which no kind of defense would preclude the use of any other.

Once it is apparent that questions about justifications *can* be raised subsequent to allegations of excuses, it becomes important whether there are any circumstances in which these issues *should* be raised in this sequence. Perhaps the cases in which it is most sensible to begin a defense with an excuse are those involving some general disability that precludes liability for any criminal offense, such as infancy or extreme mental abnormality.[37] Again, if a defendant alleges either of these disabilities, what is to be gained by first determining that he has committed a criminal offense without justification? If he loses on his infancy or insanity pleas, of course, a finding of liability will require that his conduct was unjustified.

It is not my thesis that this question cannot be answered satisfactorily. I contend only that it is important, and that criminal theorists should not be misled into avoiding it by a taxonomy that dismisses it as incoherent.

### The Rationale of the Insanity Defense

An increasing number of jurisdictions have abolished the insanity defense,[38] and many others are giving the matter serious consideration. According to the "abolitionists," the defense of insanity should be recognized only in those circumstances in which the criminal law already allows a defense from criminal liability for sane defendants, for example, ignorance and involuntariness.[39] Thus the insanity defense, when properly understood, is redundant and unnecessary.

This challenge has forced the "retentionists" to articulate the ground or basis of the insanity defense, and to explain whether and under what circumstances mental abnormality should create a special, separate exemption from criminal liability.[40] This issue cannot be resolved without addressing some of the most difficult questions in moral, political, and legal philosophy. Why is anyone excused? Why is anyone punished? How are the answers to these questions related? It seems unlikely that retentionist strategies that avoid confronting these issues can be persuasive. A taxonomy of defenses will prove its value if it can cast any light upon the intractable insanity controversy.

Herbert Fingarette has made a systematic endeavor to identify the conditions under which it is unjust to punish mentally abnormal offenders.[41] He states that "the condition that directly justifies ascribing nonresponsibility, insofar as this is justified at all, is the defendant's irrational condition of mind in committing the offense."[42] Fingarette believes he has responded to the abolitionists. If the ground or basis of the insanity defense is the irrationality of the defendant, then some mentally abnormal offenders should escape punishment even though they are neither ignorant[43] nor behave involuntarily.[44]

Of course, none of this should persuade the abolitionist unless Fingarette can show why it is unjust to punish mentally abnormal, irrational persons. Here his endeavor suffers from his misunderstanding of the taxonomy of defenses. Fingarette contends:

> Law addresses itself to those who have reached relative maturity and are acting in their right mind. . . . It makes no sense to speak of the law as addressed to the month-old infant unable to respond intelligently; and in consequence the whole panoply of associated moral sanctions is not applicable to the infant . . . The upshot is the same in the case of the mentally disabled adult . . . They are in that respect "outside" the law . . . in the sense that the accusatory process is inappropriate.[45]

In short, the plea of insanity "is not the offering of an excuse. . . . It is not a challenge to the prosecution's case but a plea to circumvent the prosecutory process."[46] Thus Fingarette believes he need not show why insanity should be recognized as an excuse; he does deems it unnecessary to address the difficult questions mentioned above.

Why does Fingarette not regard insanity as an excuse? This failure derives from his misunderstanding of the nature of defenses in general and excuses in particular. He contends that "all defensive strategies are directed to *defeating* an accusation."[47] Clearly Fingarette is mistaken here; only denials "defeat" accusations, and not all defenses are denials.

In fact, Fingarette's entire strategy for litigating the insanity defense is inconsistent with his claim that insanity does not function as an excuse. In cases in which insanity is alleged, he recommends that

> the trial jury . . . make an extremely simple sequence of basic decisions . . . The jury first decides the question as to guilt or innocence on each count . . . Only if the defendant has been found guilty on at least one count do they proceed to a consideration of the [insanity] issue.[48]

The inconsistency here should be evident. If a defendant is insane and thus, according to Fingarette, may "circumvent the prosecutory process," by what possible authority does a court first determine his guilt or innocence? The problems are even more acute. If the prosecutory process is circumvented, there can be no justification for a court order mandating commitment. These conclusions are unacceptable. No one doubts the authority of the court either to try the insane or to order commitment if statutory conditions are satisfied.

The truth of the matter is that the law is "addressed" to the sane and insane alike.[49] It is unsound to construe excuses as exceptions to the scope of offenses, as though the criminal law proscribes murder for all but the insane.[50] It is at least plausible to adopt the "implicit elements" account of justifications and contend, for example, that persons who kill in self-defense do not commit a criminal offense. But no theorist who is sensitive to the distinction between justifications and excuses would construe insanity as a justification for committing a criminal offense.[51] Once it is apparent that insanity cannot be construed as an exception to the scope of offenses, and that the criminal law is addressed to all, Fingarette is without any rationale for acquitting irrational, mentally abnormal offenders.

Thus Fingarette has not refuted the position defended by the abolitionists. Perhaps he is correct that defendants should be allowed an insanity defense when they are irrational, but his position has not been adequately defended.[52] It is unlikely that the abolitionists will be refuted by retentionist strategies that fail to construe insanity as an excuse from criminal liability.

## PROBLEMS OF CLASSIFICATION

DESPITE SUBTLE IMPROVEMENTS in our understanding of defense types, difficulties still persist in the taxonomy. At the most superficial level, the challenge is simply to place a given defense in its appropriate category.[53] This task will prove formidable.[54] At a deeper level, the problem becomes even more acute. It is one thing to be aware that any number of defenses resist facile categorization, and quite another to understand *why* these theoretically clear dichotomies should prove so stubborn in practice. Is there a single reason, or a set of reasons why so many defenses are not easily categorized? Commentators since Austin have noted the difficulties of classification, but almost no theorist has offered a principled account of why such difficulties persist.

Of course, it cannot be determined whether it is *important* to assign each particular defense to a unique category without some understanding of the uses to which this taxonomy is put. Why does it matter, for example, that a given defense is labeled a denial or an excuse? It might be thought premature to embrace a classification without appreciating what this commitment entails. Still, the prospects for *any* application of this taxonomy are remote without at least rough criteria for sorting defenses into appropriate categories. Moreover, the theorist becomes vulnerable to accusations of question-begging if he works backwards by gerrymandering the categorizations to achieve desired outcomes. Classification would then fail to function as an independent *reason* in favor of such results. Hence a case can be made to categorize defenses *before* fully understanding the uses to which these categorizations will be put. When such purposes are finally introduced, it may become appropriate to rethink earlier decisions about classification.

The taxonomy recognizes three kinds of defenses, each of which raises distinct problems when contrasted with any other. Each of these contrasts will be discussed in turn. The final subsection raises the difficult problem of why these problems are difficult.

### Denials and Justifications

Consider first the contrast between denials and justifications. Perhaps the hardest cases for purposes of applying this distinction are those involving *consent*. In a range of offenses the absence of consent can function as an element, or the presence of consent can function as a justification. One such offense is rape. Is nonconsent an element of rape, so that the offense has not occurred unless the element of nonconsent is satisfied? Or is consent a justification, so that persons given consent have a license (denied to those without consent) to commit the offense? Neither alternative should be dismissed out of hand.[55]

Many theorists who first encounter difficulties in distinguishing denials from justifications resort to ordinary language for guidance.[56] This strategy appears to yield definitive results. Few would contend that the offense of rape has been committed unless consent were absent; thus it is concluded that nonconsent functions as an element of rape. But the chief difficulty in allowing ordinary language to resolve such issues is that it threatens to categorize *all* justifications as denials, so that the class of justifications becomes empty. Even (non-mistaken) self-defense, a paradigm justification, is classified as (the absence of) an element on this approach. Although "I didn't rape her; she consented!" sounds plausible, "I didn't murder her, I acted in self-defense!" sounds equally so. The word "offense," and the names of particular offenses, seem to function in ordinary language to encompass both the elements of particular crimes and the absences of justifications. Perhaps the word "offense," as used here, should be understood as a technical term of legal art. In any case, there is room for considerable doubt that ordinary language is sufficiently sensitive to this distinction to be of much assistance in drawing it.[57]

But the decision to treat this issue as "technical" does not mean that it must be left entirely to the arbitrary discretion of technicians. There is an unfortunate tendency to allow legislatures to categorize defenses in any way they wish. Some jurisdictions may choose to treat nonconsent as an element of the offense of rape; others may prefer to regard it as a justification. Is there a "right answer" to this question? The fact that some categorizations *obviously* are incorrect shows that immediate resort to legislative discretion is premature. No one would allow a legislature to categorize a "nonkilling" as a justification for homicide, rather than to classify killing as an element. But on what principle should this absurd proposal be rejected? The legislator may hope for assistance in drawing these distinctions, and the theorist who prematurely resorts to discretion rather than principle does him a disservice. Moreover, the use of discretion cannot provide a sound basis to help resolve substantive problems in subsequent applications of these categories.[58]

Is there a preferable strategy? The only general attempt to systematically distinguish denials from justifications that does not rely heavily on "what the ordinary man would say" or place trust in the fortuities of legislative draftsmanship has been advanced by George

Fletcher. He proposes that the class of elements[59] of an offense "is determined by finding the minimal set of criteria that, in the given society, conveys a morally significant prohibition."[60] A component of liability that exceeds this minimum is then treated as (the absence of) a justification. In a given case, one decides whether to include a component of liability as an element of an offense by deciding whether the remaining set of elements constitute a "morally significant prohibition." If so, the component is treated as (the absence of) a justification; if not, it is regarded as an element.

Fletcher's (unarticulated) reason for adopting this criterion seems to be as follows. Unless the set of elements of an offense includes a "morally significant prohibition," no presumption of legal wrongdoing can arise, and it would be unjust to subject defendants to criminal liability for violating it. In short, there can be nothing to justify unless the set of elements express a coherent offense. Thus offenses should be comprised of at least the *minimal* set of elements necessary to incriminate the defendant. But why stop at the minimum? Since Fletcher does not directly address this question, an answer will have to be attributed to him. Stopping here, I suppose, guarantees that components of liability that exceed this minimum threshold are categorized as (the absences of) justifications. If offenses were comprised of the *maximum* set of components that incriminate the defendant, the class of justifications would be empty. Since a line must be drawn somewhere (if the distinction between denials and justifications is to be preserved), it is best to stop at the minimum. If a more plausible reconstruction of Fletcher's reasoning is forthcoming, it will have to be provided by Fletcher himself.

It will be helpful to consider Fletcher's own example in attempting to understand his test. He applies his criterion to conclude that consent should function as a justification for rape, rather than as (the absence of) an element. This conclusion is reached by listing, "in order of ascending incrimination," the following components of rape:

1. touching;
2. sexual contact;
3. forcible sexual contact; and
4. non-consensual, forcible sexual contact.[61]

The purpose of this list is to determine at what point on the continuum the description barely suffices to specify incriminating conduct. Additional components are treated as (the absences of) justifications.

Even if the rationale of Fletcher's list is not challenged, it is doubtful that it yields definitive results. Fletcher believes that the line between the "minimal set of elements necessary to incriminate the actor" should be drawn somewhere between components 2 and 4. But it is unclear why this should be so. He provides no support for his claim that "it is difficult to argue that touching per se is incriminating."[62] Nor does he offer much guidance to indicate when a set of components is minimally sufficient to incriminate.[63] The difficulty of ascertaining when this threshold is crossed seems no less acute than the problem the criterion was designed to resolve.

Moreover, the procedure for generating the list is mysterious. It is unlikely that a unique sequence of "incriminating elements" exists for each offense. Perhaps the offense of rape is better dissected as follows:

1. touching;
2. forcible touching;
3. forcible sexual touching; and
4. nonconsensual forcible sexual touching.

Why is one list preferable to another? Clearly, defenses will be categorized differently depending upon how this sequence is generated.

It is not at all apparent how a similar procedure could help to distinguish denials from justifications in other examples. Consider its application to a case the outcome of which almost everyone (including Fletcher) is confident: (nonmistaken) self-defense as a justification for murder. The initial difficulty is how to begin to list the components of liability in ascending order of incrimination. If "touching" heads the list for rape, I suppose that "killing" (of a human being) would head the list for murder. If so, however, *no* further components are required to render the list minimally incriminating; killing alone suffices. Thus self-defense emerges as a justification—precisely the desired outcome. The difficulty, of course, is that other components of liability always classified as elements of murder turn out to be (the absences of) justifications as well. Surely we cannot be satisfied with a test that categorizes the absence of intent as a justification for murder.[64]

The problem is not that the line may have been drawn in the wrong place, but that the test itself seems unworkable. First, the minimally incriminating core of a number of distinct offenses is identical, viz., a touching. It seems obvious that different elements differentiate, for instance, battery from rape. On Fletcher's view, however, the elements of these offenses appear to be identical, since any components of liability that differentiate them are beyond this "minimally incriminating" core and are thus assigned to the category of justifications. Moreover, the requirement that the set of elements must be *morally* incriminating is problematic in the context of offenses that are *malum prohibita*. What is "the minimal set of criteria" sufficient to "convey a morally significant prohibition" for the offense of driving on the wrong side of the street? Any immorality expressed here seems to be conveyed by nothing short of the entire offense. Could this entail that it *cannot* be justified?

It may appear that I have expended too much effort to refute a proposal with so little to recommend it. But if there is so little promise in the most thoughtful and principled attempt to distinguish denials from justifications, the several substantive applications of this distinction become suspect. Hopefully future endeavors to draw this distinction will bear more fruit.

### *Justifications and Excuses*

Perhaps the best examples to undermine confidence in the ability to distinguish justifications from excuses are those involving *duress* and *necessity*.[65] Suppose Smith threatens to rape Jones's wife unless he steals a car from White. Or suppose that Jones will suffer malnourishment on a deserted mountain unless he breaks into Black's unoccupied cabin and eats his food. Most persons would recognize Jones's defenses as valid, but where should they be located on the taxonomy? Are his *acts* permissible, or is *he* blameless despite the wrongfulness of his conduct?

Since the distinction between justifications and excuses has received more attention from philosophers than that between justifications and denials, it is disappointing to find that so little ingenuity has been brought to bear on such difficulties of categorization. Lawrence Heintz, in discussing Austin, advances "a point which, if kept in mind, resolves most questions of whether a particular defense is a justification or an excuse."[66] He proposes that "a fuller description of the event in its context" will enable us "to determine whether one is saying that all things considered it was the right thing to do *or* whether one is defending oneself by pointing out the difficulties and problems one was unable to overcome."[67] In short, if this "fuller description" pertains to the person, and shows that he is not to be blamed, the defense should be categorized as an excuse; if it pertains to the act, and shows it not to have been wrongful, the defense should be classified as a justification. Are these remarks helpful? So far as I can see, Henitz's criterion for sorting troublesome cases seems to be more like a restatement of the distinction itself than an independent means to apply it. How is the test to be used when the defendant cites both characteristics of himself *and* his act? Consider how Jones might elaborate upon his story when alleging duress or necessity. Surely he would point out the dire consequences that would have ensued had he not taken the car from White or the food from Black. Are these further details properties of Jones or his act? It is dogmatic to insist that they must be one or the other. I am skeptical that a satisfactory test for distinguishing justifications from excuses can be found in the writings of moral philosophers or legal theorists.

### Denials and Excuses

Consider finally the distinction between denials and excuses. If any pair of defenses is easy to contrast, this seems to be the likely candidate. Unfortunately, it too proves highly problematic. Cases of *involuntariness* provide the best examples of ambivalence on the part of criminal theorists. It may seem obvious that apparent criminality performed while sleepwalking or undergoing a seizure should be excused. But this apparent truism has been contested by as many criminal theorists as not, for whom the concept of an "involuntary act" has been denounced as incoherent.[68] According to this view, one who may appear to be "driving while unconscious" is not really "driving" at all.[69] Thus involuntariness is treated as a denial rather than as an excuse.

Some of the reasons for and against categorizing the defense of involuntariness as a denial or an excuse have been discussed elsewhere,[70] and I will not rehearse them here. Perhaps the most theoretically interesting argument in favor of treating involuntariness as a denial involves an analysis of the concept of action. Following the lead of Austin and Hart,[71] a number of philosophers have renounced the view that the concept of action could be analyzed into necessary and sufficient conditions. Instead action was said to be an "ascriptive and defeasible concept." An ascriptive and defeasible concept is best applied by ensuring the absence of the circumstances under which it is *in*correctly applied. Involuntariness constitutes one of several circumstances alleged to defeat the correct application of the concept of action. I will not recite the well-known difficulties with this analysis of action.[72] Instead, I will simply point out that, if correct, it threatens to destroy the distinction between denials and excuses altogether. *Any* reason for believing that a defendant should be excused for his action becomes a reason for denying that he acted at all. Even H. L. A. Hart, who originally defended an ascriptive and defeasibility analysis of action, came to recognize that excuses constitute a separate category of defenses.[73] I conclude that none of these three pairs of distinctions is immune from classificatory difficulties.

### Why the Problems?

Perhaps the greatest difficulty is to understand why the classification of so many defenses should prove so elusive. Many criminal theorists simply note the problems in categorization, but fail to explain why they exist. The issues are two: Why are so many defenses difficult to classify? And to what extent do these problems of categorization undermine the potential to use this taxonomy to shed light on substantive issues in criminal law?

Robinson is perhaps unique among criminal theorists in attempting to answer both these questions. Before describing a number of "problematic classifications," he writes:

> Consider the nature of these problematic classifications. They appear to be precisely those defenses for which proper formulation of the defense has been a matter of confusion and debate. If this is true, the fact that these defenses do not fit cleanly into one category only reinforces the scheme's usefulness. If ambiguity in classification coincides with independently generated disputes over proper formulation, it would seem to confirm that the distinctions made by the scheme are central to the ongoing criminal law theory debates, although perhaps not presently recognized as such.[74]

Is Robinson correct? Do the difficulties raised in this section coincide with "independently generated disputes over proper formulation" of a given defense? If so, how? If not, why is it so hard to categorize a defense accurately?

It is difficult to assess whether or not Robinson is correct, for it is unclear what he means by the "proper formulation" of a defense. A charitable interpretation is that the "proper formulation" of a defense is a function of whether and under what conditions that defense should be *valid*. Perhaps ambivalence about the appropriate categorization of a defense reflects uncertainty about its scope and limitations.[75] In other words, problems of classification may coincide with independent uncertainty about the very substantive issues the taxonomy is applied to help resolve. If so, Robinson's remarks are extremely suggestive.

To determine whether independent substantive debates coincide with difficulties of categorization, reconsider each of the above problems of classification. First, it is unclear whether to regard nonconsent as an element of rape, or consent as a justification. Now: What are the independent disputes about the validity of the defense of consent in cases of alleged rape? No one contests the general validity of consent as a defense to rape; nor is there debate that reasonable mistake about consent should constitute a valid defense. Controversy surrounds the question of whether *unreasonable* mistake about consent should be a valid defense.[76] The taxonomy of defenses is designed to shed light on this very sort of issue. As I will discuss in the section on inculpatory mistakes, some criminal theorists have argued that questions about the conditions under which mistake of fact constitutes a valid defense to liability depend on what that mistake is *about;* mistakes about elements of offenses may be treated differently from mistakes about other components of liability. If so, Robinson may be correct that the usefulness of the taxonomy of defenses is supported, not undermined, by such uncertainty of categorization.

Consider next the doubts about duress and necessity. Should these defenses be treated as justifications or excuses? To begin to answer this difficult question, we must identify the many independent controversies about the validity of these defenses.[77] Particularly significant, for present purposes, is the debate about the scope and limits of third party assistance. May a friend come to the assistance of a defendant who acts under duress or necessity? Suppose Jones (in the earlier examples) enlists Green's help in stealing White's car or in breaking into Black's cabin. Authorities are in disagreement about whether and under what conditions Green may borrow Jones' defense. Once again, this debate seems parallel to independent uncertainty about whether these defenses should be categorized as justifications or excuses. Most authorities who have developed a taxonomy of defenses agree that confederates may share in a defendant's justification, but not in his excuse. Robinson writes: "Assisting . . . another to engage in justified conduct should be similarly justified," but "a perpetrator's excuse . . . is clearly inapplicable to a confederate."[78] Justifications, after all, show conduct not to be wrongful, so there is no reason why they cannot be shared by confederates. Excuses, on the other hand, arise from personal characteristics of defendants that cannot intelligibly be shared. If a further refinement of the distinction between justification and excuse can clarify the difficult problem of the scope and limits of third-party assistance in cases involving necessity or duress, the development of a taxonomy of defenses will have proved its value.[79]

Consider finally the uncertainty about the proper classification of involuntariness. Is involuntariness a denial of an element, or an excuse for the commission of an offense? Again: what independent debates surround the validity of the involuntariness defense? Here there are relatively few controversies. One issue, however, is significant. Legal authorities divide about whether the burden of proof for this defense should be allocated to the prosecution or the defendant.[80] This is precisely the sort of issue the taxonomy is designed to address.

It seems fair to conclude that Robinson's thesis is highly corroborated. In each case, difficulties of categorization coincide with independent debates about the validity of defenses. Of course, the surface has barely been scratched if Robinson's thesis is to be systematically evaluated. But it seems unlikely that Robinson has told the entire story. Difficulties of classification emerge for reasons having nothing to do with indecision about the validity of defenses. Problems of categorization would not vanish if these "independently generated disputes" about the validity of defenses were resolved. Efforts to sort cases into their appropriate categories sometimes stall because of uncertainty about a number of deep, underlying philosophical problems. To identify these problems is not to solve them. But unless these problems are recognized and confronted, the usefulness of this taxonomy of defenses will fall short of the high expectations of those theorists who have developed it.

The second distinction (between justifications and excuses) raises problems that go directly to the heart of moral philosophy. To what extent should conduct be evaluated by its effects? The temptation to categorize the defenses of duress and necessity as justifications comes largely from the appeal of consequentialism. If persons are obligated (or permitted) to perform that action that produces the least harm, such defenses are likely to be counted as justifications. Consequentialism also lends itself to a view on the general problem of third-party assistance. If conduct is permissible in virtue of its effects, it is largely a matter of indifference *who* performs it. The inclination to classify these defenses as excuses derives primarily from the appeal of a nonconsequentialist, or deontological perspective. If persons are obligated to perform given actions despite their consequences, duress and necessity may at most excuse conduct that remains wrongful. Deonotologists generally attach greater significance to whether conduct is performed by one agent or another, with profound implications for the general problem of third-party assistance. Significant progress in applying this taxonomy may be delayed until good reasons are given for preferring one framework to the other.

Other difficulties threaten to undermine the taxonomy of substantive defenses at its foundation. As Fletcher recognizes, the viability of these distinctions "builds on the more basic perception of a difference between assessing the act as abstracted from the particular actor and assessing the particular actor's responsibility for the act under the circumstances."[81] But we cannot evaluate acts "as abstracted from" actors without first determining that an action has been performed. This determination, however, would take us full circle to an inquiry into the capacities and abilities of actors. It seems impossible to abstract acts from actors altogether, just as it seems impossible (and for much the same reasons) to effectively dissect the physical from the mental components of criminal offenses.

Thus the third distinction scrutinized above (between denials and excuses) will remain murky in the absence of solutions to problems in the philosophy of action. How is the concept of action to be understood? What must be true of an agent before he can be said to have performed an action? What characteristics or disabilities destroy the capacity for action? Can robots and/or animals act? Unless these terribly difficult questions are addressed, it is doubtful that a theorist can provide a principled account of when an action is excused, as opposed to when no action is performed.

Finally, the first distinction (between denials and justifications) involves puzzles from both action theory and moral philosophy. In particular, there is doubt about how actions are best described. Conduct that appears incriminating and in need of justification under some correct descriptions is not at all incriminating under other correct descriptions. Given that both descriptions are accurate, which is to be preferred? To answer such questions, more work needs to be done about the nature of conduct itself, as well as on the basis on which it is described. Otherwise, the distinction between cases in which the proscribed act is not performed and those in which the proscribed act is justified will remain blurred.

Thus caution and skepticism are advisable in attempts to use this taxonomy of defenses. Commitments to deep philosophical problems may be presupposed by applications of these distinctions. Despite these recalcitrant difficulties, Robinson's suggestive thesis merits further consideration. Perhaps little more should be said about this taxonomy of defenses without examining some of the uses to which it has been put. In the following sections I will critically discuss two (of many) such applications.

## BURDENS OF PROOF

MANY CRIMINAL THEORISTS believe that the taxonomy introduced here is of great significance in deciding whether the burden of proof[82] for a particular defense should be allocated to the prosecution or defendant.[83]

### The Traditional View

State criminal practice varies widely, but the following generalization is roughly accurate: the prosecution is required to prove each element of an offense beyond a reasonable doubt, but has much greater latitude in assigning to defendants other components of liability, that is, justifications and excuses. This generalization expresses what I will call the *traditional view*. States may (and often do) allocate burdens of proof to prosecutors for a number of justifications and excuses, but (unlike elements) are not required to do so.[84]

Although assignments of proof burdens seem to be clear examples of procedural questions, it need hardly be pointed out that here, as elsewhere, substantive considerations underlie choice of procedure. It is important to identify these substantive considerations in order to determine to what extent, if any, they are promoted by the established practice of allocating burdens by reference to the distinctions in the taxonomy. Why *should* the categorization of a defense be dispositive in determining whether the prosecution or defendant should be required to prove it? I believe that little can be said in favor of the traditional view. My strategy in this section is to sketch two alternative bases for determining where the burden of proof should lie, neither of which invokes the distinctions in the taxonomy. The usefulness of the taxonomy in helping to resolve questions about burdens of proof is undermined if either is preferable to the traditional view.

The general issue of proof allocation has been the subject of a number of recent Supreme Court decisions. In 1970 the Court held in *In re Winship* that the Constitution requires the prosecution to prove beyond a reasonable doubt "every fact necessary to constitute the crime" of which the defendant is charged.[85] Unfortunately, there is no consensus about when a given fact is "necessary to constitute [a] crime," but nothing in the opinion indicated that sweeping reforms in criminal procedure were mandated. In 1975, however, the Court in *Mullaney v. Wilbur* interpreted *Winship* to find unconstitutional the Maine practice requiring defendants to prove that homicide was based upon adequate provocation, a defense that reduced the offense from murder to manslaughter.[86] Lower courts and legal scholars expressed puzzlement about the scope of this decision. The Court added to the confusion in 1977 by deciding in *Patterson v. New York* that the State could require a defendant to bear the burden of proof for the defense of extreme emotional disturbance, which again reduced an offense from murder to manslaughter.[87] This holding did not overrule *Mullaney,* but few authorities have succeeded in reconciling them.[88] Most theorists agree that "the general understanding of *Winship* after *Patterson* is just what it was before *Mullaney*"[89]—an affirmation of the traditional view that relies heavily on the distinctions in the taxonomy of defenses. Only elements of offenses clearly "constitute the crime."

This flurry of indecisive Court activity has induced authorities to reconsider the issue of how burdens of proof *should* be allocated. Many theorists have questioned the propriety of allocating burdens depending upon whether the defense is a denial, as opposed to a justification or excuse. What is revealing, however, is the nature of their criticisms of the traditional view. Almost without exception, the traditional view is rejected on the ground that it entails what has come to be known as the "physical location theory."[90] According to this "theory," the distinction between denials and other defenses is drawn solely by reference to the literal wording of the statute: a defense is a justification or an excuse if and only if the criminal code stipulates that it is. The traditional view surely is objectionable if it entails this physical location theory. For, the criticism continues, "a legislative decision to treat a particular matter as an element of an offense or as a defense to liability may depend simply on convenience or ease in phrasing."[91] Thus the traditional view is said to rest on distinctions that are "essentially arbitrary."[92] To underscore this point, absurd consequences are said to follow from the physical location theory.[93] Clearly, a legislature should not be allowed to require defendants to prove their innocence by rewording its first-degree murder statute so that the absence of intention is described as a justification. All commentators seem to agree that the physical location theory places too much weight on the fortuities of legislative draftsmanship.

The difficulty with this objection is that it is not clear that the traditional view entails the physical location theory. The traditional view can be salvaged from difficulties based upon the physical location theory if some principled basis for categorizing defenses can be devised.[94] Most legal commentators are convinced of the impossibility of distinguishing denials from other defenses by any means other than legislative stipulation. But one should not be overly pessimistic about the prospects for success in categorizing defenses. The criticsms against the traditional view seem exaggerated; surely it is not *wholly* arbitrary that a component of liability is regarded as an element rather than as (the absence) of a justification or excuse. Again, a state could not plausibly treat a non-killing as a justification (still less as an excuse) for the commission of murder. Though malleable, these distinctions are not infinitely elastic; there is a limit to which the structure of liability can be gerrymandered to place criminal defendants at procedural disadvantages.

I will now sketch two alternatives to the traditional view, either of which seems preferable to it. Although these alternatives are incompatible, my remarks are not a defense of either view *simpliciter*. My point is that neither utilizes the distinctions recognized in the taxonomy of defenses. I conclude that it is doubtful that this taxonomy is useful as a device to help allocate burdens of proof.

### The Presumption of Innocence View

The first alternative, which I will call the "presumption of innocence" view, can be introduced by investigating which substantive policies are promoted by decisions to allocate burdens of proof to one party rather than to the other. A plethora of complicated and conflicting policies are served by this decision, but it is unnecessary to summarize them here.[95] Surely the dominant consideration[96] is a preference that several guilty defendants be acquitted rather than that one innocent defendant be punished.[97] This interest, in turn, rests upon the high premium our society places upon individual rights. The best indication of the dominance of this consideration is that in civil litigation, where it has no application, competing grounds for placing burdens of proof on defendants have much greater appeal. Once the decision to allocate proof burdens in criminal practice is understood as a device for serving this central objective, it only remains to be determined which issues bear on guilt or innocence. Now this is no easy question, but it cannot be answered by invoking the taxonomy of substantive defenses. *All* defenses, insofar as they are substantive, bear on guilt or innocence.[98] Thus the distinction between issues that must be proved by the prosecution instead of the defendant coincides more closely with the distinction between substantive and procedural defenses than with further subdivisions within the former class.

The "presumption of innocence" alternative to the traditional view favors the *Mullaney* interpretation of *Winship* from which *Patterson* retreated. It is susceptible to the criticism that the policy considerations in favor of proof allocation have been oversimplified or misidentified altogether. In particular, the requirement that the prosecution disprove all substantive defenses raised by the defendant might seem to confer an unfair advantage upon defendants at a time when our criminal justice system is perceived as losing the war against crime.[99] As a compromise to restore the adversarial balance, it might be urged that defendants prove all defenses except denials. This compromise may be sensible as a means to increase the frequency of convictions, but it hardly constitutes a principled defense of the traditional view. After all, the frequency of convictions could be increased still further by requiring defendants to prove denials as well.

A more serious objection to the "presumption of innocence" view is that it might inhibit states from recognizing new defenses,[100] or induce them to invalidate a few already in place. States might fear a drop in their conviction rate if they could not adopt a new defense without also requiring their prosecutors to disprove it beyond a reasonable doubt. In other words, the interpretation of *Winship* suggested by *Mullaney* might backfire: although proposed as a device for protecting innocent defendants, placing the burden of proof for all substantive defenses on the prosecution might actually reduce the number of defenses recognized as valid, and thus penalize the "innocent." Defendants will not welcome such "protection."

### The Greater Includes the Lesser View

If a state has the power to invalidate a defense altogether, why must it assume the burden to disprove it beyond a reasonable doubt in the event that it *does* elect to recognize it? Attempts to answer this question give rise to a second alternative to the traditional view, which I will call "the greater includes the lesser" approach.[101] It supposes that the greater power of the state to invalidate a defense altogether entails the lesser power to allocate a proof burden in any way it chooses if the defense *is* recognized. A defendant who is not even entitled to crumbs cannot complain if he receives a slice of bread rather than a whole loaf. According to this approach, the only burdens of proof that cannot be allocated to defendants are those pertaining to defenses that the state lacks the power to invalidate.

This second alternative is problematic.[102] But the important point to notice is that, like its predecessor, it does not depend upon applications of the taxonomy of defenses, since the "greater includes the lesser" view can be applied to entail that defendants may be required to disprove the elements of a given offense. A state may argue, for example, that since it has the power to enact a 35 m.p. h. speed limit, a defendant who is accused of exceeding 55 m.p. h. can be convicted on proof that he was traveling faster than 35 m.p. h., unless he can disprove that he was exceeding 55 m.p. h. By parity of reasoning, the "greater" power to punish drivers for traveling 35 m.p. h. entails the "lesser" power to punish drivers who cannot disprove that they exceeded 55 m.p. h. This argument may constitute a *reductio ad absurdum* of the "greater includes the lesser" approach. If this approach can be salvaged, I hope it is clear that its application does not require the ability to effectively categorize defenses in a taxonomy.

Though plagued with difficulties of their own, both the "presumption of innocence" and the "greater includes the lesser" alternatives seem preferable to the traditional view. Neither approach, however, utilizes the distinctions in the taxonomy of substantive defenses. Further argument is required to establish that these distinctions are useful in allocating burdens of proof. It is likely that the explanatory power of this taxonomy is to be located elsewhere.

### INCULPATORY MISTAKES

FLETCHER'S MOST INTRIGUING ARGUMENT for the practical importance of the taxonomy of defenses is made in the context of *mistakes*.[103] The problem that has bedeviled criminal theory since its inception is to provide a principled account of when mistakes have a bearing on liability. A comprehensive theory of mistakes has two parts. The first and more important part examines the *exculpatory* effect of mistakes: under what conditions are defendants *not* liable because of a false belief, when there would be no question about their *guilt* were they not mistaken?[104] The second and less important part examines the *inculpatory* effect of mistakes: under what conditions *are* defendants liable because of a false belief, when there would be no question about their *innocence* were they not mistaken?

Fletcher argues that careful attention to the taxonomy of defenses can help resolve perplexities about the inculpatory effect of mistakes. His strategy depends upon our sharing his intuitions (or considered moral judgments) about whether or not liability would be just in a number of carefully constructed hypotheticals. He describes the following three situations, each of which contains a mistake with a potential bearing on liability:

> 1. Y marries a second time in the belief that he is still married. In fact, his wife has procured a valid ex parte divorce in another jurisdiction.
> 2. C writes a letter to suspect B, inviting B to use C's car whenever B wishes. Before receiving the letter, B takes C's car with the intent to steal it.
> 3. A physician P is about to inject air into the suspect X's veins with the intent to kill him. Ignorant of P's intentions, X decides to use this opportunity to assault him. As the needle is poised, X grabs the physician and begins to choke him.[105]

According to Fletcher, the mistake is irrelevant in (1); the defendant is no more liable than he would have been were he cognizant of the truth. In (3), however, the mistake is said to be crucial; the defendant is liable although he would not have been were he aware of the facts. If the reader agrees with these two results,[106] he is prepared to confront (2). Here we are likely to be a good deal less clear about our intuitive judgments of liability. The case shares affinities with both (1) and (3), so we are pulled in opposite directions by our tendency to construct analogies with situations about which we are confident. This uncertainty should prepare us for Fletcher's theoretical resolution.

Fletcher contends that use of the taxonomy of defenses provides the most plausible means to account for our judgments about (1) and (3), while also offering insight into (2). One begins by identifying what the mistake is *about*. In (1), the mistake is about an element of the offense of bigamy. It is logically impossible to commit the offense of bigamy without a prior legally valid marriage—one's beliefs about the validity of that marriage are irrelevant. The fundamental principle of legality, *nullum poena sine lege*, precludes liability unless the conduct of the defendant satisfies each of the elements of an offense. In (3), however, the mistake is about a justification for committing the offense of assault. Each element of the offense is satisfied. Now comes the crucial premise in the analysis: "Actors may avail themselves of justifications only if they act with a justificatory intent."[107] Since the defendant lacked such an intent at the time of his alleged assault, he may not invoke a justification if he subsequently becomes aware of the facts. Liability in (3) does not violate the principle of legality, since the word "lege" in the maxim is construed to apply only to elements of offenses, and not also to (the absences of) justifications.

Armed with this analysis, Fletcher invites us to reconsider (2), about which our intuitions were ambivalent. We need to determine whether the mistake is about an element of the offense, in which case it is irrelevant and liability can be resisted because no offense has been committed, or whether the mistake is about a justification, in which case it is important and liability can be imposed without violating the fundamental principle of legality. Before applying this analysis to the problematic hypothetical, however, it is appropriate to ask whether Fletcher's approach is satisfactory thus far. Has he really provided the correct account of our intuitions in (1) and (3)?

Of course, any proposal that mistakes about elements of offenses are to be treated differently from mistakes about justifications is bound to generate opposition from those criminal theorists who are skeptical that this distinction can be drawn.[108] A legal principle that denies inculpatory force to *any* mistake does not require a distinction between denials and justifications, even *if* it does occasional violence to our intuitions. This is a significant drawback of Fletcher's approach.

Consider the crucial premise that defendants can avail themselves of a justification only if they act with "justificatory intent." What does this mean? Surprisingly, Fletcher has little to say in response, so an answer must be attributed to him. This much is clear: the lack of belief about a fact that would otherwise serve as a valid justification must imply the absence of justificatory intent. When so expressed, the crucial premise in Fletcher's argument states that a defendant cannot be justified in committing an offense unless he believes those facts in which the justification consists.

But mere belief in those facts in which the justification consists, though necessary, is probably not sufficient to comprise a justificatory intent. If belief alone sufficed, Fletcher would speak of "justificatory belief" rather than of "justificatory intent." To comprise an intent, belief must induce action, or constitute a reason for acting.[109] The necessity of this added requirement becomes evident if (3) is altered so that the defendant is aware of the facts in which the justification consists, though this belief plays no role in his conduct. In typical situations involving self-defense, the defendant commits an offense *because* he is threatened. Without this "because" relationship, it becomes less apparent that he should be allowed to profit from the defense. Suppose that patient X in Fletcher's hypothetical planned to assault physician P all along, subsequently became aware of P's intention to kill him, and reasoned: "How fortunate! Now I will be able to assault P and escape liability!" In altered hypothetical (3), the counterfactual is true that had X remained unaware of P's intent, X would have assaulted P anyway. Insofar as criminal theorists have commented upon such cases, they differ radically about what the law is or ought to be.[110] I find it difficult to comprehend why mere belief should have a bearing on liability unless it influenced conduct.[111] If Fletcher agrees, his position is to be understood as follows: a defendant cannot be justified in committing an offense unless he (a) believes those facts in which the justification consists, and (b) acts because of those beliefs.

As so construed, the surprising result is that Fletcher's position may not be about the relevance of *mistake* to liability at all. If the above analysis of justificatory intent is correct, the issue of whether or not the defendant holds any false beliefs seems to be irrelevant to Fletcher's position. What is crucial is the defendant's *motive*.[112] The claim that "actors may avail themselves of justifications only if they act with a justificatory intent" applies even to those situations in which no mistake is made. An evaluation of Fletcher's view plunges us back into the quagmire of determining when and under what conditions motive bears on criminal liability.[113] Fletcher's position is that motive is irrelevant if the defense of the accused is categorized as a denial, but material if his defense is a justification.

Surely Fletcher's analysis has promise.[114] But one should not be persuaded of the accuracy of a theoretical analysis by considering an insufficient diet of cases.[115] Are there hypotheticals in which intuitions allow justifications *despite* the lack of "justificatory intent"? Consider the following example: suppose L hates M and eagerly awaits the opportunity to kill him. When informed that M has been convicted of a capital offense, L eagerly applies for the job of electrocutioner. Suppose L plans to take advantage of this opportunity to kill M even if M is pardoned at the last minute as he waits in the electric chair. But M is not pardoned and L pulls the switch. It seems odd that L's bad motives should preclude him from being justified. M may kill notwithstanding his motives. Perhaps *some* but not *all* bad motives disallow justifications. If so, the taxonomy of defenses must be applied cautiously here. The categorization of a defense as a justification rather than as a denial is not dispositive of the question of whether a defendant who acts with a bad motive (or is mistaken) may avail himself of it.[116]

Unfortunately, the intuitions of theorists who consider such unusual hypotheticals may conflict. We should remain skeptical about Fletcher's position if it is tested primarily by its ability to explain our considered moral judgments. In fact, however, Fletcher is not content to support his approach solely by relying on shared intuitions. In addition, he constructs a number of arguments in favor of his position. None, however, is convincing.[117]

Fletcher's first argument relies on his characterization of justifications as "privileges" to commit offenses. "Privileges," in turn, are "exercised" rather than "obeyed." Next comes the crucial premise: "A conceptual analysis of 'exercising a privilege' supports the view that the act of 'exercising' or 'acting under' a privilege presupposes knowledge of the justificatory circumstances."[118] His second argument is also succinctly expressed. Here he characterizes justifications as "exceptions to prohibitory norms." He continues: "As exceptions, these claims should be available only to those who merit special treatment."[119] The requirement that persons cannot avail themselves of a justification of which they were unaware at the time of their conduct helps ensure that only those who merit "special treatment" qualify for the exception.

Both these arguments are unsound. In the first, Fletcher is curiously unmindful of his general reservations about the usefulness of ordinary language to resolve substantive problems in criminal law.[120] Moreover, no support is offered for the crucial premise that defendants cannot exercise a privilege without being aware of it. Rights constitute the clearest counterexample to this claim. Rights are exercised, not obeyed, but no one ever thought it impossible to exercise a right without being aware of it. The second argument is defective in failing to show that one can qualify for "special treatment" only by awareness of the facts in which the justification consists. Arguably, the fact that the conduct of the defendant falls under a justification is "special" enough. Moreover, there need be nothing *special* or *unusual* about acting under a justification.[121] I conclude that Fletcher's intriguing thesis is inadequately supported.

\* \* \*

The formulation and application of a taxonomy of substantive defenses is one of the most important topics contemporary theorists should address. The distinctions discussed here, only recently introduced to orthodoxy, should be further refined within revised criminal theory. Much work remains to be done. We need to know *why* the taxonomy is useful *when* it is useful, so that we are in a better position to appreciate its limitations.

## NOTES

1. John Austin, "A Plea for Excuses," in his *Philosophical Papers*, p. 123.

2. Ibid., p. 125.

3. Those criminal theorists most enthusiastic about the distinction, such as George Fletcher, complain about how textbooks, the *Model Penal Code*, and the *Encyclopedia of Crime and Justice* suffer from "indifference to the distinction." See "The Right and the Reasonable," *Harvard Law Review* 98 (1985): 949, 955.

4. Many of these so-called "procedural" defenses have a substantive rationale as well. This is especially true of entrapment. See the majority and concurring opinions in *Sorrells v. U.S.*, 287 U.S. 435 (1932).

5. In the most comprehensive and sophisticated account of criminal law defenses yet produced in Anglo-American literature, Paul Robinson originally denominated these as "nonexculpatory public policy defenses". "Criminal Law Defenses: A Systematic Analysis," *Columbia Law Review* 82 (1982): 199, 229. In his subsequent treatise he refers to them simply as "nonexculpatory defenses." See *Criminal Law Defenses*, pp. 102, 104: these defenses "are at work whenever a dismissal is based on factors other than the defendant's innocence."

6. Robinson's taxonomy includes justifications and excuses, but adds two categories he describes as "Failure of Proof Defenses" and "Offense Modifications." Ibid., p. 62. The former "consist of instances in which . . . all elements of the offense charged cannot be proven" (p. 72). Robinson himself must be unhappy with his choice of terminology here, for his references to failure of proof defenses frequently are placed in quotations as "defenses" (see pp. 70 and 72). Finally he admits that "[f]ailure of proof defenses . . . are not really defenses" (p. 123). Moreover, he dismisses most attempts to apply this distinction as "unfortunate." His category of "Offense Modifications" is said to "provide a more sophisticated account, when needed, of the harm or evil sought to be prohibited by the offense definition" (p. 77). I am unconvinced that these defenses are distinguishable from justifications. See Robinson's attempt to distinguish them on pp. 89–90.

Other commentators provide still different taxonomies. See Lawrence Heintz, "The Logic of Defenses," *American Philosophical Quarterly* 18 (1981): 243.

7. A defense is *valid* if it should succeed in reducing the punishment typically deserved for an offense; otherwise it is invalid.

8. See the discussion of the allegedly "inexcusable choice" in Rollin Perkins and Ronald Boyce, *Criminal Law*, p. 1055. Much of this controversy centers around the notorious "cannibalism lifeboat" case of *Regina v. Dudley & Stephens*, 14 Q.B.D. 273 (1884). Perkins's discussion conflates justifications with excuses by writing: "If an excuse were recognized in such a case this would declare that such an intentional killing is morally acceptable" (p. 1055).

9. Robinson contends that the theoretical and practical advantages

achieved by the Model Penal Code classification of offenses stand in "sharp contrast" to its neglect of defenses. See *Defenses*, p. 64.

10. "The distinction between offenses and defenses is perhaps the most basic distinction in criminal law that lawyers do recognize." Robinson, *Defenses*, p. 119, note 3. But see Glanville Williams, "[T]he definitional and defence elements of a crime . . . is a distinction that is impossible to draw satisfactorily. A rule creating a *defence* merely supplies additional details of the scope of the *offence*. To regard the offence as subsisting independently of its limitations and qualifications is unrealistic. The defence is a negative condition of the offence, and is therefore an integral part of it. What we regard as part of the offence and what as part of a defence depends only on traditional habits of thought or accidents of legal drafting; it should have no bearing on the important questions of criminal liability." See *Textbook of Criminal Law*, p. 138.

11. Thus the word "elements" is used here more narrowly than in *M.P.C.* §1.13(9), where it includes the absence of justifications and excuses. Most states otherwise adopting the Model Penal Code have rejected this broad definition of "elements." See Robinson, *Defenses*, pp. 67–68, note 14, and pp. 172–73, note 7. But Williams calls the Model Penal Code approach "sound." *Textbook*, p. 138.

12. See chapter 6.

13. Criminal theorists differ on the issue of whether justified conduct is laudable or merely permissible. P. J. Fitzgerald writes: "to justify an action is to show that there are circumstances such that the action, which might ordinarily be disapproved of, is in this case to be commended." See *Criminal Law and Punishment*, p. 119. In a similar vein, Robinson understands justifications to require that "harm is outweighed by the need to avoid an even greater harm or to further a greater societal interest." See *Defenses*, p. 83. These claims are controversial. Conduct is justified when it is not wrongful (i.e., when it is permissible), and not all permissible conduct need further a greater societal interest. See George Fletcher, *Rethinking Criminal Law*, pp. 769–70; and Robinson's reply, *Defenses*, p. 85, note 7. See also Joshua Dressler, "New Thoughts About the Concept of Justification in the Criminal Law: A Critique of Fletcher's Thinking and *Rethinking*," *U.C.L.A. Law Review* 32 (1984): 61.

14. Fletcher contends that "claims of justification . . . represent exceptions to the rule laid down." See "The Right Deed for the Wrong Reason," *U.C.L.A.Law Review* 23 (1975): 293, 308.

15. Judith Thomson refers to this strategy as "factual specification" in "Some Ruminations on Rights," *Arizona Law Review* 19 (1977): 45. See the thoughtful reply of W. A. Parent, "Judith Thomson and the Logic of Rights," *Philosophical Studies* 37 (1980): 405.

16. The word "privilege" is likely to mislead here, connoting some sort of special status. See this basis for a "correction" of Hohfeldian terminology in Glanville Williams, "The Concept of Legal Liberty," *Columbia Law Review* 56 (1956): 1129.

17. This confusion may be present in Fletcher, who construes justifications both as "licenses or permissions to violate the prohibitory norm" and as "exceptions to prohibitory norms." See his *Rethinking*, pp. 563 and 565.

18. H. L. A. Hart does not allow that excuses may *lessen* culpability; he requires that they must negate it altogether. See "Legal Responsibility and Excuses," in his *Punishment and Responsibility*, p. 28. This usage is a conse-

quence of his endeavor to assimilate excusing conditions to invalidating or nullifying conditions in civil law, particularly the law of contracts. Presumably the concept of a partial or incomplete nullification is incoherent. For a rejoinder to what is called an unsupported "stipulation" on the use of the word "excuse", see David Hodlcroft, "A Plea For Excuses?" *Philosophy* 44 (1969): 321. See also Austin, "Plea."

19. Robinson, *Defenses*, p. 92. He qualifies his stipulation by adding: "Mistake is the only excuse that does not require that the excusing condition be caused by a particular disability or abnormality in the actor" (p. 98, note 18). Some criminal theorists contend that the "unifying fabric [of characterizing] all the various doctrines of excuse as defects of capacity . . . has dissolved." See Peter Low, John Jeffries, and Richard Bonnie, *Criminal Law*, p. 524.

20. But see "The Rationale of the Insanity Defense," this chapter; and the categories of persons said to be "not capable of committing crimes" in *Cal.Penal Code* §26 (St. Paul: West Supp. , 1985). See also note 49.

21. Not all orthodox criminal theorists have accepted the viability of such a set of distinctions. See the criticisms in Jerome Hall, *General Principles of Criminal Law*, pp. 233–36. But see notes 24 and 49.

22. See "Problems of Classification: Denials and Justifications," this chapter. Fletcher writes: "The more compelling objection to stating the criteria of justification as negative elements of the prohibitory norm is that doing so obscures the logic of justification." See "The Right to Life," *Georgia Law Review* 13 (1979): 1371, 1384.

23. Robinson, *Substantive*, p. 101.

24. Hall, *General*, pp. 382–83.

25. Herbert Packer, "The Model Penal Code and Beyond," *Columbia Law Review* 63 (1963): 594, 596–97.

26. Robinson, *Defenses*. Vol. 2, p. 376. A. D. Woozley writes: "As a criminal offense is now typically defined, it is logically impossible for ignorance or mistake of law to excuse." See his "Negligence and Ignorance," *Philosophy* 53 (1978): 293, 303.

27. Fletcher, "Right Deed," p. 734.

28. See Robinson, *Defenses*, Vol. 2, p. 373.

29. See chapter 3.

30. Robinson, *Defenses*, p. 105.

31. Paul Robinson, "A Theory of Justification: Societal Harm as a Prerequisite for Criminal Liability," *U.C.L.A. Law Review* 23 (1975): 266, 275.

32. Fletcher contends: "Questions of excuse . . . do not arise until it is established . . . that the conduct is not justified." *Rethinking*, p. 309. Even Jerome Hall, who generally is critical of the distinction between justification and excuse, writes: "Justification often has a logical priority since excuse implies that we must first decide, 'excuse the actor for doing what?' and that may involve a decision regarding justification." See "Comment on Justification and Excuse," *American Journal of Comparative Law* 24 (1976): 638, 640.

33. Fletcher claims to draw support for this priority from "the structure of retributive thinking." See "Right and Reasonable," p. 961.

34. One theorist claims that "questions of justification have a kind of natural priority over questions of excuse," but notes that this priority is "not absolute." Kent Greenawalt, "The Perplexing Borders of Justification and Excuse," *Columbia Law Review* 84 (1984): 1897, 1899, note 6.

35. See R. Cummins, "Culpabaility and Mental Disorder," *Canadian*

*Journal of Philosophy* 10 (1980): 207, 229: "If the current condition of the defendant is such as to justify commitment, holding a trial to determine . . . culpability is simply a waste of effort."

36. Although most theorists would concur, some interesting complications are presented in Greenawalt, "Perplexing," p. 1909.

37. Perhaps this is what Hyman Gross has in mind in writing that "an excuse of mental abnormality preempts the field of excuses." See "Mental Abnormality as a Criminal Excuse," in Joel Feinberg and Hyman Gross, eds., *Philosophy of Law*, p. 482, 487.

38. Robinson, *Defenses*, Vol. 2, p. 283, note 5.

39. See Joel Feinberg, "What Is So Special About Mental Illness?", in his *Doing and Deserving*, p. 272; and Joseph Goldstein and Jay Katz, "Abolish the 'Insanity Defense'—Why Not?" *Yale Law Journal* 72 (1963): 853.

40. According to Fingarette, the question *"Why* should mental disability affect criminal responsibility . . . surprisingly, has rarely been addressed in fundamental terms." Herbert Fingarette and Ann Hasse, *Mental Disabilities and Criminal Responsibility*, p. 4. See also p. 11.

41. He surveys this issue in two books: *The Meaning of Criminal Insanity*, and Fingaratte and Hasse, ibid. Although my remarks here are highly critical, these books represent excellent discussions of the insanity defense.

42. Fingarette and Hasse, *Mental Disabilities*, p. 6.

43. Ibid., chapter 3.

44. Ibid., chapter 4.

45. Ibid., p. 208.

46. Ibid., p. 209.

47. Ibid.

48. Ibid., p. 241.

49. Hall, *General*, p. 436, note 85: "An insane person is not bound by doctrines of the criminal law." Here is a second example of confusion in Hall that derives from his failure to develop and apply a taxonomy of substantive criminal law defenses. See also "Advantages of the Taxonomy: Ignorance of Law and the Modification of Offenses," this chapter. Remarkably, Fletcher is also among those who construe the insane as "more or less . . . fall[ing] outside the scope of the criminal law." See "Right and Reasonable," p. 959.

50. But see Coke's definition of murder in J. C. Smith and Brian Hogan, *Criminal Law*, p. 273. See also Hall, "Comment," p. 644: "'Excuse' functions in the definition of crimes just as effectively as does 'justification.' " See also Robinson, *Defenses*, pp. 160–61, for a discussion of why it is important to construe insanity as an excuse.

51. See Fletcher, *Rethinking*, pp. 798–99.

52. For a response to the abolitionists, see Donald Hermann, "Assault on the Insanity Defense: Limitations on the Effectiveness and Effect of the Defense of Insanity," *Rutgers Law Journal* 14 (1983): 241.

53. Robinson remarks: "A single defense should have a single classification." *Defenses*, p. 115. But see Heintz, "Logic," p. 245: "The same condition can be cited as either an excuse or a justification." See also Greenawalt, "Perplexing," p. 1913.

54. Greenawalt concludes that "Anglo-American criminal law should not attempt to distinguish between justification and excuse in a fully systematic way." See "Perplexing," p. 1898.

55. Apparently Robinson does not find it necessary to argue that nonconsent functions as an element of the offense of rape. See *Defenses*, p.

308. It is noteworthy that he does not present a general alternative to Fletcher's test for distinguishing denials from justifications. Some criminal theorists do not believe that this distinction can or should be drawn. See Williams, *Textbook*.

56. See the position of Lord Cross in the celebrated case of *R. v. Morgan*, 2 W.L.R. 923 (1975), as discussed in Fletcher, *Rethinking*, p. 701.

57. See Fletcher, *Rethinking*, especially note 38.

58. See my discussion of the "physical location theory" in "Burdens of Proof: The Traditional View," this chapter.

59. Fletcher is critical of the use of the word "elements," and proposes use of the "term 'definition' to refer to the inculpatory dimension of wrong-doing." See *Rethinking*, pp. 552–54. Despite his criticisms, it is not clear that his use really departs from my own, inasmuch as he frequently uses the phrase "elements of the definition" (pp. 694 and 695).

60. Ibid., p. 695.

61. Ibid., p. 705.

62. Ibid.

63. In "Right Deed," p. 314, Fletcher writes: "The minimal demand on the Definition is that it state an imperative that is morally coherent under given social conditions. What makes the imperative coherent is our compre-hending the core cases of prohibited conduct. Whether there is a consensus on these core cases would seem to turn on several factors. One factor is a statistical relationship between routine and extraordinary cases. As cases of justified conduct become more and more numerous, it becomes increasingly difficult to think of the Definition as prescribing the normal, and the justification as providing the exception. In addition to statistical regularity, one needs a moral consensus supporting the wrongfulness of the condcut in these core cases. As the moral consensus breaks down, more and more exceptions are urged, until one encounters the proverbial phenomena of the exception swallowing the rule."

64. Fletcher raises a similar objection to the position of Lord Halisham in *Morgan*. See *Rethinking*, p. 703.

65. "The traditional defense of duress thus covers some behavior that is justified and other behavior that is only excused." See Greenawalt, "Per-plexing," p. 1912. See also Andrew Von Hirsch, "Lifeboat Law," *Criminal Justice Ethics* 4 (1985): 88.

66. Heintz, "Logic," p. 245.

67. Ibid., p. 246.

68. See chapter 4.

69. See *Hill v. Baxter*, 1 Q.B. 277, 283 (1958).

70. See chapters 4 and 5.

71. H. L. A. Hart, "The Ascription of Responsibility and Rights," *Proceedings of the Aristotelian Society* 49 (1948–1949): 171.

72. See G. P. Baker, "Defeasibility and Meaning," in P. M. S. Hacker and Joseph Raz, eds., *Law, Morality, and Society*, p. 20.

73. H. L. A. Hart, "Acts of Will and Responsibility," in *Punishment*, p. 90.

74. Robinson, *Defenses*, p. 106.

75. Greenawalt indicates how the formulation of a taxonomy is com-plicated by "disagreements about substantive morality." See "Perplexing," p. 1927. See his excellent discussion of the law of self-defense and the "duty" to retreat.

76. See Greenawalt, ibid., p. 1909. See also *Morgan*.

77. See Robinson, *Defenses*, pp. 45–68 and 347–72; and Fletcher, *Rethinking*, pp. 818–35. See also chapter 3.

78. Robinson, *Defenses*, pp. 172–73.

79. For an expression of skepticism, see Greenawalt, "Perplexing," pp. 1918–27. See also Von Hirsch, "Lifeboat."

80. Admittedly, questions about proof allocation may not be a function of the *validity* of a defense.

81. Fletcher, "Right and Reasonable," p. 955.

82. By "burden of proof" I mean the "risk of nonpersuasion" rather than the "burden of production." See my "The Presumption of Freedom," *Nous* 17 (1983): 345. See also Robinson, *Defenses*, pp. 129–48.

83. "The defense classifications . . . are useful, and in some instances are controlling, in determining the constitutional limitations on allocation of the burden of persuasion." Robinson, *Defenses*, p. 138.

84. "To date, there is little consensus on the appropriate allocation of the burden of persuasion within the constitutionally permissible range." Robinson, *Defenses*, p. 141.

85. 397 U.S. 358, 364 (1970).

86. 421 U.S. 684 (1975).

87. 432 U.S. 197 (1977).

88. Most authorities concur with Fletcher that "it would be a mistake to read *Patterson* as anything but a de facto overruling of *Mullany*." See *Rethinking*, p. 550. For an opposed view, see Robinson, *Defenses*, pp. 138–40. Nonetheless, Robinson finds his own attempt at reconciliation "unfortunate" (p. 139).

89. John Jeffries and Paul Stephan, "Defenses, Presumptions, and Burden of Proof in the Criminal Law," *Yale Law Journal* 88 (1979): 1325, 1342.

90. See Ronald Allen, "The Restoration of *In Re Winship:* A Comment on Burdens of Persuasion in Criminal Cases After *Patterson v. New York,*" *Michigan Law Review* 76 (1977): 30, 48: "A component of [the 'elements' theory] is the 'physical location' rule, a rule of statutory construction providing that a particular factual issue is an element of an offense only if it is incorporated into the text of the basic statute describing the offense."

91. Jeffries and Stephan, "Defenses," p. 1332.

92. Ibid., p. 1331.

93. Almost all critics of the traditional view rely on this objection. See Justice Powell's dissent in *Patterson*, p. 224, note 8. See also Barbara Underwood, "The Thumb on the Scales of Justice: Burdens of Persuasion in Criminal Cases," *Yale Law Journal* 86 (1977): 1299, 1324.

94. Alhough he is not sympathetic to the traditional view, Fletcher's attempt to provide a principled basis for distinguishing elements of an offense from justifications would immunize it from objections based on the physical location theory.

95. See Fletcher, *Rethinking*, p. 522.

96. In his concurring opinion in *Winship*, Justice Harlan writes: "I view the requirement of proof beyond a reasonable doubt in a criminal case as bottomed on a fundamental value determination of our society that it is far worse to convict an innocent man than to let a guilty man go free" (p. 372). See also E. Osenbaugh, "The Constitutionality of Affirmative Defenses to Criminal Charges," *Arkansas Law Review* 29 (1976): 429, 432. Other considerations pull in the same direction. See Underwood, "Thumb," p. 1307.

97. In the late Middle Ages, Sir John Fortescue favored a 20 to 1 ratio

in capital cases. In the seventeenth century, Hale used the ratio of 5 to 1. Blackstone raised it to 10 to 1. See Fletcher, "Two Kinds of Legal Rules: A Comparative Study of Burden-of-Persuasion Practices in Criminal Cases," *Yale Law Journal* 77 (1968): 880, 881–82.

98. Jeffries and Stephan disagree. They contend that the "presumption of innocence" rationale for the "beyond a reasonable doubt" standard is sensible only for "essential" rather than for "gratuitous . . . ingredients of the state's case." "Defenses", pp. 1346–47. For a second opposed viewpoint, see Ferdinand Dutile, "The Burden of Proof in Criminal Cases," *Notre Dame Lawyer* 55 (1979): 380, 384–85. He maintains that "mitigating factors" bear less on the "defendant's blameworthy conduct" than do "aggravating factors."

99. Especially controversial is the federal practice of requiring the prosecution to disprove insanity beyond a reasonable doubt. See Robinson, *Defenses*, p. 140, note 11.

100. See *M.P.C.* §1.12, Comment 113. Fletcher writes: "Requiring the defendant to bear 'the laboring oar' on an exculpatory issue often functions as a low-visibility device for qualifying defenses begrudgingly granted to the defendant." *Rethinking*, p. 545.

101. See Allen, "Restoration," p. 43.

102. The "greater includes the lesser" rule has been properly rejected in other contexts. Surely a state cannot argue, for example, that since it need not maintain public parks at all, it may exclude minorities from any parks it *does* elect to maintain. See *Palmer v. Thompson*, 403 U.S. 217 (1971).

103. Fletcher writes that the distinction between denials and justifications "could have concrete consequences" in "at least four areas of legal dispute," viz.: "First, it is of critical importance in deciding when external facts, standing alone, should have an exculpatory effect. Secondly, it might bear on the analysis of permissible vagueness in legal norms. Thirdly, it might bear on the allocation of power between the legislature and judiciary in the continuing development of the criminal law. And fourthly, it might be of importance in analyzing the exculpatory effect of mistakes." *Rethinking*, p. 555. Though generally critical of attempts to apply a taxonomy of substantive defenses, Greenawalt concedes that Fletcher's first purpose is important. See "Perplexing," p. 1907, note 30.

104. See chapter 3.

105. Fletcher, *Rethinking*, p. 555.

106. Robinson claims that his "own informal surveys" indicate that "[m]ost people do tend to distinguish Fletcher's case (1) from his case (3), as he has set them out, but for other reasons." Robinson, *Defenses*, Vol. 2, p. 23.

107. Fletcher, *Rethinking*, p. 557.

108. See Williams, *Textbook*.

109. Complications arise in cases of overdetermination, when either "justificatory intent" *or* bad motive would be sufficient to induce the conduct of the defendant. Some theorists gloss over these problems by referring to the defendant's "dominant motivation". See Wayne LaFave and Austin Scott, *Criminal Law*, p. 207. Some statutory codifications of self-defense address the overdetermination problem. One state requires that "the party killing must have acted under the influence of such fears alone" before he is justified in self-defense. *Cal.Penal Code* §198. See the discussion in Robinson, *Defenses*, Vol. 2, p. 17.

110. Consider: "One may harbor the most intense hatred toward another; he may court an opportunity to take his life; may rejoice while he is imbruing his hands in his heart's blood; and yet, if to save his own life, the

facts showed that he was fully justified in slaying his adversary, his malice shall not be taken into account. The principle is too plain to require amplification." *Golden v. State,* 25 Ga. 527, 532 (1858). But contrast: "Suppose a grave felony is about to be committed under such circumstances that the killing of the offender to prevent the crime would be justified by law. At that very moment he is shot and killed. If the slayer was prompted by the impulse to promote the social security by preventing the felony he is guilty of no offense. If he had no such impulse but merely acted upon the urge to satisfy an old grudge by killing a personal enemy, he is guilty of murder. The intent is the same in either case, to kill the person. The difference between innocence and guilt lies in the motive which prompted the action." Rollin Perkins, "A Rationale of Mens Rea," *Harvard Law Review* 52 (1939): 905, 932.

111. Difficult, but not impossible. LaFave and Scott write: "When an individual finds himself in a position where the law grants him the right to kill another in self-defense, it makes no difference whether his dominant motive is other than self-preservation. This does not mean, of course, that the defense can be manufactured after the event by resort to facts not known to the actor when he engaged in the conduct." *Criminal,* p. 207. They fail to explain, however, why bare knowledge is relevant when it does not influence the conduct of the defendant.

112. Robinson believes that purpose, rather than motive, is what is significant here. He attempts to distinguish them in *Defenses,* Vol. 2, pp. 17–18, note 7: "The inquiry is not simply whether he desired to do or cause x, but *why* he desired it. This is the crucial distinction between purpose and motive."

113. See chapter 5. In addition to "justificatory intent," Fletcher sometimes speaks of "meritorious intent." See "Right Deed," p. 308. I do not understand why he does not use the word "motive" here.

114. Robinson writes: "Although bad motive might bar a defendant's defense of excuse, it should not preclude the defense of justification, which focuses on the act and not on the actor's motive." See "Justification," p. 285.

115. Robinson constructs a number of hypotheticals about which he suggests our intuitions are quite different. He concludes that "Fletcher's distinction between one who does not violate a 'prohibitory norm' because an element of the inculpatory definition is not satisfied, as in A's case, and one who seeks to bring himself within an exception to the prohibitory norm by establishing a justification for otherwise prohibited action, as in C's case, does not seem to have intuitive significance here." *Defenses,* p. 25.

116. Fletcher, to his credit, expresses doubts about his own analysis, which he describes as "painstaking and far from conclusive." See *Rethinking,* p. 698. Despite his misgivings, he seems to believe that further difficulties are resolvable by refinements of the taxonomy. He concludes one paper by writing: "Refining our intuitions and honing our distinctions are the surest means of doing justice in particular cases." "Right Deed," p. 321. Also, in this context: "Skepticism both presupposes and sanctifies failure." See "Criminal Theory as an International Discipline: Reflections on the 1984 Freiburg Workshop," *Criminal Justice Ethics* 4 (1985): 60, 71.

117. Fletcher claims to have "three arguments" in favor of his view; I can find only two. The first is, at best, a refutation of an unsound argument against his view.

118. Fletcher, *Rethinking,* p. 564.

119. Ibid., p. 565.

120. See Robinson, *Defenses,* Vol. 2, p. 26, notes 27 and 28.

121. See note 16.

# 8

# *The Enforcement of Morality*

## A PUZZLING ANOMALY

SOMETIMES IT IS MORE INSIGHTFUL to focus on what a theory excludes than on what it includes. Perhaps the most remarkable aspect of orthodox criminal theory is what is missing from it. It is surprising that orthodox theorists have shown almost no concern with the issue of the scope and limits of the substantive criminal law. A discussion of this issue, and whether and to what extent moral and political philosophy should contribute to its resolution, is conspicuous by its absence. An examination of the tables of contents of the most important recent contributions to criminal theory is ample evidence of this claim. Almost no authority since Jeremy Bentham[1] treats the issue of the limits of the criminal sanction as an integral part of criminal theory. No one pretends this question is unimportant; it is difficult to imagine more fundamental issues faced by a system of criminal justice than how to determine what conduct should be criminalized, and what role moral and political arguments should play in this determination. Yet orthodox criminal theorists are strangely silent about them.

Legal authorities as a whole, of course, have not neglected these matters. Law journals include countless articles discussing whether and to what extent, for example, prostitution, abortion, or the possession of marijuana merits criminal penalties. Such discussions, however, are seldom approached by applications of the fundamental principles of criminal liability.[2] "Policy arguments," especially considerations of economic efficiency, provide the most familiar battleground here.[3] Surely the absence of an examination of these issues among orthodox theorists is not mere oversight; powerful theoretical presuppositions place them "beyond the scope" of criminal theory.

This neglect is puzzling inasmuch as criminal theory is *about* the constraints the state must observe in creating offenses. The whole point of the fundamental principles of liability is to restrict the

224

authority of the state to inflict penal sanctions. These principles express prima facie rights the government must respect in creating law. But the *kinds* of constraints imposed by orthodox theory are narrow. Suppose that horribly repressive laws were enacted that, for example, prohibited the free exercise of religion. Unless such a pernicious legislative objective were pursued by dispensing with mens rea, actus reus, etc., it could not be condemned within orthodox thought.[4]

Thus orthodox criminal theory contains a puzzling anomaly. On the one hand, it is thoroughly moral in content, expressed by a number of requirements of justice. On the other hand, it maintains a kind of moral neutrality about the issue of the substantive limits of the criminal law.[5] What principled account can be provided of the distinction between those moral limitations on state authority that are and are not the subject matter of orthodox theory? I do not believe that a satisfactory answer can be provided. This restrictrion of subject matter is essentially arbitrary. At least, this puzzling anomaly merits a more careful defense than has been provided by orthodox theorists.

Surprisingly few legal philosophers have developed detailed views about the conditions that must be satisfied before conduct may be criminalized.[6] Commentators either avoid this problem altogether, content themselves with platitudes, or admit it to be too difficult to tackle.[7] The absence of a viable theory about this issue has had a devastating impact upon criminal practice. Many social problems (examined in previous chapters) are better addressed outside the framework of the criminal law, and have placed an intolerable strain on our system of justice. Theoretical uncertainty about the legitimate uses of the criminal sanction has contributed to our failure to develop effective alternatives to deal with such issues. The theorist is without a principled objection when it is urged that the criminal justice system be employed to cope with any and all social problems.

It is my thesis that only wrongful, blameworthy, immoral conduct should be criminalized, and that such a principle should be placed at the core of revised criminal theory. This thesis is not original; it has strong intuitive appeal and is supported by arguments about the justification of punishment. Utilitarian defenses of punishment fail to establish that the state has the authority to *use* persons to promote social advantage, that is, for general or special deterrence.[8] The retributive tradition offers a more promising account, inasmuch as it restricts punishment to the *deserving*. But retributivism is not an improvement over deterrence theory unless it can explain the relationship between the class of persons who deserve punishment and the class of persons who have committed criminal offenses. Surely a person can commit an offense (without justification or excuse) and *not* deserve punishment. If the criminal law proscribes conduct that citizens have a moral right to perform, it is incomprehensible how the state can be warranted in punishing them for it.[9] Some ("legalistic") retributivists have failed to take this problem seriously.[10] Many, however, appreciate that punishment can be justified only for offenses that are wrongful, blameworthy, and immoral. Punishment, after all, expresses (and ought to express) disapproval, censure, denunciation, and reprobation.[11] These responses are totally inappropriate for conduct that is morally permissible. Thus conduct should not be criminalized without a moral and political argument that it is wrongful, as long as we take seriously the need to *justify* the punishment of persons who perform it.

Consider also the perceived failures of our criminal justice system to win the "war against crime." Perhaps the most effective strategy to reduce criminality is to ensure that the threat and use of punishment educate persons to adopt the moral norms embodied in the law.[12] This goal cannot be achieved unless offenses are widely perceived as wrongful, blameworthy, and immoral. Wider use of the criminal sanction cannot be expected to educate, but only to give rise to disrespect, resentment, and confusion.

It is crucial to understand why orthodoxy has rejected the thesis that only wrongful, blameworthy, and immoral conduct should be criminalized, without substituting a preferable alternative. Nothing inherent in orthodox theory explains its lack of commitment about the issue of the moral limits of the substantive criminal law. Criminal theory could have addressed this issue while remaining general and continuing to abstract its content from existing offenses. Presumably the vast majority of penal laws proscribe immoral conduct, just as the vast majority of statutes include a mens rea. Exceptions to this generalization could have been accommodated in the same way orthodox theory responds to any deviations from its fundamental principles.

Moreover, one might think that the fundamental requirements of liability allow, or even entail, a position on this crucial issue. Both actus reus and mens rea—the most basic principles of orthodox thought—include the concept of *reus* (guilt). Criminal theorists could have reasoned as follows: these fundamental requirements preclude liability without guilt. It is inappropriate to ascribe guilt unless conduct is wrongful; therefore, criminal sanctions may be imposed only for wrongful conduct. Thus an investigation of the conditions under which conduct is or is not wrongful should be central to orthodox theory. Moral and political philosophy is the discipline in which questions about the wrongfulness of conduct are assessed. Accordingly, criminal theory is woefully incomplete unless it acknowledges and develops its intimate connections with moral and political philosophy.

This argument is seductive; in fact, I believe it is sound. Yet nearly all recent orthodox theorists have rejected it. In brief, they have interpreted the fundamental principles of criminal liability so this argument appears unsound. The premise that requires wrongful conduct as a precondition for liability has been construed to refer to *legal* rather than to *moral* wrongdoing.[13] Since legal wrongdoing is all that is needed to ascribe guilt, orthodoxy has little to say about what kinds of conduct should or should not constitute an offense. The *reus* in actus reus and mens rea reduces to the comparatively trivial meaning of "legally wrong." *Any* kind of conduct becomes wrongful in the relevant sense if it is prohibited by law.

Notice the resultant loss to the scope and significance of criminal theory. Suppose a defendant is charged with violation of a statute proscribing the harboring of runaway slaves. On the "legally wrong" rather than the "morally wrong" interpretation of *reus,* the accused may not pursue the following line of defense: "my conduct should not give rise to liability because it violates neither the actus reus nor mens rea conditions of criminal liability, since it was not morally wrongful." The quick response of orthodox theory to this defendant is that he suffers from an interminable confusion of law and morality, and that his *reus* is established decisively by his violation of the positive statute.[14] Thus criminal theorists have deprived their discipline of much of the relevance and importance it would otherwise possess.

A moral interpretation of these fundamental principles of liability would not require a radical, unprecedented departure from ancient tenets of criminal theory. Though studies by legal historians are inconclusive, it seems likely that moral content was part of an earlier interpretation of reus. One authority concludes that mens rea "smacked strongly of moral blameworthiness" in the thirteenth century.[15] It is difficult to identify when this position was replaced by a nonmoral interpretation. In England, James Stephen's influential treatise dismissed the suggestion that "immorality is essential to crime" by noting that the requirement of mens rea "is frequently though ignorantly supposed to mean that there cannot be such a thing as legal guilt where there is no moral guilt, which is obviously untrue, as there is always a possibility of a conflict between law and morals."[16] An authority more interested in theory construction for prescriptive rather than descriptive purposes might have used Stephen's observation as a basis for recommending wholesale reform of the substantive criminal law. In America, Oliver Holmes actually celebrated the alleged "unmorality" of criminal law as representing important social progress.[17] Many contemporary theorists seem to concur.[18]

It is even less clear *why* the moral interpretation of reus was rejected. Some authorities were dissatisfied not with the moral interpretation itself, but rather with the particular gloss attached to morality within the Christian tradition. Stephen and Holmes, however, seem to have shared a different rationale. Their motivations for driving a theoretical wedge between law and morality are complex and obscure. Strongly influenced by "legal positivism," they were perhaps overly sensitive to the need that law be "objective," certain, and external. Since morality was alleged to possess none of these *desiderata,* they urged that legal terminology be dissasociated from it. If these grounds for severing criminal theory from moral and political philosophy seem less compelling today, it may be because we appreciate that the scope and application of principles of law, like those of morality, are highly controversial.[19] Contemporary legal theorists have few kind words for the "mechanical," deductive models of judicial reasoning sometimes associated with positivism. Although this earlier rationale for severing criminal theory from moral and political philosophy has been repudiated, the legacy survives in orthodox theory. David Richards notes that criminal theory "has been schizoid about the proper analysis of moral values in the law" since Holmes's time.[20]

Despite the profound influence of these 19th-century authorities, residues of the earlier moral interpretation of reus persist. Support from case law can be "multiplied indefinitely" for the proposition that mens rea means "bad faith or evil intent," "evil purpose," "evil heart," "evil disposition," "malice," or "corrupt design."[21] This is decidedly not the interpretation preferred by orthodox theorists, however. Contemporary authorities typically denounce such language as "remnants of a former era" and as "loose talk [indicating] a refusal to think seriously about the meaning of mens rea."[22] Only occasionally do theorists call for a return to the earlier interpretation of reus.[23]

Why have orthodox criminal theorists continued to attach a somewhat trivial interpretation to their fundamental principles, and consequently narrowed the significance of their discipline? Why do they use strong language condemning some kinds of injustices, while remaining silent about others? There is no simple answer to these important questions, but the following sections will provide a partial explanation. It is important to understand why contemporary pleas to reintroduce morality as the basis for penal legislation have not been warmly received.

## A FALSE START

SOMETIMES PROGRESS on an important topic is delayed because of a tendency to respond to a leading theorist who has characterized the issues in peculiar ways and steered the discussion in unfortunate directions. If the initial contributions of authorities are defective in these crucial respects, several years may be required before research is placed back on course.

Contemporary literature about the enforcement of morality provides an example of this phenomenon. Virtually all commentators who have addressed this topic in the last several years structure their work around the writings of Lord Patrick Devlin. This subject has become so closely associated with Devlin's views that it is almost impossible to divorce it from his particular interpretation. Of course, Devlin's contributions must have been insightful to merit such an extraordinary level of response. But it is lamentable that almost all the commentary on this topic constitutes either a defense or (much more commonly) an attack on his position. This is unfortunate because Devlin has characterized the issues in such a way that the most important questions are not addressed. Subsequent work that responds to Devlin, both favorably or unfavorably, has done little to remedy this defect.

Devlin begins by raising the right question: "To what extent, if at all, should the criminal law . . . concern itself with the enforcement of morals and punish . . . immorality as such?"[24] But he quickly misconstrues his own query. For he defends his answer, which is contrary to orthodoxy, by attaching a doubly curious interpretation to his inquiry. Consider first his remarkable reply to the important question "How are the moral judgements of society to be ascertained?"[25] His answer relies heavily upon the "intolerance, indignation, and disgust"[26] of the "reasonable man" or juror, who "is not expected to reason about anything, and [whose] judgement may be largely a matter of feeling . . . For my purpose . . . the moral judgements of society must be something about which any twelve men or women drawn at random might after discussion be expected to be unanimous."[27] Consider next his surprising defense of why morality, as so identified, should be enforced by the criminal law. He writes: "Society cannot ignore the morality of the individual any more than it can his loyalty; it flourishes on both and without either it dies."[28] He likens immorality to treason in its potential to destroy the very fabric of society.

Several of Devlin's critics have attacked both these platforms of his position. Why assume that the "feelings" of "reasonable persons" have anything to do with morality? Conduct that provokes "intolerance, indignation, and disgust" may not be immoral, but simply unfamiliar and threatening to established customs. A public display of interracial affection triggers these feelings in many communities, but can hardly be condemned from a moral perspective. One of the functions of an enlightened morality is to evaluate and thus improve the unexamined mores of a community. But Devlin's approach deprives morality of this critical function, for its very content is drawn by reference to these customs and mores. Thus Ronald Dworkin aptly retorts: "What is shocking and wrong is not his idea that the community's morality counts, but his idea of what counts as the community's morality."[29] Perhaps Devlin's work should be titled "the enforcement of prejudice" rather than "the enforcement of morality."

Devlin's response to why "immoral" conduct should be criminalized has also been refuted. There is little empirical evidence that the existence of a society is threatened if practices that evoke strong disapproval remain unpunished. H. L. A. Hart observes that Devlin conflates change in a society, which may follow from the introduction of new and unconventional practices, with the destruction of that society.[30] Thus Devlin has failed to answer his question of *why* society should punish alleged immorality.

Moreover, even if Devlin is correct that the social fabric will suffer if strong community sentiments are not enforced by the criminal law, it is doubtful that the results in contemporary society would meet with his personal approval. Devlin's work was motivated by his rejection of the Wolfenden Report, which recommended the decriminalization of private homosexual acts between consenting adults in Britain. Devlin seems confident that reasonable persons would unanimously feel intolerance, indignation, and disgust at this recommendation. Devlin may be a worse sociologist than a criminal theorist, for his confidence seems entirely misplaced. In fact, precious little private conduct between consenting adults would evoke such unanimously strong sentiments in modern Anglo-American societies. What Devlin apparently overlooks is that the shared morality that provides the cement of society might be one of mutual tolerance and respect.

These difficulties are familiar to legal philosophers who have examined the literature surrounding Devlin's work. What is unfortunate is that many theorists apparently believe that a refutation of Devlin has put to rest the controversy about the enforcement of morality. In fact, however, that issue has barely been touched by the response to Devlin, and his own questions have not been addressed. It should be clear that he has not been discussing the enforcement of what a philosopher understands as *morality*. Moreover, it is clear that he has failed to defend the proscription of morality *as such*. Since his arguments for criminalization depend upon the dire social consequences predicted to follow from tolerance, he has not even attempted to make a case for the enforcement of morality apart from such anticipated consequences, that is, for the enforcement of morality *as such*. Thus the critical commentary upon Devlin has not succeeded in refuting the thesis that morality should be enforced by the criminal law, but rather Devlin's doubly defective interpretation of that thesis.

## HARM

PERHAPS THE MOST effective means to understand the strengths and weaknesses of a proposal is to identify and assess alternatives to it. Devlin's invitation to enforce "morality" has been declined. What remains for the criminal law to enforce? As I have indicated, most orthodox theorists have dismissed this question as outside the scope of their discipline. Criminal theory, as they understand it, establishes only those constraints that must be observed after the decision to criminalize has been made. Nonetheless, a few more ambitious authorities have attempted to address this issue.

### Harm as a Moral and Political Principle

The most familiar alleged alternative to the enforcement of morality is the thesis that criminal law should proscribe only conduct that creates *harm*. The slogan is promising: freedom for the individual unless his conduct is harmful. Many authorities are attracted to this "harm requirement" because it seems to allow them to adopt a position about the limits of the substantive criminal law without immersing themselves in controversial and never-ending moral and political debates. In short, harm *rather* than morality is used to establish the constraints on state authority to create law.[31] As I have illustrated time and time again, many orthodox theorists suffer from "moral arguphobia"; they go to extraordinary lengths to pretend that, whatever else they may be doing, they are not developing and applying a moral or political theory. Concepts are made central to orthodox thought because they appear to be "scientific," "objective," or "factual," and harm is no exception.

There are any number of indications that orthodox criminal theorists are attracted to the harm requirement for this reason. Herbert Packer writes: "The 'harm to others' formula [should be included] in a list of limiting criteria for invocation of the criminal sanction [because] it is a way to make sure that a given form of conduct is not being subjected to the criminal sanction purely or even primarily because it is thought to be immoral."[32] Orville Snyder continually emphasizes that harm is a "fact."[33] Albon Eser lists as first among "the most important functions the harm requirement is designed to serve" its use "to distinguish criminal conduct from merely immoral behavior (i.e., from pure ethics)."[34] He continues: "the harm requirement is precisely the principle which, if properly employed, would restrain the state from punishing purely immoral wrongs."[35] Additional examples of this motivation for including the harm requirement within orthodox theory could be multiplied indefinitely.

The reader may feel he has heard all this before. These rationales in favor of the harm requirement bear a striking resemblance to those invoked in support of the causal and actus reus requirements. Chapters 5 and 6 discussed the confusion inherent in proposals to use these principles to differentiate criminal law from "pure ethics."[36] In this section I will argue that it is equally misguided to utilize the harm requirement for this purpose. The thesis that only harmful conduct should be proscribed by the criminal law does not represent a genuine *alternative* to the view that the criminal law should enforce morality, but *is* a (typically disguised) part of a moral and political theory.[37] Revised criminal theory should incorporate this thesis if it is true that only harmful conduct is wrongful. But whether or not this thesis is retained, it must be clearly understood that its application requires a fusion of criminal theory with moral and political philosophy.

Much of the controversy surrounding the harm requirement involves the law of attempts. The difficulty, of course, is that many attempts, although apparently harmless, give rise (and ought to give rise) to criminal liability. But we should now be familiar with the ingenuity of orthodox theorists, who have proposed various strategies to reconcile the law of attempts with the harm requirement. Some commentators insist that, appearances notwithstanding, all attempts legitimately proscribed by the criminal law are harmful.[38] But this usage "distorts and attenuates" the concept of harm.[39] Other theorists have rephrased the harm principle so that criminal liability requires either actual *or threatened* harm.[40] This approach, though preferable, still encounters two difficulties. First, it seemingly disallows criminal liability in the notorious cases of "impossible attempts," since such conduct does *not* create a threat of harm (in any straightforward sense).[41] Moreover, it seemingly allows criminal liability in cases of "mere preparation," since conduct that falls short of attempt may also "threaten" harm.[42]

While these perplexities are useful in introducing difficulties surrounding the harm principle, it would be misleading to infer that attempts represent the most important problems with this requirement. The more basic issue is: what constitutes harm? If this concept is fit to play the role assigned for it by orthodox theorists, there must be some criteria for identifying the interests of persons that (absent special circumstances) should be protected. The violation of these interests will be said to constitute a harm, the presence (or threat) of which is a necessary condition for the use of criminal penalties. In the absence of criteria to differentiate harmful from harmless conduct, the thesis that harm is a necessary condition for criminal liability becomes uninformative. Anyone who seriously proposes that a given kind of conduct should be criminalized is generally prepared to argue that it is harmful. If the thesis that harm is a necessary condition for the legitimate use of the criminal sanction is to function substantively, *some* such claims must be incorrect. Not *all* behavior for which criminal penalties have been proposed could be harmful.[43]

Some criminal theorists have all but turned this "harm principle" into a useless tautology. Hyman Gross is sufficiently ambitious to adopt a position on the question of what conduct should or should not be criminalized. He writes: "Some harm . . . is required of any crime validly on the books in our legal system."[44] One might reasonably expect Gross to defend some criteria for identifying harms, and to use them to criticize laws that proscribe conduct that is harmless. But he does not attempt to do so. He asks: "'What deserves to be recognized as a criminal harm?' Important as that answer is, it is not important for any investigation undertaken in this book."[45] The end result is that the concept of harm is deprived of any potential to serve as a device for rejecting laws that proscribe harmless conduct. He claims: "The term harm as we use it here, embraces everything that is regarded as an untoward state of affairs by the criminal law."[46] Someone accused of a criminal offense is in no better position to defend on the ground that his conduct was harmless than on the ground that his conduct was not *reus*. The mere fact that his conduct was prohibited by positive law is sufficient to satisfy both the harm and *reus* requirements. What was introduced as a promising basis to resist objectionable criminal laws has become a useless tautology.

Without an inventory of interests the violation of which counts as harmful, the "harm principle" is neither descriptively *nor* prescriptively useful to criminal theory. Unless one can distinguish harmful from harmless conduct, he cannot assess the accuracy of the description that the criminal law proscribes only harm. Similarly, he can have little confidence in the prescription that the criminal law *should* be used only to prevent harm. Gross's unwillingness or inability to provide an inventory of interests the violation of which is harmful might have led him to suspend judgment about the truth of the "harm principle."

If it is clear that criteria to differentiate harmful from harmless conduct are required for the "harm principle" to have any significant application, it is equally clear that such criteria are far from obvious. Harm is not an "empirical" characteristic the presence or absence of which can be detected by scientific instruments. Nor can one liken harm to obscenity by insisting that, although it cannot be defined, "I know it when I see it." The fact that reasonable persons might differ about whether conduct is harmful can be appreciated by considering the following examples, none of which involves the formidable difficulties with attempts:[47]

1. Mary opens a large supermarket across from Steve's small grocery, ruining his business.
2. Peeping Tom secretly watches Steve and Jane make love in their bedroom. Tom enjoys voyeurism, and Steve and Jane never discover they were observed.
3. Paparazzi Paul follows celebrity Steve everywhere, obnoxiously thrusting a camera in his face.
4. Sue refuses Steve's invitation to dinner, and breaks his heart.
5. Gene rapes Steve's wife.
6. John, a resident of the same state as Steve, cheats on his income tax.
7. Dan fails to throw an available life preserver to a drowning Steve.
8. Joe gives lavish gifts to each of his friends except Steve.
9. Steve is offended after witnessing a public act of homosexual intercourse.
10. Steve becomes aware that the adjacent house has been rented by homosexuals, of whom he deeply disapproves.

The question in each of these examples is whether Steve is harmed.

Each of these cases raises distinct problems. Consider (9) and (10). Most theorists attracted to a harm principle would claim that Steve's psychological distress counts as a harm in the former but not in the latter case. Few authorities invoke the harm principle to call for the decriminalization of all *public* acts between consenting adults. Some of these theorists have expended much ingenuity in attempts to explain why offense should be regarded as a harm when produced by public, but not by private acts.[48] In support of the conclusion that there is no harm in cases such as (10), Hart writes:

> A right to be protected from the distress which is inseparable from the bare knowledge that others are acting in ways you think wrong, cannot be acknowledged by anyone who recognises individual liberty as a value. . . . If distress incident to the belief that others are doing

wrong is harm, so also is the distress incident to the belief that others are doing what you do not want them to do.[49]

But Hart has not *explained* the difference between (9) and (10); he has merely restated his conviction that there *must be* a difference if the harm principle is to be preserved.[50] If the "bare knowledge" that "others are doing what you do not want them to do" in private cannot qualify as a harm, it is unclear why the offensive conduct of others becomes harmful simply because it is public. Reflection upon such cases reveals that judgments about whether conduct is to be countenanced as harmful are theory-dependent.

Upon what *kind* of theory do such judgments depend? It should be apparent that no less than a moral and political theory is needed to identify the interests of persons that (absent special circumstances) should be immune from violation. Only moral reasoning can hope to explain why the violation of some of Steve's interests should be counted as harms deemed worthy of protection while others should not.

It is understandable that Gross would not attempt to solve the formidable problem of identifying the legitimate interests the state is warranted in protecting. But the resultant failure to think deeply and seriously about the concept of harm can foster the misapprehension that it is amenable to a factual, empirical analysis.[51] Those moral and political philosophers who have developed the most sophisticated accounts of the concept of harm are less likely to make this mistake. Joel Feinberg's remark shows insight:

> Legislators must decide not only *whether* to use the harm principle . . . but also *how* to use it in cases of merely minor harms, moderately probable harms, reasonable and unreasonable risks of harm, aggregative harms, harms to some interests preventable only at the cost of harms to other interests irreconcilable with them, structured competitive harms, accumulative harms, and so on. Solutions to these problems cannot be provided by the harm principle in its simply stated form, but absolutely require the help of supplementary principles, some of which represent controversial moral decisions and maxims of justice.[52]

It would be a serious mistake to suppose that the need for moral criteria to differentiate harmfulness from harmlessness arises because of a small number of troublesome borderline cases. A moral and political theory is required to justify whether and under what circumstances the criminal law should recognize a harm even in cases of physical injuries. Typically the harm principle is expressed to allow personal freedom in the absence of harm *to others*. Many authorities appeal to the principle *volenti fit non injuria* in an attempt to argue that the criminal law should not proscribe harm to oneself.[53] Clearly the "objective," physical component of a wound can be equally severe whether or not it is self-inflicted. The claim that the criminal law should allow harm to oneself is normative; its truth depends upon the assessment of a moral and political theory that includes such perplexing notions as autonomy.[54] Only moral and political reasoning can decide whether the *volenti* principle should be accepted. The harm principle, after all, should be invoked to "prevent only those harms that are wrongs."[55] If a robber murders Steve, we all agree that he has been harmed, not because we do not employ moral criteria of harmfulness, but because the application of such criteria to this case is beyond serious dispute. We are so accustomed to moral issues being complex that we forget they remain moral even when they are simple.

### Mill and the Harm Principle

Thus the "harm principle" *is* a moral and political principle. Its foremost historical champion, John Stuart Mill, was clear about this point. His awareness that this principle is moral in content emerges, first, from the kind of defense he constructed for it, and second, from his formulation of other principles he believed to be equivalent to it. *On Liberty* provides an extended defense of the harm principle in which Mill claimed to "forego any advantage which could be derived to my argument from the idea of abstract right as a thing independent of utility. I regard utility as the ultimate appeal on all ethical questions."[56] Mill recognized that a moral principle requires a moral defense. Moreover, Mill's various restatements of the harm principle remove any doubt about its moral content. He believes conduct becomes eligible for censure when "a person is led to violate a distinct and assignable obligation to any other person,"[57] or when it damages "the interests of one another, or rather certain interests which . . . ought to be considered as rights."[58] The obligations and rights to which Mill refers here are *moral:* they cannot (without circularity) be *legal* obligations or rights, since the whole point of his enterprise is to determine what our legal obligations and rights should be.

Whether or not Mill succeeds in defending the harm principle is quite another matter. It is a commonplace to contend that a moral theory that appeals only to consequences (such as harms) to appraise conduct is seriously deficient.[59] Mill himself may have been aware of the limitations of a consequentialist morality; his defense of the harm principle, despite his disclaimers, appears suspiciously nonutilitarian at points.[60] In any case, success or failure must be assessed according to however one evaluates moral and political theories. Appeals to a harm principle cannot spare criminal theorists the burden of engaging in moral and political argument.

If it is clear that Mill is defending a moral principle, much that has been written about *On Liberty* is misleading. The standard interpretation of Mill is that he "gave an emphatic negative answer in his essay *On Liberty*" to the question "is it morally permissible to enforce morality as such?"[61] It is true that Mill opposed the criminalization of harmless conduct believed by society to be immoral. But his opposition could not have been grounded on a belief that the state had no business enforcing morality, since morality is used as the basis for deciding what conduct *should* be criminalized.[62] Instead, it is plausible to interpret Mill as believing that there *are* no "harmless immoralities." Society should not enforce harmless immorality, because there is no such thing to enforce. Mill indeed opposed the enforcement of conventional or popular morality, but only because he rejected the adequacy of such "morality," not because he opposed the enforcement of morality itself.

The legacy of Mill can be invoked to support the conclusion that if the concept of harm is useful in establishing the limits of the substantive criminal law, it is not because it represents an *alternative* to the claim that morality should be enforced.[63] The thesis that the criminal sanction should be used solely to proscribe harm is attractive only insofar as harmful conduct is morally wrongful. While Devlin identified immoral conduct by reference to the attitudes of "reasonable persons," defenders of the harm principle (sometimes unwittingly) presuppose a moral and political theory to differentiate harmful from harmless conduct. Only the content of the enforced morality differs. Orthodox theorists are sadly mistaken if they are attracted to a harm principle because it allows them to adopt a position about the limits of the substantive criminal law while resisting the "infection" of criminal theory with moral and political philosophy.

## LIBERALISM AND NEUTRALITY

ONCE IT IS CLEAR that the harm principle does not represent a genuine alternative to the enforcement of morality, and the issue is severed from its unfortunate association with the peculiar views of Lord Devlin, the controversy can be expressed anew: what can be said for or against the thesis that the state should use morality to establish the limits of the substantive criminal law?

Orthodox criminal theorists per se have contributed surprisingly little to this debate. Instead, the dispute surrounding liberalism provides the political context in which this question has most often been discussed.[64] Perhaps no single thread ties together all the diverse views that have been described as liberal. But much of the liberal tradition has defended a conception of the state as morally *neutral,* enforcing no particular theory of moral goodness over competitors. The political philosophy of liberalism, construed as state commitment to moral neutrality, is of fundamental importance for criminal theory. As so understood, liberalism opposes the synthesis between moral and political philosophy and criminal theory proposed here. For if it can be shown that neutrality is an ideal toward which political institutions should aspire, it seems obvious that the criminal justice system is a sensible place to begin. No component of a political system is as coercive as its system of criminal justice. If deviations from neutrality by political institutions are pernicious in general, they are likely to be especially objectionable here. According to this tradition, the criminal law should decline the invitation to enforce morality because of this breach of neutrality.

This conception of the liberal state as morally neutral has been defended by a number of contemporary political theorists. According to Ronald Dworkin, the liberal state "must be neutral on what might be called the question of the good life."[65] Bruce Ackerman contends that in the liberal state "no reason is a good reason [for exercises of political power] if it requires the power holder to assert (a) that his conception of the good life is better than that asserted by his fellow citizens, *or* (b) that, regardless of his conception of the good, he is intrinsically superior to one or more of his fellow citizens."[66] Michael Sandel identifies the "core thesis" of liberalism as the view that "society, being composed of a plurality of persons, each with his own aims, interests, and conceptions of the good, is best arranged when it is governed by principles that do not *themselves* presuppose any particular conception of the good."[67]

"Realists" sometimes retort that complete neutrality is utopian: political authorities can always be counted upon to favor their own conception of the good. Thus neutrality is dismissed as an unattainable myth. But this sweeping rejection of the ideal of neutrality should not give serious pause to its defenders. States can be compared and contrasted to the degree that they approximate neutrality, even if total neutrality is impossible. As long as neutrality is admitted as desirable, it is worthwhile to evaluate states to the extent that they approach it. Eventually the realist must retreat from claims about what is possible to an examination of what is desirable.

What can be said in favor of regarding moral neutrality as a goal toward which political institutions in general, and systems of criminal law in particular, should strive? Liberal theorists divide into two distinct camps in answering this question. These defenses differ about whether neutrality is to be construed as a *moral* value.

### Liberal Neutrality as the Absence of Morality

It should come as no surprise that liberal neutrality, construed as the absence of commitment about moral and political controversies, would be found attractive. Many theorists are drawn toward this conception of neutrality because of a belief in *moral skepticism.* There are countless varieties of moral skepticism. Each is said to support state neutrality because of our alleged inability to effectively distinguish right from wrong. State enforcement of morality presupposes that value preferences can be rationally defended; since they cannot, the only acceptable alternative is neutrality.

Many theorists are quite confused about the connection between moral skepticism and a preference for liberal neutrality. Uncertainty and ambivalence about whether the tolerance of liberals is defensible as a moral position can be traced to the work of anthropologists such as Ruth Benedict. A profound moral skepticism pervades her work; she claims that the mores of distinct societies are evaluatively "incommensurable."[68] She repudiates any rational procedure to evaluate the mores of a culture. The lesson she hopes will be learned from her investigations of cultural diversity is that we should be *tolerant* and less arrogant in assuming that the values of others are inferior to our own. All mores, she concludes, are "equally valid."[69] Benedict's liberal sentiments are laudable; unfortunately, they are incompatible with the premises on which they are based. If the mores of a culture happen to include intolerance, and there is no rational basis to evaluate mores, there can be no ground for condemning intolerance. Yet she combines a professed moral skepticism about societal values with a defense of the virtue of tolerance. Benedict may have deluded herself into believing that skepticism supports liberalism by failing to notice that judgments of equal validity are essentially comparative. The claim that the mores of culture A are superior or inferior to those of culture B is clearly comparative; but so too is the claim that the mores of cultures A and B are "equally valid." A consistent moral skeptic must profess no preference either for equality or inequality, tolerance or intolerance. Liberalism is not the consequence of a view that discredits the coherence of cross-cultural comparisons. If one hopes to defend the superiority of liberalism, it will not do to impugn the rationality of comparative standards.

What conclusions about the limits of the substantive criminal law and enforcement of morality can be drawn from moral skepticism? Liberals frequently invoke skepticism as a reason to oppose controversial interferences in personal liberty. Since we cannot know, for example, whether abortion is immoral, it would be unwise to criminalize it. This strategy, however, fails to explain why *any* interferences with liberty are condoned. No state professes skepticism about the wrongness of murder or rape. A state that consistently embraces skepticism has no basis for enacting *any* penal legislation whatever. Anarchism may be the only political philosophy available to a pervasive skeptic.

The specter of anarchism generally induces liberals to retreat from their professed skepticism. *Some* knowledge of the good is presupposed by criminal legislation of which liberals approve. The burden confronting such theorists is to provide a principled account of the distinction between matters about which it is and is not possible to possess moral knowledge. The most familiar (though not the only) compromise of the skeptical liberal is to claim moral knowledge solely of *instrumental* goods.

The details of instrumentalist theories of the good vary among liberal theorists, but most embody (roughly) the following insight. Individuals are in radical disagreement about what purposes or goals are worthy of pursuit, and the liberal state should exhibit no favoritism toward any such conception. But each person is alike in *having* purposes or goals. Thus all persons share an interest in protection from interferences with *whatever* purposes or goals they may have. Political institutions do not breach their promise of neutrality if they limit criminal penalties to conduct that interferes with the abilities of persons to pursue *any* of their diverse purposes or goals.

Many of the great liberals of this century have constructed elaborate defenses of instrumentalist theories of the good alleged to be consistent with state neutrality about ends. It would be simplistic to suppose that a single argument could suffice to refute them all. Nonetheless, at least six general difficulties should give pause to each.

First, the project of defending moral skepticism about ends but not means is worth undertaking only if there are good reasons to embrace skepticism about ends. If the chief motivation in favor of skepticism about ends is to avoid moral and political controversy, it is sobering to discover that disagreement about means may be no less intractable. Many contemporary debates in criminal procedure illustrate the extent of these disputes, although I have not discussed them here.

Moreover, it is unlikely that liberals favor *no* constraints on what purposes or goals are legitimate.[70] Consider the thorny question of what duties living persons owe members of future generations. Actions performed now will change the opportunities available to the unborn. For example, we can decrease the possibility that future persons will ever enjoy the experience of seeing a live lion or tiger. Or we can increase the likelihood that future persons will suffer from cancer. Surely foreclosure of some of these "opportunities" is desirable. It seems clear that "to be fair to our children and to our children's children, we must act on some conception of what they *should* want."[71]

Neutrality about ends is susceptible to a third difficulty. Even if the liberal state approximates neutrality, we can rest assured that other social institutions do not.[72] There may be good reason to allow the values enforced by political institutions to compensate for those adopted by nonpolitical institutions. A capitalistic economy rewards, for example, skill, beauty, musicality, effort, and luck. Those persons with none of these characteristics are likely to experience hardship. A political system that neglects these unfortunates under the guise of neutrality is simply deferring to the values of nonpolitical institutions. A state genuinely committed to neutrality might be partial in attempting to ameliorate the hardship caused by nonpolitical institutions that are blatantly nonneutral. The limitations upon state action in this direction are illustrated by controversies surrounding preferential hiring of minorities. But there is little reason to insist that the state should be singled out as the sole social institution to be constrained by neutrality.

In addition, there is a need to decide about *whose* purposes and ends the state should be neutral. The immediate inclination is to respond that neutrality should be observed toward *everyone*. But what political units are contemplated by this reply? The problem is not merely to decide how animals, infants and idiots are to be accommodated, formidable though these difficulties may be. The more fundamental issue is to justify treatment of the *individual* as the basic political unit. This bias toward individualism is not the only possible alternative. The chief competitor to liberalism is utilitarianism, in which the ultimate concern is for collective rather than individual welfare. In commenting upon the consequences for individuals if utilitarianism were implemented as state policy, Ackerman confidently asserts: "Nobody in his right mind would consent to such degradation."[73] Perhaps not. But this dismissal of utilitarianism is curious when coupled with a commitment to neutrality. There is little doubt that moral and political values are required in any demonstration that the liberal concern for the individual is preferable to the utilitarian concern for the collective. Thus the liberal is not morally neutral in his favoritism toward the individual as the basic political unit.

Moreover, the state is hardly neutral in its attitude and response to criminals. State neutrality toward personal ends is difficult to reconcile with the existence of the institution of punishment, since criminal sanctions obviously interfere with the life plans of offenders. Much ingenuity has been expended to show how impositions of punishment are compatible with the liberal promise of neutrality.[74] Yet these attempts are more ingenious than convincing. It is more candid to admit that punishment expresses the nonneutral condemnation of a community.[75]

Finally, how can a commitment to equality be squared with neutrality? Recall Ruth Benedict's apparent confusion that judgments of equality, unlike those of superiority or inferiority, are not value-laden and thus immune from moral skepticism. A similar confusion is evident in contemporary liberal theorists as well. Ackerman writes: "Neutrality forbids me from saying that I'm any better than you are; it doesn't prevent me from saying that I'm at least as good."[76] What might be called a *presumption of equality* is operative throughout his entire work. "Rationality," as understood by Ackerman, requires that "whenever anybody questions the legitimacy of another's power, the power holder must respond . . . by giving a reason that explains why he is more entitled to the resource than the questioner is."[77] But if one asks why power should be distributed *equally,* no comparable justification is required, for "the burden of articulation [is placed] squarely upon those who seek an inegalitarian distribution of worldly advantage."[78] Such presumptions, of course, are transparent substitutes for arguments.[79] Their use fosters the pretense that one point of view is preferable to another when nothing persuasive is said on either side. But a preference for equality (like inequality) must be supported by argument, not the ad hominem that inequality is irrational. It is likely that any such argument will breach the promise of neutrality.

### Liberal Neutrality as Morality

The above considerations warrant doubt that liberal neutrality can be defended without an appeal to moral and political values. A number of liberals, of course, are well aware of this fact. Dworkin identifies liberalism with the requirement "that government must be neutral on what might be called the question of the good life."[80] He repeats the familiar connection between neutrality and equality: a state treats its citizens as equals when it shows no favoritism toward some conceptions of the good over others. His arguments in favor of neutrality and equality, however, differ considerably from those discussed thus far. Dworkin is no moral skeptic; neutrality and equality are not adopted because they represent a lack of commitment in an area where genuine knowledge is unattainable. Instead, neutrality and equality are embraced as the most defensible moral and political alternative. He writes: "Liberalism cannot be based on scepticism. Its constitutive morality provides that human beings must be treated as equals by their government, not because there is no right and wrong in political morality, but because that is what is right."[81]

Dworkin is notoriously elusive in defending these judgments of political morality. Sometimes he seems content merely to identify the moral theory that underlies and is presupposed by our Constitution. To reject neutrality and liberalism, as interpreted by Dworkin, is tantamount to a repudiation of the moral theory embodied in the Constitution, and ultimately of the Constitution itself.[82] When pressed to probe more deeply, however, he supports neutrality by a conception of equality derived from "the vague but powerful idea of human dignity . . . associated with Kant."[83] It would be unfair if this passing reference were interpreted to imply Dworkin's commitment to the whole corpus of Kant's moral philosophy. But this remark suggests a better understanding of liberalism than is provided by those who identify it with a promise of political neutrality. One need not specialize in Kantian exegesis to appreciate how a plausible moral defense of equality might be constructed. Kant believed that all persons (unlike animals) are entitled to be treated with equal concern and respect because they possess a comparable degree of moral autonomy. Persons are alike in their freedom to formulate goals, interests, purposes, desires, and the like. Thus the autonomy of persons is the basis for regarding them as equals; a nonautonomous being has no claim to be treated with equal concern and respect. In the Kantian tradition, therefore, autonomy and equality come as a package. It is disingenuous to appeal to that tradition as a basis for equality while not recognizing the comparable importance of autonomy.[84]

Liberalism should not be understood as a political theory professing neutrality about what is good. Instead, it should be construed as a theory that attaches a high premium on the liberty of autonomous persons. A number of values compete for significance in the political arena, and difficult questions arise when these values conflict. This book has focused on many such controversies, and liberals are not neutral about them. They will respond by placing an especially heavy (though not dispositive) weight on the freedom, liberty, and autonomy of citizens.

This interpretation of the core of liberalism has a number of advantages. First, it comports with the etymology of the word. According to Maurice Cranston, a liberal "is a person who believes in liberty, as a nudist is a person who believes in nudity."[85] Second, it explains why liberals are not of a single mind about complex political issues. Often it is unclear which side of a given controversy should be favored by one who places a high premium on personal liberty.[86] Finally, it accounts for why a definition of liberalism as political neutrality is seductive. If a liberal encourages individual freedom and the resultant diversity of lifestyles, it may appear that he is neutral among them.

For present purposes, it is not important to *defend* liberalism as understood along the lines sketched above. The crucial point is to recognize what *kind* of defense is required if liberalism is acceptable. A moral and political argument is required to justify the elevation of one value (liberty) over others in the political arena. Liberals should not retreat behind a shallow skepticism that repudiates moral argumentation entirely, or pretend that neutrality does not require a moral defense. It is clear that "defenders of the liberal state must either accept the burden of substantive justification or abandon their enterprise altogether."[87] Thus, as with the harm principle, liberalism does not represent an *alternative* to the thesis that morality should be enforced; it *is* a theory of political morality. An adequate defense of liberalism must demonstrate why the moral values embodied in liberalism are the right values to enforce.

Since I have argued that criminal theory has no viable alternative but to incorporate a substantive moral and political philosophy, the options are to abandon liberalism (construed as state neutrality) or to reinterpret it. The latter approach seems preferable. A moral and political philosophy that emphasizes the importance of liberty explains the significance of the rights respected by the fundamental requirements of criminal liability. These rights are likely to receive their most jealous protection within a liberal framework.[88] Liberalism, as here understood, represents the moral and political tradition with which I believe it is most promising to fuse revised criminal theory.

There is no warrant for disqualifying an evaluation of liberalism and its competitors from the scope of criminal theory. The suppositions that moral and political philosophy is not a credible discipline, or that a criminal theory can be embraced without adopting a stand on moral and political issues, have done a great disservice. Both have contributed to the silence of orthodox theorists about the issue of the limits of the substantive criminal law. Once these suppositions are rejected, there is no reason why positions on these issues cannot be incorporated into criminal theory. I am painfully aware that the mere call for a fusion between criminal theory and moral and political philosophy does not describe the details of this synthesis, and only a very small step has been taken here. But many of the resources for attaining this fusion are already present; revised criminal theorists need only take advantage of them.

### NOTES

1. See Jeremy Bentham, *An Introduction to the Principles of Morals and Legislation.*
2. An exception is Herbert Packer, *The Limits of the Criminal Sanction.*

Even Packer, however, is careful to avoid excessive moral and political argumentation. For a more recent exception, see David Richards, *Sex, Drugs, Death, and the Law.*

3. Richards describes as "remarkable" the obsession with efficiency in decriminalization arguments. Ibid., p. 84. Another writer describes the debate as "largely an in-house quarrel among utilitarians." See Noel Reynolds, "The Enforcement of Morals and the Rule of Law," *Georgia Law Review* 11 (1979): 1325.

4. Three caveats: First, I do not mean to imply that any and all legislative objectives are consistent with the fundamental principles of criminal liability. Second, standards other than the fundamental principles, such as those contained in the Bill of Rights, preclude many substantive injustices. Finally, it might be thought that the harm requirement prevents illegitimate legislative objectives. See "Harm," this chapter.

5. "The general part of the criminal law . . . is 'topic-neutral.' " Michael Moore, "The Moral and Metaphysical Sources of the Criminal Law," in J. Roland Pennock and John Chapman, eds., *Nomos XXVII: Criminal Justice,* pp. 11, 14.

6. Notable exceptions include John Kleinig, "Crime and the Concept of Harm," *American Philosophical Quarterly* 15 (1978): 32; and Lawrence Becker, "Criminal Attempt and the Theory of the Law of Crimes," *Philosophy and Public Affairs* 3 (1974): 262. It is noteworthy that Joel Feinberg's *Harm to Others,* the most ambitious and sophisticated treatment of "the moral limits of the criminal law," makes no systematic attempt to differentiate between criminal and noncriminal harms.

7. See the comments in Jeffrie Murphy and Jules Coleman, *The Philosophy of Law,* pp. 122–23.

8. Many legal philosophers have made this point. See Jeffrie Murphy, "Marxism and Retribution," *Philosophy and Public Affairs* 2 (1973): 217.

9. See Daniel Farrell, "Paying the Price: Justifiable Civil Disobedience and the Problem of Punishment," *Philosophy and Public Affairs* 6 (1977): 165.

10. See J. D. Mabbott, "Punishment," *Mind* 48 (1939): 150. Mabbott seems to believe punishment is deserved by the commission of *any* conduct the state designates as criminal.

11. See Joel Feinberg, "The Expressive Function of Punsishment," in his *Doing and Deserving,* p. 95; Andrew Von Hirsch, *Past or Future Crimes?* pp. 55–56; and Neil MacCormick, *Legal Rights and Social Democracy,* p. 33.

12. See Jan Gorecki, *A Theory of Criminal Justice.*

13. See the impoverished interpretation of *reus* in J. C. Smith and Brian Hogan, *Criminal Law,* p. 30; and in Glanville Williams, *Criminal Law: The General Part;* and also in Williams, *Textbook of Criminal Law,* p. 147.

14. The position I defend should not be misinterpreted as a version of "natural law." I am not arguing that a statute proscribing what is morally permissible *cannot* be law, but that it *should* not be law.

15. Francis Sayre, "Mens Rea," *Harvard Law Review* 45 (1932): 974, 988.

16. James Stephen, *A History of the Criminal Law of England,* pp. 94–95.

17. Oliver Wendell Holmes, *The Common Law,* p. 41.

18. Among the latest to question the need "to preserve the moral infrastructure of the criminal law," at least in the context of the insanity defense, is Norval Morris, *Madness and the Criminal Law,* p. 63.

19. See Ronald Dworkin, "Can Rights Be Controversial?" in his *Taking Rights Seriously,* p. 279.

20. David Richards, "Human Rights and the Moral Foundations of the Substantive Criminal Law," *Georgia Law Review* 13 (1979): 1395, 1400.

21. See the references in Peter Low, John Jeffries, and Richard Bonnie, *Criminal Law*, pp. 206–7.

22. Ibid., p. 207.

23. "[W]e should return to the earlier concept of *mens rea* as stating a principle that a man who is morally free from blame is not liable to punishment." Peter Brett, *An Inquiry Into Criminal Guilt*, p. 70.

24. Patrick Devlin, *The Enforcement of Morals*, p. 2.

25. Ibid., p. 14.

26. Ibid., p. 17.

27. Ibid., p. 15.

28. Ibid., p. 22.

29. Ronald Dworkin, "Liberty and Moralism" in *Taking Rights Seriously*, p. 255.

30. H. L. A. Hart, "Immorality and Treason," in Richard Wasserstrom, ed., *Morality and the Law*, p. 49.

31. "There are those who believe that their conception of the good life should be reflected in the basic structure of society; and there are those who believe that people should be free to pursue their own conception of the good, so long as they do not harm others." Laurence Thomas, "Law, Morality, and Our Psychological Nature," in David Braybrooke, ed., *Social Justice*, p. 111.

32. Packer, *Limits*, p. 267.

33. Orvil Snyder, *Preface to Jurisprudence*, p. 523.

34. Albon Eser, "The Principle of 'Harm' in the Concept of Crime," *Duquesne University Law Review* 4 (1966): 345, 346.

35. Ibid., p. 367.

36. See chapters 5 and 6.

37. Many philosophers might be surprised to learn that few orthodox theorists share their opinion that that the requirement of harm is a moral and political principle.

38. Hyman Gross, *A Theory of Criminal Justice*, pp. 127–29; Becker, "Criminal Attempt;" and Kleinig, "Crime and the Concept."

39. Barbara Levenbook, "Prohibiting Attempts and Preparations," *University of Missouri at Kansas City Law Review* 49 (1980): 41, 45.

40. This is the orthodox formulation. But see Levenbook, ibid.

41. This issue has attracted an extraordinary level of commentary. See, for example, Arnold Enker, "Impossibility in Criminal Attempts—Legality and the Legal Process," *University of Minnesota Law Review* 53 (1969): 665.

42. See Levenbook, "Prohibiting."

43. See John Hodson, *The Ethics of Legal Coercion*, p. 18.

44. Gross, *Theory*, p. 114.

45. Ibid., p. 122.

46. Ibid., p. 78.

47. In the course of examining a number of "puzzling cases," Feinberg observes: "it has become far from evident just which crimes now on the books satisfy the harm principle and which do not. That confusion can only be dispelled by a careful analysis of the concept of harm." *Harm*, p. 13. He adds (p. 65): "we are forced to refine our analysis by stipulation since the vagueness cannot be tolerated in a concept that is to be put to such important normative uses."

48. See Joel Feinberg, *Offense to Others.*

49. H. L. A. Hart, *Law, Liberty, and Morality,* p. 47.

50. See David Conway, "Law, Liberty and Indecency," *Philosophy* 49 (1974): 135.

51. Gross himself recognizes the necessity to supplement his work with moral and political argumentation. See *Theory,* p. 115.

52. Feinberg, *Harm,* p. 187.

53. See the discussion in Joel Feinberg, "Legal Paternalism," *Canadian Journal of Philosophy* 1 (1971): 1.

54. See my "Paternalism and Autonomy," *Philosophy and Public Affairs* 10 (1980): 27.

55. Feinberg, *Harm,* pp. 35–36. See also Hodson, *Ethics,* p. 25.

56. John Stuart Mill, *Utilitarianism, Liberty, and Representative Government,* p. 97.

57. Ibid., p. 185.

58. Ibid., p. 177.

59. See Samuel Scheffler, *The Rejection of Consequentialism.*

60. See Robert P. Wolff, *The Poverty of Liberalism.*

61. Hart, *Law, Liberty,* p. 4.

62. Mill writes: "The idea of penal sanction, which is the essence of law, enters . . . into . . . any kind of wrong. We do not call anything wrong, unless we mean to imply that a person ought to be punished in some way for doing it." See *Utilitarianism, Liberty,* p. 59.

63. "The starting-point for discussion of the question [of the enforcement of morality] is to recognize that it is itself a question of morality . . . 'harm' is itself a morally loaded concept." MacCormick, *Legal Rights,* pp. 18, 29. See also Hodson, Ethics, p. 26.

64. "The issues of the Hart-Devlin controversy reflect in a microcosm . . . the continued viability of liberalism." Thomas Grey, *The Legal Enforcement of Morality,* p. 9.

65. Ronald Dworkin, "Liberalism," in Stuart Hampshire, ed., *Public and Private Morality,* p. 127. In a later essay, Dworkin characterizes the liberal stance as remaining "neutral in matters of *personal* morality." See "Neutrality, Equality, and Liberalism," in Douglas MacLean and Claudia Mills, eds., *Liberalism Reconsidered,* p. 1 (emphasis added).

66. Bruce Ackerman, *Social Justice in the Liberal State,* p. 11.

67. Michael Sandel, *Liberalism and the Limits of Justice,* p. 1.

68. Ruth Benedict, *Patterns of Culture,* p. 55.

69. Ibid., p. 278.

70. "Each . . . contemporary liberal theorist begins by promising to do without a substantive theory of the good; each ends by betraying that promise." William Galston, "Defending Liberalism," *American Political Science Review* 76 (1982): 625.

71. Mark Sagoff, "Liberalism and Law," in MacLean and Mills, *Liberalism,* pp. 12, 15.

72. See Joseph Raz, "Liberalism, Autonomy, and the Politics of Neutral Concern," in Peter French, et al., eds., *Midwest Studies in Philosophy* 7 (1982): 89.

73. Ackerman, *Social,* p. 343.

74. See Herbert Morris, "Persons and Punishment," *Monist* 52 (1968): 475. According to Von Hirsch, a value-free orientation has been an obstacle to justice in sentencing policy. See *Past or Future,* p. 149.

75. See note 11.

76. Ackerman, *Social,* p. 15.

77. Ibid., p. 4.

78. Ibid., p. 16.

79. See my "The Presumption of Freedom," *Nous* 17 (1983): 345.

80. Dworkin, "Public and Private," p. 127.

81. Ibid., p. 142.

82. Ronald Dworkin, "Taking Rights Seriously," in *Taking Rights Seriously,* p. 184.

83. Ibid., p. 198.

84. See my "Ronald Dworkin and the Right to Liberty," *Ethics* 90 (1979): 121.

85. Maurice Cranston, *Freedom: A New Analysis,* p. 65.

86. See Gerald Dworkin, "Is More Choice Better Than Less?" in French, *Midwest,* p. 47.

87. Galston, "Defending," p. 627.

88. Of course, I have not *argued* that competing moral and political traditions might not succeed as well.

# Bibliography

Abbate, Fred. "The Conspiracy Doctrine: A Critique." *Philosophy and Public Affairs* 3 (1974): 295.

Ackerman, Bruce. *Social Justice in the Liberal State.* New Haven: Yale University Press, 1982.

Adams, Robert. "Involuntary Sins," *Philosophical Review* 94 (1985): 3.

Allen, Ronald. "The Restoration of *In Re Winship:* A Comment on Burdens of Persuasion in Criminal Cases After *Patterson v. New York.*" *Michigan Law Review* 76 (1977): 30.

Amsterdam, Anthony. "Federal Constitutional Restrictions on the Punishment of Crimes of Status, Crimes of General Obnoxiousness, Crimes of Displeasing Police Officers, and the Like." *Criminal Law Bulletin* 3 (1967): 205.

Anscombe, Elizabeth. *Intention.* Ithaca: Cornell University Press, 1958.

Archbold. *Archbold's Criminal Pleading, Evidence, and Practice,* 37th ed. 1969.

Ashford, Harold, and Risinger, D. Michael. "Presumptions, Assumptions, and Due Process in Criminal Cases: A Theoretical Overview." *Yale Law Journal* 79 (1969): 165.

Ashworth, A. "Reason, Logic, and Criminal Liability." *Law Quarterly Review* 91 (1975): 102.

Austin, John. *Lectures on Jurisprudence.* [1861] 4th ed. London: John Murray, 1873.

Austin, John. "A Plea for Excuses." In *Philosophical Papers.* Oxford: Clarendon Press, 1961. P. 123.

Baker, G. P. "Defeasibility and Meaning." In P. M. S. Hacker and Joseph Raz, eds., *Law, Morality, and Society.* Oxford: Clarendon Press, 1977. P. 20.

Bayles, Michael. *Principles of Legislation.* Detroit: Wayne State University Press, 1978.

―――. "Character, Purpose, and Criminal Responsibility." *Law and Philosophy* 1 (1982): 5.

Becker, Lawrence. "Criminal Attempt and the Theory of the Law of Crimes." *Philosophy and Public Affairs* 3 (1974): 262.

Benedict, Ruth. *Patterns of Culture.* Boston: Houghton Mifflin, 1934.

Bentham, Jeremy. *An Introduction to the Principles of Morals and Legislation.* [1789] London: Methuen, 1982.

Beynon, Helen. "Doctors as Murderers." *Criminal Law Review* (1982): 17.

Black, Charles. *Capital Punishment.* 2d ed. New York: W. W. Norton, 1981.

249

Blackstone, William. *Commentaries*. [1765] Chicago: University of Chicago Press, 1979.

Blair, Christen. "Constitutional Limitations on the Lesser Included Offense Doctrine." *American Criminal Law Review* 21 (1984): 445.

Brand, Miles. "The Language of Not Doing." *American Philosophical Quarterly* 8 (1971): 49.

Brandt, Richard. "Blameworthiness and Obligation." In Abe Melden, ed., *Essays in Moral Philosophy*. Seattle: University of Washington Press, 1958.

Brett, Peter. *An Inquiry Into Criminal Guilt*. London: Sweet & Maxwell, 1963.

Broder, Dale, and Merson, Robert. *"Robinson v. California:* An Abbreviated Study." *American Criminal Law Quarterly* 3 (1965): 203.

Burdick, William. *The Law of Crime*. Albany: M. Bender & Co., 1946.

Cass, Ronald. "Ignorance of the Law: A Maxim Reexamined." *William and Mary Law Review* 17 (1976): 671.

Chisholm, Roderick. *Person and Object*. London: Allen & Unwin, 1976.

Clark, William, and Marshall, William. *A Treatise on the Law of Crimes*. Chicago: Callaghan & Co., 1952.

Cohen, L. Jonathan. "Who Is Starving Whom?" *Theoria* 47 (1981): 65.

Colvin, Eric. "Codification and Reform of the Intoxication Defense." *Criminal Law Review* 26 (1983): 43.

Conway, David. "Law, Liberty, and Indecency." *Philosophy* 49 (1974): 135.

Cook, Walter. "Act, Intention, and Motive in the Criminal Law." *Yale Law Journal* 26 (1917): 645.

Coval, S.; Smith, J.; and Burns, Peter. "The Concept of Action and Its Juridical Significance." *University of Toronto Law Journal* 30 (1980): 199.

Cranston, Maurice. *Freedom: A New Analysis*. London: Longmans, Green, & Co., 1953.

Cuomo, Anthony. "Mens Rea and Status Criminality." *Southern California Law Review* 40 (1967): 463.

Cummins, R. "Culpability and Mental Disorder." *Canadian Journal of Philosophy* 10 (1980): 207.

Dan-Cohen, Meir. "Decision Rules and Conduct Rules: On Acoustic Separation in the Criminal Law." *Harvard Law Review* 97 (1984): 625.

D'Arcy, Eric. *Human Acts*. Oxford: Clarendon Press, 1966.

Davidson, Donald. "Actions, Reasons, and Causes." *Journal of Philosophy* 60 (1963): 685.

Davis, Nancy. "The Priority of Avoiding Harm." In Bonnie Steinbock, ed., *Killing and Letting Die*. Englewood Cliffs: Prentice-Hall, 1980. P. 172.

Devlin, Patrick. *The Enforcement of Morals*. Oxford: Oxford University Press, 1965.

Dressler, Joshua. "New Thoughts About the Concept of Justification in the Criminal Law: A Critique of Fletcher's Thinking and *Rethinking*." *University of California at Los Angeles Law Review* 32 (1984): 61.

Dutile, Ferdinand. "The Burden of Proof in Criminal Cases." *Notre Dame Lawyer* 55 (1979): 380.

Dworkin, Gerald. "Is More Choice Better Than Less?" In Peter French, Theodore Vehling, and Howard Wettstein, eds., *Midwest Studies in Philosophy*, vol. 7. Minneapolis: University of Minnesota Press, 1982. P. 47.

Dworkin, Gerald, and Blumenfeld, David. "Punishment for Intentions." *Mind* 75 (1966): 396.

Dworkin, Ronald. *Taking Rights Seriously.* Cambridge: Harvard University Press, 1977.

———. "Liberalism." In Stuart Hampshire, ed., *Public and Private Morality.* Cambridge: Cambridge University Press, 1978. P. 127.

———. "Neutrality, Equality, and Liberalism." In Douglas MacLean and Claudia Mills, eds., *Liberalism Reconsidered.* Totowa: Rowman & Allanheld, 1983. P. 1.

Edwards, J. "Automatism and Criminal Responsibility." *Modern Law Review* 21 (1958): 375.

Ely, John. *Democracy and Distrust.* Cambridge: Harvard University Press, 1980.

The English Law Commission. *Criminal Law, Report on Defenses of General Application.* 1977.

Enker, Arnold. "Impossibility in Criminal Attempts—Legality and the Legal Process." *University of Minnesota Law Review* 53 (1969): 665.

Epstein, Richard. *A Theory of Strict Liability.* San Francisco: Cato Institute, 1980.

Erlinder, C. Peter. "Mens Rea, Due Process, and the Supreme Court: Toward a Constitutional Doctrine of Substantive Criminal Law." *American Journal of Criminal Law* 9 (1981): 163.

Eser, Albin. "The Principle of 'Harm' in the Concept of Crime." *Duquesne University Law Review* 4 (1966): 345.

Farrell, Daniel. "Paying the Price: Justifiable Civil Disobedience and the Problem of Punishment." *Philosophy and Public Affairs* 6 (1977): 165.

Feinberg, Joel. *Doing and Deserving.* Princeton: Princeton University Press, 1970.

———. "Legal Paternalism." *Canadian Journal of Philosophy* 1 (1971): 1.

———. *Harm to Others.* New York: Oxford University Press, 1984.

———. "The Moral and Legal Responsibility of the Bad Samaritan." *Criminal Justice Ethics* 3 (1984): 56.

———. *Offense to Others.* New York: Oxford University Press, 1985.

Fingarette, Herbert. *The Meaning of Criminal Insanity.* Berkeley: University of California Press, 1972.

———. "Addiction and Criminal Responsibility." *Yale Law Journal* 84 (1975): 413.

Fingarette, Herbert, and Hasse, Ann. *Mental Disabilities and Criminal Responsibility.* Berkeley: University of California Press, 1979.

Fischer, John. "Responsibility and Control." *Journal of Philosophy* 79 (1982): 24.

Fitzgerald, P. J. "Voluntary and Involuntary Acts." In Anthony Guest, ed., *Oxford Essays in Jurisprudence.* 1st Ser. London: Oxford University Press, 1961. P. 1.

———. *Criminal Law and Punishment.* Oxford: Clarendon Press, 1962.

——— "Acting and Refraining." *Analysis* 37 (1967): 133.

Fletcher, George. "Prolonging Life: Some Legal Considerations." *Washington Law Review* 42 (1967): 999.

———. "Two Kinds of Legal Rules: A Comparative Study of Burden-of-Persuasion Practices in Criminal Cases." *Yale Law Journal* 77 (1968): 880.

———. "The Right Deed for the Wrong Reason." *University of California at Los Angeles Law Review* 23 (1975): 293.

———. *Rethinking Criminal Law.* Boston: Little, Brown, & Co., 1978.

———. "The Right to Life." *Georgia Law Review* 13 (1979): 1371.

————. "Some Unwise Reflections on Discretion." *Law and Contemporary Problems* 47 (1984): 269.

————. "Criminal Theory as an International Discipline: Reflections on the Freiburg Workshop." *Criminal Justice Ethics* 3 (1985): 60.

————. "The Right and the Reasonable." *Harvard Law Review* 98 (1985): 949.

Foot, Philippa. "Euthanasia." *Philosophy and Public Affairs* 6 (1977): 85.

Frankena, William. "Obligation and Ability." In Max Black, ed., *Philosophical Analysis*. Ithaca: Cornell University Press, 1950. P. 157.

Frankfurt, Harry. "Alternate Possibilities and Moral Responsibility." *Journal of Philosophy* 66 (1969): 829.

————. "Freedom of the Will and the Concept of a Person." *Journal of Philosophy* 68 (1971): 5.

Frey, R. G., ed. *Utility and Rights*. Minneapolis: University of Minnesota Press, 1984.

Fuller, Lon. *The Morality of Law*. New Haven: Yale University Press, 1964.

Galston, William. "Defending Liberalism." *American Political Science Review* 76 (1982): 625.

Geach, Peter. *Mental Acts*. London: Routledge & Kegan Paul, 1957.

Gettier, Edmund. "Is Justified True Belief Knowledge?" *Analysis* 23 (1963): 121.

Gewirth, Alan. *Reason and Morality*. Chicago: University of Chicago Press, 1979.

————. "Are There Any Absolute Rights?" *Philosophical Quarterly* 31 (1981): 1.

Glazebrook, P. "Should We Have a Law of Attempted Crime?" *Law Quarterly Review* 85 (1969): 28.

————. "The Necessity Plea: English Criminal Law." *Cambridge Law Journal* 30 (1972): 87.

Goldstein, Abe. "Conspiracy to Defraud the United States." *Yale Law Journal* 68 (1959): 405.

Goldstein, Joseph, and Katz, Jay. "Abolish the 'Insanity Defense'—Why Not?" *Yale Law Journal* 72 (1963): 853.

Goode, Matthew. "Some Thoughts on the Present State of the 'Defence' of Intoxication." *Criminal Law Journal* 8 (1984): 104.

Gorecki, Jan. *A Theory of Criminal Justice*. New York: Columbia University Press, 1979.

Gorr, Michael. "Omissions." *Tulane Studies in Philosophy* 28 (1979): 93.

Green, O. Harvey. "Killing and Letting Die." *American Philosophical Quarterly* 17 (1980): 195.

Greenawalt, Kent. "The Perplexing Borders of Justification and Excuse." *Columbia Law Review* 84 (1984): 1897.

Grey, Thomas. *The Legal Enforcement of Morality*. New York: Random House, 1980.

Gross, Hyman. *A Theory of Criminal Justice*. New York: Oxford University Press, 1979.

————. "Mental Abnormality as a Criminal Excuse." In Joel Feinberg and Hyman Gross, eds., *Philosophy of Law*. 2d ed. Belmont: Wadsworth Publishing Co., 1980. P. 482.

Hall, Jerome. *General Principles of Criminal Law*. 2d ed. Indianapolis: Bobbs-Merrill, 1960.

————. *Foundations of Jurisprudence*. Indianapolis: Bobbs-Merrill, 1973.

————. "Comment on Justification and Excuse." *American Journal of Comparative Law* 24 (1976): 638.

Hare, R. M. *The Language of Morals*. Oxford: Oxford University Press, 1952.

Harris, John. "The Marxist Conception of Violence." *Philosophy and Public Affairs* 3 (1974): 192.

————. "Bad Samaritans Cause Harm." *Philosophical Quarterly* 32 (1982): 60.

Hart, H. L. A. "The Ascription of Responsibility and Rights." *Proceedings of the Aristotelian Society* 49 (1948–49): P. 171.

————. *The Concept of Law*. Oxford: Oxford University Press, 1961.

————. *Law, Liberty, and Morality*. New York: Vintage Books, 1963.

————. *Punishment and Responsibility*. New York: Oxford University Press, 1968.

————. "Immorality and Treason." In Richard Wasserstrom, ed., *Morality and the Law*. Belmont: Wadsworth Publishing Co., 1971. P. 49.

Hart, H. L. A., and Honoré, A. M. *Causation in the Law*. Oxford: Oxford University Press, 1959.

Heintz, Lawrence. "The Logic of Defenses." *American Philosophical Quarterly* 18 (1981): 243.

Hermann, Donald. "Assault on the Insanity Defense: Limitations on the Effectiveness and Effect of the Defense of Insanity." *Rutgers Law Journal* 14 (1983): 241.

Hitchler, W. "The Physical Element of Crime." *Dickenson Law Review* 39 (1934): 95.

Hodlcroft, David. "A Plea For Excuses?" *Philosophy* 44 (1969): 321.

Hodson, John. *The Ethics of Legal Coercion*. Dordrecht: D. Reidel, 1983.

Holmes, Oliver Wendell. *The Common Law*. [1881] Boston: Little, Brown, & Co., 1963.

Hughes, Graham. "Criminal Omissions." *Yale Law Journal* 67 (1958): 590.

————. "Criminal Responsibility." *Stanford Law Review* 16 (1964): 470.

Husak, Douglas. "Ronald Dworkin and the Right to Liberty." *Ethics* 90 (1979): 121.

————. "Paternalism and Autonomy." *Philosophy and Public Affairs* 10 (1980): 27.

————. "The Presumption of Freedom." *Nous* 17 (1983): 345.

Jacobs, Francis. *Criminal Responsibility*. London: Weidenfeld & Nicolson, 1971.

Jeffries, John, and Stephan, Paul. "Defenses, Presumptions, and Burdens of Proof in the Criminal Law." *Yale Law Journal* 88 (1979): 1325.

Kadish, Sanford. "The Decline of Innocence." *Cambridge Law Journal* 26 (1968): 273.

————, ed., *Encyclopedia of Crime and Justice*. New York: Free Press, 1983.

Kamisar, Yale. "Some Nonreligious Views Against Proposed 'Mercy-Killing' Legislation. *Minnesota Law Review* 42 (1958): 969.

Keener, William. *Selections on Jurisprudence*. St. Paul: West Publishing Co., 1896.

Keller, Robert. "Constitutional Law: Cruel and Unusual Punishment." *Buffalo Law Review* 18 (1969): 337.

Kelman, Mark. "Interpretive Construction in the Substantive Criminal Law." *Stanford Law Review* 33 (1981): 591.

Kennedy, I. M. "Switching-off Life Support Machines: The Legal Implications." *Criminal Law Review* (1977), p. 443.

Kenny, Courtney. *Outlines of Criminal Law* [1902] 19th ed. London: Cambridge University Press, 1966.

Kirchheimer, Otto. "Criminal Omissions." *Harvard Law Review* 55 (1942): 615.

Kleinig, John. "Good Samaritanism." *Philosphy and Public Affairs* 5 (1976): 382.

————. "Crime and the Concept of Harm." *American Philosophical Quarterly* 15 (1978): 32.

Lacey, Forrest. "Vagrancy and Other Crimes of Personal Condition." *Harvard Law Review* 66 (1953): 1203.

LaFave, Wayne, and Scott, Austin. *Criminal Law.* St. Paul: West Publishing Co., 1972.

————. *Substantive Criminal Law.* St. Paul: West Publishing Co., 1986.

Levenbook, Barbara. "Prohibiting Attempts and Preparations." *University of Missouri at Kansas City Law Review* 49 (1980): 41.

Louisell, David, and Hazard, Geoffrey. "Insanity as a Defense in the Bifurcated Trial." *California Law Review* 49 (1961): 805.

Low, Peter; Jeffries, John; and Bonnie, Richard. *Criminal Law.* Mineola: Foundation Press, 1982.

Lynch, A. C. E. "The Mental Element in the Actus Reus." *Law Quarterly Review* 98 (1982): 109.

Mabbott, J. D. "Punishment." *Mind* 48 (1939): 150.

Macauley, Thomas. "Notes on the Indian Penal Code." In *Works of Lord Macauley.* Trevelyan, ed., Vol. 7, 1866). P. 493.

MacCormick, Neil. *Legal Rights and Social Democracy.* Oxford: Clarendon Press, 1982.

Mack, Eric. "Causing and Failing to Prevent." *Southwestern Journal of Philosophy* 7 (1976): 83.

————. "Bad Samaritanism and the Causation of Harm." *Philosophy and Public Affairs* 9 (1980): 230.

Marston, Geoffrey. "Contemporaneity of Act and Intention in Crimes." *Law Quarterly Review* 86 (1970): 208.

McNiece, Harold, and Thornton, John. "Affirmative Duties in Tort." *Yale Law Journal* 58 (1949): 1272.

Mill, John Stuart. *Utilitarianism, Liberty, and Representative Government.* New York: E. P. Dutton and Co., 1951.

Miller, Justin. *Criminal Law.* St. Paul: West Publishing Co., 1934.

Moore, Michael. "The Moral and Metaphysical Sources of the Criminal Law." In J. Roland Pennock and John Chapman, eds., *Nomos 27: Criminal Justice.* New York: New York University Press, 1985. P. 11.

Morawetz, Thomas. "Book Review." *Georgia Law Review* 13 (1979): 1558.

Morillo, Carolyn. "Comments on Gorr and Green." *Tulane Studies in Philosophy* 28 (1979): 125.

Morris, Herbert. "Book Review." *Stanford Law Review* 13 (1960): 185.

————. "Persons and Punishment." *Monist* 52 (1968): 475.

————. "Punishment for Thoughts." In Robert Summers, ed., *Essays in Legal Philosophy.* Berkeley: University of California Press, 1968. P. 95.

Morris, Norval. *Madness and the Criminal Law.* Chicago: University of Chicago Press, 1983.

Muller, Gerhard. "On Common Law Mens Rea." *Minnesota Law Review* 42 (1955): 1043.

Murphy, Jeffrie. "Marxism and Retribution." *Philosophy and Public Affairs* 2 (1973): 217.

————. "Involuntary Acts and Criminal Liability." In Murphy, *Retribution, Justice, and Therapy.* Dordrecht: D. Reidel, 1979, P. 116.

Murphy, Jeffrie, and Coleman, Jules. *The Philosophy of Law.* Totowa: Rowman & Allanheld, 1984.

Murtaugh, John. "Status Offenses and Due Process of Law." *Fordham Law Review* 36 (1967): 51.

Note: "Graduated Responsibility as an Alternative to Current Tests of Determining Criminal Capacity." *Maine Law Review* 25 (1973): 343.

Note: "Alcohol Abuse and the Law." *Harvard Law Review* 94 (1981): 1660.

Nozick, Robert. *Anarchy, State, and Utopia.* New York: Basic Books, 1974.

O'Connor, D. "The Voluntary Act." *Medical Science Law* 15 (1975): 31.

O'Doherty, E. "Men, Criminals, and Responsibility." *Irish Jurist* 1 (1966): 285.

Osenbaugh, E. "The Constitutionality of Affirmative Defenses to Criminal Charges." *Arkansas Law Review* 29 (1976): 429.

Packer, Herbert. "Mens Rea and the Supreme Court." *Supreme Court Review* (1962): 107.

————. "The Model Penal Code and Beyond." *Columbia Law Review* 63 (1963): 594.

————. *The Limits of the Criminal Sanction.* Stanford: Stanford University Press, 1968.

Parent, W. A. "Judith Thomson and the Logic of Rights." *Philosophical Studies* 37 (1980): 405.

Pattenden, Rosemary. *The Judge, Discretion, and the Criminal Trial.* Oxford: Clarendon Press, 1982.

Perkins, Rollin. "Negative Acts in the Criminal Law." *Iowa Law Review* 22 (1937): 659.

————. "Ignorance or Mistake of Law Revisited." *Utah Law Review* 3 (1980): 473.

————. "Criminal Liability Without Fault: A Disquieting Trend." *Iowa Law Review* 68 (1983): 1067.

Perkins, Rollin, and Boyce, Ronald. *Criminal Law.* 3d.ed. Mineola: Foundation Press, 1982.

Pohlman, H. L. *Justice Oliver Wendell Holmes and Utilitarian Jurisprudence.* Cambridge: Harvard University Press, 1984.

Prior, A. N. "The Virtue of the Act and the Virtue of the Agent." *Philosophy* 26 (1951): 121.

Prosser, William. *Torts.* 4th. ed. St. Paul: West Publishing Co., 1971.

Rachels, James. "Active and Passive Euthanasia." *New England Journal of Medicine* 292 (1975): 78.

Ramsey, Paul. *The Patient as Person.* New Haven: Yale University Press, 1970.

Rawls, John. "Two Concepts of Rules." *Philosophical Review* 64 (1955): 3.

———. *A Theory of Justice*. Cambridge: Harvard University Press, 1971.

Raz, Joseph. "Legal Principles and the Limits of the Law." *Yale Law Journal* 81 (1972): 823.

———. "Liberalism, Autonomy, and the Politics of Neutral Concern." In Peter French, et. al., eds., *Midwest Studies in Philosophy*, Vol. 7, 1982. P. 89.

Reynolds, Noel. "The Enforcement of Morals and the Rule of Law." *Georgia Law Review* 11 (1977): 1325.

Richards, David. *The Moral Criticism of Law*. Encino: Dickenson Publishing Co., 1977.

———. "Human Rights and the Moral Foundations of the Substantive Criminal Law." *Georgia Law Review* 13 (1979): 1395.

———. *Sex, Drugs, Death, and the Law*. Totowa: Rowman & Littlefield, 1982.

Robinson, Paul. "A Theory of Justification: Societal Harm as a Prerequisite for Criminal Liability." *University of California at Los Angeles Law Review* 23 (1975): 261.

———. "Criminal Law Defenses: A Systematic Analysis." *Columbia Law Review* 82 (1982): 199.

———. *Criminal Law Defenses*. St. Paul: West Publishing Co., 1984.

———. "Causing the Conditions of One's Own Defense: A Study of the Limits of Theory in Criminal Law Doctrine." *Virginia Law Review* 71 (1985): 1.

Ryu, Paul. "Causation in Criminal Law." *University of Pennsylvania Law Review* 106 (1958): 773.

Sagoff, Mark. "Liberalism and Law." In Douglas MacLean and Claudia Mills, eds., *Liberalism Reconsidered*. Totowa: Rowman & Allanheld, 1983. P. 12.

Salmond, John. *Jurisprudence*. [1902] 11th. ed. London: Sweet & Maxwell, 1957.

Sandel, Michael. *Liberalism and the Limits of Justice*. Cambridge: Cambridge University Press, 1982.

Sayre, Francis. "Criminal Attempts." *Harvard Law Review* 41 (1928): 821.

———. "Criminal Responsibility for the Acts of Another." *Yale Law Journal* 43 (1930): 689.

———. "Mens Rea," 45 *Harvard Law Review* (1932), p. 974.

———. "Public Welfare Offenses." *Columbia Law Review* 37 (1937): 55.

Scanlon, T. M. "Quality of Will and the Value of Choice." (forthcoming)

Scheffler, Samuel. *The Rejection of Consequentialism*. Oxford: Clarendon Press, 1982.

Schulhofer, Stephen. "Harm and Punishment: A Critique of Emphasis on the Results of Conduct in the Criminal Law." *University of Pennsylvania Law Review* 122 (1974): 1497.

Searle, John. "Prime Facie Obligations." In Joseph Raz, ed., *Practical Reasoning*. New York: Oxford University Press, 1978. P. 81.

Sherry, Arthur. "Vagrants, Rogues, and Vagabonds—Old Concepts in Need of Revision." *California Law Review* 48 (1960): 557.

Silber, John. "Being and Doing: A Study of Status Responsibility and Voluntary Responsibility." *University of Chicago Law Review* 35 (1967): 47.

Silving, Helen. *Constituent Elements of Crime.* Springfield: Charles Thomas, 1967.

————. *Criminal Justice.* Buffalo: W. S. Hein, 1971.

Sim, P. "The Involuntary Actus Reus." *Modern Law Review* 25 (1962): 741.

Skilton, Robert. "The Requisite Act in Criminal Attempt." *University of Pittsburg Law Review* 3 (1973): 308.

Smith, J. C. "Subjective or Objective? Ups and Downs of the Test of Criminal Liability in England." *Villanova Law Review* 27 (1981–1982): 1179.

————. "Commentary." *Criminal Law Review* (1982): 527.

————. "Liability for Omissions in the Criminal Law." *Journal of Legal Studies* 4 (1984): 88.

Smith, J. C., and Hogan, Brian. *Criminal Law.* 5th ed. London: Butterworth & Co., 1983.

Snyder, Orville. *Criminal Justice.* New York: Prentice-Hall, 1953.

————. *Preface to Jurisprudence.* Indianapolis: Bobbs-Merrill, 1954.

Stephen, James. *A History of the Criminal Law of England.* New York: Burt Franklin, 1883.

Stevenson, Mike. "Chronic Alcoholism and Criminal Responsibility." *Gonzaga Law Review* 4 (1969): 336.

Stocker, Michael. "Responsibility, Especially For Beliefs." *Mind* 91 (1982): 398.

Stuart, Donald. "The Actus Reus in Attempts." *Criminal Law Review* (1970): 505.

Taylor, Charles. "Responsibility for Self." In Amelie Rorty, ed., *The Identities of Persons.* Berkeley: University of California Press, 1976. P. 281.

Thomas, Laurence. "Law, Morality, and Our Psychological Nature." In David Braybrooke, ed., *Social Justice.* Bowling Green: Bowling Green University Press, 1982. P. 111.

Thomson, Judith. *Acts and Other Events.* Ithaca: Cornell University Press, 1977.

————. "Some Ruminations on Rights." *Arizona Law Review* 19 (1978): 45.

Tonry, Michael. "Criminal Law: The Missing Element in Sentencing Reform." *Vanderbilt Law Review* 35 (1982): 607.

Tooley, Michael. "An Irrelevant Consideration: Killing Versus Letting Die." In Bonnie Steinbock, ed., *Killing and Letting Die.* Englewood: Prentice-Hall, 1980. P. 56.

Torcia: *Wharton's Criminal Law.* 14th ed. Rochester: Lawyers Cooperative Publishing Co., 1978.

Trammell, Richard. "A Criterion for Determining Negativity and Positivity of Duties." *Tulane Studies in Philosophy* 33 (1985): 75.

Turner, J. "Attempts to Commit Crimes." *Cambridge Law Journal* 5 (1934): 230.

Underwood, Barbara. "The Thumb on the Scales of Justice: Burdens of Persuasion in Criminal Cases." *Yale Law Journal* 86 (1977): 1299.

van Inwagen, Peter. "Ability and Responsibility." *Philosophical Review* 87 (1978): 201.

Von Hirsch, Andrew. *Doing Justice.* New York: Farrar, Straus & Giroux, 1976.

———. "Desert and Previous Convictions in Sentencing." *University of Minnesota Law Review* 65 (1981): 591.

———. *Past or Future Crimes?* New Brunswick: Rutgers University Press, 1985.

———. "Lifeboat Law." *Criminal Justice Ethics* 4 (1985): 88.

Warnock, G. J. "Review: On Guilt and Innocence." *Nous* 14 (1980): 134.

Wasik, Martin. "Partial Excuses." *Modern Law Review* 45 (1982): 516.

———. "Excuses at the Sentencing Stage." *Criminal Law Review* (1983), p. 450.

Wasserstrom, Richard. "Strict Liability in the Criminal Law." *Stanford Law Review* 12 (1960): 731.

Weinrib, Ernest. "The Case for a Duty to Rescue." *Yale Law Journal* 90 (1980): 247.

Weinryb, Elazar. "Omissions and Responsibility." *Philosophical Quarterly* 30 (1980): 1.

Wells, Celia. "Swatting the Subjectivist Bug." *Criminal Law Review* (1982): 209.

White, Alan. *Grounds of Liability.* Oxford: Clarendon Press, 1985.

Williams, Bernard. "Deciding to Believe." In Williams, *Problems of the Self,* London: Cambridge University Press, 1973. P. 136.

Williams, Glanville. "The Concept of Legal Liberty." *Columbia Law Review* 56 (1956): 1129.

———. " 'Mercy-Killing' Legislation—A Rejoinder." *Minnesota Law Review* 42 (1958): 1043.

———. *Criminal Law: The General Part.* 2d. ed. London: Stevens & Sons, 1961.

———. "Criminal Assault—Parking on a Copper's Foot." *Cambridge Law Journal* (1969), p. 16.

———. "Letter to the Editor." *Criminal Law Review* (1982), p. 773.

———. *Textbook of Criminal Law.* 2d. ed. London: Stevens & Sons, 1983.

Wolff, Robert P. *The Poverty of Liberalism.* Boston: Beacon Press, 1968.

Wootton, Barbara. *Crime and the Criminal Law.* London: Stevens & Sons, 1963.

Woozley, A. D. "Negligence and Ignorance." *Philosophy* 53 (1978): 293.

Zimmerman, Michael. *An Essay On Human Action.* New York: Peter Lang, 1984.

———. "Sharing Responsibility." *American Philosophical Quarterly* 22 (1985): 115.

———. *An Essay on Moral Responsibility.* (forthcoming)

———. "Negligence and Moral Responsibility." *Nous.* (forthcoming)

# Index

negligence and, 11–12, 66, 132–35, 150*n*.
proposed abolition of, 52–53
social protection versus, 3
strict liability and, 137, 138, 139, 140, 141
unreasonable mistake of fact and, 61–63
voluntary intoxication and, 53–56, 69–70, 73–74*n*., 75*n*.
Mill, John Stuart, 236–37
Misdemeanor, felony differentiated from, 20–21
Mistakes
exculpatory, 212
inculpatory, 211–15, 222–23*n*.
reasonable, 62–63
unreasonable, 61–63
Model Penal Code
attempted offense definition of, 95
classification of offenses by, 216–17*n*.
criminality liability terms of, 10, 13, 22
culpability terms of, 126, 127
discretion definition of, 65
mens rea definition of, 33
proximate cause terms of, 163
Moral philosophy
action-guiding nature of, 129–32, 150*n*.
control principle and, 131–32
criminal law and, 4–6, 226–28
orthodox criminal theory and, 128–32, 150*n*.
Moral rights
criminal liability and, 30–39
criminal theory and, 35–39
justice and, 30–34
Moral skepticism, 239–40, 242
Morality
agent, 130
law differentiated from, 128–32
of moral wrongs, 128–32
Morality, enforcement of, 224–27
harm and, 231–37, 245*n*.
liberal neutrality and, 238–44
liberalism and, 237–44
Motive
intention differentiated from, 144–46, 154–55*n*.
irrelevance of, 143–48, 154–55*n*.

justification and, 214–15, 223*n*.
*Mullaney* v. *Wilbur,* 208, 210, 221*n*.
Murder
actus reus of, 124–25
attempted, 123
elements of, 188, 189
as felony, 70, 77*n*.
intentional, 126
by omission, 157, 158–59, 160–61, 171–72, 181*n*.
self-defense and, 189, 192, 195, 199, 201

**N**

Necessity
as choice of lesser evils, 66–69
as justification, 202–3, 205, 206, 216*n*.
Negligence, criminal
comparative, 43
criminal liability for, 65–66, 79, 132–36, 150*n*., 151–52*n*.
discretion regarding, 65–66, 76*n*.
fault and, 132, 133–36
mens rea and, 11–12, 132–35, 150*n*.
omissions as, 84–85
orthodox criminal theory of, 132–36
recklessness differentiated from, 135, 151*n*.
Neutrality, liberal, 238–44, 247*n*.
Noncriminal offense, 3
*Nulla sine lege,* 7–8
*Nullum poena sine lege,* 212–15

**O**

Obligation, moral versus legal, 128–32, 168
Offense(s), criminal. *See also* Conduct, criminal; Crime; specific offenses
concept of, 125–26
defense and, 188–90, 217*n*.
elements of, 42, 126, 188–89, 200, 201–2, 217*n*., 220*n*.
lesser included, 43
orthodox model of, 41–42, 122–28
Offense modification, 192–93, 216*n*.
Omissions